Praise for
THROUGH GOD'S EYES

Ancient wisdom and deep knowing echo through these pages. This stunning book reverberates with the amazing grace, profound strength, and compassionate love of the Divine. Like a good friend, you will consult this book over and over in the course of a lifetime; this inspired work is a rare treasure.

—JANIS AMATUZIO, MD,
AUTHOR OF *FOREVER OURS* AND *BEYOND KNOWING*

Regardless of how you conceive the Absolute—as God, Goddess, Allah, Universe, or simply as a sense of cosmic beauty and order—your belief will be enriched by *Through God's Eyes*. This fine book is a refreshing departure from the preachy ideology of religious dogmatism. It reveals the richness, complexity, and meaning of everyday life, warts and all.

—LARRY DOSSEY, MD,
AUTHOR OF *THE POWER OF PREMONITIONS*

This is a book that makes the wisdom of the ages and sages accessible to everyone. I know from experience it speaks the truth about human potential and will help the reader to connect with a higher consciousness and see through God's eyes too. If we all live the message some day the world will no longer be chaotic but will be healed and at peace despite the difficulties life presents us with. This is a guidebook for a troubled world.

—BERNIE SIEGEL, MD,
AUTHOR OF *A BOOK OF MIRACLES* AND
365 PRESCRIPTIONS FOR THE SOUL

This is really a remarkable book! To be inspired is one thing, yet to find yourself immersed in an understanding of your relationship with the Divine is life changing. I'll read it again, and again!

—DAVID WAGNER,
AUTHOR OF *LIFE AS A DAYMAKER*

One of the most important books I've ever read. An incredible compilation of spiritual wisdom and insight. It's the owner's manual God should give you when you're born.

—ROBERT PETERSON,
AUTHOR OF *OUT OF BODY EXPERIENCES*

This ambitious book deserves a place on the nightstand of anyone committed to living the richest life possible. Phil Bolsta has gathered the wisdom of the ages and organized it in a wonderfully useful way. This is a book that will make you think, contemplate, and, most certainly, add positive insights that could just change your life.

—BARBARA J. WINTER,
AUTHOR OF *MAKING A LIVING WITHOUT A JOB*

I am very happy to see Phil's ideas take form in this book. Over the years his dedication to serving people and bringing truth to light has been persistent, honest, and real. Many hearts and souls have been touched by his work and this honesty. Over the years I have watched him walk deeply with the ideas in this book. It has taken form as his journey and the essential life lessons that have caused him to develop into the beautiful soul that he is. I am honored that my story about the beauty of the death of the gazelle had such an impact on Phil and feel blessed that he has traveled so far with it [see "About the Title" on page xv]. I pray that all of us have the blessings to be able to perceive reality through the eyes of God and to experience the existence of the Divine within us and within every event that occurs in our lives. Thanks, Phil, for opening the doors again so that many people may taste the fragrance of this reality.

—IBRAHIM JAFFE, MD,
FOUNDER OF THE UNIVERSITY OF SPIRITUAL HEALING & SUFISM

Phil Bolsta has strung together a brilliant selection of jewels in a necklace of timeless quotes amplified with his perceptive commentary. In *Through God's Eyes* there is a logical flow from section to section so the whole can be read as narrative or each section can be contemplated and absorbed on its own. A wonderful tool on the journey of uncovering and revealing more of Self.

—LARRY CHANG,
AUTHOR OF *WISDOM FOR THE SOUL: FIVE MILLENNIA OF PRESCRIPTIONS FOR SPIRITUAL HEALING*

What a fine web this author weaves. Whereas at first we believe ourselves to be dwarves standing on the shoulders of giants, we awaken and realize we are that which we seek. May you enjoy the labyrinth contained within. Walk slowly. Feel the love and move so ever intently, gently from the shadows into the soulshine. *Through God's Eyes* reminds us that there is no end, so be here now.

—TIM MIEJAN,
EDITOR AND PUBLISHER OF *THE EDGE: SOUL OF THE CITIES*

Through Gods Eyes is a master work. It is proof that God's angels here on Earth, who see with his eyes, love with his heart, and speak with his voice have numbered in the hundreds. Phil Bolsta's ability to weave these voices together as a unified whole is sheer genius. This book will be a handbook companion to be read over and over for those on a spiritual path.

—RHYS THOMAS,
RHYS THOMAS INSTITUTE OF ENERGY MEDICINE

Through God's Eyes could be subtitled *CliffsNotes for Your Soul*. Each "note" and quote of inspiration will stir your soul to take action in the appropriate direction for your highest good. I recommend this book to everyone who desires a saner, healthier, and happier existence.

—DONALD SCHNELL,
AUTHOR OF *THE INITIATION*

In *Through God's Eyes*, Phil Bolsta masterfully weaves wisdom from others with his personal stories of growth and challenge, giving the reader powerful tools for living a joyful, creative, and spirit-filled life.

—KATHRYN HARWIG,
AUTHOR OF *THE RETURN OF INTUITION*

Phil's pure and loving spirit shines through in the inspiring spiritual guidance he shares in *Through God's Eyes*. No matter where you are on the spiritual path, you will find beautifully written passages that will speak to your heart and soul.

—LAURIE BAUM, MSW,
AUTHOR OF *SACRED MYSTERIES OF EGYPT* AND
EVERYTHING YOU NEED TO KNOW ABOUT YOUR ASTROLOGY SIGN

I can't imagine the hours and hours Phil put into composing this book. I love the quotes from these beautifully gifted people and I especially love Phil's personal stories at the end of each chapter. This book is a wonderful contribution for anyone searching for their spiritual roots.

—ECHO BODINE,
AUTHOR OF *LOOK FOR THE GOOD AND YOU'LL FIND GOD*

In this work of spiritual artistry, Phil Bolsta has filtered and sifted the wisdom of the ages both ancient and contemporary, secular and religious, spiritual and scientific into coherent and cohesive collections and then arranged those collections into a clear path for anyone who wishes to walk a deeper, more awakened spiritual journey through life. His commentaries and real-life anecdotes add just the right clarity to bring each area of reflection into the here-and-now.

—LORI ANNE YANG,
FOUNDER AND CEO OF MAMMASTE, LLC

At first glance, this monstrous 538-page book appears to be a collection of inspirational quotes from cultural icons as well as sages throughout the ages. However, as you read the book carefully, you will be pleasantly surprised to discover that it actually provides a detailed road map for your spiritual quest for a meaningful and harmonious life. Here lies the genius of Bolsta—he makes the profound look simple and his simple steps can lead to profound changes in individuals and society. I recommend this book to anyone with an interest in spirituality and service to mankind, regardless of their faith tradition.

—DR. PAUL WONG,
AUTHOR OF *THE HUMAN QUEST FOR MEANING*

For my friend James,
who helps others navigate,
with equal mastery,
both their practical & their
spiritual world.

Richard

THROUGH
GOD'S
EYES

May peace, love and joy be the dearest
of friends.

*Phil
Bolsta*

THROUGH
GOD'S
EYES

Finding Peace and Purpose
in a Troubled World

PHIL BOLSTA

COVER PHOTO: The Helix Nebula is a large planetary nebula (the gaseous envelope ejected by a dying, sun-like star) located in the constellation Aquarius. This image was produced from data generated by the Space Telescope Science Institute.

Quotes by Paramahansa Yogananda, Swami Sri Yukteswar, Lahiri Mahasaya, Sri Daya Mata, and Sri Gyanamata used with permission from Self-Realization Fellowship, Los Angeles, California (yogananda-srf.org). See page 517 for sources of these quotes.

The quote about attitude on page 290 is used by permission of Charles R. Swindoll. Copyright © 1981, 1982 by Charles R. Swindoll, Inc. All rights are reserved worldwide.

The poem "Faith" on page 417 used by permission of Patrick Overton.

FIRST EDITION MAY 2012

16   15   14   13   12   5   4   3   2   1

Library of Congress Control Number: 2012938337

ISBN 13: 978-0-9840328-2-2

Manufactured in the United States of America.
Designed by James Monroe Design, LLC.

For information about special purchases or custom editions,
please contact:

James Monroe Publishing, LLC.
7236 Bald Eagle Lane
Willow River, Minnesota 55795

www.jamesmonroedesign.com

To Erin
If life held nothing else for me
I'd look back with no regret,
For you have walked the earth
And I'm forever in your debt

To Abe
Through you, a cherished dream for my daughter
has found full expression

To Carrie Sheeran
A promise is a promise

CONTENTS

THREE: *You Are Beautiful and You Are Loved* 55

Your soul, that spark of the Infinite within you, is perfect and magnificent. You are boundless joy, you are inexhaustible love, you are indescribable beauty.

FOUR: *Your Choice Is Love or Fear* 83

Your every thought, word, and action spring from either love or fear. The nature of your choices determines the quality of your life.

NINE: *Pursue Your Right Livelihood* 225
When you are aligned with Spirit and long to do meaningful work, the world is in need of whatever it is you need to do.

TEN: *Fulfill Your Destiny* 253
When you are ready to know your life's purpose, it will reveal itself by taking up residence in your conscious mind.

When you surrender to Divine Will with unwavering faith and trust, every moment becomes a gift.

Detaching from outcomes does not mean that you are apathetic and unmotivated. Quite the contrary. Detachment means that you care deeply, but from an objective, enlightened perspective.

ABOUT THE TITLE

The title *Through God's Eyes* reflects a pivotal moment of personal enlightenment. At a 1998 weekend workshop, Dr. Ibrahim Jaffe, founder of the University of Spiritual Healing & Sufism, shared a life-changing story with his students. He said that after watching a TV nature program in which a lion savagely ripped apart a gazelle, he had been distraught. Retreating into meditation, he implored God, *How could you allow such carnage and tragedy to exist?* He told us that the response he received humbled him and restored his faith in Divine Intelligence: "I felt and saw through inner revelation how this incident was experienced from a higher level as pure love and that it was beautiful beyond description."

Ibrahim explained that this world may appear cruel and harsh to our unenlightened eyes, but even the brutality inherent in the animal kingdom has meaning, purpose, and a stark beauty all its own. Indeed, looking through God's eyes, we see that simply by living our lives, we all serve each other in ways both simple and profound. From that day on, I challenged myself to see the world through God's eyes—to the extent that I could, of course—so that I too could witness every moment unfolding with beauty, love, and perfection.

Granted, that is much easier said than done, especially on days when I am the gazelle. That's why every chapter contains reminders urging you to look through God's eyes. I've found that the more I train myself to view the world in this way, the more peaceful and grounded I become. It then becomes easier to follow the core teaching of the ancient wisdom presented in these pages:

*With love and devotion, align your will with Divine Will
and be a source of love, hope, and healing energy to
all who cross your path.*

It is my greatest hope that learning to see the world through God's eyes inspires you to break free from the prison of human perception, welcome peace, love, and joy as your dearest friends, and become a more positive and powerful force for good in the world.

READER'S GUIDE

Whether you are a novice spiritual seeker or have been pursuing enlightenment for decades, you likely will not plow through this book in two or three sittings. It is designed to be read a quote, a page, or a chapter at a time to allow for absorption and contemplation.

Whether you frequently reference this book or glance at it every few months, whether you start on page one or flip it open randomly, whether you read for a few minutes or a few hours, I hope you come away inspired and with something worthwhile to ponder.

I offer a personal life story at the end of every chapter. Hopefully, my own experiences will make each chapter's principles more relatable and give you ideas on how to apply them in your own life.

Following each story are twelve self-reflection questions intended to spur self-exploration, build self-awareness, and heighten your appreciation and enjoyment of life. Your answers to these questions will be uniquely your own. The answers that are right for you may not be right for another; in fact, they may be right for you for only a short while.

I included a bonus chapter on affirmations because the daily practice of affirmations accelerated my own spiritual growth quickly and effectively. Today, no matter where I am or what I am doing, affirmations keep me centered, grounded, and connected to the loving energy that surrounds and sustains us. I've listed sample affirmations as guidance to help you write your own.

Please note that I use the word "God" throughout for the sake of consistency and convenience, fully recognizing that there are probably as many interpretations of God as there are people reading this book. Many people view God as the source of all existence, many others as existence itself. Whether you view God as a being, a universal intelligence, a force, or any other type of form or formless entity, I trust that you will substitute the name, term, or reference for "God" that you are most comfortable with each time you come across the word.

Truth is one, sages call it by different names.

—RIG VEDA

Also, I have made all mentions of God gender-neutral except for references within the quotes of other people. Our human notions of gender are woefully inadequate to describe an intelligence that is present in every atom of creation.

A quick biography of each person quoted in this book can be found at GodsEyesBios.com. Sources of quotes from Self-Realization Fellowship publications can be found on page 517. Sources of all quotes used in this book can be found at GodsEyesQuotes.com, which will be updated frequently because identifying who said what, when, and where is a never-ending project. Any corrections or new information with regard to bios or quote attributions would be greatly appreciated. You can reach me at GodsEyes@me.com.

FOREWORD
by Caroline Myss

I love this book, beginning with the title all the way through to the final word. Rarely have I been as enthralled by a piece of work as I am by Phil Bolsta's remarkable *Through God's Eyes*. Each time I opened it to read a few pages, I found that I could not stop. I told myself, "Just one more page," but inevitably I kept on reading, even though I had read many of the chapters before. Part of the exquisite beauty of this book is that you will want to read it again and again. Such is the gift of genuine inspiration and grace.

Yet another reason I love this book is that I am enamored with prayer, reflection, contemplation, and wisdom. We live in a society that is starving and indeed suffering from the absence of all four of those sacred practices—and it shows. *Through God's Eyes* presents immeasurable opportunities for prayer, reflection, and spiritual inquiry, all threaded together by a continuum of wise teachings in such a way that the reader is brought into a gentle state of contemplation with ease. You will find yourself wanting to reflect on the insightful writings of the numerous mystics, theologians, philosophers, poets, scientists, and writers that Phil has cleverly gathered together. Over two pages, for example, he blends the wisdom of Henry David Thoreau, C. S. Lewis, Deepak Chopra, Rabindranath Tagore, and my personal favorite, Teresa of Avila. I could create a weekend workshop centered around the stunning offerings—presented on just two pages of this remarkable book—by these five individuals.

Phil alternates these inspiring quotes with his own perceptive and finely crafted narrative. Consider this observation from one of the pages mentioned above: "You boldly and confidently move forward, trusting that Divine Intelligence is directing you to the people, situations, and events that will serve your highest good."

Who doesn't need to know that? Whose life is not better for having faith in such guidance? It's worth pausing for ten minutes in the midst of a busy day to close your eyes and ask yourself, "What do I trust in this world? Do I truly believe in a God that I trust? If not, then what do I believe in?"

I love this book because I know all too well how much people need this book. I know that prayer, or reflective sacred thought, is the most powerful force we have available to us as human beings. I also know that few truths are as difficult to understand or to believe as that one. I've had more than one person ask me, "Do you have any prayers that work?" hoping that I would have a magic quick-fix formula that a person could use to make his or her life just feel better. But life is not like that and prayer is not magic. Prayer and contemplation are about taking the time to understand who we are and why we make the choices we do. As a result, we learn more about ourselves, our inner nature, and how to exist in harmony with the wisdom of life.

For the past ten years, I've conducted workshops on prayer and healing. Before that, I avoided doing workshops on either subject, as I was deeply aware of the contradiction that existed in the consciousness movement that allowed for "energy" discussions but not prayerful ones. Then, as my work became more directly involved with classical mystical theology, I introduced healing and prayer. No one was more surprised than I was by the healings that took place during workshops dedicated to my book, *Entering the Castle*, which was inspired by the writings of Teresa of Avila. Time after time, as people opened themselves to the silent power of grace and healing, they experienced profound physical as well as emotional healings. I wish I had had Phil's book on hand as a gift to give these wonderful people after such profound workshops. His book feeds the open soul. His book feeds the soul seeking healing. And his book is a comfort to the soul going through the dark night.

I love this book because it is timeless and it is for everyone. *Through God's Eyes* is an enlightened piece of work that is an essential read for all people who are truly devoted to the care and refinement of their soul. I will add that I feel privileged to write the Foreword for Phil not just because I believe so strongly in this book, but also because he has been a friend for twenty years. Phil is a contemporary mystic, a man whose life is a living commitment to spiritual service. I am honored to know him.

—Caroline Myss
Author of *Anatomy of the Spirit, Entering the Castle,* and *Defy Gravity*
September 2012

ACKNOWLEDGMENTS

When the idea for this book first tapped me on the shoulder more than a dozen years ago, I never imagined it would evolve into what it has become. Its size, scope, and quality is directly attributable to the insightful, no-holds-barred feedback I received from a number of wise and generous friends.

Those friends include Bill Arnold, Lisa Baldwin, Christopher Barbour, Ann Bauer, Laurie Baum, Rachel Bird, Russ Blixt, Eric Christopher, Marta Crothers, Jecenia Hidalgo, Alyssa Kalmoe, Mark Lovett, John C. A. Manley, Sarah Moran, Iva Petrova, Deb Reilly, and Judy Szamos.

Special thanks to my reviewer all-stars, who soared above and beyond the call of duty: Paul Bullis, Nancy Gronlund, Marcia Hines, Erin O'Rourke, Bob Peterson, Russ Peterson, Dave Ply, Roberto Velasco, Sandra Winieski, and Lori Anne Yang.

Special thanks also to:

- Caroline Myss for her friendship and support, and for making time in her insanely hectic schedule to write the Foreword.

- Dr. Larry Dossey for his wise counsel on the nature of energy and prayer.

- Coleman Barks for his kindness in helping me identify sources of Rumi quotations.

- Frank Parlato, Jr. for providing extensive details about Swami Vivekananda quotations.

- Jay Monroe for his kindness, his generosity, and his world-class book designing expertise.

- Preston and Liz Palmer for their great friendship, and to Preston for his photographic prowess.

- Greg Maki for his good-hearted nature and his superb illustration skills.

- Geri Hall for her faith, friendship, and astonishing generosity.

- Paul Streitz for his unconditional friendship, good humor, and stalwart support.

- Kathleen Moore for her unwavering belief in me.

INTRODUCTION

This is the book I longed to read as I took my first tentative steps down a spiritual path. I assumed that someone had laid out all the spiritual principles I was learning in a logical, organized, and engaging way. Surely there had to be one book that explained how all of these principles interact, how to weave them together into a cohesive worldview, and how to practically apply this spiritual wisdom to daily life.

I found plenty of fascinating books filled with valuable insights and information, but I always came away with more questions than answers. As I struggled to piece together what living a spiritual life looked like, I felt like I was standing in a giant library where all the books were strewn on the floor. The book I was looking for, the book that would speak to my soul, was not among them.

I vowed to write such a book someday. After all, if I was searching for it, surely other like-minded souls were too. I felt I was well suited to the task. As a writer, I specialize in bringing clarity and order to complex subject matter—and spirituality is as complex as it gets. Above all, this subject touched my heart and called to me like no other.

As I walked my path and began connecting the dots, I saw an age-old framework forming that was as elegant as it was beautiful—everything fit together, flowed together, and sang together in pure harmony. Eventually, after years of research and study, I felt capable of interpreting and articulating this worldview, which for thousands of years has been enlightening spiritual seekers about the meaning and purpose of life and the vastness of human potential.

In other words, I am not the source of this information. I am merely a resource for gathering, organizing, and presenting it in a way that makes it accessible and relatable to ordinary people like me who are living ordinary lives while pondering extraordinary questions.

As the book began taking shape, I sensed that it already existed, perfect and complete, in a higher realm. All I had to do was search for the relevant concepts and quotes that were scattered throughout generations of cultures across the globe. Next, I had to sort everything out and piece it all together into a giant cosmic jigsaw puzzle.

There was no question about the format to use. I was intuitively guided to alternate the comments and quotes so that they supported, built upon, and flowed into each other. A quote may expand on the concept that precedes it or it may introduce the brief commentary that follows. I appreciated the initial impression of my agent, Barbara Neighbors Deal, who said, "As I was reading, I kept having this mental image of your text as a shimmering, fine gold chain, with the quotations as beautifully set jewels on the necklace."

Though your interpretation of spiritual concepts may differ from mine, I hope this book prompts you to examine and clarify your own beliefs about spirituality and your place in the world. I will consider this book a success if it inspires you to live more consciously, love more consistently, and greet each morning with joy and gratitude.

> *Believe nothing, no matter where you read it, or who said it, no matter if I have said it, unless it agrees with your own reason and your own common sense.*
>
> —BUDDHA

ONE

RETHINK YOUR WORLDVIEW

*The universe is full of magical things
patiently waiting for our wits to grow sharper.*

—Eden Phillpotts

RETHINK YOUR WORLDVIEW

Whether you feel stressed or blessed, whether you seek information or inspiration, examining your core beliefs about God and the Universe can radically transform and enrich your life.

> *One's first step in wisdom is to question everything—and one's last is to come to terms with everything.*
>
> —GEORG C. LICHTENBERG

COSMIC CROSSROADS

Let's start with the fundamentals. Do you view the Universe as a friendly, orderly realm and God as a benevolent, merciful presence? Or do you see the world as a harsh, unforgiving place and God as a thunderbolt-hurling, punishing force?

> *What can be seen on earth points to neither the total absence nor the obvious presence of divinity, but to the presence of a hidden God. Everything bears this mark.*
>
> —BLAISE PASCAL

Do you question the very existence of God? Do you believe the workings of the Universe are random and capricious and that life intrinsically lacks meaning and purpose?

> *Were there no God, we would be in this glorious world with grateful hearts and no one to thank.*
>
> —CHRISTINA ROSSETTI

Do you demand irrefutable evidence of God's presence that your senses and science can observe and measure?

> *One can search the brain with a microscope and not find the mind, and can search the stars with a telescope and not find God.*
>
> —J. GUSTAV WHITE

Will you reject the notion that God has a plan for the world until every last aspect of that plan has been revealed to you?

> *In the search for truth there are certain questions that are not important. Of what material is the universe constructed? Is the universe eternal? Are there limits or not to the universe? . . . If a man were to postpone his search and practice for Enlightenment until such questions were solved, he would die before he found the path.*
>
> —BUDDHA

That day will never come. The only certain statement we can make about God is that we can never be certain about any aspect of God.

> *Something unknown is doing we don't know what.*
>
> —SIR ARTHUR STANLEY EDDINGTON

The rest of your life hinges on the road you choose at this cosmic crossroads. Why? The way you look at the world influences your thoughts, which in turn influence your choices, your actions, and how you conduct your life.

> *It is never too late to learn what it is always necessary to know.*
>
> —LUCIUS ANNAEUS SENECA

Therefore, shifting from fearing God to embracing the Hindu rishis' teachings that God is synonymous with bliss, love, truth, and beauty will organically lead to a more positive, loving life.

> *Love is beauty and beauty is truth, and that is why in the beauty of a flower we can see the truth of the universe.*
>
> —BUDDHA

Science cannot objectively define God through experimentation because every subject's perception of God would be, by definition, subjective.

> *God is like a mirror. The mirror never changes but everybody who looks at it sees a different face.*
>
> —MIDRASH TANHAMA

Those who worship the scientific method on the altar of infallibility will continue to be at loggerheads with faith because faith, by definition, is beyond the scope of science.

> *When faith is supported by facts or by logic it ceases to be faith.*
>
> —EDITH HAMILTON

Science's inability to detect God's signature says more about science than it does about God.

> *Physics is mathematical, not because we know so much about the physical world, but because we know so little: it is only its mathematical properties that we can discover.*
>
> —BERTRAND RUSSELL

Like all seekers of truth, mathematicians and scientists will find God only by setting aside their formulas and test tubes and turning their attention within.

> *To them that ask, where have you seen the Gods, or how do you know for certain there are Gods, that you are so devout in their worship? I answer: Neither have I ever seen my own soul, and yet I respect and honor it.*
>
> —MARCUS AURELIUS

God is discovered not through technology, research, and analysis, but by looking into the eyes of the next person you see.

> *Let none turn over books or roam the stars in quest of God who sees him not in man.*
>
> —JOHANN KASPAR LAVATER

Science may never prove the existence of God, but anyone who has ever felt God's presence has all the proof they need.

Not being known doesn't stop the truth from being true.

—RICHARD BACH

SAGES THROUGH THE AGES

While some may argue that belief in God requires a leap of faith, great philosophers throughout history have reasoned that the existence of Divine Intelligence is logical and inescapable.

> *All I have seen teaches me to trust the Creator for all I have not seen.*
>
> —RALPH WALDO EMERSON

Thirty-three centuries ago, Egyptian Pharaoh Akhenaten beheld confirmation of God's presence in everything from the simplest of creatures to the vastness of the Universe.

> *Casteth he his eye towards the clouds, findeth he not the heavens full of his wonders? looketh he down to the earth, doth not the worm proclaim, "Less than omnipotence could not have formed me!"*
>
> —AKHENATON

A thousand years later, Aristotle argued that all of creation is imbued with inherent purpose, and that the synthesis of order, direction, and continual motion in the Universe cannot be a by-product of chance.

> *I cannot imagine how the clockwork of the universe can exist without a clockmaker.*
>
> —VOLTAIRE

Sixteen more centuries passed before Italian theologian and priest Thomas Aquinas wrote that it was not fortuitous but by design that things which lack knowledge are consistently directed toward a particular end. Just as the arrow is directed by the archer, so are all natural things in existence directed by God.

Look at the facts of the world. You see a continual and progressive
triumph of the right. I do not pretend to understand the moral
universe, the arc is a long one, my eye reaches but little ways.
I cannot calculate the curve and complete the figure by the
experience of sight; I can divine it by conscience. But from what
I see I am sure it bends towards justice. Things refuse to be
mismanaged long.

—THEODORE PARKER

Three hundred fifty years later, Francis Bacon, an English philosopher and the father of inductive reasoning and the scientific method, concluded that expanding your vision inevitably leads to evidence of God's handiwork.

It is true, that a little philosophy inclineth man's mind to atheism;
but depth in philosophy bringeth men's minds about to religion:
for while the mind of man looketh upon second causes scattered,
it may sometimes rest in them, and go no further; but when it
beholdeth the chain of them confederate, and linked together, it
must needs fly to Providence and Deity.

—FRANCIS BACON

Nineteenth-century Danish philosopher and theologian Søren Kierkegaard agreed, adding that expansion of vision can refer to a microcosm as well as a macrocosm.

God's providence is great precisely in small things; whereas for
men there is something lacking here—just as lace seen through
a microscope is irregular and unlovely, but the texture of nature
under the same scrutiny proves to be more and more ingenious.

—SØREN KIERKEGAARD

In response to a letter from a child who asked if scientists pray, iconic physicist Albert Einstein wrote that "Every one who is seriously involved in the pursuit of science becomes convinced that a spirit is manifest in the laws of the universe—a spirit vastly superior to that of man."

The scientist is possessed by a sense of universal causation....
His religious feeling takes the form of a rapturous amazement at
the harmony of natural law, which reveals an intelligence of such
superiority that, compared with it, all the systematic thinking
and acting of human beings is an utterly insignificant reflection....
It is beyond question closely akin to that which has possessed the
religious geniuses of all ages.

—ALBERT EINSTEIN

Since the dawn of time, those perceptive souls with the eye of an artist and the heart of a poet have leveraged the full force of their creative powers to rejoice in God's grandeur.

Earth's crammed with heaven,
And every common bush afire with God.

—ELIZABETH BARRETT BROWNING

Whether pharaoh, priest, philosopher, physicist, or poet, those who viewed the world through God's eyes have long recognized the premise of divinity and the promise of infinity in the most ordinary events, encounters, and experiences.

I think that the leaf of a tree, the meanest insect on which we
trample, are, in themselves, arguments more conclusive than any
which can be advanced, that some vast intellect animates infinity.

—PERCY BYSSHE SHELLEY

FIRST STEPS

You begin to live more consciously when you stop assuming that what you believe is unquestionably the way things are.

A belief system is nothing more than a thought you've thought over
and over again.

—WAYNE DYER

Challenging the verity of what you were taught by your parents, religious leaders, or other well-meaning authority figures may be emotionally wrenching.

> *There will come a time when you believe everything is finished.*
> *That will be the beginning.*
>
> —LOUIS L'AMOUR

Yet drilling down to the essence of what you believe—with all the honesty and courage you can muster—and questioning every idea you have about God are prerequisites for living an authentic life.

> *I tore myself away from the safe comfort of certainties through my*
> *love for the truth; and truth rewarded me.*
>
> —SIMONE DE BEAUVOIR

Even if you emerge with your original belief system intact, your efforts will have been worthwhile. For you will now believe what you believe through conscious choice rather than unconscious acceptance.

> *Some people have a hard time understanding how God can exist.*
> *They don't seem to have a problem believing that everything*
> *started with an explosion from a tiny point at the center of the*
> *universe. But, where did that tiny point come from? It takes as*
> *much faith to believe that the universe came from nothing as it*
> *does to believe that an intelligent eternal being created it.*
>
> —DUANE ALAN HAHN

If, however, your longstanding beliefs crumble to ashes when held up to the light, you must be willing to scatter them to the winds and never look back.

> *If a thousand old beliefs were ruined in our march to truth, we*
> *must still march on.*
>
> —REV. STOPFORD A. BROOKE

Where to begin? It does not matter—just take that first step and keep moving. Are you a bookstore browser? Stroll over to the spirituality section or do your browsing online. Do you prefer talking to those who possess the knowledge and wisdom that you want for yourself? Seek out the counsel of well-informed acquaintances or approach a leader at your place of worship. Does casual conversation with peers appeal to you? Check out a lecture or seminar on consciousness and introduce yourself to like-minded attendees. Is self-reflection your pathway to realization? Take frequent, contemplative nature walks to sift through all the new ideas you encounter.

> *Wherever you are is the entry point.*
>
> —KABIR

Each author, each speaker, each fellow traveler you bump into will refer you to other publications, other seminars, other methodologies. Hold on to the concepts that resonate with you; set aside the rest.

> *When you are deluded and full of doubt, even a thousand books of scripture are not enough. When you have realized understanding, even one word is too much.*
>
> —FEN-YANG SHAN-CHAO

PACE YOURSELF

Do not expect immediate illumination. Focus only on today's efforts, for the journey is every bit as important as the destination.

> *He who would leap high must take a long run.*
>
> —DANISH PROVERB

Rare is the spiritual aspirant who instantaneously experiences and effortlessly sustains blissful union with the Source of all that is.

> *There are very few human beings who receive the truth, complete and staggering, by instant illumination. Most of them acquire it fragment by fragment, on a small scale, by successive developments, cellularly, like a laborious mosaic.*
>
> —ANAÏS NIN

Indeed, your first exposure to unfamiliar spiritual teachings may uproot your belief system and leave you reeling from information overload.

> *Looking up gives light,*
> *though at first it makes you dizzy.*
>
> —RUMI

Even if you are consumed by the desire to devour every spiritual book you can find, you may "hit the wall" if you try to take in too much too soon.

> *The vast ocean of truth can be measured only according to the*
> *capacity of one's own cup of intelligence and perception.*
>
> —PARAMAHANSA YOGANANDA

Inevitably, it dawns on you that you have not been contemplating spiritual questions for quite some time.

> *Be not afraid of growing slowly, be afraid only of standing still.*
>
> —CHINESE PROVERB

You may find it difficult to restoke your enthusiasm for enlightenment. Not to worry, that is a common and natural progression.

> *Flowers do not force their way with great strife. Flowers open to*
> *perfection slowly in the sun. . . . Don't be in a hurry about spiritual*
> *matters. Go step by step, and be very sure.*
>
> —WHITE EAGLE

It takes time to expand the capacity of your consciousness. Pace yourself, and the day will come when you can skillfully drink in new ideas, integrate them into your perspective, and most importantly, reflect them in your relationships with others and with God.

> *Spiritual growth results from absorbing and digesting truth and putting it to practice in daily life.*
>
> —WHITE EAGLE

Take all the time you need. God has infinite patience and the laws of the Universe will continue to operate.

> *If you understand, things are just as they are; if you do not understand, things are just as they are.*
>
> —ZEN PROVERB

A word of caution: Watch out for a disconnect between *learning* these principles and *living* them.

> *However many holy words you read, however many you speak, what good will they do you if you do not act upon them?*
>
> —BUDDHA

Be wary of becoming so enamored with thinking and talking about these concepts that you downplay the need to put them into practice.

> *It is so fatally easy to confuse an aesthetic appreciation of the spiritual life with the life itself—to dream that you have waked, washed, and dressed and then to find yourself still in bed.*
>
> —C. S. LEWIS

FORGING AHEAD

As you accept the notion of Divine Intelligence at work in the world, your awareness of and appreciation for the perfection of Universal Law gradually expands.

I have observed the power of the watermelon seed. It has the power of drawing from the ground and through itself 200,000 times its weight. When you can tell me how it takes this material and out of it colors an outside surface beyond the imitation of art, and then forms inside of it a white rind and within that again a red heart, thickly inlaid with black seeds, each one of which in turn is capable of drawing through itself 200,000 times its weight— when you can explain to me the mystery of the watermelon, you can ask me to explain the mystery of God.

—WILLIAM JENNINGS BRYAN

As you expand the scope of your awareness, the scope of your non-awareness expands as well.

Real knowledge is to know the extent of one's ignorance.

—CONFUCIUS

You glimpse the vastness of how much there is to know and humbly realize how little of it you comprehend.

As a human being, one has been endowed with just enough intelligence to be able to see clearly how utterly inadequate that intelligence is when confronted with what exists.

—ALBERT EINSTEIN

Know that a day filled with one *Eureka!* moment after another represents but a single drop in the ocean of all there is to know.

Between our birth and death we may touch understanding,
As a moth brushes a window with its wing.

—CHRISTOPHER FRY

If answers to crucial questions continue to elude you, do not despair. Rather, be delighted that there is so much yet to learn.

*I would like to beg you, dear Sir, as well as I can, to have patience
with everything unresolved in your heart and to try and love* the
questions themselves *as if they were locked rooms or books
written in a very foreign language. Don't search for the answers,
which could not be given to you now, because you would not be
able to live them. And the point is, to live everything. Live the
questions now. Perhaps then, someday far in the future, you will
gradually, without even noticing it, live your way into the answer.*

—RAINER MARIA RILKE

Think of yourself as a radio trying to tune in to higher spiritual frequencies. Keeping
yourself plugged into the Divine current deepens and enriches your understanding of
how the Universe operates.

The snow falls, each flake in its appropriate place.

—ZEN PROVERB

Upgrading your circuits through harmonious thinking and living is a lifelong process.
Every day brings exciting new opportunities for growth.

*The possession of knowledge does not kill the sense of wonder and
mystery. There is always more mystery.*

—ANAÏS NIN

Be kind to yourself and do not get discouraged when you slip up. Taking two steps
forward and one step back still moves you in the right direction.

*Never discourage anyone who continually makes progress, no
matter how slow.*

—PLATO

When you are ready to learn more, the Universe will make arrangements and the
appropriate opportunities will present themselves.

Going slowly does not prevent arriving.

—NIGERIAN PROVERB

In truth, there is never a time when you are *not* presented with such opportunities, because you are always ready to take a step forward.

> *Don't go through life, grow through life.*
>
> —ERIC BUTTERWORTH

Every step forward leads to another step, and another step beyond that. Push complacency to the side of the road and keep walking.

> *By God, don't linger*
> *in any spiritual benefit you have gained,*
> *but yearn for more—like one suffering from illness*
> *whose thirst for water is never quenched.*
> *This Divine Court is the Plane of the Infinite.*
> *Leave the seat of honor behind;*
> *let the Way be your seat of honor.*
>
> —RUMI

Enlightened souls who have come before us have planted signposts along the way. Such guidance is invaluable, yet your path is uniquely your own.

> *Looking for God is like seeking a path in a field of snow; if there is no path and you are looking for one, walk across it and there is your path.*
>
> —THOMAS MERTON

Do not look for your path; it does not yet exist. Your path takes shape with every step you take.

> *Wayfarer, the only way*
> *is your footsteps, there is no other.*
> *Wayfarer, there is no way,*
> *you make the way as you go.*
>
> —ANTONIO MACHADO

By virtue of attaining a blissful, unbroken state of God-union, these contemporary saints can effortlessly perform miracles that defy the laws of physics. Yet the general public will remain unaware of their existence.

> *Those who say, do not know; those who know, do not say.*
>
> —Lao Tzu

By definition, those who have achieved union with Divine Consciousness have transcended the ego. The notion that these selfless saints would flaunt their abilities is unthinkable; holiness and humility walk hand in hand.

> *If I were to display the powers God has given me, I could draw thousands. But the path to God is not a circus. I gave the powers back to God, and I never use them unless He tells me to. My mission is to awaken love for God in the soul of man. I prefer a soul to a crowd, and I love crowds of souls.*
>
> —Paramahansa Yogananda

We must view these masters not as great *exceptions* but as great *examples* of what is possible when human consciousness is expanded to receive the Divine.

> *Jesus, like Krishna and Buddha, symbolizes what human nature can become. Are we only to adore them? They are showing us what we can be. We are not to worship them; we are to become them, and then go farther.*
>
> —Swami Rama

Christians, for example, are better served by striving to become more *Christ-like* (through internal enlightenment) instead of more *like Christ* (through external action). As they become more Christ-like, they will naturally act in ways that are more like Christ.

> *He that believeth in Me, the works that I do he shall do also; and greater works than these shall he do.*
>
> —Jesus of Nazareth
> John 14:12

ENLIGHTENMENT AWAITS

Imagine discovering that an elaborate jigsaw puzzle is covering your entire dining room table. As a human being, your initial view of the world is akin to looking at a small corner piece of that puzzle and thinking it is the whole puzzle. As awareness builds and evidence mounts, you begin believing that there is a larger puzzle to contend with. Apply enough diligence and devotion and you experience self-realization, the intuitive knowing that you yourself are every piece of the puzzle. Further purify your mind, heart, and spirit, and you may reach enlightenment, the state of authentically being and living that truth.

> *In the world's audience hall, the simple blade of grass sits on the same carpet with the sunbeam and the stars of midnight.*
>
> —RABINDRANATH TAGORE

The four steps to enlightenment, then, are learning, believing, knowing, and being. Each of these steps demands more courage and faith than the one before. Their order is absolute—none may be leapfrogged.

> *There are no shortcuts to any place worth going.*
>
> —BEVERLY SILLS

The chasm between believing and knowing can be traversed with a single bound. It is the distinction between faith that flows from intellectually knowing *about* God versus intuitively knowing God's *presence*.

> *It has pleased God that divine verities should not enter the heart through the understanding, but the understanding through the heart.*
>
> —BLAISE PASCAL

In a famous 1959 BBC interview, host John Freeman asked Carl Jung, the founder of analytical psychology, "Do you now believe in God?" Jung responded, "I don't need to believe . . . I know."

> *Faith is like radar that sees through the fog—the reality of things at a distance that the human eye cannot see.*
>
> —CORRIE TEN BOOM

Self-realization dawns when you realize through direct contact with God that your self is one with the Divine Self in body, mind, and spirit.

> *Faith is not a thing to grasp, it is a state to grow to.*
>
> —Mahatma Gandhi

This exalted state of conscious unity with the Divine cannot be explained; it can only be experienced.

> *Words end where truth begins.*
>
> —Unknown

Humbly acknowledging that God is beyond knowing does not alter your conviction— you know that you know God.

> *Faith is a knowledge within the heart, beyond the reach of proof.*
>
> —Kahlil Gibran

The paradox is that even when you know that you know God, you know that you do not know God.

> *God is not what you imagine or what you think you understand.*
> *If you understand you have failed.*
>
> —Saint Augustine

Claiming that you know God implies that you understand God and, by extension, God's plan for you.

> *What is demanded of man is not, as some existential philosophers*
> *teach, to endure the meaninglessness of life, but rather to bear his*
> *incapacity to grasp its unconditional meaningfulness in rational*
> *terms.*
>
> —Viktor Frankl

The best that you can hope for is to experience the peace beyond all understanding that comes from feeling God's loving presence in every moment.

And I say to mankind, Be not curious about God,
For I who am curious about each am not curious about God . . .
I hear and behold God in every object, yet understand God not
in the least.

—WALT WHITMAN

THE JOURNEY'S END

The step-by-step transformation from ignorance to cosmic consciousness is vividly portrayed in the blockbuster movie, *The Matrix*. In the beginning, Neo, the central character, is clueless that his world is an elaborate fabrication. Exposed to the truth, he continues to resist until the existence of a different reality can no longer be ignored. Over time, he wraps his mind around the concept until it is fully integrated into his consciousness. Finally, as his life hangs in the balance, he experiences an epiphany and becomes one with the cosmos.

If your knowledge of fire has been turned to certainty by words
alone, then seek to be cooked by the fire itself.
Don't abide in borrowed certainty.
There is no real certainty until you burn;
if you wish for this, sit down in the fire.

—RUMI

Neo's journey—fictional, yes, but symbolic of great truths—demonstrates that a path relying solely on research, rationality, and reflection has its limits.

Reality divided by reason always leaves a remainder. After
everything has been said about the universe, after the entire world
has been transformed on the basis of scientific knowledge into a
hierarchical structure of ever-widening systems, we are still left
with a profound sense of mystery. . . . This luminous experience
of the impenetrable mystery is common to all the scientists,
philosophers, and mystics of the highest rank. The scientist calls
it the mystery of Nature. The philosopher calls it the mystery of
Being. The mystic calls it the mystery of the Spirit.

—HARIDAS CHAUDHURI

Indeed, the mind, which relies on the senses for its information, is fundamentally unable to lead you to God.

> *We have no sense that can reveal knowledge of Him; the senses give knowledge only of His manifestations. No thought or inference can enable us to know Him as He truly is, for thought cannot go beyond the data of the senses; it can only arrange and interpret the impressions of the senses.*
>
> —Paramahansa Yogananda

While you may intellectually accept the existence of God as an idea, this idea is like all ideas: a detached mental construct unable to satisfy your deep longing for love and connection.

> *Faith is an oasis in the heart which will never be reached by the caravan of thinking.*
>
> —Kahlil Gibran

Although logic and reason are indispensable pillars of a civilized life, the finite mind is incapable of perceiving that which is infinite.

> *Some like to understand what they believe in. Others like to believe in what they understand.*
>
> —Stanislaw Jerzy Lec

Your search for God will find fulfillment only if you are willing to leap beyond your intellect into the arms of faith.

> *Faith is a sounder guide than reason. Reason can go only so far, but faith has no limits.*
>
> —Blaise Pascal

Life becomes willing to reveal its mysteries when you become aware of that which exists beyond your awareness.

> *It is one of the commonest of mistakes to consider that the limit of
> our power of perception is also the limit of all there is to perceive.*
>
> —C. W. LEADBEATER

Your journey will be uneven. There will be effortless days when the sun is shining and birds are singing, but there will also be dark nights when the road is perilous and a chill wind blows. Press on.

> *If you don't invite God to be your summer Guest, He won't come
> in the winter of your life.*
>
> —LAHIRI MAHASAYA

You need not make the journey alone. By all means, follow the teachings of a God-enlightened guru or other spiritual teacher, as long as you view your teacher as a gateway to your destination and not the destination itself.

> *I am but a finger pointing at the moon. Don't look at me; look at
> the moon.*
>
> —BODHIDHARMA

As your attunement with the Divine current grows ever stronger, so too does your yearning for God.

> *There is a God-shaped vacuum in every heart.*
>
> —BLAISE PASCAL

Surrender to this longing. Let it consume you. Live your life so that everything you think, say, and do brings you ever nearer to God.

> *Do not seek illumination unless you seek it as a man whose hair is
> on fire seeks a pond.*
>
> —SRI RAMAKRISHNA

You are on the right path when you find yourself spontaneously reflecting the warmth and tenderness of Divine love to every soul you encounter.

A religious awakening which does not awaken the sleeper to love
has roused him in vain.

—JESSAMYN WEST

Every day in which you joyously dive into the ocean of Divine love rewards you with one more day of experiencing the ever-new joy of heaven on earth.

All the way to heaven is heaven.

—SAINT CATHERINE OF SIENA

Close your mind to the existence of God, and you close the door to a wondrous new dimension bursting with untold opportunities to welcome even more peace, joy, and love into your heart.

Remember this. When people choose to withdraw far from a fire,
the fire continues to give warmth, but they grow cold. When
people choose to withdraw far from light, the light continues to be
bright in itself but they are in darkness. This is also the case when
people withdraw from God.

—SAINT AUGUSTINE

You must come to God through your own free will. If God appeared today in human form to erase all doubt about the existence of God, many would bow down out of fear or obligation instead of faith and devotion.

There will never be conclusive proof that God exists because that
would take away your freedom to believe that there is no God.

—DUANE ALAN HAHN

Do not for a moment think you are not worthy of the journey. Enlightenment is no longer the exclusive domain of robed renunciates in secluded monasteries.

We have been too content with allocating the high places of spirituality to the few names of a far-off past, and with assigning the muddy depths to humanity in general. We forget our own divine nature. For we too can approach Jesus, become Buddha-like or win the wisdom of a Plato.

—PAUL BRUNTON

From time immemorial, it was believed that many are called but few are chosen. All, in fact, are called.

All know the Way; few actually walk it.

—BODHIDHARMA

Will you choose to respond to that call with the limited logic of your mind or the limitless love in your heart?

Throw your heart over the fence and the rest will follow.

—NORMAN VINCENT PEALE

Ultimately, the path to enlightenment circles back to you. You are not only the seeker on the journey, you are the journey itself as well as the journey's end.

The path that you follow is not about going somewhere, but about coming back to you. Over and over again. Only this time, you are awake to who that is and the life that you are living.

—ANGEL KYODO WILLIAMS

There has never been a better time, there will never be a better time, to begin looking at the world through God's eyes.

There is only one time when it is essential to awaken. That time is now.

—BUDDHA

RETHINK YOUR WORLDVIEW
Living the Lesson

I had always striven to be the life of the party in high school and college, cracking jokes and hamming it up. In my mid-twenties, as the fog of immaturity began lifting, I became dimly aware that the self-absorbed world I inhabited had been sheltering me from the hard work of growing up. It's only a slight exaggeration to say that ten years out of high school, I still possessed the social graces and life skills of a teenage boy.

I began dreading parties, especially those where intelligent conversation was expected. Surrounded by smart, successful people, I felt like a one-man island of ignorance, disconnected from everyone and largely ignored. No wonder others had no interest in talking to me; I had nothing to say. I had grown stagnant.

Then I picked up Shirley MacLaine's book, *Out on a Limb*. I was amazed, excited, and inspired by her metaphysical adventures: her reunion with a mysterious messenger, her out-of body experience, her work with a spiritual medium. I didn't know what "enlightenment" was, but I knew I wanted to experience it for myself. A whole new world had opened up to me. This wasn't a spiritual alarm clock ringing, it was a four-alarm fire.

I sought out more books about spirituality: *Love, Medicine & Miracles* by Dr. Bernie Siegel; *Creating Money: Keys to Abundance* by Sanaya Roman and Duane Packer; *Creative Visualization* by Shakti Gawain. The concepts I encountered in these and other books were wild, outrageous, and mind-boggling; yet on some level they all resonated with me.

As my mind opened and my heart expanded, life lovingly spread her arms to receive me. I looked at people differently; I was less judgmental and selfish, more loving and compassionate. There was more depth to me.

As maturity beckoned, I heard the first faint urgings of my life's work, calling to me from the far reaches of my consciousness. I found my voice and began actively writing for the first time since childhood. I finally had something to say.

Six months after my thirty-fifth birthday, I was at work when a subtle shift occurred. All the spiritual principles I had learned decided they had mingled long enough; in a heartbeat, they coalesced and migrated from my head to my heart. There was no *Eureka!* moment; I just suddenly felt calmer, wiser, more peaceful and happy. I remember thinking, *Oh, now I get it. This is what it's supposed to feel like.* Instinctively, I knew that an exciting new chapter of life had begun.

Today, nineteen years later, the memory of that day makes me smile—the kind of tender, doting smile I had given my daughter when she proudly showed me the A she received on her second-grade essay. At thirty-five, I was still pretty clueless, but at least I was headed in the right direction. Who knows? Perhaps in another nineteen years, I will look back at the person I am today and chuckle again at how little I really knew.

I sure hope so.

RETHINK YOUR WORLDVIEW
Self-Reflection Questions

- Why or why not is the complexity of the Universe evidence of Divine Intelligence at work?

- What evidence tells me that God is friendly, hostile, or indifferent?

- Why do I believe or disbelieve that God has a plan for each of us and for all of humanity?

- If I encounter information that clashes with my conception of God, how open am I to rethinking my position?

- Have I chosen my beliefs about God or have I accepted what I've been told to believe?

- What makes me so sure that there is or is not a world existing beyond my five senses?

- How does my relationship with God affect my relationships with others?

- In what ways might I not be as enlightened as I think I am?

- How can faith and intuition co-exist with logic and rational analysis?

- How strong is the longing within me to know and love God more deeply?

- Why am I worthy of God's love?

- What steps can I take to deepen my relationship with God?

TWO

YOU ARE NOT SEPARATE FROM GOD

God enters by a private door into every individual.

—RALPH WALDO EMERSON

YOU ARE NOT SEPARATE FROM GOD

The very life force within you is a Divine spark, an extension of God, of Spirit. Though you cannot claim to be God, God's Divine essence is your birthright.

> *However many generations in your mortal ancestry, no matter what race or people you represent, the pedigree of your spirit can be written on a single line. You are a child of God!*
>
> —BOYD K. PACKER

A DROP OF GOD

Spirit is the Source of all that is and all that ever will be. All of creation flows from Spirit and will ultimately flow back into Spirit. Nothing exists beyond the limits of Spirit because Spirit is limitless and infinite.

> *All are but parts of one stupendous whole,*
> *Whose body Nature is, and God the soul.*
>
> —ALEXANDER POPE

Your soul, the individualized God force within you, is but a wave of spirit in the vast ocean of Spirit.

> *Your soul is the part of you that is universal and individual at the same time, and it is a reflection of all other souls.*
>
> —DEEPAK CHOPRA

Just as a wave is not the ocean itself, still it is of the ocean and has all the characteristics of the ocean.

> *The wave cannot say, "I am the ocean," because the ocean can exist without the wave. But the ocean can say, "I am the wave," because the wave cannot exist without the ocean.*
>
> —PARAMAHANSA YOGANANDA

Just as the ocean is behind every individual wave, so is God behind every breath you take.

> *You are never alone or helpless. The force that guides the stars*
> *guides you too.*
>
> —Shrii Shrii Anandamurti

In truth, stating that your soul is within you is taking poetic license; your body does not *contain* your soul. It is more accurate to say that your body inhabits your soul than that your soul inhabits your body.

> *You don't* have *a soul . . . You* are *a soul. You* have *a body,*
> *temporarily.*
>
> —Walter M. Miller, Jr.

Your soul is a perfect reflection of God. It has always existed and will always exist. It is timeless, unchangeable, and everlasting.

> *You are as old as God and as young as the morning.*
>
> —Hilda Charlton

To paraphrase the Bhagavad Gita, the holiest of ancient Hindu scriptures, the eternal soul cannot be burned by fire, drowned by water, or pierced by any weapon.

> *I am so fully convinced that the soul is indestructible, and that its*
> *activity will continue through eternity. It is like the sun, which*
> *seems to our earthly eyes to set in night, but is in reality gone to*
> *diffuse its light elsewhere.*
>
> —Johann Wolfgang von Goethe

Your soul is the gateway to eternity. Look within your own soul and you will glimpse the inexpressible beauty that awaits you on the other side of creation.

> *The soul is the mirror of an indestructible universe.*
>
> —Gottfried Leibniz

Your soul expresses itself as spirit, ceaselessly urging you to take flight, to soar toward the heavens and dance ecstatically among the stars.

> *I have a brightness in my soul, which strains toward Heaven. I am like a bird!*
>
> —JENNY LIND

CONNECTED TO ALL OF CREATION

The only distance between you and God is the thought that there is distance between you and God.

> *You are a drop of God in a sea of God.*
>
> —DONALD SCHNELL

God is not just present in every human being. There is no thing and no place where God is not.

> *God is that Supreme Intelligence which governs everything.*
>
> —ANCIENT WISDOM

If you believe that God is not present within you, you go through life disconnected from the very essence that sustains you.

> *To think you are separate from God is to remain separate from your own being.*
>
> —D. M. STREET

Expand the scope of your vision by looking through God's eyes, and no matter what you look at, it will be brimming over with God's loving presence.

> *If in thirst you drink water from a cup, you see God in it. Those who are not in love with God will see only their own faces in it.*
>
> —RUMI

If nothing is separate from God, then at the deepest level we are all connected to every atom of creation.

> *Seen from a divine perspective, God is the center of the universe, and that center is everywhere. In those moments when you feel most deeply in touch with God, you naturally experience yourself as being at the very center of everything.*
>
> —HUSTON SMITH

All that separates us from others, as Indian yogi Paramahansa Yogananda noted, are "partitions of ego consciousness."

> *All souls are one. Each is a spark of the original soul. And this soul is inherent in all souls.*
>
> —HASIDIC WISDOM

As Hindu scriptures state, at its deepest level creation is indivisible. Every thought, every action is a cause whose effect echoes endlessly throughout the Universe.

> *My brother asked the birds to forgive him; that sounds senseless, but it is right; for all is like an ocean, all is flowing and bending; a touch in one place sets up movement at the other end of the earth. It may be senseless to beg forgiveness of the birds, but birds would be happier at your side—a little happier anyway—and children and all animals, if you were nobler than you are now.*
>
> —FYODOR DOSTOYEVSKY

The complex web of Divine energy that we call the Universe is referred to in quantum physics by such names as the Unified Field, Quantum Hologram, Consciousness Grid, Field of Potential, or Nonlocal Intelligence.

> *Humankind has not woven the web of life. We are but one thread within it. Whatever we do to the web, we do to ourselves. All things are bound together. All things connect.*
>
> —TED PERRY

The more we learn about the workings of the Universe, the closer we move to circling back to what we already instinctively know.

> *The quantum hologram has always been here; it is everywhere*
> *all the time; and it appears to have what Western scientists are*
> *now calling "intelligence." Except for the language, this field*
> *sounds very similar to what the ancients called God.*
>
> —GREGG BRADEN

Alternative medicine pioneer Deepak Chopra describes the conscious energy field that sustains us as "literally an expression of the mind of God."

> *The world has not to be put in order: the world is order incarnate.*
> *It is for us to put ourselves in unison with this order.*
>
> —HENRY MILLER

Indeed, the Unified Field, which connects everything in the Universe to everything else beyond space and time, is the manifestation of consciousness itself.

> *One Nature, perfect and pervading, circulates in all natures;*
> *One Reality, all comprehensive, contains within itself all realities;*
> *The one moon reflects itself wherever there is a sheet of water,*
> *And all the moons in the waters are embraced within the one*
> *moon.*
>
> —YUNG-CHIA TA-SHIH

Given that psychiatrist and author Dr. David. R. Hawkins defines consciousness as "an impersonal quality of Divinity expressed as awareness," think of God as an acronym for Governing Omnipresent Divinity. God is all that is unmanifested, expressing itself through all that is manifest.

> *Then comes the faith and the insight that All is God. And the*
> *darkness of "the world of confusion," of the confusion of good and*
> *evil, retreats from our sight. One still realizes that the world is as*
> *it was, but it does not matter, it does not affect one's faith.*
>
> —RABBI ABRAHAM J. HESCHEL

DREAMING THE DREAM

Hinduism takes the concept of the Unified Field a step further by viewing the material world as a dream of God's, a projection of cosmic consciousness. Vishnu, a deity exalted as the highest God in the Bhagavad Gita, is portrayed as the Divine Dreamer of the world dream.

> *One does not dream: one is dreamed. We "undergo" the dream, we are the objects.*
>
> —CARL JUNG

We are not separate from God, and so we dream the dream along with God. The dream and the dreamer are one and the same.

> *We are literally God exploring God's Self in an infinite Dance of Life.*
>
> —MELLEN-THOMAS BENEDICT

What we call reality is but a dreamscape within Reality, the Divine realm where peace, love, and beauty reign.

> *Nothing real can be threatened. Nothing unreal exists. Herein lies the peace of God.*
>
> —A COURSE IN MIRACLES

The notion that all of creation emanates from—and exists within—the mind of God supports the contention that time is an illusion, a human-made construct.

> *For us believing physicists, the distinction between past, present, and future is only a stubbornly persistent illusion.*
>
> —ALBERT EINSTEIN

Anchored in time-bound reality, we genuflect in front of life's hourglass, unaware that time exists only as a thought, made real only because we are thinking it.

It is the mind, it is thought that creates time. Thought is time, and whatever thought projects must be of time; therefore, thought cannot possibly go beyond itself. To discover what is beyond time, thought must come to an end.

—JIDDU KRISHNAMURTI

This mind-bending hypothesis, increasingly embraced by theoretical physicists, holds that everything that has happened, or ever will happen, is happening *now*.

The future is only the past again, entered through another gate.

—ARTHUR WING PINERO

The controversy over time can be settled by noting the distinction between reality and Reality. Space and time are confined to the physical world (reality). In the realms beyond mortal consciousness (Reality), there is only the Eternal Now.

Time, then, is much like a hologram ... There's no beginning or end to a hologram, it's already everywhere, complete—in fact, the appearance of being "unfinished" is part of its completeness. ... Our perception of events happening in time is analogous to a traveler watching the landscape unfold before him. But to say that the landscape unfolds before the traveler is merely a figure of speech—nothing is actually unfolding; nothing is actually becoming manifest. There's only the progression of awareness.

—DR. DAVID R. HAWKINS

In looking at the world through God's eyes, we become awake in the dream, awed by the unity, timelessness, and perfection of Reality.

Time is the substance of which I am made. Time is a river which sweeps me along, but I am the river; it is a tiger which mangles me, but I am the tiger; it is a fire which consumes me, but I am the fire.

—JORGE LUIS BORGES

In his book, *Vibrational Medicine*, Dr. Richard Gerber describes all matter as "frozen light," light which has been slowed down and become solid. This light, the light of Divine Consciousness, can be compared to the light emanating from a movie projector.

As moving pictures are sustained by a beam of light coming from the projection booth of a movie house, so are all of us sustained by the Cosmic Beam, the Divine Light pouring from the projection booth of Eternity.

—Paramahansa Yogananda

The forms projected on the screen appear separate from one another; but try to grab an object from the screen and you discover that, just as all creation is but a single Divine thought, the lifelike reality on the screen is produced by a single beam of light.

The external world of physics has thus become a world of shadows. In removing our illusions we have removed the substance, for indeed we have seen that substance is one of the greatest of our illusions.

—Sir Arthur Stanley Eddington

Switch off the projector of God's mind and we would cease to exist as surely as celluloid characters vanish when the movie projector is unplugged.

So impossible is it for the world to continue without God that if God were able to forget the world it would instantly disappear.

—Søren Kierkegaard

This world may be a dream of God's, but, by design, we who live in the physical world view it as bracingly real and rife with meaning and purpose.

I believe in a spiritual world—not as anything separate from this world—but as its innermost truth. With the breath we draw we must always feel this truth, that we are living in God.

—Rabindranath Tagore

Perhaps when we leave this life behind, we will "awaken" to a more advanced plane of existence, a vibrationally superior dimension that serves as yet another screen for the manifestation of projected Light.

*We sometimes congratulate ourselves at the moment of waking
from a troubled dream: it may be so the moment after death.*

—NATHANIEL HAWTHORNE

In that transcendent moment, we may very well look back at this existence as a dream,
just as we awaken every morning and look back with amusement or relief at the dreams
that seemed so real in our sleeping hours.

*The mind looks at unity and sees diversity; it looks at what is
timeless and reports transience. And in fact the percepts of its
experience are diverse and transient; on this level of experience,
separateness is real. Our mistake is in taking this for ultimate
reality, like the dreamer thinking that nothing is real except his
dream.*

—EKNATH EASWARAN

THE SOUL OF THE WHOLE

While the Source behind everything in the material world is changeless and eternal,
the material world itself is ultimately ephemeral.

*Everything you see has its roots in the Unseen world.
The forms may change, yet the essence remains the same.
Every wondrous sight will vanish, every sweet word will fade.
But do not be disheartened,
The Source they come from is eternal—
Growing, branching out, giving new life and new joy.
Why do you weep?—
That Source is within you.
And this whole world is springing up from it.*

—RUMI

Great masters throughout the ages have taught: *That which is real is that which never
changes.*

A human being is a part of the whole, called by us "Universe,"
a part limited in time and space. He experiences himself, his
thoughts, and feelings as something separate from the rest—
a kind of optical delusion of his consciousness. The striving to
free oneself from this delusion is the one issue of true religion.
Not to nourish it but to try to overcome it is the way to reach
the attainable measure of peace of mind.

—ALBERT EINSTEIN

We awaken to that reality when we learn to see the world through God's eyes instead of our own.

They say to me in their awakening, "You and the world you live in
are but a grain of sand upon the infinite shore of an infinite sea."
And in my dream I say to them, "I am the infinite sea, and all
worlds are but grains of sand upon my shore."

—KAHLIL GIBRAN

EGO vs. SPIRIT

You will not elevate your awareness until you align yourself more with your spirit than with your ego.

Ego is to the true self what a flashlight is to a spotlight.

—JOHN BRADSHAW

Ego and spirit are polar opposites. When the soul aligns itself with the mind and body, it unconsciously manifests as ego.

Imagine a ray of sunlight that has forgotten it is an inseparable
part of the sun and deludes itself into believing it has to fight for
survival and create and cling to an identity other than the sun.
Would the death of this delusion not be incredibly liberating?

—ECKHART TOLLE

When the soul realizes its Divine nature, it transcends the body-consciousness of the ego, and spirit joyously aligns with Spirit.

> *Come out into the broad open light of day, come out from the little*
> *narrow paths, for how can the infinite soul rest content to live and*
> *die in small ruts? Come out into the universe of Light. Everything*
> *in the universe is yours, stretch out your arms and embrace it*
> *with love.*
>
> —SWAMI VIVEKANANDA

The difference between your ego and your spirit is the difference between thinking and awareness. Thinking is realization via the self-contained content of your mind. Awareness is Self-realization via conscious attunement with Divine Intelligence.

> *The essence of who you are is consciousness. When consciousness*
> *(you) becomes completely identified with thinking and thus forgets*
> *its essential nature, it loses itself in thought.*
>
> —ECKHART TOLLE

When you look through God's eyes, you see the context of life. When you look through your eyes, you see the content of life.

> *The most common ego identifications have to do with possessions,*
> *the work you do, social status and recognition, knowledge and*
> *education, physical appearance, special abilities, relationships,*
> *personal and family history, belief systems, and often also*
> *political, nationalistic, racial, religious, and other collective*
> *identifications. None of these is you.*
>
> —ECKHART TOLLE

What your ego sees is not an intelligent, orderly Universe populated by divine beings, but a projection of a deeply flawed worldview based on your own experiences, biases, and judgments.

> *Judgment means that you view the world as you are, rather than*
> *as it is.*
>
> —WAYNE DYER

By focusing solely on the material world and believing only in the reality you can confirm with your five senses, you forget your Divine heritage.

> *It is the ultimate human paradox that man's dependence on*
> *perception precludes his being able to know his own identity.*
>
> —Dr. David R. Hawkins

Look to the outer world and you see yourself as a human being. Look to your inner world and you see yourself as a spiritual being.

> *We behold what we are, and we are what we behold.*
>
> —John of Ruysbroeck

Ego cunningly shields your eyes from the light of Spirit that ceaselessly bathes you in its loving, protective glow.

> *Nothing hath separated us from God but our own will, or rather*
> *our own will is our separation from God.*
>
> —William Law

Yet despite your ego's best efforts, you can never fully tune out the gentle but persistent stirrings of your soul.

> *When I am bound by nature, by name and form, by time, space,*
> *and causality, I do not know what I truly am. But even in this*
> *bondage my real Self is not completely lost. I strain against the*
> *bonds; one by one they break, and I become conscious of my*
> *innate grandeur.*
>
> —Swami Vivekananda

When you identify with ego, with separateness and scarcity, you see yourself as alone and vulnerable in an unfriendly world.

> *For it's only the illusion of individuality that is the origin of all*
> *suffering—when one realizes that one is the universe, complete*
> *and at one with all that is, forever without end, then no further*
> *suffering is possible.*
>
> —Dr. David R. Hawkins

Transcend your ego, and you discover that behind every perceived separation from Spirit is a doorway to the Divine.

> *Two prisoners whose cells adjoin communicate with each other by*
> *knocking on the wall. The wall is the thing which separates them*
> *but it is also their means of communication. It is the same with us*
> *and God. Every separation is a link.*
>
> —Simone Weil

Lose yourself in ego and you unconsciously act selfishly. Lose yourself in Spirit and you consciously act selflessly.

> *Once you get hold of selflessness, you'll be dragged from your ego*
> *and freed from many traps.*
> *Come, return to the root of the root of your self.*
>
> —Rumi

Ego directs you to judge others by the way they look and act. Spirit urges you to look past superficialities and honor the Divine essence in all.

> *As we persist in judging one another by what we appear to be, we*
> *are all taking part in a great masquerade.*
>
> —Joel Goldsmith

The voice of your spirit sings out, "One for all, and all for one." The voice of your ego smugly announces, "It's all about me."

> *Ego has a voracious appetite, the more you feed it, the hungrier*
> *it gets.*
>
> —Nathaniel Bronner, Jr.

Only God-illumined souls vanquish the ego altogether. The rest of us must rely on daily discipline and eternal vigilance to keep our ego in check.

> *If you want to reach a state of bliss, then go beyond your ego and the internal dialogue. Make a decision to relinquish the need to control, the need to be approved, and the need to judge. Those are the three things the ego is doing all the time. It's very important to be aware of them every time they come up.*
>
> —DEEPAK CHOPRA

The challenge is maintaining the right balance of ego and spirit so that your spirit is firmly in command, like a parent lovingly guiding a child. Like a child, your ego is motivated by the need for attention, validation, and independence.

> *There is a point where destiny and chaos walk hand in hand, when ego and soul force become one, when your ego becomes a servant of the soul.*
>
> —CAROLINE MYSS

If your ego is driving your quest for enlightenment, enlightenment will remain forever beyond your reach.

> *The attainment of enlightenment from ego's point of view is extreme death, the death of self, the death of me and mine, the death of the watcher. It is the ultimate and final disappointment.*
>
> —CHÖGYAM TRUNGPA

If your only desire is loving and serving God, enlightenment waits patiently and lovingly on the other side of devotion.

> *Out of an unrestricted love for God arises the willingness to surrender all motives, except to serve God completely. To be the servant of God becomes one's goal rather than enlightenment.*
>
> —DR. DAVID R. HAWKINS

Switch your allegiance from your ego to your spirit, and pressure and struggling give way to peace and serenity.

When you move from ego to spirit, you go from striving to arriving.

—WAYNE DYER

The more you empty yourself of your ego and your own self-importance, the more room there is to welcome your spirit.

The very foundation of the spiritual life is humility. Without humility the cup of one's consciousness is so filled with "I, I, I" that there is no room for "Thou, Thou, Thou."

—SRI DAYA MATA

But beware: Like an incumbent politician who is all bluster and no substance, your ego is programmed for self-preservation at all costs.

The ego is simultaneously enamored with its self-appointed magnitude and terrified at its real ineptness.

—ALAN COHEN

Back your ego into a corner and it can slither out like a seductive snake, shrewdly tempting you back toward the sense pleasures of the material world and away from the soul pleasures of the spiritual path.

A whole person is one who has both walked with God and wrestled with the devil.

—CARL JUNG

The wise spiritual aspirant discerns the difference between self-destructive pleasures and those earthly delights that inspire one's spirit to soar to ever greater heights of exultation.

I believe God made me for a purpose, but he also made me fast. And when I run I feel his pleasure.

—ERIC LIDDELL

Your spirit is the angel on your left shoulder, reassuring you that you are a perfect creation of God, that you already have everything you need.

> *For I can see in your eyes*
> *That you are exquisitely woven with the finest silk and wool*
> *And that Pattern upon your soul has the signature of God*
> *And all your moods and colors of love*
> *Come from His Divine vats of dye and gold.*
>
> —HAFIZ

Your ego is the devil on your right shoulder, incessantly whispering that you are stronger or weaker than others, that you are entitled to or are unworthy of riches, that you must always look out for number one or for everyone but yourself.

> *Unworthiness is simply a case of mistaken identify.*
>
> —ALAN COHEN

Steeped in abundance, spirit shares and is always content. Cowering in scarcity, ego takes and is never satisfied.

> *You are spiritually whole, complete and perfect, and your success*
> *and happiness in life will be in direct proportion to your ability to*
> *accept this truth about yourself.*
>
> —DR. ROBERT ANTHONY

No matter how great your effort to live completely in Spirit, your ego is like a beach ball held under water; one slip, and it shoots to the surface to reassert its dominance.

> *I came out alone on my way to my tryst. But who is this that*
> *follows me in the silent dark? I move aside to avoid his presence*
> *but I escape him not.*
> *He makes the dust rise from the earth with his swagger; he adds*
> *his loud voice to every word that I utter.*
> *He is my own little self, my lord, he knows no shame; but I am*
> *ashamed to come to thy door in his company.*
>
> —RABINDRANATH TAGORE

As you submerge your ego under the waters of Self-realization while simultaneously lifting your eyes to behold the face of God, earthly desires loosen their hold on you.

> *All earthly delights are sweeter in expectation than enjoyment;*
> *but all spiritual pleasures more in fruition than expectation.*
>
> —FRANÇOIS FÉNELON

As awareness expands, you periodically ask yourself, *Is what I'm doing serving God?* You remind yourself daily to be a "servant of Spirit" instead of an "emperor of ego."

> *It is on the anvil of this gross earth that struggling man must*
> *hammer out the imperishable gold of spiritual identity.*
>
> —PARAMAHANSA YOGANANDA

As the ego's power diminishes, so too does the fear of death, both consciously and unconsciously.

> *Everyone is so afraid of death, but the real Sufis just laugh:*
> *nothing tyrannizes their hearts.*
> *What strikes the oyster shell doesn't damage the pearl.*
>
> —RUMI

At the body's final breath, the God-illumined soul discards its "earth suit" as if it were tossing a dirty shirt in the hamper.

> *Life must be played by ear—which is only to say that we must*
> *trust, not symbolic rules and linear principles, but our brains or*
> *natures. Yet this must bring one back to the faith that nature*
> *makes no mistake. In such a universe a decision which results in*
> *one's own death is not a mistake: it is simply a way of dying at the*
> *right moment.*
>
> —ALAN WATTS

RELIGION AND SPIRITUALITY

Historically, the belief that we are separate from God was the chief differentiator between spirituality and most of the world's major religions. Over the last few decades, however, many faiths have embraced a more spiritual point of view.

> *If you don't have a temple in your heart, you'll never find your heart in a temple.*
>
> —SUFI WISDOM

Organized religion typically represents God as an external entity while spirituality portrays the Divine as an integral aspect of our humanity.

> *The world is filled with hungry souls who famish in the very presence of the bread of life; men die searching for the very God who lives within them. Men seek for the treasures of the kingdom with yearning hearts and weary feet when they are all within the immediate grasp of living faith.*
>
> —THE URANTIA BOOK 159:3.8

Both paths offer rich rewards. Some religious followers find deep meaning in celebrating and paying homage to their family heritage. Some spiritual seekers find peace and purpose in celebrating and honoring their Divine heritage.

> *Religion is a house; spirit is the air that flows through and around it.*
>
> —TOM GEGAX

Both paths have pitfalls. Organized religion plays a vital role in building community yet often positions itself as an indispensable intermediary between worshipers and God.

> *The religious community is essential, for alone our vision is too narrow to see all that must be seen, and our power too limited to do all that must be done. But together, our vision widens and our strength is renewed.*
>
> —MARK MORRISON-REED

Spirituality encourages direct contact with God; yet, without a disciplined commitment to self-awareness, seekers on the road to truth may miss the turn for humility and veer off toward arrogance.

> *Once the game is over, the king and the pawn go back in the*
> *same box.*
>
> —ITALIAN PROVERB

Traditionally, religion has been sociological and institutional while spirituality is individual and personal.

> *People in the West don't understand that a path of spirituality is*
> *not the same as professing a religion. One is built on experience,*
> *the other is accepted on faith.*
>
> —SWAMI RAMA

Many organized religions demand that you follow an external set of rules based on the experience of others, while spirituality encourages you to seek your own experiences through inner exploration and discovery.

> *Men substitute tradition for the living experience of the love of God.*
> *They talk and think as though walking with God was attained by*
> *walking in the footsteps of men who walked with God.*
>
> —WILLIAM CHARLES BRAITHWAITE

Organized religion is all about the depths of your beliefs. Spirituality is all about the depths of your consciousness.

> *Sometimes people get the mistaken notion that spirituality is a*
> *separate department of life, the penthouse of our existence. But*
> *rightly understood, it is a vital awareness that pervades all realms*
> *of our being.*
>
> —BROTHER DAVID STEINDL-RAST

Dogma preaches to us *about* God while spirituality teaches us to *achieve* God consciousness.

Many a doctrine is like a window pane. We see truth through it
but it divides us from truth.

—KAHLIL GIBRAN

While religious dogma may stifle self-expression, spiritual devotees often take great truths such as "God and I are one" out of context, misinterpret them, and apply them in ways that honor their ego rather than their spirit.

The world is a kind of spiritual kindergarten where millions of
bewildered infants are trying to spell God with the wrong blocks.

—EDWIN ARLINGTON ROBINSON

Organized religion has often been presented as a closed, hierarchical system. In such a structure, all questions lead to official explanations and individual interpretation is discouraged.

Believe those who are seeking the truth; doubt those who find it.

—ANDRÉ GIDE

Spirituality is an open, multifarious path with many questions leading to answers that cannot be fully grasped in the questioner's current state of consciousness. Individual evolvement is mandatory.

It is impossible for a man to begin to learn that which he thinks
that he knows.

—EPICTETUS

Religion and spirituality complement each other when religion is positioned not as a filter for rigidly interpreting God, but as a foundation for reaching out to God.

One of the main functions of formalized religion is to protect
people against a direct experience of God.

—CARL JUNG

Many organized religions assert that their method of worship is the only true path to God while ancient spiritual wisdom maintains that all rivers lead to the same ocean. Thus, when conflict arises, religion tends to divide while spirituality typically unites.

> *God made Truth with many doors to welcome every believer who knocks on them.*
>
> —KAHLIL GIBRAN

Enlightened seekers honor differing religious or spiritual views and celebrate the similarities in the core teachings of the world's major faiths.

> *Truth is a river that is always splitting up into arms that reunite. Islanded between the arms, the inhabitants argue for a lifetime as to which is the main river.*
>
> —CYRIL CONNOLLY

As we leave this world, no matter what our beliefs may be, we must all pass over the same bridge to whatever awaits us on the other side.

> *Faith does not change your destination.*
>
> —DUANE ALAN HAHN

HEAVEN ON EARTH

As they breathe their last, sinners and scoundrels are not consigned to burn in hellfire for all eternity. Hell is not a physical reality; it is a delusionary state of consciousness produced by our belief that we are separate from God—and the reflection of that consciousness in the life we create for ourselves here on earth.

> *The mind is its own place, and in itself Can make a Heav'n of Hell, a Hell of Heav'n.*
>
> —JOHN MILTON

God does not punish you; you punish yourself when you ignore God's Universal Laws of harmonious living.

> *We are our own devils; we drive ourselves out of our Edens.*
>
> —JOHANN WOLFGANG VON GOETHE

When you think, speak, or act dishonorably, your intuition drags you into court and your conscience hands down the verdict: guilty as charged.

> *The torture of a bad conscience is the hell of a living soul.*
>
> —JOHN CALVIN

The more you rationalize your unscrupulous intentions, the further away you drift on the ocean of delusion. The more you excuse your improper behavior, the higher rise the flames of your self-made purgatory.

> *The world of the ego is like a house of mirrors through which the ego wanders, lost and confused, as it chases the images in one mirror after another. Human life is characterized by endless trials and errors to escape the maze. At times, for many people, and possibly for most, the world of mirrors becomes a house of horrors that gets worse and worse. The only way out of the circuitous wanderings is through the pursuit of spiritual truth.*
>
> —DR. DAVID R. HAWKINS

All the while, your soul yearns to transcend the errors of your ego and reclaim its Divine stature.

> *Oh, then, soul, most beautiful among all the creatures, so anxious to know the dwelling place of your Beloved that you may go in quest of Him and be united with Him, now we are telling you that you yourself are His dwelling and His secret chamber and hiding place.*
>
> —SAINT JOHN OF THE CROSS

You need not struggle to find God. All you need to do is remember who and what you are.

> It is not difficult to find God. It is impossible to avoid God. There is nowhere (now here) where God is not.
>
> —DEEPAK CHOPRA

That *Aha!* moment—when you yank aside the curtain of illusion and embrace your Divine nature—is the moment you realize that heaven is a state of consciousness.

> The Kingdom of God cometh not with outward show. Neither shall they say, "Lo, it is here!" or "Lo, it is there!" For behold, the Kingdom of God is within you.
>
> —JESUS OF NAZARETH
> LUKE 17: 20-21

In that exultant moment, the sky of your consciousness is set ablaze with the rejoicing of a thousand suns.

> True enlightenment is nothing but the nature of one's own self being fully realized.
>
> —HIS HOLINESS THE 14TH DALAI LAMA

All of creation embraces you as the heavens call out a silent, joyous greeting: *Welcome home.*

> God-realization is the most natural thing there is. The amazing and incomprehensible fact is not that you *can* become conscious of God but that you *are* not conscious of God.
>
> —ECKHART TOLLE

YOU ARE NOT SEPARATE FROM GOD
Living the Lesson

Whenever I meet somebody new, my ego starts poking at me like a little kid, badgering me to blurt out something impressive so the person I'm talking to will find me interesting and special and worth listening to.

I monitor myself continually in social situations, and can see my ego barreling toward me from a mile away. Most of the time, I'm able to step in front of it and deflect it, but sometimes it crashes through my defenses and I find myself saying things like, "Yes, I wrote about that in my book."

On the way home from a social gathering, I mentally scan my "ego vs. spirit" scorecard. On a good night, my ego gets shut out and I congratulate myself on my restraint. On a typical night, I cringe as I recall gratuitously referencing my recent achievements and dropping a few names.

It's maddening! Even when I'm asking the other person questions about themselves and listening intently and genuinely, I'm constantly swatting my ego away. Yes, it's certainly acceptable, even advisable, to share information about yourself during social encounters, but only when asked and only to inform, not impress.

It's helpful to remind myself that the person I'm talking to is as much a child of God as I am. Focusing on their inner divinity snaps me out of my self-absorbed mindset and naturally produces feelings of curiosity, empathy, and love. I'm getting more vigilant about doing this because I much prefer being a sender of affection than the center of attention.

YOU ARE NOT SEPARATE FROM GOD
Self-Reflection Questions

- What makes me so sure that I share a divine connection with God or that I am separate and distinct from God?

- What is the nature of the connection I share with other human beings?

- In what ways am I connected to all of creation?

- What argument can I make for or against the idea that this life is but a dream of God?

- How can I break free from the constraints of time-bound reality and live with a greater sense of timelessness?

- What in this Universe is changeless and eternal?

- Do I define myself in terms of my spirit or of my mind and body, and how can I maintain a healthy balance?

- How do my experiences, biases, and judgments color the way I see the world?

- How can I train myself to be less self-absorbed and start living more consciously and selflessly?

- How can I do a better job of balancing sense pleasures and spiritual pleasures?

- How can I keep my ego in check so I can resist the urge to control, impress, and judge others?

- What appeals to me and what turns me off about religion and about spirituality?

THREE

YOU ARE BEAUTIFUL AND YOU ARE LOVED

Did we but know how much God loves us,
we should die of joy.

—UNKNOWN SAINT

YOU ARE BEAUTIFUL AND YOU ARE LOVED

Imagine a trusted friend approaching you, gazing into your eyes, and whispering, "You are beautiful and you are loved." You may vigorously protest, yet the truth and power of those seven words will resonate deep within your soul.

> *Your task is not to seek for love, but merely to seek and find all of the barriers within yourself that you have built against it.*
>
> —A COURSE IN MIRACLES

THE LIGHT INSIDE YOU

Your soul, that spark of the Infinite within you, always has been and always will be perfect and magnificent.

> *All the powers in the universe are already ours. It is we who have put our hands before our eyes and cry that it is dark.*
>
> —SWAMI VIVEKANANDA

You are boundless joy, you are inexhaustible love, you are indescribable beauty. That is who you are. That is who you will always be.

> *You are a wildflower, a beauty unsurpassed. In each soul is the unique imprint of the grace of God.*
>
> —PARAMAHANSA YOGANANDA

If you could gaze into a magical mirror that reflected your true essence, you would be awed by the pure, radiant beauty of your soul.

> *Love is a state of Being. Your love is not outside; it is deep within you. You can never lose it, and it cannot leave you.*
>
> —ECKHART TOLLE

There is more love in your heart than all the pain that could ever touch you. There is more joy in your heart than all the sadness you could ever face. There is more beauty in your heart than all the ugliness you could ever encounter.

> *As we look not back nor forward, but deep within, we see a light*
> *that is greater than the darkness of the world.*
>
> —MARIANNE WILLIAMSON

Call forth this God-force within, embody it and express it with your every thought and deed, and the pieces of your life begin to effortlessly fall into place.

> *Manifest the divinity within you, and everything will be*
> *harmoniously arranged around it.*
>
> —SWAMI VIVEKANANDA

GOD'S LIMITLESS LOVE

As soon as you accept that you are bathed in God's loving consciousness in every moment, you open your heart to knowing true peace.

> *A person desperately searching for love is like a fish desperately*
> *searching for water.*
>
> —DEEPAK CHOPRA

Welcome God's love into your life and you awaken to a whole new way of being in the world. The air smells sweeter, every soul you meet offers a secret smile, and the most ordinary of moments shimmers with artistry and promise.

> *That which God said to the rose,*
> *and caused it to laugh in full-blown beauty,*
> *He said to my heart,*
> *and made it a hundred times more beautiful.*
>
> —RUMI

Knowing you are divinely loved enriches your life beyond measure, and provides the strength and courage you need to persevere through any difficulty.

> *Who, being loved, is poor?*
>
> —OSCAR WILDE

Until you look through God's eyes and see the incandescent beauty in your own soul, you can appreciate the beauty of the external world only from a distance.

> *Though we travel the world over to find the beautiful, we must carry it with us, or we find it not.*
>
> —RALPH WALDO EMERSON

God loves you unceasingly and unconditionally. You may forget God, but God will never forget you.

> *God loves each of us as if there were only one of us.*
>
> —SAINT AUGUSTINE

No matter what mistakes you have made, you have been and will always be cherished by God. God is pure love, and pure love can express itself only in purely loving ways.

> *We have been loved since before the beginning.*
>
> —JULIAN OF NORWICH

In those sublime moments when you experience God's tender embrace, you are blessed with a glimpse of the infinite depth and magnitude of God's love.

> *You felt that there is a love which transcends all sense and understanding, and that this love is not the love with which you love God but the love with which God loves you.*
>
> —SØREN KIERKEGAARD

God's limitless love for you is the celestial music of your soul. Every moment presents a fresh opportunity to express it, to give voice to it, to let it burst forth in celebratory song.

Everyone shows harmony or disharmony according to how open he is to the music of the universe. The more one is open to all that is beautiful and harmonious, the more one's life is tuned to that universal harmony and the more one will show a friendly attitude towards everyone one meets. One's very atmosphere will create music around one.

—HAZRAT INAYAT KHAN

When it is time for you to leave this earth and return to God, you will be welcomed with open arms and a love so overwhelming as to be beyond imagining.

The supreme happiness of life is the conviction that we are loved.

—VICTOR HUGO

It follows that if you are beautiful and loved, then so is every other person you come into contact with.

If you don't find God in the next person you meet, it is a waste of time looking for him further.

—MAHATMA GANDHI

When you recognize God in another, you recognize yourself as well, for your Divine essence is indistinguishable from the Divine essence of another.

My friend, you and I shall remain strangers unto life,
And unto one another, and each unto himself,
Until the day when you shall speak and I shall listen
Deeming your voice my own voice;
And when I shall stand before you
Thinking myself standing before a mirror.

—KAHLIL GIBRAN

Helping someone perceive their innate divinity, to understand that they too have a pivotal role to play in the evolution of humankind, is perhaps the greatest gift you can give to another.

A person's single most important task is to discover the divinity of ordinary things, ordinary lives, and ordinary minds.

—Aldous Huxley

When the opportunity arises to deliver this message to someone in need of hearing it, choose your words carefully so that they are appropriate for both the recipient and the situation.

The greatest good you can do for another is not just to share your riches, but to reveal to him his own.

—Benjamin Disraeli

THE BLESSINGS OF FRIENDSHIP

Just as each soul is a unique gift to the world, every friend that God sends your way is a priceless gift in your life.

Friendship is a thing most necessary to life, since without friends no one would choose to live, though possessed of all other advantages.

—Aristotle

Each of your friends is a singular expression of God's love for you, a reflection of your relationship with the Divine.

Human friendship is the echo of God's friendship.

—Paramahansa Yogananda

Good friends expand your capacity for love and are a constant reminder of God's blessings.

Let God love you through others and let God love others through you.

—D. M. Street

Through friendship, you learn compassion, forgiveness, and accountability. Every friend helps shape you into the person you are capable of becoming.

> *Each friend represents a world in us, a world possibly not born*
> *until they arrive, and it is only by this meeting that a new world*
> *is born.*
>
> —ANAÏS NIN

A deep, abiding friendship is the most precious of jewels, provided it springs from the purest of intentions.

> *That friendship will not continue to the end that is begun for*
> *an end.*
>
> —FRANCIS QUARLES

Friendship must be kept pristine at all costs, free of even the slightest hint of deceit or manipulation.

> *Friendship is always a sweet responsibility, never an opportunity.*
>
> —KAHLIL GIBRAN

True friends recognize and revere a soul connection that feels as fresh as the morning dew and as timeless as a starry sky.

> *Depth of friendship does not depend on length of acquaintance.*
>
> —RABINDRANATH TAGORE

A real friend is always with you in spirit, no matter how many years or miles may separate you.

> *When you part from your friend, you grieve not;*
> *For that which you love most in him may be clearer in his absence,*
> *as the mountain to the climber is clearer from the plain.*
>
> —KAHLIL GIBRAN

Every encounter with a close friend is a homecoming, a sweet reminder of all that is right with the world.

> *A friend may well be reckoned the masterpiece of nature.*
>
> —RALPH WALDO EMERSON

A trusted friend is a safe haven, a home away from home, where you feel secure enough to be authentic and trusting enough to be vulnerable.

> *Talking with a friend is nothing else but thinking aloud.*
>
> —JOSEPH ADDISON

When fear and doubt rest heavily upon your shoulders, your friends will lift your spirits by telling you the truth of who you really are.

> *We do not believe in ourselves until someone reveals that deep inside us something is valuable, worth listening to, worthy of our trust, sacred to our touch. Once we believe in ourselves we can risk curiosity, wonder, spontaneous delight, or any experience that reveals the human spirit.*
>
> —E. E. CUMMINGS

A dear friend will listen with an open mind, love with an open heart, and comfort with open arms.

> *Sometimes being a friend means mastering the art of timing. There is a time for silence. A time to let go and allow people to hurl themselves into their own destiny. And a time to prepare to pick up the pieces when it's all over.*
>
> —GLORIA NAYLOR

In your darkest moments, a faithful friend will silently and tenderly offer you a shoulder to lean on, to cry on, to rest on, until you are replenished and ready to face the world again.

*When we honestly ask ourselves which persons in our lives mean
the most to us, we often find that it is those who, instead of giving
much advice, solutions, or cures, have chosen rather to share our
pain and touch our wounds with a gentle and tender hand. The
friend who can be silent with us in a moment of despair or
confusion, who can stay with us in an hour of grief and
bereavement, who can tolerate not-knowing, not-curing,
not-healing and face with us the reality of our powerlessness,
that is the friend who cares.*

—HENRI NOUWEN

The best friends both comfort and challenge you. They not only see who you are, but who you can become.

*The only service a friend can really render is to keep up your
courage by holding up to you a mirror in which you can see
a noble image of yourself.*

—GEORGE BERNARD SHAW

A good friend will tell you what you need to hear when you need to hear it, knowing that compassionate candor strengthens any friendship worth having.

An honest answer is like a kiss of friendship.

—PROVERBS 24:26

A real friend is on the same wavelength, so you need not guard your words. Even if you do not say what you mean, your friend will know what you mean to say.

*Oh, the comfort—the inexpressible comfort of feeling safe with
a person—having neither to weigh thoughts nor measure words,
but pouring them all right out, just as they are, chaff and grain
together; certain that a faithful hand will take and sift them, keep
what is worth keeping, and then with the breath of kindness blow
the rest away.*

—DINAH MARIA CRAIK

The best of friends communicate intuitively, heart to heart, far beyond the limits of what mere words can express.

> *The language of Friendship is not words, but meanings. It is an intelligence above language.*
>
> —HENRY DAVID THOREAU

When disputes with friends crop up, rise above the circumstances of the moment. Imbue your words and actions with reverence for the divine bond of friendship that blesses you both.

> *The flower that follows the sun does so even on cloudy days.*
>
> —ROBERT LEIGHTON

If someone you consider a friend betrays you, do not withdraw from the world. If you had not experienced the pain of friendship lost, you would not be able to fully appreciate the joy of true friendship.

> *People are lonely because they build walls instead of bridges.*
>
> —JOSEPH FORT NEWTON

Trusted friends do more than answer your calls during a crisis. They roll up their sleeves and pitch in with the heavy lifting.

> *Too many people are ready to carry the stool when the piano needs moving.*
>
> —UNKNOWN

Knowing there are friends who will rush to our side at 3 AM, no questions asked, brings us more comfort and gratitude than all the riches of the world.

> *It is not so much our friends' help that helps us as the confident knowledge that they will help us.*
>
> —EPICURUS

There is no magic formula for friendship, yet friendship is magical. The bond that unites two friends is as mysterious as it is certain.

> *If you press me to say why I loved him, I can say no more than*
> *because he was he, and I was I.*
>
> —MICHEL DE MONTAIGNE

True friends imprint their essences on each other's souls. Even as your tears and laughter recede into the swirling mists of memories lost, the heart holds dear every unspoken expression of love that has ever passed between you.

> *When you meet your friend on the roadside or in the market place,*
> *let the spirit in you move your lips and direct your tongue.*
> *Let the voice within your voice speak to the ear of his ear;*
> *For his soul will keep the truth of your heart as the taste of the*
> *wine is remembered*
> *When the color is forgotten and the vessel is no more.*
>
> —KAHLIL GIBRAN

Lifelong friendships are irreplaceable. Cherish your friends and lavish them with attention, for we know not what tomorrow may bring.

> *Hold a true friend with both your hands.*
>
> —NIGERIAN PROVERB

In your final days, will you fondly remember your business dealings or will you gratefully recall those blessed moments when you loved and were loved in the company of your dearest friends?

> *Carve your name on hearts, and not on marble.*
>
> —CHARLES HADDON SPURGEON

A LIFE OF DEVOTION

God, your greatest friend, lovingly guides you in every moment, but makes no demands and has no expectations.

> *God wants to win back his own flowers as gifts from man's hand.*
> —RABINDRANATH TAGORE

Yet the more you open your heart to Spirit, the greater your desire to give to God the one gift that you, and you alone, can offer: your love.

> *Of all earthly music, that which reaches the furthest into heaven is the beating of a loving heart.*
> —HENRY WARD BEECHER

As Indian saint Sri Mata Amritanandamayi Devi noted, offering God anything other than your love is like showing a candle to the sun.

> *God is not in need of anything, but all things are in need of Him.*
> —MARCIANUS ARISTIDES

Just as a parent treasures every expression of affection from a beloved child, so too is God touched by your every expression of loving devotion.

> *There are thoughts which are prayers. There are moments when, whatever the posture of the body, the soul is on its knees.*
> —VICTOR HUGO

What is devotion? It is the unceasing practice of acknowledging God's presence, with the ultimate goal of living your life as one long prayer.

> *As impossible as it is for us to take a breath in the morning large enough to last us until noon, so impossible is it to pray in the morning in such a way as to last us until noon. . . . Let your prayers ascend to Him constantly, audibly or silently, as circumstances throughout the day permit.*
> —OLE HALLESBY

Is it possible to maintain awareness of God's presence in every moment? Think of it this way: When you fall in love, you hold the thought of your beloved in the back of your mind throughout the day, even while concentrating on difficult tasks. When you fall in love with the Divine Beloved, the joy of God communion is never far from your thoughts.

> *Our daily worship of God is not really the process of gradual*
> *acquisition of him, but the daily process of surrendering ourselves,*
> *removing all obstacles to union and extending our consciousness*
> *of him in devotion and service, in goodness and in love.*
>
> —RABINDRANATH TAGORE

The greater your peace, the easier it becomes to feel God's presence. It is not outer activity but inner restlessness that distracts you from God.

> *No matter which way you turn a compass, its needle points to the*
> *north. So it is with the true yogi. Immersed he may be in many*
> *outer activities, but his mind is always on the Lord.*
>
> —PARAMAHANSA YOGANANDA

Visual reminders can help keep your attention focused on, and your mind attuned to, Divine Consciousness. Find images of the manifestations of God—Divine Mother, Heavenly Father, Jesus, Krishna, Buddha—that speak to your heart. Place them in your home, in your wallet, on your computer screen, and anywhere else you are likely to see them.

> *That in order to form a habit of conversing with God continually,*
> *and referring all we do to Him, we must at first apply to Him with*
> *some diligence: but that after a little care we should find His love*
> *inwardly excite us to it without any difficulty.*
>
> —BROTHER LAWRENCE

Welcome God into your heart and your consciousness, and you will be graced and embraced by God's loving, comforting presence.

And thou shalt love the Lord thy God with all thy heart, and with all thy soul, and with all thy mind, and with all thy strength: this is the first commandment.

—JESUS OF NAZARETH
MARK 12:30

There are countless ways to practice devotion. Two of the most prevalent are prayer and meditation. Prayer is when you talk to God; meditation is when God talks to you.

In your silence God's silence ceases.

—PARAMAHANSA YOGANANDA

THE POWER OF PRAYER

Devotional prayer does not seek God's help in granting wishes. It is a heartfelt plea for eternal, unbroken attunement with Divine Will.

Prayer is not an asking. It is a longing of the soul.

—MAHATMA GANDHI

Prayer is a natural outgrowth of faith, an inevitable testament to your trust in Divine mercy and kindness.

Faith is the fountain of prayer, and prayer should be nothing else but faith exercised.

—THOMAS MANTON

Your every urge to pray, no matter when, no matter where, is a prayer unto itself. Each spontaneous expression of praise and thanksgiving is a powerful reminder of God's love for you.

Prayer is, for me, an outburst from the heart; it is a simple glance darted upwards to Heaven; it is a cry of gratitude and of love in the midst of trial as in the midst of joy!

—SAINT THÉRÈSE OF LISIEUX

Begin your prayer by silently expressing your love and devotion for God in the language of your heart.

> *When thou prayest, rather let thy heart be without words, than thy words without a heart.*
>
> —JOHN BUNYAN

Your words are far less important than the purity and intensity of your yearning for Divine communion.

> *There is a mighty lot of difference between saying prayers and praying.*
>
> —JOHN G. LAKE

What you are thinking during the course of your prayer pales in significance to what you are feeling.

> *If you pray to God as though your heart and mind will burst with longing, He will respond.*
>
> —PARAMAHANSA YOGANANDA

After sending up your soul call, thank God for all your many blessings or simply sit in silence and bask in the warmth of God's holy, healing presence.

> *Grow flowers of gratitude in the soil of prayer.*
>
> —TERRI GUILLEMETS

In this state, you transcend the circumstances of everyday life and experience the joy of a personal relationship with God.

> *O Father, when I was blind I found not a door that led to Thee. Thou hast healed my eyes; now I discover doors everywhere; the hearts of flowers, the voices of friendship, memories of lovely experiences.*
>
> *Each gust of my prayer opens a new entrance to the vast temple of Thy presence.*
>
> —PARAMAHANSA YOGANANDA

Your expressions of eternal love and gratitude take on a life of their own. The energy you put forth travels to where it is needed most.

> *To give thanks in solitude is enough. Thanksgiving has wings and goes where it must go. Your prayer knows much more about it than you do.*
>
> —VICTOR HUGO

If you do feel compelled to ask for something, ask for deeper understanding that furthers your spiritual progress.

> *Prayer is not asking for what you think you want but asking to be changed in ways you can't imagine.*
>
> —KATHLEEN NORRIS

Before ending your prayer, ask how you can be of service. Trust that you will be guided to recognize opportunities to serve in the days, months, and years to come.

> *O, do not pray for easy lives. Pray to be stronger men! Do not pray for tasks equal to your powers. Pray for powers equal to your tasks!*
>
> —PHILLIPS BROOKS

If you wish to know whether God has responded to your prayer, you will find the answer within your own heart.

> *Who rises from prayer a better man, his prayer is answered.*
>
> —GEORGE MEREDITH

Greet and end each day with prayer, and in time you will feel God's presence in all your waking hours.

> *Let prayer be the key of the morning, and the bolt at the night.*
>
> —PHILIP HENRY

Ultimately, you will not know peace until there is congruency between your words while you are on your knees and your actions while you are on your feet.

We must alter our lives, in order to alter our hearts, for it is
impossible to live one way, and pray another.

—WILLIAM LAW

Consistent prayer generates a virtuous circle. Every prayer elevates your consciousness, which brings you closer to God, which brings you greater peace and deepens your devotion, which inspires you to pray more frequently.

Our praying, to be strong, must be buttressed by holy living. . . .
The life of faith perfects the prayer of faith.

—E. M. BOUNDS

MEDITATE AND KNOW GOD

Like prayer, meditation enables you to communicate with God, but in a much deeper way.

When the five senses and the mind are stilled, when the reasoning
intellect rests in silence, then begins the highest path.

—THE KATHA UPANISHAD

Meditation quiets the mind, calms the senses, opens the heart, and prepares you to receive Divine Consciousness.

Meditation is therefore the art of suspending verbal and symbolic
thinking for a time, somewhat as a courteous audience will stop
talking when a concert is about to begin.

—ALAN WATTS

Sitting to meditate is a physical expression of your desire to dissolve into God's loving embrace, to blissfully melt back into the Source from whence you came.

We shall not cease from exploration
And the end of all our exploring
Will be to arrive where we started
And know the place for the first time.

—T. S. Eliot

Paramahansa Yogananda, author of the spiritual classic, *Autobiography of a Yogi*, wrote that meditation enables us to dive ever more deeply into the boundless ocean of God's presence.

It is only when you go deep within, in meditation, that you
suddenly realize how completely you had forgotten what you really
are. You will be astonished to find what a tremendous gap there is
beyond ordinary consciousness, which is of the world, and that
consciousness in which you feel that just behind the restless mind,
just behind the limited physical awareness, is a vast realm of
divine awareness, of divine bliss.

—Sri Daya Mata

Yogananda described meditation as the turning on of the inner switch that fills the body with the Divine current.

I shut my eyes in order to see.

—Paul Gauguin

Through the spiritual science of meditation, you can experience the peace of direct personal contact with God.

Meditation is not a means to an end. It is both the means and
the end.

—Jiddu Krishnamurti

When your love, devotion, and yearning reach sufficient intensity, the curtains of maya will part and you will perceive God in the specific form or divine quality that resonates most deeply within your heart.

In whatever way a devotee worships Me, in that way do I come to him.

—BHAGAVAD GITA 7:21

Meditation is not an emptying of the mind. It is the highest form of concentration in which the mind is focused entirely on God.

We need to find God, and he cannot be found in noise and restlessness. God is the friend of silence. See how nature—trees, flowers, grass—grows in silence; see the stars, the moon and the sun, how they move in silence.

—MOTHER TERESA

In this heightened state, we drop our body-mind consciousness and know ourselves to be divine beings in our own right.

The sun shines, but if I close my eyes I see only darkness. When I open my eyes, the sunlight is there. It was always there; the darkness existed merely because I had my eyes closed. That is the way it is with the light of God's presence. Your eyes are closed; but if you open your spiritual eye by meditation, you will behold Him shining within you and everywhere.

—PARAMAHANSA YOGANANDA

We see our own spirit reflected in all of creation and the Spirit behind all of creation reflected in us.

Meditation will bring you sensitivity, a great sense of belonging to the world. It is our world—the stars are ours, and we are not foreigners here. We belong intrinsically to existence. We are part of it, we are the heart *of it.*

—OSHO

Meditation must be entered into with pure intent and infinite patience. God will respond in God's time, not yours.

Striving, striving, one day behold! the Divine Goal.

—LAHIRI MAHASAYA

During meditation, do not be discouraged if your attention drifts and worldly thoughts intrude. Simply begin again as if you had just begun.

> *If the heart wanders or is distracted, bring it back to the point quite gently and replace it tenderly in its Master's presence. And even if you did nothing during the whole of your hour but bring your heart back and place it again in Our Lord's presence, though it went away every time you brought it back, your hour would be very well employed.*
>
> —SAINT FRANCIS DE SALES

Continue your practice faithfully, with no expectations, and cherish whatever blessings come your way.

> *Do not entertain hopes for realization, but practice all your life .*
>
> —MILAREPA

In that glorious moment when you first feel the loving warmth of God's response, you find to your great delight that the yearning for communion has been mutual.

> *If you follow the way of meditation that we teach, you shall find that one day, when you are least expecting it, God will drop both His hands to lift you up. It is not only that you are seeking God, but that God is seeking you—more than you are seeking Him.*
>
> —PARAMAHANSA YOGANANDA

Briefly sit in silence and solitude after completing your practice in order to build a bridge of serenity between your meditation and the impatient world that awaits your return.

> *Silence is a solvent that destroys personality, and gives us leave to be great and universal.*
>
> —RALPH WALDO EMERSON

In time, with enough patience and practice, you will be able to access a deep inner stillness wherever you happen to be, no matter what is happening around you.

> *The ideal man is he who, in the midst of the greatest silence and solitude, finds the intensest activity, and in the midst of the intensest activity finds the silence and solitude of the desert.*
>
> —SWAMI VIVEKANANDA

What we call happiness is negligible compared to the inner peace and exultation of spirit we attain in meditation. Happiness, the province of the ego, is fleeting. Joy, the natural state of the soul, is infinite and eternal.

> *Still your mind in me, still yourself in me, and without doubt you shall be united with me, Lord of Love, dwelling in your heart.*
>
> —BHAGAVAD GITA 12:8

Close your eyes and recall a moment of indescribable beauty in your life. Remember how you longed to carry that moment forever in your heart so you could return to it at will? The bliss of that experience waits for you just beyond the gateway of meditation, where it melts into loving union with the ever-new joy of God's limitless love.

> *By meditation we connect the little joy of the soul with the vast joy of the Spirit.*
>
> —PARAMAHANSA YOGANANDA

Enriching your inner life is only half the equation. If the peace and unconditional love you feel in meditation is not expressed through your every action, then you are not truly living a spiritual life.

> *Let no one be deluded that a knowledge of the path can substitute for putting one foot in front of the other.*
>
> —MARY CAROLINE RICHARDS

Meditation teaches you how to be, in Yogananda's words, "calmly active and actively calm."

*Calmness of mind does not mean you should stop your activity.
Real calmness should be found in activity itself.*

—SHUNRYU SUZUKI

The goal of meditation is not to avoid the world, but to live in it more consciously and fully in ways that serve humanity.

*We don't sit in meditation to become good meditators. We sit in
meditation so that we'll be more awake in our lives.*

—PEMA CHÖDRÖN

SURRENDERING TO DIVINE WILL

In the Bhagavad Gita, Hinduism's definitive guide to the science of Self-realization, devotion is referred to as shraddha, the natural inclination of the heart to turn toward its Source in faith and surrender.

*To replace human order with divine chaos in a trusting way is
called surrender.*

—CAROLINE MYSS

Surrendering means you recognize that whatever is, *is.* Deny that what is, *is,* and your self-deception can only end badly.

*When you argue with reality, you lose—but only 100 percent of
the time.*

—BYRON KATIE

Accepting that you cannot change what cannot be changed enables you to objectively deal with and overcome whatever challenge is in front of you, free of judgment and emotional resistance.

It is so. It cannot be otherwise.

—INSCRIPTION ON THE RUINS OF A
FIFTEENTH-CENTURY CATHEDRAL IN AMSTERDAM

The word "surrender" raises a red flag for people who believe their life will unravel unless they stay on top of every last detail as only they can.

> *Surrender is the simple but profound wisdom of* yielding to *rather than* opposing *the flow of life.*
>
> —ECKHART TOLLE

Attempting to exert control over every aspect of your life is like swimming upstream—progress is slow and difficult.

> *When you struggle against this moment, you're actually struggling against the entire universe.*
>
> —DEEPAK CHOPRA

Choose to receive God's grace and you begin swimming *with* the current. You are in the flow, and life gets easier.

> *He who is in harmony with Nature hits the mark without effort and apprehends the truth without thinking.*
>
> —CONFUCIUS

Surrendering to Divine Will does not mean you are sacrificing your free will or diminishing your capacity to reason and act.

> *As your faith is strengthened you will find that there is no longer the need to have a sense of control, that things will flow as they will, and that you will flow with them, to your great delight and benefit.*
>
> —EMMANUEL TENEY

By humbly pledging to surrender your will to Divine Will, you are tacitly agreeing to carry out God's will by courageously and honorably striving to realize your full potential.

> *The winds of grace are always blowing, but it is you that must raise your sails.*
>
> —RABINDRANATH TAGORE

Your attunement with Divine Will strengthens your resolve to live purposefully and reinforces your capacity to do, to achieve, to become.

> *Believe in the nature within you, the divine nature, that you are in very deed a son or daughter of the living God. There is something of divinity with you, something that stands high and tall and noble.*
>
> —GORDON B. HINCKLEY

By surrendering, you are not admitting that your life is unmanageable. You are trusting that God has a better plan for your life than you do, that omniscient Spirit sees far beyond the finite vision of your ego.

> *I used to pray that God would do this or that. Now I pray that God will make His will known to me.*
>
> —SOONG MAY-LING

What you are actually surrendering is your self-centeredness and the belief that you are alone and unprotected in an uncaring, unforgiving world.

> *Forgetfulness of self is remembrance of God.*
>
> —BAYAZID AL-BISTAMI

Fully accepting God's unconditional love requires unconditional receptivity, which requires unconditional surrender.

> *Receive, O Lord, my entire liberty, memory, understanding, and my whole will. All that I have and possess, thou hast given me, and to thee I restore them. Give me only your love and your grace, and I will be satisfied; I desire nothing more.*
>
> —SAINT IGNATIUS OF LOYOLA

Surrendering is nothing more than a homecoming, a recognition that your will aligns with Divine Will as naturally as a child's hand fits into its mother's.

Everything is in God's hands, and you are His tool to be used by Him as He pleases. Try to grasp the significance of "all is His," and you will immediately feel free from all burdens. What will be the result of your surrender to Him? None will seem alien, all will be your very own, your Self.

—ANANDAMAYI MA

Aligning your will with God's will calls forth your own inherent divinity and dissolves any blocks between your consciousness and Divine Consciousness.

The bodily food we take is changed into us, but the spiritual food we receive changes us into itself, hence love divine is not preserved in us, otherwise there would be two. Divine love preserves us in itself as one in the same.

—MEISTER ECKHART

Living your life for God flows naturally out of your surrender to, and alignment with, Divine Will. The more tightly your arms are wrapped around your ego, the less authentically you can serve Spirit.

Ask to be the servant of the Lord, a vehicle of divine love, a channel of God's will. Ask for direction and divine assistance and surrender all personal will through devotion. Dedicate one's life to the service of God. Choose love and peace above all other options. Commit to the goal of unconditional love and compassion for all life in all its expression and surrender all judgment to God.

—DR. DAVID R. HAWKINS

Surrendering to Divine Will generates a virtuous circle. By relinquishing control, you become more trusting, which frees up your attention for the present moment, which heightens your awareness of the beauty that surrounds you, which assures you of the perfection of Divine Intelligence, which strengthens your devotion, which naturally leads to joyous surrender to God.

Don't seek God in temples. He is close to you. He is within you. Only you should surrender to Him and you will rise above happiness and unhappiness.

—LEO TOLSTOY

Surrender your power to God and you realize that the power you wielded in the material world was an illusion, a false sense of superiority created by your ego to ensure its survival.

> *The most exquisite paradox*
> *as soon as you give it all up*
> *you can have it all*
> *How about that one?*
> *As long as you want power*
> *You can't have it.*
> *The minute you don't want power*
> *you'll have more than you ever dreamed*
> *possible.*
>
> —RAM DASS

The more you invest in this illusory ego-based power, the more you distance yourself from the only power that matters.

> *Power over others is weakness disguised as strength. True power is*
> *within, and it is available to you now.*
>
> —ECKHART TOLLE

Surrender unconditionally to the Source of all that is and know the beauty, power, and freedom of living life as an unceasing love poem to God.

> *When we know love matters more than anything, and we know*
> *that nothing else really matters, we move into the state of*
> *surrender. Surrender does not diminish our power, it enhances it.*
>
> —SARA PADDISON

YOU ARE BEAUTIFUL AND YOU ARE LOVED
Living the Lesson

My friend Jia was in despair. She had walked away from a great job as a research scientist in her early forties to pursue her dream of earning a medical degree in the U.S.; her credentials as a doctor in her native China were not recognized in America.

Jia has a kind heart, endless compassion, a keen intellect, and an astonishing work ethic. However, medical school was not going well; the head of her program was treating her harshly, advising her to drop out and telling her she would never make it as a doctor. Jia kept giving her best but felt lonely, isolated, and ostracized by her fellow students.

At ten o'clock one night, I was passing by Jia's neighborhood on my way home, so I swung by her house and rang the bell. Jia opened the door looking sad and forlorn. I told her that I could only stay a couple of minutes and that I had just come over to tell her something.

I took her hand and gently said, "You are beautiful and you are loved." Her face began to crumble and she collapsed in my arms, sobbing on my shoulder. I held her for a minute or two until she composed herself. I didn't leave until she assured me she was okay.

We all need to be reminded that we are beautiful and we are loved because it is so easy to forget. Even if those words offered only a few minutes of comfort to Jia, stopping by was well worth the effort.

Jia did leave that school, but only because she realized it was the wrong program, the wrong people, and the wrong path for her. After painstaking research, she was accepted into a program in a neighboring state, where she was beloved by the staff and students and emerged as the superstar of her class.

Today, Jia is blessed with a husband who loves her and sees her as beautiful, and is a practicing physician on the West Coast, leading the life she dreamed of and worked so hard to achieve.

YOU ARE BEAUTIFUL AND YOU ARE LOVED
Self-Reflection Questions

- How would I feel if someone told me I was beautiful and I was loved?

- How can I increase my awareness of God's presence?

- Why do I believe or disbelieve that God loves me unconditionally?

- How can I remind myself to look for the beauty in other people?

- How can I demonstrate to those closest to me that I cherish their friendship?

- How can I be a better friend?

- What are some of the ways my friends and I are authentic with each other?

- In what ways am I a better person because of my friendships?

- How can I do a better job of expressing my love and devotion to God?

- What steps can I take to expand my prayer life?

- How can I fit a regular meditation practice into my life?

- Why should I or should I not put my life in God's hands?

FOUR

YOUR CHOICE IS LOVE OR FEAR

Love is heaven and fear is hell.
Where you place your attention is where you live.

—ALAN COHEN

YOUR CHOICE IS LOVE OR FEAR

Your every thought, word, and action spring from either love or fear. The nature of your choices determines the quality of your life.

> *The platform from which you act—faith or fear—determines*
> *your results more than the actions themselves.*
>
> —ALAN COHEN

ONE OR THE OTHER

Love is the whisper of the Divine, ceaselessly calling creation back toward the Creator. Your every loving thought resonates with the essence of love itself and strengthens your vibrational connection with all that is.

> *Love is the only reality and it is not a mere sentiment. It is the*
> *ultimate truth that lies at the heart of creation.*
>
> —RABINDRANATH TAGORE

Fear expresses itself as anger, intimidation, insecurity, despair, self-loathing, or any other emotion or behavior not grounded in love.

> *There are no guarantees.*
> *From the viewpoint of fear*
> *none are strong enough.*
> *From the viewpoint of love*
> *none are necessary.*
>
> —PAT RODEGAST (EMMANUEL)

When you choose love, you are coming from your heart and declaring that you trust God to handle the consequences.

> *On the ocean of life let your mind be the ship and your heart be*
> *the compass.*
>
> —JAMES MANNING

When you choose fear, you are coming from your head and assuming that you can manage the situation better than God can.

> *The heart has its reasons which reason knows nothing of.*
>
> —BLAISE PASCAL

Choose love, and you are being proactive; you are making things happen, living a life of choice, and getting better.

> *To work in the world lovingly means that we are defining what we will be for, rather than reacting to what we are against.*
>
> —CHRISTINA BALDWIN

Choose fear, and you are being reactive; you are letting things happen, living a life of chance, and getting bitter.

> *A life of reaction is a life of slavery, intellectually and spiritually. One must fight for a life of action, not reaction.*
>
> —RITA MAE BROWN

Choose love and you share your authentic self with the world. Choose fear and you conceal your true identity from others and, worse yet, from yourself.

> *Love takes off the masks that we fear we cannot live without and know we cannot live within.*
>
> —JAMES BALDWIN

Choose fear, and you will forever be searching for happiness and fulfillment through other people, possessions, and experiences. Choose love, and you discover unimaginable bliss within your own heart.

> *Everyone chases after happiness, not noticing that happiness is at their heels.*
>
> —BERTOLT BRECHT

Choose love, and you serenely welcome whatever gifts are delivered to your door. Choose fear, and you affirm that you do not trust what tomorrow may bring.

> *Love is a fruit in season at all times, and within reach of every hand.*
>
> —MOTHER TERESA

Choose love and you are illuminating your future with the radiant promise of undreamed-of possibilities.

> *Life is a magic vase filled to the brim; so made that you cannot dip into it nor draw from it; but it overflows into the hand that drops treasures into it—drop in malice and it overflows hate; drop in charity and it overflows love.*
>
> —JOHN RUSKIN

Choose fear and you are casting a pallor over your state of mind and all the days that remain to you.

> *Fear is that little darkroom where negatives are developed.*
>
> —MICHAEL PRITCHARD

Choose love, and your words and actions help heal the world. Choose fear, and your own world becomes a less hospitable place to live.

> *Speak when you are angry and you will make the best speech you will ever regret.*
>
> —AMBROSE BIERCE

Choose fear, and peace remains a stranger. Choose love, and peace gathers you tenderly in its arms.

> *The trick is in what one emphasizes. We either make ourselves miserable, or we make ourselves strong. The amount of work is the same.*
>
> —CARLOS CASTANEDA

WE ARE ALL LOVE

Love is the language of God. Love *is* God. You exist because of love. You exist to share love. You exist to *be* love.

> *Love is life. All, everything that I understand, I understand only because I love. Everything is, everything exists, only because I love. Everything is united by it alone. Love is God, and to die means that I, a particle of love, shall return to the general and eternal source.*
>
> —LEO TOLSTOY

We all have within us a Divine spark. We all share God's DNA. Love is your very nature, the essence of who you are.

> *He who is filled with love is filled with God himself.*
>
> —SAINT AUGUSTINE

Love is evidence of God's presence within you. Your every loving thought melts you ever more deeply into Divine Mother's welcoming arms.

> *The best way to know God is to love many things.*
>
> —VINCENT VAN GOGH

Love is far more than a choice you make or an emotion you feel. Love is the life force of the Universe.

> *The essence of love isn't a feeling—it is a state of being. Or to be more exact, it is the state in which you are in contact with Being.*
>
> —DEEPAK CHOPRA

Love is the elemental energy that created and sustains creation itself. Whoever taps into its power walks hand in hand with God.

Someday when men have conquered the winds, the waves, the tides, and gravity, they will harness for God the energies of love, and then, for the second time in the history of the world, man will have discovered fire.

—PIERRE TEILHARD DE CHARDIN

With each step toward enlightenment, choosing love becomes less of a choice and more of a natural expression of who you are.

As you ascend, your love will turn to ecstasy. . . . Ecstasy is the final stage of intimacy with yourself.

—DEEPAK CHOPRA

Ultimately, love defies definition. Every expression of love, every sensation of being loved, is as unique as the individual experiencing it.

That love is all there is
Is all we know of love.

—EMILY DICKINSON

LOVE CIRCLES BACK

We are individual waves in the ocean of Spirit, yet we are inseparably connected to each other and through each other in the Unified Field.

The fundamental delusion of humanity is to suppose that I am here and you are out there .

—YASUTANI HAKUUN

We all come from and will return to the one Source. By definition then, we are all one, so whatever you do for others, you do for yourself.

Celebrate another's gain as your own, and yours will soon follow.

—ALAN COHEN

Therefore, when you choose to be loving, you will receive love in return, both in this life and beyond.

> *Love, and you shall be loved. All love is mathematically just, as much as the two sides of an algebraic equation.*
>
> —RALPH WALDO EMERSON

How does this principle affect you on a practical basis? Author and speaker Dannion Brinkley offers a compelling example. While undergoing a near-death experience after being struck by lightning, Brinkley found himself receiving a life review in which he relived every emotion from every encounter he ever had on earth. The process was then repeated, except this time he experienced the emotions of the people with whom he had interacted.

> *The Game of Life is a game of boomerangs. Man's thoughts, deeds and words return to him sooner or later, with astounding accuracy.*
>
> —FLORENCE SCOVEL SHINN

Today, when appropriate, Brinkley greets those who cross his path with a long, lingering, loving hug, a gesture that is at once selfless and selfish.

> *Now you will daily give and give, and the great stores of your love will not lessen thereby: for this is the miracle that happens every time to those who really love: the more they give, the more they possess of that precious nourishing love from which flowers and children have their strength and which could help all human beings if they would take it without doubting.*
>
> —RAINER MARIA RILKE

Brinkley explains that, since his hugs are always returned in kind, he is looking forward to receiving all that love and gratitude twice over in his next life review.

> *Give, and it shall be given to you. . . . For with the same measure that ye give to others, it shall be measured to you again.*
>
> —JESUS OF NAZARETH
> LUKE 6:38

HALLOWED GROUND

If your purpose on this earth is to learn and practice unconditional love, then all your relationships become hallowed ground.

> *For it is only face to face with the god enthroned in the innermost*
> *shrine of the other that the god hidden in me will consent to appear.*
>
> —FELIX ADLER

Wherever love goes, honor and respect follow. Instead of gossiping about another's flaws, you say only what you would be comfortable saying in their presence.

> *There is so much good in the worst of us,*
> *And so much bad in the best of us,*
> *That it behooves all of us*
> *Not to talk about the rest of us.*
>
> —UNKNOWN

Psychiatrist and author Gerald Jampolsky wrote that, in every encounter you have with another human being, that person is either offering love to you or is in need of love from you.

> *What we do from joy expresses love; what we do from fear calls*
> *for love.*
>
> —ALAN COHEN

Imagine looking at the world through such a lens and recognizing that every time someone treats you in an unloving way, you have the honor and the privilege of providing love to that person, love which they are in desperate need of.

> *Deep down, even the most hardened criminal is starving for the*
> *same thing that motivates the innocent baby: love and acceptance.*
>
> —LILY FAIRCHILDE

Consciously choose to be more loving, and your first thought when meeting someone new changes from *What can I get from this person?* to *What can I give to this person?*

*You will find as you look back upon your life that the moments
that stand out, the moments when you have really lived, are the
moments when you have done things in a spirit of love.*

—HENRY DRUMMOND

Expressing love does not require you to speak the word "love." Those who drink in your loving energy will often reflect it back more powerfully and authentically than words could ever convey.

*Do the meanings of the heart swim in the streams of our
conversations, and do they matter most when they're glimpsed
through deep water, and never caught?*

—RICHARD BACH

Nor do you need to be demonstratively loving, which could be misinterpreted. Choosing love may simply mean projecting a loving presence during the course of your interactions.

*Let my soul smile through my heart and let my heart smile
through my eyes, that I may scatter Thy rich smiles in sad hearts.*

—PARAMAHANSA YOGANANDA

Your loving intentions may dissolve the wall of fear that so many people erect to protect themselves from the self-serving desires of others.

What comes from the heart goes to the heart.

—SAMUEL TAYLOR COLERIDGE

THE GOD IN OTHERS

Imagine a child, alone and frightened, wishing it were home, knowing that all will be well, that it will be loved, cherished, and protected when it is safe in its mother's arms. That child is you. That child is the next person you meet. That child is every person who has been or ever will be born.

The essence of spirituality is to love God supremely and to love all souls as a part of Him.

—SRI DAYA MATA

When you come from love, when you *are* love, you are joyously humbled by the beauty and magnificence of every soul.

Those who do not love feel superior to everyone else.
Those who love feel equal to everyone else.
Those who love much gladly take the lower place.

—CARLO CARRETTO

Train yourself to see the beauty and presence of God in others by practicing this exercise the next time you are in public: For five minutes, bathe everyone you see in love and light.

The beauty that addresses itself to the eyes is only the spell of the moment; the eye of the body is not always that of the soul.

—GEORGE SAND

Honoring the Divine nature of others is far more than a passing kindness. In that recognition lies the salvation of the world.

Only spiritual consciousness—realization of God's presence in oneself and in every other living being—can save the world. I see no chance for peace without it. Begin with yourself. There is no time to waste. It is your duty to do your part to bring God's kingdom on earth.

—PARAMAHANSA YOGANANDA

Seeing the world through God's eyes, you see no more strangers, only dear friends you have not yet met.

Then it was as if I suddenly saw the secret beauty of their hearts, the depths of their hearts where neither sin nor desire nor self-knowledge can reach, the core of their reality, the person that each one is in God's eyes. If only they could all see themselves as they really are. If only we could see each other that way all the time. There would be no more war, no more hatred, no more cruelty, no more greed. . . . I suppose the big problem would be that we would fall down and worship each other.

—THOMAS MERTON

Does choosing love in every encounter mean that you love all people equally? Only when you are impersonally serving as a channel for Divine love. Human love is more personal and intimate. Divine love flows *through* the heart; human love flows *from* the heart.

All a sane man can ever think about is giving love.

—HAFIZ

A CRY FOR LOVE

Why wouldn't you come from love in every encounter? For most of us, it is because our ego gets in the way. In looking out for our own self-interest, we become blind to the needs of others.

While God waits for His temple to be built of love, men bring stones.

—RABINDRANATH TAGORE

We get so caught up in our own lives, we forget that when people are treated with love and respect, they tend to respond in loving and respectful ways.

Beginning today, treat everyone you meet, friend or foe, loved one or stranger, as if they were going to be dead at midnight. Extend to each person, no matter how trivial the contact, all the care and kindness and understanding and love that you can muster, and do it with no thought of any reward. Your life will never be the same again.

—OG MANDINO

When we come from ego, we sit in constant judgment of others. Yet even when our criticism is justified, we must remind ourselves that fear-based behavior is a cry for love.

The child who acts unlovable is the child who most needs to be loved.

—CATHY RINDNER TEMPELSMAN

Judgment turns to rage when we feel attacked or victimized. At such times, choosing love over anger seems unthinkable. But choose it we must.

Hesitate in a moment of anger and prevent a year of grief.

—CHINESE PROVERB

You will not learn how to choose love in every moment until you learn to love those who act in unloving ways.

Love means to love that which is unlovable, or it is no virtue at all.

—G. K. CHESTERTON

Respond to negativity in kind and you are turning away from God and rejecting the joy and peace that could heal you both. Instead, the battle escalates and both parties become casualties.

In this world, hate never yet dispelled hate. Only love dispels hate.

—BUDDHA

Granted, if you are physically attacked, you must defend yourself. But that too is loving; you are fighting back out of love for your own life, for your loved ones, and for the unfinished work you were called here to do. If you hurt the other person, yet know in your heart you did what you had to do and no more, you can walk away with a clear conscience.

> *Though defensive violence will always be "a sad necessity" in the*
> *eyes of men of principle, it would be still more unfortunate if*
> *wrongdoers should dominate just men.*
>
> —SAINT AUGUSTINE

If it is only your beliefs and values that are challenged, respond not by defending but by transcending. Lashing out against your perceived adversary only perpetuates the vicious circle of anger and fear.

> *Whenever anyone has offended me, I try to raise my soul so high*
> *that the offense cannot reach it.*
>
> —RENÉ DESCARTES

Fear is a papier-mâché wall standing between you and the breathtaking beauty of the life you were born to lead.

> *Overcome fear, behold wonder.*
>
> —RICHARD BACH

Open your heart and you open up your life as well, breaking free of the shackles of your fears and inhibitions.

> *Ultimately we know deeply that the other side of every fear is*
> *freedom.*
>
> —MARILYN FERGUSON

Let love light your path or you will lose your way, stumbling around in the shadows of delusion.

> *This sky where we live*
> *Is no place to lose your wings*
> *So love, love, love.*
>
> —HAFIZ

Live harmoniously with Divine love, and you will effortlessly find yourself thinking and expressing the right thoughts in the right place at the right time.

> *Love, and do what you will.*
>
> —SAINT AUGUSTINE

If you have ever felt deprived of love, do not allow those painful memories to block the healing flow of unconditional love from your heart to others.

> *We are not held back by the love we didn't receive in the past, but by the love we're not extending in the present.*
>
> —MARIANNE WILLIAMSON

Suppressing your loving instincts is unnatural and unhealthy. Living authentically with a loving heart is your natural state and the very foundation of wellness.

> *Our well-being is dependent on our giving love. It is not about what comes back; it is about what goes out.*
>
> —ALAN COHEN

No matter how dire the circumstances, responding with love is always an option. Living consciously carries with it the awareness of that option—and the responsibility to choose it.

> *We who lived in concentration camps can remember the men who walked through the huts comforting others, giving away their last piece of bread. They may have been few in number, but they offer sufficient proof that everything can be taken from a man but one thing: the last of the human freedoms—to choose one's attitude in any given set of circumstances, to choose one's own way.*
>
> —VIKTOR FRANKL

BROADCASTING LOVE

Our attempts to love unconditionally are often sabotaged by our ego. Why? The ego's dominance depends on the belief that we are separate from God. And what is God? Unconditional love. The nearer we get to God, the more desperate our ego becomes.

> *The reason that ego and love are not compatible comes down to this: you cannot take your ego into the unknown, where love wants to lead. If you follow love, your life will become uncertain, and the ego craves certainty.*
>
> —DEEPAK CHOPRA

Human love is limited, Divine love is limitless. When you draw solely on your own reservoir of love, you risk exhausting your resources, which can leave you feeling frustrated and guilty for failing to sustain your loving intentions.

> *Miracles can be defined as shifts in perception that remove the blocks to our awareness of love's presence.*
>
> —GERALD JAMPOLSKY

Resolve to be a vessel, a channel, an instrument of unconditional Divine love. Then, instead of depleting your own limited reserves, you will be a conduit for the inexhaustible love of God.

> *Be so drunk with the love of God that you will know nothing but God; and give that love to all.*
>
> —PARAMAHANSA YOGANANDA

How do you do that? Get your ego, your "self," out of the way so that you are fully present and available to serve.

> *The moment you become aware of the ego in you, it is strictly speaking no longer the ego, but just an old, conditioned mind-pattern. Ego implies unawareness. Awareness and ego cannot coexist.*
>
> —ECKHART TOLLE

Practice silencing your ego by closing your eyes and imagining that you are floating near the ceiling, dispassionately looking down on your physical body.

> *Through self-observation, more presence comes into your life automatically. The moment you realize you are not present, you are present.*
>
> —ECKHART TOLLE

Becoming aware of your awareness and identifying with your spiritual essence instead of your body-bound ego enables you to "step out from behind your eyes" and serve as a conscious witness to your own life.

> *The aim of life is to live, and to live means to be aware, joyously, drunkenly, serenely, divinely aware. In this state of god-like awareness one sings; in this realm the world exists as poem.*
>
> —HENRY MILLER

Consciousness is a continuum, ranging from complete non-awareness to unity with the Divine Mind.

> *The key to growth is the introduction of higher dimensions of consciousness into our awareness.*
>
> —VILAYAT INAYAT KHAN

Your level of consciousness is defined by your level of self-awareness, presence, and alignment with the Source of all that is.

> *Be what you are. This is the first step toward becoming better than you are.*
>
> —JULIUS CHARLES HARE

When your level of consciousness reaches critical mass, you can metaphorically step aside and let the deep love of God flow through your body as if it were a radio tuned to a Divine frequency.

*Love is based not on how you act or feel but on your level of
awareness.*

—DEEPAK CHOPRA

Broadcasting love energetically attracts the attention of others, even those who are
simply passing by. Many will instinctively respond by reflecting love back to you with
a smile.

Every person has light within that responds to the light in others.

—QUAKER WISDOM

Whenever you feel out of attunement and all you can broadcast is static, visualize
God—in whatever form resonates with you—standing next to whomever or whatever
is challenging you. Imagine God smiling lovingly at you and gently whispering,
"Choose love."

To love someone means to see him as God intended him.

—FYODOR DOSTOYEVSKY

The more attuned you are to the Divine current, the more electrifying life becomes and
the greater your desire to reach out to others in joy and fellowship.

*Let us endeavor so to live that when we come to die even the
undertaker will be sorry.*

—MARK TWAIN

Radiating love expands your heart, which in turn expands your consciousness, which
in turn expands your understanding of how to live more fully in the world.

*I live my life in widening circles that reach out across the world.
I may not ever complete the last one, but I give myself to it.*

—RAINER MARIA RILKE

SELFLESS SERVICE

How do you move from fear to love? Reaching out in service helps. When your storehouse of joy feels dark and empty, the simple act of helping another human being can magically replenish your inventory.

> *To complain that life has no joys, while there is a single creature whom we can relieve by our bounty, assist by our counsels, or enliven by our presence, is to lament the loss of that which we possess, and is just as rational as to die of thirst with the cup in our hands.*
>
> —WILLIAM MELMOTH

Assisting someone in need takes your mind off your own troubles, assuages your yearning for meaning and purpose, and reconnects you to the heartbeat of humanity.

> *Helping someone else takes you out of your head—where fear and doubt dwell—and puts you back into your heart. You'll discover . . . that you are part of a larger family that needs you.*
>
> —ARIANE DE BONVOISIN

What does serving others look like? Begin by simply asking yourself what you can do to make another person feel cared for and valued.

> *So in everything, do to others what you would have them do to you.*
>
> —JESUS OF NAZARETH
> MATTHEW 7:12

As you grow more comfortable seeing the world through God's eyes, you naturally view others with greater empathy, love, and compassion.

> *Cultivate the desire to do for others as you would do for your own loved ones. Expand the little cup of your love into an ocean of love divine for all beings.*
>
> —SRI DAYA MATA

When your shift from self-centered to other-centered clicks into place, you cannot look anywhere without seeing opportunities to help, comfort, or inspire others.

> *The only way to be loved is to be and to appear lovely; to possess*
> *and display kindness, benevolence, tenderness; to be free from*
> *selfishness and to be alive to the welfare of others.*
>
> —JOHN JAY

The more you align yourself with Divine love, the more you yearn for others to experience the joy and peace that love has brought you.

> *Fear is the cheapest room in the house.*
> *I would like to see you living in better conditions.*
>
> —HAFIZ

As you evolve into an instrument of God's love, your mere presence becomes an act of service.

> *Live in such a way that those who know you but don't know God*
> *will come to know God because they know you.*
>
> —UNKNOWN

Others will be divinely directed to cross your path so that your beacon of love can set their flickering lanterns ablaze.

> *Thousands of candles can be lighted from a single candle, and the*
> *life of the candle will not be shortened. Happiness never decreases*
> *by being shared.*
>
> —BUDDHA

Kindle the light in others and your own heart glows ever more brightly. The more you give of your love, the more love you have to give.

> *We cannot hold a torch to light another's path without*
> *brightening our own.*
>
> —BEN SWEETLAND

The loving energy flowing through you not only heals others, it heals your own mind, body, and spirit as well.

> There is no exercise better for the heart than reaching down and lifting people up.
>
> —JOHN ANDREW HOLMES

Love purifies whatever it touches. Where once there was disease and dysfunction, love restores vitality and harmony.

> Where there is great love there are always miracles.
>
> —WILLA CATHER

Serving others is love in action, as long as it is not tainted by your ego's desire for recognition.

> Everybody can be great. Because everybody can serve. You don't have to have a college degree to serve. You don't have to make your subject and your verb agree to serve. . . . You only need a heart full of grace, a soul generated by love.
>
> —MARTIN LUTHER KING, JR.

Doing good deeds so others think of you as someone who does good deeds keeps you tightly entwined in the arms of ego, oblivious to Spirit's welcoming embrace.

> He who is too busy doing good finds no time to be good.
>
> —RABINDRANATH TAGORE

You are acting selfishly when your service flows from the promptings of your ego, your focus is on what you can get, and you walk away feeling unappreciated and resentful.

> The faraway sun, seemingly small in the sky, radiates beyond its sphere to give us light and warmth. The stars share with us the joy of their jewel-like luster. All of God's expressions in nature send out a vibration that in some way serves the world. You are His highest creation; what are you doing to reach out beyond yourself?
>
> —PARAMAHANSA YOGANANDA

You are acting selflessly when your service flows from the purity of your spirit, your focus is on what you can give, and you walk away feeling happy and peaceful.

> *My God! grant that my bounty may be a clear and transparent*
> *river, flowing from pure charity, and uncontaminated by self-love,*
> *ambition, or interest.*
>
> —CHRISTIAN SCRIVER

Ego is always out for itself. Love has no ulterior motives, and no agenda other than to do God's work.

> *Do all the good you can,*
> *By all the means you can,*
> *In all the ways you can,*
> *In all the places you can,*
> *At all the times you can,*
> *To all the people you can,*
> *As long as ever you can.*
>
> —JOHN WESLEY

Service to others is an effect, not a cause; it flows naturally out of your devotion and surrender to God.

> *Compassion is the seed that grows into the giving tree of selfless*
> *service.*
>
> —UNKNOWN

Acting selflessly is paradoxically a selfish path because it is a gateway to personal peace, fulfillment, and attunement with the Divine current.

> *I slept and dreamt that life was joy.*
> *I awoke and saw that life was service.*
> *I acted and behold, service was joy.*
>
> —RABINDRANATH TAGORE

At the same time, loving your own life is a selfless gift to humanity that energetically serves the greater good.

> *I want to be thoroughly used up when I die, for the harder I work,
> the more I live. I rejoice in life for its own sake. Life is no "brief
> candle" for me. It is a sort of splendid torch, which I have got hold
> of for the moment; and I want to make it burn as brightly as
> possible before handing it on to future generations.*
>
> —GEORGE BERNARD SHAW

Awaken to the joy of service, and serving others transitions from being a conscious choice to an instinctive driving force.

> *True heroism is remarkably sober, very undramatic. It is not the
> urge to surpass all others at whatever cost, but the urge to serve
> others at whatever cost.*
>
> —ARTHUR ASHE

LOVING YOUR SELF

Of course, devoting every moment to serving others is neither advisable nor possible. You must choose love for yourself as well by engaging in enlightened self-care—proper diet, exercise, sleep, and other healthful activities.

> *I celebrate myself, and sing myself.*
>
> —WALT WHITMAN

Neglect your own body, mind, and spirit, and you limit your capacity to lovingly care for others.

> *If you aren't good at loving yourself, you will have a difficult time
> loving anyone, since you'll resent the time and energy you give
> them that you aren't even giving to yourself.*
>
> —BARBARA DE ANGELIS

Inadequately caring for your own needs can project a conviction of low self-worth, which may foster an environment in which others expect your service and take you for granted.

> There is a basket of fresh bread on your head, and yet you go door
> to door asking for crusts.
> Knock on your inner door. No other.
>
> —RUMI

Low self-esteem can generate a downward spiral in which you increasingly focus on the needs of others not out of a genuine desire to serve but as a socially acceptable way to avoid the perceived pain of self-discovery.

> How much easier is self sacrifice than self-realization!
>
> —ERIC HOFFER

Achieving a healthy balance between attention to self and attention to others requires great awareness and wisdom.

> If I am not for myself, who will be for me?
> And if I am for myself alone, what am I?
> And if not now, when?
>
> —RABBI HILLEL

If you lean more toward self-loathing than self-love, consider how you feel about your friends. You love them even though they, like you, are imperfect, have hurt others, and regret past actions.

> Love is blind; friendship closes its eyes.
>
> —FRENCH PROVERB

If you can unconditionally love your friends despite their flaws, you can learn to extend the same kindness toward yourself.

*You yourself, as much as anybody in the entire universe, deserve
your love and affection.*

—BUDDHA

Love your flaws, your insecurities, your negative thoughts and feelings, and one day soon you may be startled to see a more positive and confident you smiling back in the mirror.

*Love all of what you call your "imperfections." You don't change
them by denying or hating them. You change them by loving them.
As you love your negative feelings they can evolve into their
positive expressions. Love all your thoughts, even those that are
limited or fearful. Think of them as small children needing your
love and reassurance.*

—SANAYA ROMAN

Looking through God's eyes can help you see yourself as God sees you and treat yourself as God treats you—with love, compassion, and endless patience.

*Love is what we were born with. Fear is what we have learned
here.*

—MARIANNE WILLIAMSON

Love yourself and you naturally begin loving others, God, and life itself in ways that someone with low self-esteem cannot begin to comprehend.

*Self-love is not opposed to the love of other people. You cannot
really love yourself and really do yourself a favor without doing
other people a favor, and vice versa.*

—DR. KARL MENNINGER

So which will you choose, love or fear? Choose love, and you are charting a new course, creating better outcomes, transcending the circumstances at hand, and appreciating all the gifts that life has to offer.

Love is the Law of God. You live that you may learn to love. You love that you may learn to live. No other lesson is required of Man.

—MIKHAIL NAIMY

Choose fear, and you are acting out old scripts, falling prey to bad habits, holding fast to patterns of behavior that no longer serve you, and taking life's most precious gifts for granted.

He who does good comes to the temple gate,
he who loves reaches the shrine.

—RABINDRANATH TAGORE

May you choose love. It is a wonderful place to live. When your time on earth is done, all that will matter is how much love is in your heart. Why wait another minute to begin living that truth?

A loving heart is the truest wisdom.

—CHARLES DICKENS

YOUR CHOICE IS LOVE OR FEAR
Living the Lesson

Not long after reading Gerald Jampolsky's observation that every person we meet is in need of love from us or offering love to us, I walked into my gym and saw Bill, a member I knew fairly well. He was doing standing calf raises with his back to me. Impulsively, I wrapped my weight belt around his forehead as a goofy way of saying hello. He was not pleased. He whipped around and, in so many words, most of which are unprintable, told me he would punch my face in if I ever did that again.

Instead of reacting on the same level of consciousness—"Oh, yeah? Take your best shot, you jerk!"—I thought, *Cool! Here's my chance to see if this love stuff really works!* I immediately began radiating love from my heart and bathing Bill in its healing glow. I also tried to apologize, but he turned away, muttering angrily.

After hanging up my jacket in the locker room, I headed to the pull-up bar and began my workout. I dropped down from the bar just in time to see Bill striding purposefully toward me from the other side of the gym. "I mean it, Phil," he fumed. "If you ever do that again, I'll drag you out to the parking lot and pummel you." With that, he spun around and stormed away.

This time I followed him, choosing to pump love instead of iron. "Bill," I called out, catching up to him, "I'm very sorry. I had no idea you would be so upset. It won't happen again." I continued apologizing until he turned to face me. "My sister used to do stuff like that to me," he sputtered. "And I hated it."

Bingo. Bill's outburst had nothing to do with me; I had inadvertently triggered a painful childhood memory. What happened in the next moment was astonishing: The heavy, dark cloud of negative energy that had engulfed him simply vanished. It was as if a magician had uttered "Abracadabra!" and instantaneously replaced a violent thunderstorm with sunny skies.

I tried to apologize one more time, but Bill cut me off. "Don't worry about it," he said calmly, dismissing the whole incident with a wave of his hand. "No big deal." An hour later, we were both in the locker room, preparing to leave. "So long, Phil," he called out. "Have a good day."

Wow. If I had responded to Bill's anger in kind, the confrontation may have escalated out of control. Even worse, from that day forward the tension would have been thick between us, and my enjoyment of going to the gym every morning would have been tinged with dread. Instead, love healed our conflict, it healed our relationship, and it may have even healed the pain Bill had been carrying around since childhood. That was the day I stopped looking at love as a choice, and embraced it as a way of life.

YOUR CHOICE IS LOVE OR FEAR
Self-Reflection Questions

- Do I generally interact with the world from a place of fear or love, and why?

- What would happen if I started trusting God to guide me through stressful situations?

- In what ways am I waiting for life to come to me instead of taking the initiative to fully engage in life?

- What would it take for me to feel more peace in my heart?

- How can I be warmer and more compassionate with others?

- How can I make a habit out of recognizing the presence of God in others?

- How can I do a better job of focusing on others during conversations instead of looking for opportunities to turn the spotlight back on myself?

- How can I stop myself from judging others for not acting like I think they should?

- When does my anger get the best of me, and what can I do about it?

- How can I shift my mindset so that I no longer feel emotionally drained from interacting with certain people?

- When I help somebody, am I truly being selfless or am I looking for ego strokes?

- Why or why not do I feel other people are more worthy of love than I am?

FIVE

FOLLOW YOUR GUIDANCE

God speaks as softly as possible,
and as loudly as necessary.

—Rafi Zabor

FOLLOW YOUR GUIDANCE

Divine Intelligence speaks to you through the voice of your intuition. While some people hear this voice more clearly, it is accessible to anyone who chooses to listen.

> *How do these geese know when to fly to the sun? Who tells them the seasons? How do we, humans, know when it is time to move on? How do we know when to go? As with the migrant birds, so surely with us, there is a voice within, if only we would listen to it, that tells us so certainly when to go forth into the unknown.*
>
> —ELISABETH KÜBLER-ROSS

PURE KNOWING

Intuition is pure truth, pure knowing. It is Truth with a capital T. It knows all there is and all there ever will be to know.

> *Intuition is the clear conception of the whole at once.*
>
> —JOHANN KASPAR LAVATER

You recognize your intuition as truth because it strikes a chord of harmony within you and resonates with your inner divinity.

> *We are not human beings having a spiritual experience, we are spiritual beings having a human experience.*
>
> —PIERRE TEILLHARD DE CHARDIN

Intuitive guidance accounts for one of life's most profound paradoxes: You already know the answer to every question you can ask.

> *My Lord, why do I storm heaven for answers that are already in my heart? . . .*
> *O Lead me to the beyond within.*
>
> —SISTER MACRINA WIEDERKEHR

Your intuition may even initiate the question to draw your attention to an answer in need of discovery.

> *God speaks to all individuals through what happens to them moment by moment.*
>
> —JEAN-PIERRE DE CAUSSADE

Socrates stated more than twenty-four hundred years ago that "learning" could be more accurately described as "remembering."

> *Forget everything you have learned and you will remember everything you have forgotten.*
>
> —ALAN COHEN

Check in with this inner knowing for confirmation before making an important decision or tackling a challenge. It is your channel to Divine Wisdom.

> *You know nothing till intuition agrees.*
>
> —RICHARD BACH

INTUITIVE AWARENESS

Your conscience flows from and is an expression of your intuition, which in turn flows from and is an expression of Divine Consciousness.

> *Conscience is God's presence in man.*
>
> —EMANUEL SWEDENBORG

You may "hear" the voice of conscience, of intuition, any number of ways, perhaps as an unpleasant feeling in the pit of your stomach, a flash of insight, or a nudge in the right direction.

> *The voice of conscience is so delicate that it is easy to stifle it; but it is also so clear that it is impossible to mistake it.*
>
> —MADAME DE STAËL

Your intuition often expresses itself not as a thought in your mind, but as a feeling in your body or as an unexplainable sensation.

> *The mind can assert anything, and pretend it has proved it. My beliefs I test on my body, on my intuitional consciousness, and when I get a response there, then I accept.*
>
> —D. H. LAWRENCE

Trust that feeling, honor that sensation, listen carefully to the message it conveys. If it causes you discomfort, be grateful: it has manifested to protect you from yourself.

> *Every time I've done something that doesn't feel right, it's ended up not being right.*
>
> —MARIO CUOMO

As intuitive awareness deepens, your inner alarm system will sound off whenever you find yourself in a situation that does not serve your highest good.

> *The power of intuitive understanding will protect you from harm until the end of your days.*
>
> —LAO TZU

Heighten your awareness and you enhance not only your spiritual well-being, but your emotional and physical health as well.

> *The more consciousness you bring into the body, the stronger the immune system becomes. It is as if every cell awakens and rejoices.*
>
> —ECKHART TOLLE

As you learn to live more consciously, you will find that you can intuitively scan your inner landscape for signs of discord.

> *The task of making sense of ourselves and our behavior requires that we acknowledge there can be as much value in the blink of an eye as in months of rational analysis.*
>
> —MALCOLM GLADWELL

You feel calmer and more centered. Before long, you swear you can feel God's hand at your back, gently directing you.

> *There is no way to peace; peace is the way.*
>
> —A. J. MUSTE

The pieces of your life start falling into place. You greet each new situation with optimism and enthusiasm.

> *None live so easily, so pleasantly, as those that live by faith.*
>
> —MATTHEW HENRY

Your daily activities may remain constant, but you perform them more mindfully and reverently.

> *Before enlightenment, chop wood, carry water. After enlightenment, chop wood, carry water.*
>
> —ZEN PROVERB

INTUITION AND INTELLECT

The more you trust in your ability to tune in to your intuitive wisdom, the easier it will be to access it. Relying on logic alone to guide your actions will take you only so far.

> *If we listened to our intellect, we'd never have a love affair. We'd never have a friendship. We'd never go into business, because we'd be cynical. Well, that's nonsense. You've got to jump off cliffs all the time and build your wings on the way down.*
>
> —RAY BRADBURY

A great intellect is a great blessing. It can also be a great curse if it blocks you from accessing the wisdom of your heart.

> *The intelligent man who is proud of his intelligence is like a*
> *condemned man who is proud of his large cell.*
>
> —SIMONE WEIL

Your intellectual decisions are biased by the quality of your knowledge, the influence of your belief system, and your unique psychological profile.

> *Watch out for intellect, because it knows so much it knows nothing*
> *and leaves you hanging upside down, mouthing knowledge as your*
> *heart falls out of your mouth.*
>
> —ANNE SEXTON

Your intuitive promptings bypass these personal biases and harmonize your actions with Universal Intelligence.

> *You have to be able to do what your mind would give you logical*
> *reasons to not do. You have to be everything your soul beckons you*
> *to be and everything your mind tells you to be cautious about.*
>
> —CAROLINE MYSS

Intuitive guidance manifests as inner resolve that cannot be explained by intellectual argument alone.

> *For those who believe, no proof is necessary. For those who don't*
> *believe, no proof is possible.*
>
> —STUART CHASE

Yet neither can you rely solely on your inner voice. You are at your best when your conscious intellect operates in tandem with your superconscious intuition.

> *It is always with excitement that I wake up in the morning*
> *wondering what my intuition will toss up to me, like gifts from*
> *the sea. I work with it and rely on it. It's my partner.*
>
> —DR. JONAS SALK

If you cannot discern intuition from intellect, continue to walk your path; every day brings greater clarity and insight.

> *If we are facing in the right direction, all we have to do is keep on walking.*
>
> —BUDDHIST PROVERB

ACCEPTANCE AND TRUST

If your inner voice is only the faintest of whispers, retreat to an empty room, dim the lights, sit quietly, breathe deeply, and turn your attention inward.

> *Put your ear down close to your soul and listen hard.*
>
> —ANNE SEXTON

The challenge is not to further develop your intuition but to hear, accept, and apply the information you are already being given.

> *God gives you the dots. Connecting them is up to you.*
>
> —DANE STAUFFER

Honor the promptings of your inner life, and your outer life will naturally unfold with beauty and purpose.

> *If the single man plant himself indomitably on his instincts, and there abide, the huge world will come round to him.*
>
> —RALPH WALDO EMERSON

Intuitive navigation always steers you in the direction of your dreams, toward a richer, more fulfilling, more abundant life.

The more and more each is impelled by that which is intuitive, or the relying upon the soul force within, the greater, the farther, the deeper, the broader, the more constructive may be the result.

—EDGAR CAYCE

Heed your guidance and follow it faithfully, and each step will reveal itself in divine right order.

Faith is taking the first step even when you don't see the whole staircase.

—MARTIN LUTHER KING, JR.

It does not matter if the journey's end is cloaked in fog; every step forward burns off a bit more haze.

There is no advancement to him who stands trembling because he cannot see the end from the beginning.

—E. J. KLEMME

The courage to honor your guidance requires a unique blend of faith, hope, trust, and obedience—faith that you are being pointed in the right direction, hope that the outcome will be rewarding, trust that it will, and obedience to the Divine force that operates in your best interests.

Courage can't see around corners, but goes around them anyway.

—MIGNON MCLAUGHLIN

Muffle your courage and you may be forever haunted by the dim realization that the life you dreamed of was once yours for the taking.

The regret that comes down
like a fine ash
year after year
is the shadow of what
we did not dare.

—MARGE PIERCY

RESISTING AND RATIONALIZING

Argue with your intuition, rationalize it away, or drown it out with mental chatter, and you may not notice any repercussions.

> *There is a criterion by which you can judge whether the thoughts you are thinking and the things you are doing are right for you. The criterion is:* Have they brought you inner peace? *If they have not, there is something wrong with them.*
>
> —PEACE PILGRIM

Yet the more you tune out your inner guidance, the further you drift away from the placid waters of Divine union.

> *When conscience is our friend, all is peace; but if once offended, farewell to the tranquil mind.*
>
> —MARY MONTAGU

At the very least, disregarding your guidance will ensure that you experience life as a series of locked doors and dead-end roads.

> *There are two kinds of people: those who say to God, "Thy will be done," and those to whom God says, "All right, then, have it your way."*
>
> —C. S. LEWIS

Ignoring your intuition and forging stubbornly ahead on your own is inevitably self-defeating.

> *God without you won't; you without God can't.*
>
> —DESMOND TUTU

Then again, you cannot tune out your intuition completely. Some part of you is always aware, always listening.

We may perhaps, through belief in our own most patent rectitude, succeed in escaping all adverse criticism and in deceiving ourselves. But deep down below the surface of the average conscience, a still small voice says to us: "Something is out of tune."

—CARL JUNG

No matter how mightily you resist, you cannot help but periodically recognize the loving wisdom that is guiding you.

Men occasionally stumble over the truth, but most of them pick themselves up and hurry off as if nothing had happened.

—WINSTON CHURCHILL

INTUITION AND INDEPENDENCE

Your conscience is the bridge between your body-bound ego and the infinite wisdom of Spirit. Block out your conscience, and you disable your moral compass.

The person that loses their conscience has nothing left worth keeping.

—IZAAK WALTON

Stifle your conscience and you risk falling prey to someone who, consciously or not, may overwrite your vision for your life with their own.

No man is great enough or wise enough for any of us to surrender our destiny to. The only way in which anyone can lead us is to restore to us the belief in our own guidance.

—HENRY MILLER

You relinquish your power when you abandon your instincts and place your trust in others to lead you through the moral thickets of life.

As soon as you trust yourself, you will know how to live.

—JOHANN WOLFGANG VON GOETHE

Even if the person advising you has your best interests at heart and is someone you know and trust, Divine Omniscience always trumps human reason.

Don't listen to friends when the Friend inside you says, "Do this."

—MAHATMA GANDHI

We have much to learn from those who are wiser and more experienced, yet their truth may not be your truth.

Blessed are the ears that catch the accents of divine whispering, and pay no heed to the murmurings of this world.

—THOMAS À KEMPIS

Only you can feel the stirrings of your heart. Only you can peer into the depths of your soul.

Your highest right knows all futures. Listen to its whisper and find that the prize ahead is your own greatest happiness.

—RICHARD BACH

Your intuition is your independence. If the voice within is drowned out by the white noise of guilt, regret, and other negative emotions, your life is not and will not be your own.

There is something in every one of you that waits and listens for the sound of the genuine in yourself. It is the only true guide you will ever have. And if you cannot hear it, you will all of your life spend your days on the end of strings that somebody else pulls.

—HOWARD THURMAN

INTUITION vs. EGO

The purity of your conscience is compromised to the extent that it is influenced by your ego. A pure conscience directs you to make the right choice. A conscience clouded by ego allows you to make the choice you prefer.

> *You have to leave the city of your comfort and go into the*
> *wilderness of your intuition. . . . What you'll discover will be*
> *wonderful. What you'll discover will be yourself.*
>
> —ALAN ALDA

As soon as you step aside and clear the way for, as spiritual teacher and author Eckhart Tolle termed it, "the knower in you who dwells behind the thinker," you ratchet up your consciousness and loosen your ego's grip on your conscience.

> *Intuition comes very close to clairvoyance; it appears to be the*
> *extrasensory perception of reality.*
>
> —ALEXIS CARREL

As conscience shrugs off the influence of your ego and comes into greater alignment with Spirit, the voice of conscience begins sounding like the whisper of angels.

> *Behold, I send an Angel before thee, to keep thee in the way, and to*
> *bring thee into the place which I have prepared.*
>
> —EXODUS 23:20

The more grounded and peaceful you become, the easier it will be to distinguish your intuition from your ego.

> *Spiritual truth, then, is universally true and without variation*
> *through time or place. It always brings peace, harmony, accord,*
> *love, compassion, and mercy. Truth can be identified by these*
> *qualities. All else is the invention of the ego.*
>
> —DR. DAVID R. HAWKINS

Turn your attention outward and your ego will jump into action, drowning out the voice of divinely guided intuition with storms of relentless mental chatter and emotional upheaval.

> *There are always two voices sounding in our ears, the voice of fear and the voice of confidence. One is the clamor of the senses, the other is the whispering of the higher self.*
>
> —CHARLES B. NEWCOMB

Feeling emotion along with a thought is a clue that the thought is not an intuitive message.

> *Intuition speaks without emotion and with no value judgment attached to it. I am able to receive an intuitive message as if I am watching a movie that doesn't involve me.*
>
> —KATHRYN HARWIG

It is your ego that is responsible for the admonishments still rattling around in your head from your family, your sixth-grade teacher, your mean-spirited boss, and all the other well-intentioned or horribly misguided authority figures from your past or present.

> *If you hear a voice within you saying, "You are not a painter," then by all means paint, boy, and that voice will be silenced.*
>
> —VINCENT VAN GOGH

Ego encourages you to act selfishly or from a position of superiority or inferiority, typically expressing itself as fear, judgment, or a sense of entitlement.

> *Fear is static that prevents me from hearing my intuition.*
>
> —HUGH PRATHER

If the message you are hearing encourages you to attack anything or anyone, it is your ego speaking.

The ego always seeks to divide and separate. The Holy Spirit always seeks to unify and heal.

—A COURSE IN MIRACLES

Intuitive guidance, by definition, nudges you toward what is good, what is right, what is helpful.

Whenever conscience speaks with a divided, uncertain, and disputed voice, it is not yet the voice of God. Descend still deeper into yourself, until you hear nothing but a clear and undivided voice, a voice which does away with doubt and brings with it persuasion, light, and serenity.

—HENRI FRÉDÉRIC AMIEL

Divinely inspired intuition urges you, without exception, to act with love and compassion, to be of service to humankind.

Nothing is true that forces me to exclude.

—ALBERT CAMUS

A dedication to serving others does not mean that your life is not your own. It means looking through God's eyes for opportunities to be of service while following and honoring your own guidance.

A man does not have to be an angel in order to be a saint.

—NORMAN COUSINS

Know that on the deepest level, there is no distinction between what is best and most helpful to you and what is best and most helpful to others.

It is one of the most beautiful compensations of this life that no one can sincerely try to help another without helping himself.

—CHARLES DUDLEY WARNER

INFINITE PATIENCE

Diverting course on a moment's notice to follow your guidance can take time, a precious commodity these days.

> *Those who make the worst use of their time are the first to*
> *complain of its brevity.*
>
> —Jean de La Bruyère

Yet the more time you devote to pursuing what you feel guided to pursue, the more time you seem to have for everything else.

> *It is familiarity with life that makes time speed quickly. When*
> *every day is a step in the unknown, as for children, the days*
> *are long with gathering of experience.*
>
> —George Gissing

You are alive with the joy of learning, discovering, and experiencing life as it was meant to be lived.

> *Every second is of infinite value.*
>
> —Johann Wolfgang von Goethe

You may find yourself shifting from being chronically late to feeling like you have all the time in the world.

> *The butterfly counts not months but moments, and has time*
> *enough.*
>
> —Rabindranath Tagore

It has been said that a wise person never rushes. That makes sense. Hurrying disturbs your connection with the Divine current, creating mental static that throws you out of sync.

> *He who forces time is forced back by time but he who yields to time finds time standing at his side.*
>
> —THE TALMUD

The more you hurry, the more scattered your thoughts become and the more likely you are to overlook important details, bump into furniture, knock things over, and find yourself doubling back to retrieve forgotten items.

> *Those in a hurry do not arrive.*
>
> —ZEN PROVERB

Resolve to practice infinite patience. Acting slowly and deliberately helps you stay anchored in the present moment and notice what is in need of noticing.

> *We say we waste time, but that is impossible. We waste ourselves.*
>
> —ALICE BLOCH

You always have time for whatever you put first. When you are tuned in to Divine guidance, time becomes your trusted ally.

> *If a man has a great deal to put in them, a day will have a hundred pockets.*
>
> —FRIEDRICH NIETZSCHE

The more you value time, the more you value life. With reverence and gratitude, you quietly celebrate every moment, every breath.

> *A man who dares waste one hour of time has not discovered the value of life.*
>
> —CHARLES DARWIN

Ultimately, whatever time you spend acting on Divine direction is dwarfed by the time you would have wasted by making poor choices, false starts, and wrong turns.

Whoever travels without a guide
needs two hundred years for a two-day journey.

—RUMI

INTUITIVE ARTISTRY

Intuition is the wellspring of creative inspiration. Every artistic achievement originated with the same creative impulse that birthed all of existence.

> *To the artist is sometimes granted a sudden, transient insight*
> *which serves in this matter for experience. A flash, and where*
> *previously the brain held a dead fact, the soul grasps a living*
> *truth! At moments we are all artists.*

—ARNOLD BENNETT

Encourage this creative impulse to take root inside you, allow it to consume you, that it may find full expression through you.

> *What is genius but the mind, heart, and art of God shining to the*
> *world through an open window?*

—ALAN COHEN

Every time you act on a creative urge, your mind links with the Divine Mind and the life force of the Universe is yours to command.

> *I touch God in my song as the hill touches the far-away sea with*
> *its waterfall.*

—RABINDRANATH TAGORE

Divine inspiration is so powerful that it instantly erases the word "impossible" from your vocabulary.

> *The person who says it cannot be done should not interrupt the person doing it.*
>
> —CHINESE PROVERB

Trusting in the Divine force that lovingly urges you to create and evolve, you are invigorated, not intimidated, by each new challenge.

> *I am always doing something I can not do, in order that I may learn how to do it.*
>
> —PABLO PICASSO

You stay true to your vision, knowing that you compromise the integrity of whatever you create when you allow a conflicting point of view to influence your work.

> *None of us will ever accomplish anything excellent or commanding except when he listens to this whisper which is heard by him alone.*
>
> —RALPH WALDO EMERSON

In those transcendent, pure moments when a gifted artist's brush, violin, voice, or pen seems commanded by the very hand of God, the resulting masterpiece leaves us breathless, for we intuitively recognize it as beyond the scope of ordinary human achievement.

> *Just as the sun is infinitely brighter than a candle flame, there is infinitely more intelligence in Being than in your mind.*
>
> —ECKHART TOLLE

NO ACCIDENTS

Your angelic emissaries are with you always, guiding you with infinite wisdom and deep love.

Whatever inspires, also guides and protects.

—RICHARD BACH

The implications of this realization are staggering. If God is guiding you with infinite intelligence and inexhaustible love, that means that nothing is random or accidental.

When it is time to learn patience, God has an amazing ability to lengthen bank lines.

—JAMES KEELEY

Hold on to that thought the next time your grocery bag breaks in the parking lot, or you knock over a lamp at home, or you trip on the sidewalk and sprain your ankle.

Now and then I go about pitying myself and all the while my soul is being blown by great winds across the sky.

—OJIBWAY WISDOM

You are not having an unlucky day. You are not being punished. You are not a victim of haphazard events. Stay open, stay positive, and stay alert, for God is redirecting you.

Sometimes when things seem to be going wrong, they are going right for reasons you are yet to understand.

—ALAN COHEN

In the aftermath of such "mishaps," you will meet people you otherwise would not have met, have experiences you would have missed, and be exposed to opportunities for spiritual growth you would not have encountered.

Let a benevolent universe have its way, and you will recognize a bigger plan than you understood when you looked through the eyes of fear.

—ALAN COHEN

Your "misfortune" may also be a form of protection. Dr. Bernie Siegel tells the story of a man racing to the airport to catch a plane for an important business meeting. His tire blows out on the freeway; by the time he changes it his flight is long gone. Frenzied and disheveled, he curses the gods, only to find out later that the plane crashed and all aboard had perished. That flat tire turned out to be a life-saving gift, one that undoubtedly sparked an intense period of reflection and reassessment.

> *Sell your cleverness, and purchase bewilderment.*
>
> —RUMI

An incident is neither positive nor negative; its meaning depends entirely on how you interpret it.

> *There's no disaster that can't become a blessing, and no blessing that can't become a disaster.*
>
> —RICHARD BACH

An old Chinese Taoist story illustrates how changing an event's context changes its meaning: A poor farmer's only horse ran away. "That's awful," said a neighbor. The farmer said, "We'll see." The horse returned with a herd of wild horses. "That's wonderful," said the neighbor. The farmer said, "We'll see." The farmer's son was thrown by one of the new horses and broke his leg. "That's awful," said the neighbor. The farmer said, "We'll see." The next day an army contingent searching the province for recruits rejected the farmer's injured son. "That's wonderful," said the neighbor. The farmer said, "We'll see." And so on.

> *It is not possible to judge any event as simply fortunate or unfortunate, good or bad. It is like the old story about the farmer and the horse [see above]. You must travel throughout all of time and space to know the true impact of any event. Every success contains some difficulties, and every failure contributes to increased wisdom or future success. Every event is both fortunate and unfortunate. Fortunate and unfortunate, good and bad, exist only in our perceptions.*
>
> —THICH NHAT HANH

Instead of passing judgment on what comes your way and, as author and medical intuitive Caroline Myss says, "mourning the absence of perfection in your life," challenge yourself to view unexpected incidents as necessary steps toward fulfilling your life's purpose.

True understanding is to see the events of life in this way: "You are here for my benefit, though rumor paints you otherwise." And everything is turned to one's advantage when he greets a situation like this: "You are the very thing I was looking for." Truly, whatever arises in life is the right material to bring about your growth and the growth of those around you. This, in a word, is art—and this art we call "life" is a practice suitable to both men and gods. Everything contains some special purpose and a hidden blessing. What then could be strange or arduous, when all of life is here to greet you like an old and faithful friend?

—MARCUS AURELIUS

In time, you learn to welcome whatever is in front of you with these three words always on your lips: "As you wish."

Life has no other discipline to impose, if we would but realize it, than to accept life unquestioningly. Everything we shut our eyes to, everything we run away from, everything we deny, denigrate or despise, serves to defeat us in the end. What seems nasty, painful, evil can become a source of beauty, joy and strength, if faced with open mind. Every moment is a golden one for him who has the vision to recognize it as such.

—HENRY MILLER

Look through God's eyes and you understand that it matters not what life brings to you. What matters is what you bring to life.

The very thing I call pleasurable today, tomorrow under better circumstances I may call pain. The fire that warms us can also consume us; it is not the fault of the fire.

—SWAMI VIVEKANANDA

Follow your guidance with courage and conviction and you will know a deep measure of peace no matter how the consequences play out.

Courage is the price which life exacts for granting peace.

—AMELIA EARHART

ONE SONG

If God is guiding each of us with infinite wisdom and inexhaustible love, it follows that God is an organizing force bringing divine order to the Universe, and that you are loved and supported no matter how you choose to exercise your free will.

> *There is a force of love present everywhere, and it can be trusted to bring your own life into order and peace.*
>
> —DEEPAK CHOPRA

The ancients' six-word definition of God—*that Supreme Intelligence which governs everything*—aligns perfectly with the characterization of the Universe as a unified field of conscious, Divine energy in which every atom is connected to every other atom.

> *The world looks like a multiplication-table, or a mathematical equation, which, turn it how you will, balances itself. Take what figure you will, its exact value, nor more nor less, still returns to you. Every secret is told, every crime is punished, every virtue rewarded, every wrong redressed, in silence and certainty.*
>
> —RALPH WALDO EMERSON

The Universe, as a clever observer so poetically noted, is "one song"—uni (*one*) verse (*song*)—and every atom sings from the same songbook.

> *Thou canst not stir a flower*
> *Without troubling of a star.*
>
> —FRANCIS JOSEPH THOMPSON

The ripples you create by following your guidance touch countless lives and produce cascading waves of consequences that will influence generations yet to come.

> *Every action of our lives touches on some chord that will vibrate in eternity.*
>
> —EDWIN HUBBELL CHAPIN

Every time you act on your guidance, you add love and peace to the world and subtly influence the course of human history.

> *Never doubt that you can change history. You already have.*
>
> —MARGE PIERCY

Your every action alters the nature of collective consciousness, the self-aware "database" composed of the cumulative awareness, beliefs, intelligence, and wisdom of every person on the planet.

> *Nothing is more powerful than an individual acting out of his*
> *conscience, thus helping to bring the collective conscience to life.*
>
> —NORMAN COUSINS

A HIGHER PURPOSE AT WORK

Divine Intelligence works with you to co-create every encounter and every event in your life. Every moment is saturated with meaning and purpose.

> *Curses and blessings do not come through gates, but man himself*
> *invites their arrival.*
>
> —T'AI-SHANG KAN-YING P'IEN

The idea that there is a loving guidance at work in the Universe is much easier to accept when life is going well.

> *When the oak is felled the whole forest echoes with its fall, but*
> *a hundred acorns are sown in silence by an unnoticed breeze.*
>
> —THOMAS CARLYLE

In times of misfortune or grief, it can be difficult to accept those five familiar words invariably offered by well-meaning friends: *Everything happens for a reason.*

> *When life looks like it's falling apart, it may just be falling in place.*
>
> —BEVERLY SOLOMON

When our world seems especially dark, it does not seem possible that such a statement can be true. We reject it as a rationalization intended to help us cope with disappointment and loss.

> *The eternal mystery of the world is its comprehensibility. . . . The fact that it is comprehensible is a miracle.*
>
> —ALBERT EINSTEIN

Yet if you could rise above your circumstances and look through God's eyes, you would see that your life is unfolding precisely as it must to serve your highest good and the highest good of all concerned.

> *Every object and being in the universe is a jar overfilled with wisdom and beauty.*
>
> —RUMI

Even if you are skeptical that a particular event has meaning, acting as if it does imbues the event with meaning. How? If you look for possible reasons you will find them, which paves the way for fresh insights and opportunities for growth. Ultimately, if the only meaning an event has is the meaning you assign to it, it is meaning nonetheless.

> *If God exists, he is perfect; if he is perfect, he is wise, powerful and just; if he is wise and powerful, all is well.*
>
> —JEAN-JACQUES ROUSSEAU

Skepticism is natural, for the magnitude and magnificence of Divine guidance is too vast for us to grasp. No matter; life does not depend on human understanding for it to unfold in wisdom.

> *When we look ahead, we see only chaos. When we look behind, we see only order.*
>
> —CAROLINE MYSS

You might be able to see around the corner that lies ahead, but not around the next corner or the countless corners beyond that. Ah, but God can.

> *I have learned that faith means trusting in advance what will*
> *make sense only in reverse.*
>
> —PHILIP YANCEY

GOD'S VOICE

When you act in accordance with your inner guidance, your energy vibrates at a higher, finer rate and you come into greater alignment with the Source of all that is.

> *A good conscience is to the soul what health is to the body; it*
> *preserves a constant ease and serenity within us, and more than*
> *countervails all the calamities and afflictions which can possibly*
> *befall us.*
>
> —JOSEPH ADDISON

The greater your harmony with this Universal Life Force, the closer you approach the peace that surpasses all understanding.

> *Let the water settle; you will see the moon and stars mirrored in*
> *your being.*
>
> —RUMI

Listen to your conscience and you perceive a fine line between your actions and God's actions. Listen more deeply and you discover that there is no line at all.

> *Let us work as if success depended upon ourselves alone, but*
> *with heartfelt conviction that we are doing nothing, and God*
> *everything.*
>
> —SAINT IGNATIUS OF LOYOLA

Cultivate the discipline and commitment to abide by the voice of God within, and you serve as an instrument of Divine Will, allowing God to act through you.

One of the goals of authentic spiritual work is to embrace our inner divinity and embody a sense of the transcendent. To the extent that we can do this, we diminish any potential conflict between God's will and our own.

—DR. LARRY DOSSEY

Follow your guidance faithfully and eventually you become one with it; God's voice becomes your voice.

Lord, I will reason, I will will, I will act; but guide Thou my reason, will, and activity to the right thing I should do.

—PARAMAHANSA YOGANANDA

In this exalted state of consciousness, you effortlessly see the world through God's eyes and act instinctively on God's behalf.

Lord, make me an instrument of Your peace.
Where there is hatred let me sow love;
Where there is injury, pardon;
Where there is doubt, faith;
Where there is despair, hope;
Where there is darkness, light; and
Where there is sadness, joy.
Oh divine Master, grant that I may not so much
Seek to be consoled as to console;
To be understood as to understand;
To be loved as to love.

—SAINT FRANCIS OF ASSISI

The moment you experience blissful unity with All That Is is the moment you release every burden, every worry, and joyously awaken to a higher consciousness.

Someday perhaps the inner light will shine forth from us, and then we'll need no other light.

—JOHANN WOLFGANG VON GOETHE

FOLLOW YOUR GUIDANCE
Living the Lesson

Pursuing a career as a freelance writer meant taking a big chance at a time when I couldn't afford to take big chances. My inner voice, however, told me that I couldn't afford *not* to take that chance—there was too much at stake. Exactly what was at stake I didn't know; all I knew was that I was being pushed and prodded by a force that would not take no for an answer.

I knew if I could just get that first break, I'd be on my way. I sent samples of my work to every magazine and business I could think of, hoping it wouldn't take too long for that first domino to fall.

Then Todd Manzi called. He and I had met at the gym and become friends. Todd had established a one-person marketing agency and wanted to know if I could write an ad for a local homebuilder. It was a rush job, so I went home, wrote the copy, and handed it over to Todd two hours later.

The day after the ad was printed in the *Minneapolis Star Tribune*, I dropped off a résumé and samples (including the hot-off-the-press ad) at a nearby ad agency. Half an hour later, the creative director called. She said she had been impressed with that ad in the newspaper and had wondered who had written it.

She hired me to write a lively corporate history for a client, which ended up as a four-page insert in the *Star Tribune*. I used that piece as a sample to open doors with other prospective clients. I also expanded the history project into a feature article for a local business magazine.

As time went by, I traced a number of important assignments back to that first ad I had written for Todd. One referral led to another, which led to another, and soon I was getting steady work. The more I put myself out there, the more good things happened. I felt like I was in the flow, with the entire Universe conspiring on my behalf.

I've thanked Todd profusely over the years for giving me that first important break, but I still harbor hopes of doing something especially meaningful for him one day. I'm not sure what that will look like, but I do know what it will be accompanied by—a nice new box of dominoes.

FOLLOW YOUR GUIDANCE
Self-Reflection Questions

- In what ways does my inner guidance make itself known?

- Why do I trust that my conscience is pointing me in the right direction?

- What can I do to get more in touch with my inner guidance?

- How can I summon the courage to faithfully follow my guidance?

- How would my life change if I slowed down, stayed anchored in God, and created more time in my life?

- How does following my guidance affect my relationship with God?

- In what situations am I more likely to "argue" with my intuition and ignore its guidance?

- What are the dangers in tuning out my conscience and placing my trust in the guidance of others?

- If logic tells me one thing and intuition tells me another, which am I more apt to follow and why?

- How can I be sure that I am listening to my intuition instead of hearing what I want to hear?

- Why do I believe or disbelieve that everything happens for a reason?

- How can I remind myself to look for God's fingerprints on whatever comes my way?

SIX

FOCUS ON BEING, NOT DOING

Often, people attempt to live their lives backward:
They try to have more things, or more money, in order to do more of what they want,
so that they will be happier. The way it actually works is the reverse.
You must first be who you really are, then do what you need to do,
in order to have what you want.

—Shakti Gawain

FOCUS ON BEING, NOT DOING

We are human beings, not human doings. Pour all your efforts into doing while neglecting the art of being, and yours will be a life out of balance.

> *If we look at the path, we do not see the sky.*
>
> —NATIVE AMERICAN PROVERB

REARRANGING PRIORITIES

How you relate to the outer world is a reflection of your inner world. A chaotic inner life manifests as a chaotic outer life.

> *When we do not find peace of mind in ourselves it is useless to seek it elsewhere.*
>
> —FRANÇOIS DE LA ROCHEFOUCAULD

Avoiding introspection only fans the flames of cause and effect. Ignore a smoldering brush fire in your inner world and you inevitably find yourself battling a four-alarm blaze in your outer world.

> *When an inner situation is not made conscious, it appears outside as fate.*
>
> —CARL JUNG

Tragically, many people get so absorbed in the demands of daily life that they lose touch with themselves.

> *There exists in most men a poet who died young, whom the man survived.*
>
> —CHARLES AUGUSTIN SAINTE-BEUVE

They focus exclusively on what they can do instead of who they can be. They hitch their wagon to ego, unaware that Spirit walks patiently beside them.

So you can walk on water? You are no better than a twig floating on a puddle. You can fly through the air? You are no better than this gnat buzzing around my head. Master your own heart then maybe you can be somebody.

—ARABIC WISDOM

Single-mindedly focusing on what you can do, achieve, and acquire, all the while ignoring your soul's yearning for deeper connection with the Source of all that is, is a tragedy of epic proportion.

For whosoever will save his life shall lose it; but whosoever shall lose his life for My sake and the gospel's, the same shall save it. For what shall it profit a man if he shall gain the whole world, and lose his own soul?

—JESUS OF NAZARETH
MARK 8:35-36

The essence of who you are is not defined by how you earn a paycheck or how you spend your leisure time. What matters is who you are *being* while you are doing those activities.

Your duty is to be, and not to be this or that.

—SRI RAMANA MAHARSHI

Going through life disconnected from your spirit is like driving a race car with a broken steering wheel; you find yourself veering off course and occasionally crashing into walls.

The level of structure that people seek always is in direct ratio to the amount of chaos they have inside.

—TOM ROBBINS

Shifting your focus from doing to being does not mean that you do away with doing. It means that you recognize that doing *flows* from being.

A cheery relaxation is man's natural state, just as nature itself is relaxed. A waterfall is concerned only with being itself, not with doing something it considers waterfall-like.

—VERNON HOWARD

Prioritize being over doing, and doing what needs to be done becomes more effortless and enjoyable.

One must not lose sight of practical matters in order to pursue spiritual ones. The superior person maintains a proper balance.

—I CHING

LIVING CONSCIOUSLY

You live harmoniously when you reconcile doing and being by performing every action with mindfulness and conscious intent.

Anything less than a conscious commitment to the important is an unconscious commitment to the unimportant.

—STEPHEN R. COVEY

Emphasize doing and your attention can get stuck in the past or the future. Emphasize being and you root yourself fully and gloriously in the present moment.

It is the privilege of living to be aware of a curtain's fold or the intonation of a human voice. To be acutely, agonizingly conscious of the moment that is always present and always passing.

—MARYA MANNES

Striving to live more consciously and with greater presence expands your capacity to simply *be*.

When you become conscious of Being, what is really happening
is that Being becomes conscious of itself. When Being becomes
conscious of itself—that's presence. Since Being, consciousness,
and life are synonymous, we could say that presence means
consciousness becoming conscious of itself, or life attaining
self-consciousness.

—ECKHART TOLLE

Move through life unconsciously and "being" remains a foreign concept, obscured from view by a relentless emphasis on activity.

At some point early in our lives, we decide just how conscious we
wish to be. We establish a threshold of awareness. We choose how
stark a truth we are willing to admit into consciousness, how
readily we will examine contradictions in our lives and beliefs,
how deeply we wish to penetrate. Our brains can censor what we
see and hear, we can filter reality to suit our level of courage. At
every crossroads we make the choice again for greater or lesser
awareness.

—MARILYN FERGUSON

Keep your foot on the gas, and the beauty that otherwise would touch your heart and stir your soul becomes nothing more than a blur in your rearview mirror.

How narrow is the vision that exalts the busyness of the ant above
the singing of the grasshopper.

—KAHLIL GIBRAN

Look beyond your "To Do" list and create a "To Be" list. Begin it by writing down the qualities your ideal self would possess. Perhaps your list includes such traits as being loving, kind, nurturing, generous, honest, and reliable.

It is not how much we do, but how much love we put into the
doing. And it is not how much we give, but how much love we
put into the giving. To God, there is nothing small.

—MOTHER TERESA

Monitor your behavior and train yourself to stop thinking, saying, or doing anything not in harmony with your vision.

> *Let the beauty we love be what we do.*
>
> —RUMI

Imagine yourself evolving and gradually embodying these qualities. Challenge yourself to think and act from your future self's perspective. The more often you do, the closer you move to becoming that which you imagined.

> *The living self has one purpose only: to come into its own fullness of being, as a tree comes into full blossom, or a bird into spring beauty, or a tiger into lustre.*
>
> —D. H. LAWRENCE

You become your priorities. Who you are today is the return on investment of every thought, every desire, every action that was entered into the ledger of your life.

> *You have given your life to become the person you are today. Was it worth it?*
>
> —RICHARD BACH

SILENCE AND SOLITUDE

Reshaping your inner world and living more consciously begins with self-reflection and self-appraisal.

> *The life which is unexamined is not worth living.*
>
> —SOCRATES

Taking internal inventory requires time alone and a willingness to ask and answer pointed, and perhaps painful, questions.

*It is easier to sail many thousand miles through cold and storm
and cannibals, in a government ship, with five hundred men and
boys to assist one, than it is to explore the private sea, the Atlantic
and Pacific Ocean of one's being alone.*

—HENRY DAVID THOREAU

You cannot get to know yourself in a meaningful way until you become comfortable with yourself in silence. Only in silence can your true self fully reveal itself to you.

*The more powerful and original a mind, the more it will incline
towards the religion of solitude.*

—ALDOUS HUXLEY

Lower yourself into a pool of silence, wait for the sediment of your daily life to settle, then peer down into the depths of your own being.

*Confucius said, "Men cannot see their reflection in running water
but only in still water. Only that which is still in itself can still the
seekers of stillness." . . . If water derives lucidity from stillness, how
much more the faculties of the mind! The mind of the sage, being
in repose, becomes the mirror of the universe.*

—CHUANG TZU

There are more mysteries in the boundless world within you than there are lifetimes to discover and understand them all.

*What is necessary, after all, is only this: solitude, vast inner
solitude. To walk inside yourself and meet no one for hours—
that is what you must be able to attain.*

—RAINER MARIA RILKE

If you are always on the go, the notion of taking time for quiet reflection may feel uncomfortable. Yet silence is your natural state.

We all have within us a center of stillness surrounded by silence.

—DAG HAMMARSKJÖLD

It may take a few attempts before you are able to sit quietly and breathe deeply without feeling anxious.

> *All man's miseries derive from not being able to sit quietly in a*
> *room alone.*
>
> —BLAISE PASCAL

Done mindfully, sitting in silence delivers you fully into the present moment, washing away your troubles and synchronizing your breathing with the heartbeat of creation.

> *Solitude is a silent storm that breaks down all our dead branches;*
> *Yet it sends our living roots deeper into the living heart of the*
> *living earth.*
>
> —KAHLIL GIBRAN

Be still long enough and the Universe opens the door to itself, revealing its secrets and beckoning you within.

> *You do not need to leave your room. Remain sitting at your table*
> *and listen. Do not even listen, simply wait. Do not even wait, be*
> *quiet, still, and solitary. The world will freely offer itself to you to*
> *be unmasked, it has no choice, it will roll in ecstasy at your feet.*
>
> —FRANZ KAFKA

It is a natural progression. Solitude brings silence. Silence brings stillness. Stillness brings peace. Peace brings liberation.

> *True stillness comes naturally through moments of solitude where*
> *we allow our minds to settle. Just as water seeks its own level, the*
> *mind will gravitate toward the holy. Muddy water will become*
> *clear if allowed to stand undisturbed, and so too will the mind*
> *become clear if it is allowed to be still.*
>
> —DENG MING-DAO

Practice being silent and peaceful every day. Early morning, before your mind kicks into high gear, is an ideal time for stillness.

Silence is as full of potential wisdom and wit as the unhewn marble of great sculpture.

—ALDOUS HUXLEY

Begin by silently expressing love, devotion, and yearning, and allow yourself to be blanketed in God's presence.

Be still, and know that I am God.

—PSALMS 46:10

Silently, with a pure heart, ask God questions about your life. Then be still and listen for the answers.

Stillness is the altar of Spirit.

—PARAMAHANSA YOGANANDA

A mind distracted by random thoughts darting about like fireflies is unable to discern the silent but unmistakable presence of God.

To the mind that is still, the whole universe surrenders.

—LAO TZU

Longer periods of solitude—a weekend retreat, perhaps—can extend and expand your presence and enrich your self-knowledge.

Our language has wisely sensed those two sides of man's being alone. It has created the word "loneliness" to express the pain of being alone. And it has created the word "solitude" to express the glory of being alone.

—PAUL TILLICH

The more alone you are, the less alone you are, for there are fewer distractions keeping you from deepening your relationship with yourself and with God.

A wise man is never less alone than when he is alone.

—JONATHAN SWIFT

Wherever you find yourself, love and honor your solitude, and your solitude will love and honor you back.

> *But your solitude will be a support and a home for you, even in the*
> *midst of very unfamiliar circumstances, and from it you will find*
> *all your paths.*
>
> —RAINER MARIA RILKE

A WORK IN PROGRESS

Spiritual growth requires daily recommitment. Great changes will occur when you resolve to be a little more positive, a little more loving, every day.

> *Paths cannot be taught, they can only be taken.*
>
> —ZEN PROVERB

A daily spiritual practice can elevate your consciousness, instill a sense of harmony with life's rhythms, and promote a subtle but enduring state of joy and gratitude.

> *But what is happiness except the simple harmony between a man*
> *and the life he leads?*
>
> —ALBERT CAMUS

The operative word is "daily." You cannot maintain a higher consciousness by meditating, chanting, praying, or reading inspirational content sporadically. You might as well prepare for a career as a concert pianist by playing ten minutes of Mozart every other day.

> *We must all suffer one of two things: the pain of discipline or the*
> *pain of regret or disappointment.*
>
> —JIM ROHN

You will likely find that the pleasure of self-discovery quickly becomes self-motivating. Each meditation beckons you to go deeper; each exhilarating new book leads to another; each session of affirmations ends too soon.

You cannot teach a man anything; you can only help him to find it within himself.

—GALILEO GALILEI

Yes, implementing a regular practice can be daunting, but putting it off indefinitely can result in a life that just doesn't work very well.

No God, no peace. Know God, know peace.

—UNKNOWN

View yourself as a work in progress. Take great satisfaction in how far you have come, but recognize that the more you learn, the more work there is yet to do.

You are neither the child you were, nor the old person you will become.

—BUDDHIST PROVERB

Inevitably, life's day-to-day demands will distract even the most dedicated of seekers. Not to worry, just try to keep the lapses brief. The longer the detour, the more difficult it will be to steer back on course.

He who interrupts the course of his spiritual exercises and prayer, is like a man who allows a bird to escape from his hand; he can hardly catch it again.

—SAINT JOHN OF THE CROSS

There will come a time when you look back at your younger self, and marvel at the gap between who you were then and who you are today.

We may discover that we are most ourselves when we are furthest from the self we think we ought to be.

—THOMAS MOORE

Travel far enough, and you will reach a crossroads. You will have to choose between retreating to the safety and comfort of life as you knew it, or severing all ties with that existence and forging bravely ahead into the vast unknown.

One does not discover new lands without consenting to lose sight of the shore for a very long time.

—ANDRÉ GIDE

This does not necessarily mean you must bid farewell to the life you have lived; but it does mean that you are genuinely willing to do so if that is what it takes to truly know God.

The important thing is this: to be able at any moment to sacrifice what we are for what we could become.

—CHARLES DU BOS

Granted, it is likely that you will outgrow some relationships. The good news is, you will meet new friends with whom you will relate more deeply and more authentically.

When you affirm your own rightness in the universe, then you co-operate with others easily and automatically as part of your own nature. You, being yourself, helps others be themselves.

—JANE ROBERTS (SETH)

The even better news is, you will never be alone because you will also be deepening your relationship with God.

God loves me so much he will accept me just as I am, but he loves me too much to leave me that way.

—LEIGHTON FORD

AWAKENING TO YOUR POWER

You will have the power to transform your life the moment you realize that you have always had the power to do so.

All the buddhas of all the ages have been telling you a very simple fact: Be—don't try to become. Within these two words, be and becoming, your whole life is contained. Being is enlightenment, becoming is ignorance.

—Osho

Dorothy could have clicked the heels of her ruby slippers together three times as soon as she arrived in Oz, but she had to experience the richness of life's adventures before she could awaken to and fully appreciate her heart's desire.

I've continued to recognize the power individuals have to change virtually anything and everything in their lives in an instant. I've learned that the resources we need to turn our dreams into reality are within us, merely waiting for the day when we decide to wake up and claim our birthright.

—Anthony Robbins

You do not have to wander through the desert, climb the Himalayas, or melt a wicked witch. Go within and you will find that you are already home.

There is no need to run outside for better seeing, nor to peer from a window. Rather abide at the center of your being; for the more you leave it, the less you learn. Search your heart and see if he is wise who takes each turn: the way to do is to be.

—Lao Tzu

While the quest for enlightenment typically begins with study, introspection, and reflection, completing the journey requires that all your doing, learning, and thinking give way to simply being.

If you endeavor to embrace the Way through much learning, the Way will not be understood. If you observe the Way with simplicity of heart, great indeed is this Way.

—Buddha

SACRED MOMENTS

Live with greater reverence and you begin noticing subtle evidence of Divine guidance at work. You bump into an old friend who had popped into your mind an hour before. You receive an unexpected check that is precisely the amount you need to get your car repaired. A chance encounter in a restaurant leads to a terrific job opportunity.

When I'm trusting and being myself as fully as possible,
everything in my life reflects this by falling into place easily
and working smoothly.

—SHAKTI GAWAIN

Taken separately, these happenings can be dismissed as happy coincidences. Yet as your consciousness expands, such incidents seem to occur with greater frequency. In truth, you had simply failed to notice them as they flitted by the screen of your conscious mind.

Coincidences are God's way of remaining anonymous.

—UNKNOWN

Gradually, it dawns on you that luck has nothing to do with it. You are in sync with life's rhythms and, as Wayne Dyer put it, "collaborating with fate."

I seem to have been only like a boy playing on the seashore, and
diverting myself in now and then finding a smoother pebble or a
prettier shell than ordinary, whilst the great ocean of truth lay all
undiscovered before me.

—ISAAC NEWTON

Carl Jung coined the term "synchronicity" to explain these meaningful coincidences, this evidence of the sacred in everyday life.

Although we talk so much about coincidence, we do not really
believe in it. In our heart of hearts we think better of the universe;
we are secretly convinced that it is not such a slipshod, haphazard
affair, that everything in it has meaning.

—J. B. PRIESTLY

You begin looking for the sacred moments that currently lie just beyond your vision. The greater your awareness, the less mysterious are the ways of the Universe.

> *Every blade of grass has its angel that bends over it and whispers, "Grow, grow."*
>
> —THE TALMUD

The more pure your intent, the more consistently you see the world through God's eyes. In response, the Unified Field reorients itself to align with and support your higher-frequency consciousness.

> *As you open your awareness, life will improve of itself, you won't even have to try. It's a beautiful paradox: the more you open your consciousness, the fewer unpleasant events intrude themselves into your awareness.*
>
> —THADDEUS GOLAS

The answers to lifelong questions quietly approach, tap you on the shoulder, and point the way.

> *The mystery of life is not a problem to be solved, it is a reality to be experienced.*
>
> —JOHANNES JACOBUS VAN DER LEEUW

HUMILITY AND HARMONY

While you discern that life is unfolding perfectly, you do not make the egotistical, spiritually arrogant assumption that you yourself are perfect.

> *There is no worse sickness for the soul,*
> *O you who are proud, than this pretense of perfection.*
>
> —RUMI

On a soul level, of course, you are indeed perfect, but your spiritual development in the physical world requires humility and surrender; humility is the absence of ego, which clears the way for surrender to Spirit.

> *If we had strength and faith enough to trust ourselves entirely to*
> *God and to follow Him simply wherever He should lead us, we*
> *would have no need of any great effort of mind to reach perfection.*
>
> —FRANÇOIS FÉNELON

Humility in no way implies inability, inferiority, or insignificance. Those who surrender to Spirit discover that in humility lies true strength and empowerment.

> *In form, you are and will always be inferior to some, superior to*
> *others. In essence, you are neither inferior nor superior to anyone.*
> *True self-esteem and true humility arise out of that realization.*
> *In the eyes of the ego, self-esteem and humility are contradictory.*
> *In truth, they are one and the same.*
>
> —ECKHART TOLLE

Step into genuine humility—located at the opposite end of the spectrum from insecurity and unworthiness—and you instantly transition from unconscious identification with ego to conscious alignment with Spirit.

> *The true way to be humble is not to stoop till you are smaller than*
> *yourself, but to stand at your real height against some higher*
> *nature that shall show you what the real smallness of your greatest*
> *greatness is.*
>
> —PHILLIPS BROOKS

Anchored in Spirit, you strive to live as simply and humbly as circumstances allow, recognizing that removing unnecessary distractions helps you maintain your focus on what truly has value.

To live content with small means; to seek elegance rather than luxury, and refinement rather than fashion; to be worthy, not respectable, and wealthy, not rich; to listen to stars and birds, babes and sages, with open heart; to study hard; to think quietly, act frankly, talk gently, await occasions, hurry never; in a word, to let the spiritual, unbidden and unconscious, grow up through the common—this is my symphony.

—WILLIAM HENRY CHANNING

You are more emotionally available to others and more vigilant about savoring life's beauty and perfection throughout each day.

Life is not measured by the number of breaths we take, but by the moments that take our breath away.

—UNKNOWN

Every day becomes a celebration, and every person who crosses your path is changed by your joyous outpouring of hope, love, and healing energy.

When you were born, you cried, and the world rejoiced. Live your life in such a manner that when you die, the world cries and you rejoice.

—KABIR

Your mindset switches from *What does this person think of me and how can I get what I want?* to *Why has God sent this person to me and how can we serve each other?*

If I have been of service, if I have glimpsed more of the nature and essence of ultimate good, if I am inspired to reach wider horizons of thought and action, if I am at peace with myself, it has been a successful day.

—ALEX NOBLE

Viewing the fulfillment of your potential as a sacred contract, you walk confidently and purposefully into your very best self.

Our deepest fear is not that we are inadequate. Our deepest fear is that we are powerful beyond measure. It is our light, not our darkness, that most frightens us. We ask ourselves, Who am I to be brilliant, gorgeous, talented, fabulous? Actually, who are you not to be? You are a child of God. Your playing small doesn't serve the world. There's nothing enlightened about shrinking so that other people won't feel insecure around you. We are all meant to shine, as children do. We were born to make manifest the glory of God that is within us. It's not just in some of us; it's in everyone. And as we let our own light shine, we unconsciously give other people permission to do the same. As we're liberated from our own fear, our presence automatically liberates others.

—Marianne Williamson

TOLERANCE AND JUDGMENT

It sounds paradoxical, but spiritual growth simultaneously renders you more tolerant and less tolerant.

It is only imperfection that complains of what is imperfect. The more perfect we are, the more gentle and quiet we become towards the defects of others.

—Joseph Addison

You are more tolerant because you recognize that God is present in all and that the next person you see may be delivering a life-altering message meant just for you.

Everyone is God speaking.
Why not be polite and listen to him?

—Hafiz

Just as spiritual development engenders humility, humility engenders tolerance. You recognize that you are no more entitled to special treatment than anyone else.

If we wish to live honorable lives—we will give to every other
human being every right that we claim for ourselves.

—ROBERT G. INGERSOLL

The greater your tolerance, the less judgmental you are. You understand and appreciate that we each must learn our own lessons in our own way in our own time.

The person you consider ignorant and insignificant is the one
who came from God, that he might learn bliss from grief and
knowledge from gloom.

—KAHLIL GIBRAN

You are also less tolerant because you are more protective of your time, not wishing to squander precious hours with people or activities unless you are deepening your relationships, genuinely enjoying yourself, or advancing your life's work.

An invariable result of genuine spiritual development . . . As
regards people, it is quite possible to love them more and at the
same time to like them less.

—GALE WEBBE

CHOOSING HAPPINESS

Aristotle concluded that the motive for everything we do is to find happiness. Yet happiness need not be sought. You can simply *be* happy.

There is no way to happiness; happiness is the way.

—BUDDHA

Striving for happiness is counterproductive. The belief that happiness will be yours when certain obstacles are surmounted is itself a certain obstacle to happiness.

The search for happiness is one of the chief sources of unhappiness.

—ERIC HOFFER

Expecting to find happiness in external conditions is like expecting to grasp a sparkling jewel by reaching into the mirror that reflects it.

> *We look everywhere for happiness, forgetting that it's in our own little plot of land. We have our own acres of diamonds but we don't know it.*
>
> —OG MANDINO

Happiness cannot be pursued because it is not in front of you for you to follow but within you for you to find.

> *Happiness is a butterfly, which, when pursued, is always just beyond your grasp, but which, if you will sit down quietly, may alight upon you.*
>
> —NATHANIEL HAWTHORNE

At the same time, happiness is in pursuit of *you* in the guise of divinely orchestrated opportunities designed to turn your attention within.

> *Ever since Happiness heard your name,*
> *It has been running through the streets*
> *Trying to find you.*
>
> —HAFIZ

Happiness is not a destination; it is a state of mind, a sense of well-being. It is something to be embraced, not chased.

> *Happiness is not a station you arrive at, but a manner of traveling.*
>
> —MARGARET LEE RUNBECK

Any happiness you derive from attaining, achieving, or overcoming is destined to be short-lived. Deep, lasting happiness springs from cherishing who you already are and what you already have.

*Yes, there is a Nirvanah; it is in leading your sheep to a green
pasture, and in putting your child to sleep, and in writing the last
line of your poem.*

—KAHLIL GIBRAN

Happiness flows naturally and abundantly from a peaceful heart. All the happiness you
could ever hope for is as close to you as your next breath.

The time to be happy is now. The place to be happy is here.

—ROBERT G. INGERSOLL

A HALLOWED TRUST

The more centered and peaceful you are, the more effortlessly you see the world
through God's eyes.

*The appearance of things change according to the emotions, and
thus we see magic and beauty in them, while the magic and beauty
are really in ourselves.*

—KAHLIL GIBRAN

Joy becomes your constant companion, compassion floods your soul, and you are
keenly aware of God's loving presence in and around you.

God loves to see in me, not his servant, but himself who serves all.

—RABINDRANATH TAGORE

You view your relationship with God as a hallowed trust that must be kept pure. You
pledge to think love, speak love, *be* love.

Abandon yourself into the arms of love.

—UNKNOWN SAINT

The face you show to God and the face you show to the world are in harmony. You instinctively monitor your thoughts and actions so that nothing disturbs your alignment with the Divine Mind.

> *When you bow deeply to the universe, it bows back; when you call out the name of God, it echoes inside you.*
>
> —MORIHEI UESHIBA

You resolve to be an ambassador of Divine light and love so that when others see and hear you, they see and hear God.

> *As human beings, our greatness lies not so much in being able to remake the world outside us ... as in being able to remake ourselves.*
>
> —MICHAEL N. NAGLER

Intoxicated with the ever-new joy of deep communion with God, you radiate mental sunshine.

> *Happiness cannot be traveled to, owned, earned, worn, or consumed. Happiness is the spiritual experience of living every minute with love, grace, and gratitude.*
>
> —DENIS WAITLEY

Others take notice as surely as if you were visibly glowing and sporting wings. Your peaceful countenance speaks louder than words.

> *What you* are *stands over you the while, and thunders so that I cannot hear what you say to the contrary.*
>
> —RALPH WALDO EMERSON

In fact, you need not speak at all. Commenting on Jesus' statement about coming into this world to "bear witness unto the truth," Paramahansa Yogananda wrote, "A child of God 'bears witness' *by his life.* He embodies truth; if he expound it also, that is generous redundancy."

Preach the gospel all the time. If necessary, use words.

—SAINT FRANCIS OF ASSISI

A CALL TO RISE

The beckoning whisper of Spirit is a call to rise, to be a source of love and light to the world, to humbly be of service to God and humankind.

> *The highest form of spiritual work is the realization of the essence of man. . . . You never learn the answer; you can only become the answer.*

—RICHARD ROSE

Life begins anew when you joyously acknowledge that everything you do is for God and that everything you have is from God.

> *Give all you are, all you have, nothing more is asked of you but also nothing less.*

—MIRRA ALFASSA (THE MOTHER)

When you live to please God instead of seeking to please your own ego, your thoughts, words, and actions become spiritualized, and any division between your material and spiritual efforts is dissolved.

> *In the degree that we are filled with this Spirit of Peace by thus opening ourselves to its inflow does it pour through us, so that we carry it with us wherever we go. In the degree that we thus open ourselves do we become magnets to attract peace from all sources; and in the degree that we attract and embody it in ourselves are we able to give it forth to others. We can in this way become such perfect embodiments of peace that wherever we go we are continually shedding benedictions.*

—RALPH WALDO TRINE

As you transform the way you show up in the world, divine blessings ceaselessly shower down to guide your way.

> *Every man who becomes heartily and understandingly a channel of the Divine beneficence, is enriched through every league of his life. Perennial satisfaction springs around and within him with perennial verdure. Flowers of gratitude and gladness bloom all along his pathway, and the melodious gurgle of the blessings he bears is echoed back by the melodious waves of the recipient stream.*
>
> —Josiah Gilbert Holland

You gradually identify more with your Divine heritage than with your body-bound personality.

> *Live in the nowhere that you came from, even though you have an address here.*
>
> —Rumi

As the veil of maya drops away, enlightenment dawns, and you see the world and your role in it with fresh eyes.

> *We are all prisoners but some of us are in cells with windows and some without.*
>
> —Kahlil Gibran

One day you notice that you are in this world, but not of it. And the things that once caused you pain can no longer touch you.

> *I have told you these things, so that in me you may have peace. In this world you will have trouble. But take heart! I have overcome the world.*
>
> —Jesus of Nazareth,
> John 16:33

The external details of your life, which once may have consumed your attention, are now little more than an afterthought.

> *You shall be free indeed when your days are not without a care nor*
> *your nights without a want and a grief,*
> *But rather when these things girdle your life and yet you rise above*
> *them naked and unbound.*
>
> —KAHLIL GIBRAN

But beware: Enlightenment does not confer entitlement. If enlightenment is to be maintained, it must be earned moment to moment.

> *As far as the Buddha Nature is concerned, there is no difference*
> *between sinner and sage ... One enlightened thought and one is a*
> *Buddha, one foolish thought and one is again an ordinary person.*
>
> —HUI NENG

The richer your inner life, the less you fear the end of life. Death is viewed as just another of life's mysteries to explore.

> *I said to Life, "I would hear Death speak."*
> *And Life raised her voice a little higher and said,*
> *"You hear him now."*
>
> —KAHLIL GIBRAN

Whenever death comes calling, you will serenely leave this world, content that you have led a life well lived.

> *The fear of death follows from the fear of life. A man who lives*
> *fully is prepared to die at any time.*
>
> —MARK TWAIN

FOCUS ON BEING, NOT DOING
Living the Lesson

I had fun making a three-minute video to promote my book, *Sixty Seconds: One Moment Changes Everything*. I wrote the script and enlisted the help of Jeff Goodson and Holly Schroeder, two talented and generous friends. When we got together for filming, Holly interviewed me as if we were on a TV talk show. After Jeff's typically superb editing, I posted the video on my website—only to trash it a few hours later.

Why? From the start, I was leery of my acting ability. The more I tried to sound natural, the more I came off as rehearsed and inauthentic. Wondering if I was just being too hard on myself, I posted the video on my site and asked my ex-wife (whom I'm still very close to) and our daughter to critique it.

Their judgment was swift and brutally honest, which was exactly what I expected and hoped for. They both urged me to remove the video immediately because the inauthenticity of my performance was not consistent with the authenticity of my message and my work. I am grateful that they pulled no punches. I don't want people to tell me what they think I want to hear, I want them to tell me what I need to hear.

As an author who needed to establish a public presence, I knew I had a lot to learn and that I would stumble occasionally. As former NFL quarterback Don Meredith observed, "The higher you climb on the flagpole, the more people see your rear end." But I also knew I wouldn't be able to do the work I feel called to do unless I took that risk.

So up I go on the flagpole, and nothing will stop me from climbing as high as I can. I've got work to do, work that I feel is important, work that can help and heal others. So what if I take a pratfall now and then? I'll just get up, dust myself off, and figure out a better way to do what needs to be done. After all, it's not about me, it's about the work.

I apologized to Jeff and Holly and asked if they'd be willing to try again, only this time with Holly narrating a TV magazine-type piece in which I don't have to talk at all. Both of them graciously agreed. Holly is a much better actor than I could ever hope to be so I was better off leaving the heavy lifting to her.

As for me, I'll just try to be the best me I can be, thanks to a steady diet of reality checks from my family and friends. Now if you'll excuse me, I've got some flagpole climbing to do.

FOCUS ON BEING, NOT DOING
Self-Reflection Questions

- Am I more likely to derive my identify through my external activities and accomplishments or through my internal sense of self?

- When I feel peaceful, how do my perceptions about the outer world change?

- How can I make my happiness less dependent on having the right job, the right relationship, or the right amount of money or recognition?

- How can I prevent my thoughts from darting off in all directions?

- How can I be more aware of who I am being in the midst of what I am doing?

- What would I like to change about the way I present myself to the world?

- How can I determine what questions I should ask myself that I may not want to hear the answers to?

- What are three things I can do today that will help me be more loving and positive?

- What will it take for me to implement a daily spiritual discipline and stick to it?

- How can I challenge myself to step out of my comfort zone so I can fully step into who I am capable of being?

- How would living more simply enable me to live more authentically?

- How can I expand my awareness to become more cognizant of how I can be of service to others?

SEVEN

EXTERNAL SECURITY IS AN ILLUSION

Shop for security over happiness and you buy it,
at that price.

—Richard Bach

EXTERNAL SECURITY IS AN ILLUSION

Many people live their lives on automatic pilot. They put in their time. They go through the motions. The years fly by. All in the name of security—job security, financial security, marital security.

> *Security is when everything is settled, when nothing can happen to you; security is the denial of life.*
>
> —GERMAINE GREER

A FALSE IDENTITY

Material wealth is a worthy goal, but a capricious one. Your house, car, and savings account can be swept away in an instant by a medical crisis, natural disaster, economic crash, or business deal gone bad.

> *Security is not in having things; it's in handling things.*
>
> —UNKNOWN

Can financial security truly bring peace of mind? It can, to some degree—but it cannot provide a deep, enduring sense of meaning and purpose.

> *Possession of material riches without inner peace is like dying of thirst while bathing in a lake.*
>
> —PARAMAHANSA YOGANANDA

Those whose wealth and status are assured often experience a surprising and unsettling lack of fulfillment and a growing awareness that something of greater importance has eluded them.

> *I think everybody should get rich and famous and do everything they ever dreamed of so they can see that it's not the answer.*
>
> —JIM CARREY

Similarly, your job status can prove as ethereal as the wind. Losing a job is especially challenging for those whose identity and self-worth are inseparable from their work life.

> *People wish to be settled: only as far as they are unsettled is there any hope for them.*
>
> —RALPH WALDO EMERSON

People who define themselves exclusively by the work they do often wither away shortly after retirement. Without a job, they do not know who they are.

> *Men go abroad to admire the heights of mountains, the mighty billows of the sea, the broad tides of rivers, the compass of the ocean, and the circuits of the stars, and pass themselves by.*
>
> —SAINT AUGUSTINE

Place your security in the hands of others and your future is anything but secure. The best parts of you will lay dormant, their yearning for expression gradually eroding into fitful dreams of what might have been.

> *Don't tell me that my security comes from somebody else! Tell me I'm responsible. Tell me security is a by-product of the gift I give of my skill and my learning and my love into the world. Tell me security comes from an idea given time and care.*
>
> —RICHARD BACH

CHANGE AND COMPLACENCY

What we seek in the name of security is the avoidance of the unexpected, the assurance of the known over the unknown, and the guarantee of comfort.

> *It's not so much that we're afraid of change or so in love with the old ways, but it's that place in between that we fear . . . . It's like being between trapezes. It's Linus when his blanket is in the dryer. There's nothing to hold on to.*
>
> —MARILYN FERGUSON

If you have achieved a comfortable level of security, you may not even entertain the notion that the ground could shift beneath you at a moment's notice.

> *Would that life were like the shadow cast by a wall or a tree; but it*
> *is like the shadow of a bird in flight.*
>
> —THE TALMUD

Fear of change and the yearning for stability can dim your awareness, dull your alertness, and lull you into complacency. Hence, the first subtle signs of danger may not register.

> *We are never more in danger than when we think ourselves most*
> *secure, nor in reality more secure than when we seem to be most in*
> *danger.*
>
> —WILLIAM COWPER

Desperately throw your arms around all that you are attached to in this life, and change will rear back its head and roar with laughter.

> *Security is a false god; begin making sacrifices to it and you are*
> *lost.*
>
> —PAUL BOWLES

Run from change and it will find you. Better to stand your ground and lift up your arms in calm surrender.

> *Security is mostly a superstition. It does not exist in nature, nor do*
> *the children of men as a whole experience it. . . . Avoiding danger*
> *is no safer in the long run than outright exposure . The fearful are*
> *caught as often as the bold.*
>
> —HELEN KELLER

Change is a demanding but well-intentioned teacher, for a life of comfort too often degenerates into stagnation and unfulfilled promise.

Life is always either a tightrope or a feather bed. Give me the tightrope.

—EDITH WHARTON

Far away, shimmering on the water under the setting sun, is your potential. Break out of the prison of comfort and security and swim out to meet it.

All that we do
Is touched with ocean, yet we remain
On the shore of what we know.

—RICHARD WILBUR

Know that in the deepest part of uncomfortable circumstances stands the gateway to self-awareness and personal power.

Everything will change when your desire to move on exceeds your desire to hold on.

—ALAN COHEN

Befriending change triggers a quest for self-discovery and a hunger for new experiences that deliver a richer, more authentic sense of security than the hollow promises of material comforts.

Security can only be achieved through constant change, through the wise discarding of old ideas that have outlived their usefulness, and through the adapting of others to current facts.

—WILLIAM O. DOUGLAS

FEAR AND CONSEQUENCES

By definition, the craving for external security leads to a life lived in fear. After all, if you desperately want something, you will desperately fear losing it once you have it.

There is fear as long as you want to be secure—secure in your
marriage, secure in your job, in your position, in your
responsibility, secure in your ideas, in your beliefs, secure in
your relationship to the world or in your relationship to God.
The moment the mind seeks security or gratification in any
form, at any level, there is bound to be fear.

—JIDDU KRISHNAMURTI

Obsessed with holding on to what you have, you may not only fail to recognize life-enriching opportunities, you may view them as threats to what you are so fiercely protecting.

The walls that we build around ourselves both mentally and
physically give us the dangerous false illusion that we are safe,
but there's no such thing as a wall that cannot be torn down.
When we invest ourselves in the idea that we have erected this
wall for protection, we naturally make enemies of anything on
the other side of the wall.

—ANGEL KYODO WILLIAMS

Who you are is independent of what you have and what you do. If those things were taken from you but you had not yet discovered they were gone, you would be unaffected.

If I am what I have and if what I have is lost, who then am I?

—ERICH FROMM

It is your reaction to a loss, not the loss itself, that causes you to think you are less than you were.

It's a good thing to have all the props pulled out from under us
occasionally. It gives us some sense of what is rock under our feet,
and what is sand.

—MADELEINE L'ENGLE

Accelerate the process of finding yourself, of realizing who you are without all the trappings of life, by imagining what living with only the bare necessities would look and feel like.

> *Security depends not so much upon how much you have, as upon how much you can do without.*
>
> —Joseph Wood Krutch

Allowing events in the external world to shape and define your internal world is an act of self-delusion that always leads to suffering.

> *Each one has to find his peace from within. And peace to be real must be unaffected by outside circumstances.*
>
> —Mahatma Gandhi

External security does not bring peace. Rather, peace brings internal security, which renders external security superfluous.

> *Slowly, painfully, I have learned that peace of mind may transform a cottage into a spacious manor hall; the want of it can make a regal park an imprisoning nutshell.*
>
> —Joshua Loth Liebman

You must lose the fear of losing what you fear to lose. Free yourself by turning your attention from what might be lost to your fear of losing it.

> *Any life truly lived is a risky business, and if one puts up too many fences against the risks one ends by shutting out life itself.*
>
> —Kenneth S. Davis

Each layer of fear you peel away gives you a deeper understanding of why fear is not to be feared.

*Begin challenging your own assumptions. Your assumptions are
your windows on the world. Scrub them off every once in a while,
or the light won't come in.*

—ALAN ALDA

When you do experience a loss, reflect not on *what* has left but on *why* it has left. There is always a reason.

*You have learnt something. That always feels at first as if you had
lost something.*

—GEORGE BERNARD SHAW

Trust that whatever has left your life has fulfilled its purpose and no longer serves your best interests.

I make the most of all that comes and the least of all that goes.

—SARA TEASDALE

The loss of what you valued so dearly creates room in your life for something of even greater value and meaning.

*When the heart weeps for what it has lost, the spirit laughs for
what it has found.*

—SUFI WISDOM

Seek stability in that which is unstable and there will be no trace of your footprints on the path that leads to purpose and peace.

The way to be safe, is never to be secure.

—FRANCIS QUARLES

Embedded in every loss is the lesson that the only obstacle between you and peace is the belief that there is an obstacle between you and peace.

Peace is our real nature. We spoil it. What is required is that we cease to spoil it. We are not going to create peace anew. There is space in a hall, for instance. We fill up the place with various articles. If we want space, all that we need do is to remove all those articles, and we get space. Similarly if we remove all the rubbish, all the thoughts, from our minds, the peace will become manifest. That which is obstructing the peace has to be removed. Peace is the only reality.

—SRI RAMANA MAHARSHI

KNOWLEDGE vs. WISDOM

The journey toward true security begins when you shift your focus from the external world of knowledge and achievement to the internal world of wisdom and experience.

Never mistake knowledge for wisdom. One helps you make a living; the other helps you make a life.

—SANDRA CAREY

Knowledge is the shovel; wisdom is the buried treasure. Knowledge leads to higher comprehension; wisdom leads to higher consciousness.

Intuition isn't the enemy, but the ally, of reason.

—JOHN KORD LAGEMANN

Knowledge is ever-changing; it is the calling card of the intellect. Wisdom is timeless; it is the common sense of the soul.

Intelligence complicates; wisdom simplifies.

—MASON COOLEY

Knowledge is rational truth; it often discounts true wisdom. Wisdom is intuitive truth; it always discerns true knowledge.

The intuitive mind is a sacred gift and the rational mind is a faithful servant. We have created a society that honors the servant and has forgotten the gift.

—BOB SAMPLES

Our outer world offers access to limited knowledge; our inner world offers access to limitless wisdom.

The seat of knowledge is in the head; of wisdom, in the heart.

—WILLIAM HAZLITT

Knowledge is attained from an external source; wisdom is generated from an internal knowing.

When you reach the end of what you should know, you will be at the beginning of what you should sense.

—KAHLIL GIBRAN

Knowledge grows from information and investigation; wisdom flows from introspection and intuition.

Knowledge is proud that he has learned so much; Wisdom is humble that he knows no more.

—WILLIAM COWPER

Knowledge is cerebral—it is acquired through study; wisdom is Divine—it is awakened through experience.

Science is organized knowledge. Wisdom is organized life.

—IMMANUEL KANT

Ego engages the outer world by urging you to expand your knowledge. Spirit enriches your inner world by nudging you to explore your wisdom.

It is the province of knowledge to speak and it is the privilege of wisdom to listen.

—OLIVER WENDELL HOLMES

Knowledge is transferrable and directly conveyed; wisdom is transformative and divinely conferred.

Strive to close the eyes of the body and open those of the soul and look into your own heart.

—SAINT TERESA OF AVILA

Knowledge is gleaned by combing through diverse resources; wisdom is gained by communing with Divine Consciousness.

Knowledge is power, but wisdom is peace.

—ALAN COHEN

THE DEEP DIVE

To transmute knowledge into wisdom, you must scale the wall of your restless thoughts and dive headfirst into the uncharted waters of your inner world.

There is one spectacle grander than the sea, that is the sky; there is one spectacle grander than the sky, that is the interior of the soul.

—VICTOR HUGO

Take a deep breath and plunge beneath the surface. There, far beyond your comfort zone, life-altering insights and experiences await.

There is only one great adventure and that is inward toward the self.

—HENRY MILLER

If the water is murky and discoveries are few, you are in shallow waters. Gather your courage and venture further out into the lake of introspection.

> *If you don't discover the pearl by one or two divings, don't blame*
> *the ocean; find fault with your diving. You haven't yet plunged*
> *deep enough.*
>
> —PARAMAHANSA YOGANANDA

If your self-image continues to cower on shore, light a match to it. Peer into the blaze and you will find freedom laughing joyously amidst the flames.

> *You must wish to consume yourself in your own flame: how could*
> *you wish to become new unless you had first become ashes!*
>
> —FRIEDRICH NIETZSCHE

Your internal expedition may be both thrilling and terrifying. Welcome your uneasiness; ask it to reveal its secrets.

> *All uncertainty is fruitful . . . so long as it is accompanied by the*
> *wish to understand.*
>
> —ANTONIO MACHADO

Brace yourself. Stripping away layers of anger, denial, defensiveness, and guilt requires unflinching honesty and a willingness to completely rebuild your emotional identity.

> *Growth demands a temporary surrender of security.*
>
> —GAIL SHEEHY

Cast aside any remorse about being the person you used to be or about doing the things you used to do.

> *You can rake the muck this way, rake the muck that way—it will*
> *always be muck. Have I sinned or have I not sinned? In the time*
> *I am brooding over it, I could be stringing pearls for the delight of*
> *heaven.*
>
> —HASIDIC WISDOM

All the experiences of your life, even those you may regret the most, conspired perfectly to deliver you to the brink of awakening.

> *Before I travelled my road I was my road.*
>
> —ANTONIO PORCHIA

When you are certain you can dig no deeper, dig deeper. When you are satisfied you can walk no further, walk further. Each revelation points the way to revelations yet to come.

> *Never, never rest contented with any circle of ideas, but always be certain that a wider one is still possible.*
>
> —RICHARD JEFFERIES

Take heart: every barrier you break through means there is that much less blocking you from all you are capable of becoming.

> *When I let go of what I am, I become what I might be.*
>
> —LAO TZU

Inevitably, you will discover that not only are you more than you imagined, you are more than you ever could have imagined.

> *I can't give you any advice but this: to go into yourself and see how deep the place is from which your life flows.*
>
> —RAINER MARIA RILKE

Turn from this inward journey and you will forever be imprisoned by what you perceive as random circumstances beyond your control.

> *The man who has no inner life is a slave of his surroundings, as the barometer is the obedient servant of the air at rest, and the weathercock the humble servant of the air in motion.*
>
> —HENRI FRÉDÉRIC AMIEL

PASSION AND POSSIBILITIES

Enthusiasm builds as you glimpse the infinite beauty and joy that await you just beyond the far reaches of your consciousness.

> *If you can take care of the internal, you can easily take care of the external. Then you can avoid the infernal and latch on to the eternal.*
>
> —JOSEPH LOWERY

You are no longer satisfied being dissatisfied. You embrace continual self-improvement instead of consistent self-criticism.

> *Remove the rock from your shoe rather than learn to limp comfortably.*
>
> —STEPHEN C. PAUL

You praise rather than blame. You look for solutions instead of excuses. You see opportunities instead of obstacles.

> *A man will be* imprisoned *in a room with a door that's unlocked and opens inwards; as long as it does not occur to him to* pull *rather than push it.*
>
> —LUDWIG WITTGENSTEIN

Your fears take a back seat to your dreams. You greet each day with passion instead of passiveness.

> *Anything I've ever done that ultimately was worthwhile initially scared me to death.*
>
> —BETTY BENDER

You are more comfortable in your own skin and more confident in your ability to add value to your work, your relationships, and the world at large.

> *Character—the willingness to accept responsibility for one's own life—is the source from which self-respect springs.*
>
> —JOAN DIDION

You do not hesitate to reinvent yourself when presented with exciting new possibilities.

> *There is no security on this earth. There is only opportunity.*
>
> —DOUGLAS MACARTHUR

You interpret the adage "Let go and let God" as "*Let go* of what no longer serves me and *let God* lead me to live the life I was born to live."

> *It takes a lot of courage to release the familiar and seemingly secure, to embrace the new. But there is no real security in what is no longer meaningful. There is more security in the adventurous and exciting, for in movement there is life, and in change there is power.*
>
> —ALAN COHEN

A QUANTUM LEAP

You know you have made a quantum leap in consciousness when you look back at the life you had so recently led and feel like you are watching somebody else's life.

> *Only in growth, reform, and change, paradoxically enough, is true security to be found.*
>
> —ANNE MORROW LINDBERGH

As self-awareness grows, your mind and heart are purified. As your heart opens and your mind clears, you see further into the boundless depths of Spirit. You are at peace with who you are and your place in the world.

The best way to make your dreams come true is to wake up.

—Paul Valery

When peace becomes your dearest friend, you are liberated from the urgings of your ego. You are free to be fully present, authentic, and whole.

> *Like water, which can clearly mirror the sky and the trees only so long as its surface is undisturbed, the mind can only reflect the true image of the Self when it is tranquil and wholly relaxed.*
>
> —Indra Devi

Your appetite for ego gratification subsides as your appreciation for peace, beauty, and life itself expands.

> *They deem me mad because I will not sell my days for gold;*
> *And I deem them mad because they think my days have a price.*
>
> —Kahlil Gibran

The greater your self-awareness and self-knowledge, the greater your empathy for others.

> *Each of us really understands in others only those feelings he is capable of producing himself.*
>
> —André Gide

Your capacity to hold and project love and compassion expands. You become a healing presence to all who cross your path.

> *A good example is like a bell that calls many to church.*
>
> —Danish proverb

Do not delay your transformation. The sooner you step into the shoes of who you are capable of becoming, the sooner you will be a powerful force for good in the world.

Begin now to be what you will be hereafter.

—Saint Jerome

The planet is in desperate need of virtuous, kind-hearted people whom others can gaze upon and think, *So that is what's possible.*

If you would lift me, you must be on higher ground.

—Ralph Waldo Emerson

STANDING UNSHAKEN

When you are firmly anchored in God, you know that whatever you must face, you will not be facing it alone.

Security is not the absence of danger, but the presence of God, no matter what the danger.

—Unknown

The placid lake of your God-attuned equanimity is undisturbed by the pebbles of chaos and crisis.

So love God inwardly that nothing will ever be able to touch you outwardly.

—Paramahansa Yogananda

Remaining centered and calm, even when outside circumstances are chaotic, prevents you from plugging into illusions of the material world that take your spirit with them.

What lies behind us and what lies before us are small matters compared to what lies within us.

—Ralph Waldo Emerson

Ultimately, real security is trusting that you have the faith, strength, and courage to rise above any challenge.

Faith alone defends. Life is either a daring adventure or nothing.
To keep our faces toward change and behave like free spirits in the
presence of fate is strength undefeatable.

—HELEN KELLER

Waiting on the other side of every trial and tribulation is the liberating realization that you were as strong and as brave as you hoped you would be.

Every time you meet a situation, though you may think at the
time it is an impossibility and you go through the tortures of the
damned, once you have met it and lived through it you find that
forever after you are freer than you ever were before.

—ELEANOR ROOSEVELT

As Paramahansa Yogananda wrote, when you can "stand unshaken midst the crash of breaking worlds," then nothing can touch you where you live, and nothing of value can be taken from you.

Live in the midst of the battle of life. Anyone can keep calm in
a cave or when asleep. Stand in the whirl and madness of action
and reach the Centre. If you have found the Centre, you cannot
be moved.

—SWAMI VIVEKANANDA

Of course, only a God-realized saint can maintain perfect equanimity when faced with great personal tragedy.

Quiet minds cannot be perplexed or frightened, but go on in
fortune or misfortune at their own private pace, like a clock
during a thunderstorm.

—ROBERT LOUIS STEVENSON

Yogananda's eloquent vision is an ideal worth striving for, but one that few will fully realize.

Herein lies the whole secret of Existence. Waves may roll over the surface and tempest rage, but deep down there is the stratum of infinite calmness, infinite peace, and infinite bliss.

—SWAMI VIVEKANANDA

Yet never lose sight that no matter what life brings, you are loved and cared for beyond all imagining.

Be like the bird that, halting in her flight
Awhile, on boughs too slight,
Feels them give way beneath her and yet sings,
Knowing that she hath wings.

—VICTOR HUGO

THE REALITY OF REINCARNATION

The notion of external security as a holy grail starts unraveling when reincarnation is added to the mix.

When one man dies, one chapter is not torn out of the book, but translated into a better language.

—JOHN DONNE

Looking through God's eyes, we see that the only valuables we can take with us after our final breath are love, wisdom, and other soul qualities.

I know I am deathless . . .
I laugh at what you call dissolution,
And I know the amplitude of time.

—WALT WHITMAN

If we lived only one lifetime, an argument could be made that the Universe is a chaotic, random crapshoot that renders any spiritual insight, and indeed our very existence, as ultimately insignificant.

Reincarnation contains a most comforting explanation of reality by means of which Indian thought surmounts difficulties which baffle the thinkers of Europe.

—ALBERT SCHWEITZER

Reincarnation is consistent with the concept of a benevolent Universe in that you are given unlimited opportunities to learn what you need to learn, atone for your errors, and complete your soul's work.

My life often seemed to me like a story that has no beginning and no end. I had the feeling that I was an historical fragment, an excerpt for which the preceding and succeeding text was missing. I could well imagine that I might have lived in former centuries and there encountered questions I was not yet able to answer; that I had been born again because I had not fulfilled the task given to me.

—CARL JUNG

Reincarnation tells us that failure is temporary, success is assured, and every experience has value. What a liberating, euphoric epiphany!

If you realize that all things change, there is nothing you will try to hold on to. If you are not afraid of dying, there is nothing you cannot achieve.

—LAO TZU

Over the course of innumerable lifetimes, you must experience the full range of what it means to be human.

You only live once—but it's forever.

—ALAN COHEN

Life can be viewed as a giant Bingo card of experiences on which every space must be filled with the essence of one of the tragedies or triumphs of life.

As long as you are not aware of the continual law of Die and
Be Again, you are merely a vague guest on a dark Earth.

—JOHANN WOLFGANG VON GOETHE

Some may view reincarnation as a lifetime pass for goofing off. After all, why work on enlightenment today when you can put it off, well, pretty much forever? Fine, take your time; this inclination is self-correcting no matter how many lifetimes you breeze through. A child with an unlimited free pass in a vast amusement park will tire of it soon enough.

All the great and true spiritual masters offer their devotees a
tangible spiritual realization of a greater reality, and a destiny
greater than merely mortal, material existence. Divine realization
Itself—perfect happiness itself, complete awakening from the
dream of mortal, limited existence—is the greatest of all human
destinies, and the destiny for which every heart longs.

—ADI DA SMARAJ

There is no procrastination penalty except perhaps an occasional fleeting sense of regret. Eventually, you will heed the inner urge to lift your gaze heavenward.

The oldest wisdom in the world tells us that we can consciously
unite with the divine while in this body, for this is man really born.
If he misses his destiny, Nature is not in a hurry; she will catch
him some day and compel him to fulfill her secret purpose.

—SARVEPALLI RADHAKRISHNAN

The moment you stop hitting life's snooze button and open your eyes to the beauty and joy that awaits you, you will marvel that you waited so long to awaken.

A person does not have to be behind bars to be a prisoner. People
can be prisoners of their own concepts and ideas. They can be
slaves to their own selves.

—PREM RAWAT (MAHARAJI)

Just as your childhood memories are stored within you, so are memories of your previous lives. While they may not be accessible, they are an integral part of who you are, shaping you and guiding you through all the many roles you play in the endless drama of life.

> *I did not begin when I was born, nor when I was conceived. I have*
> *been growing, developing, through incalculable myriads of*
> *millenniums.... All my previous selves have their voices, echoes,*
> *promptings in me.... Oh, incalculable times again shall I be born.*
>
> —JACK LONDON

Each incarnation allows us to begin anew so that we keep our focus on the lessons waiting for us in this life, undistracted by past events, memories, and relationships.

> *As we have thousands of dreams in this life, so this our life is one*
> *of thousands of such lives, into which we enter from this more real,*
> *actual, true life, from which we emerge, entering into this life, and*
> *to which we return, when we die. Our life is one of the dreams of*
> *that more real life, and so forth, ad infinitum, up to the one, last,*
> *real life,—the life of God.*
>
> —LEO TOLSTOY

Reincarnation accounts for why you are drawn to certain people, why on some level you "recognize" each other when meeting for the first time. There is unfinished business between you that requires resolution.

> *You meet someone and you're sure you were lovers in a past life.*
> *After two weeks with them, you realize why you haven't kept in*
> *touch for the last two thousand years.*
>
> —AL CLEATHEN

KARMIC LAW

Call it karma, or reaping what you sow, or what goes around comes around. Every action generates a reaction in the Unified Field, which extends beyond the reach of space and time.

> *With every deed you are sowing a seed,*
> *Though the harvest you may not see.*
>
> —ELLA WHEELER WILCOX

Karma is not positive or negative, it is simply purposeful. Actions that are harmonious with Divine Will produce desirable results; inharmonious actions produce undesirable results.

> *If you plant turnips you will not harvest grapes.*
>
> —AKAN (WEST AFRICAN) PROVERB

Your every action is a cosmic tennis ball served into the court of Divine Intelligence. Every shot is impartially volleyed back—the law of cause and effect always demands its due.

> *Every Cause has its Effect; every Effect has its Cause; everything*
> *happens according to Law; Chance is but a name for Law not*
> *recognized; there are many planes of causation, but nothing*
> *escapes the Law.*
>
> —THE KYBALION

Indeed, your every thought, word, and action weaves yet another indestructible strand in the web of life.

> *Life is like a cash register in that every account, every thought,*
> *every deed, like every sale, is registered and recorded.*
>
> —FULTON J. SHEEN

Karma is the lifeblood of all your relationships, from your briefest encounters to your deepest friendships.

*Ye live not for yourselves; ye cannot live for yourselves; a thousand
fibers connect you with your fellow-men, and along those fibers, as
along sympathetic threads, run your actions as causes, and return
to you as effects.*

—HENRY MELVILL

Karmic consequences are certain but unpredictable. The same cause may affect two
people's karmas very differently based on their prior karma, their pre-incarnation
agreements, and an infinite number of other variables that all coalesce into effects that
serve the highest good of each individual.

*The law of karma states simply that every event is both a cause and
an effect. Every act has consequences of a similar kind, which in
turn have further consequences and so on; and every act, every
karma, is also the consequence of some previous karma.*

—EKNATH EASWARAN

Reincarnation and karma explain why God's plan for you is ultimately determined by
the exercise of your own free will.

*Though God is the Creator and Sustainer of man, He has
ordained the law of cause and effect, or karma, to govern life
so that man himself is the judge of his own actions.*

—PARAMAHANSA YOGANANDA

God provides the canvas and unceasing guidance, but leaves the painting of your life
up to you.

*You have your brush, you have your colors, you paint paradise,
then in you go.*

—NIKOS KAZANTZAKIS

If God directly interfered in any way, not only would you be deprived of valuable experiences, but the application of karmic law would be disrupted.

It is hard to sneak a look at God's cards. But that he would choose to play dice with the world . . . is something I cannot believe for a single moment.

—ALBERT EINSTEIN

While the Universe renders no judgment on your actions, do not assume that anything goes, that God's loving detachment is a handy "get out of jail free" card.

There are in nature neither rewards nor punishments—there are consequences.

—ROBERT G. INGERSOLL

There are karmic consequences for every choice you make, whether you are held accountable in this life or in a future incarnation.

In the course of natural righteousness, each man, by his thoughts and actions, becomes the molder of his destiny. Whatever universal energies he himself, wisely or unwisely, has set in motion must return to him as their starting point, like a circle inexorably completing itself.

—PARAMAHANSA YOGANANDA

Reincarnation enhances your tolerance of others because you understand that we are all at different stages of soul development with different paths to travel and different karmic influences to contend with.

I cannot think of permanent enmity between man and man, and believing as I do in the theory of rebirth, I live in the hope that if not in this birth, in some other birth I shall be able to hug all humanity in friendly embrace.

—MAHATMA GANDHI

Karma cannot be sidestepped but it can be transcended through earnest, unwavering spiritual practice. Devotees who have achieved Self-realization may have many or all of their karmic debts mitigated or forgiven.

> *Seeds of past karma cannot germinate if they are roasted in the fires of divine wisdom.*
>
> —PARAMAHANSA YOGANANDA

God-illumined souls break free from the revolving wheel of reincarnation and melt in loving union with Divine Consciousness.

> *But they for whom I am the supreme goal, who do all work renouncing self for me and meditate on me with single-hearted devotion, these I will swiftly rescue from the fragment's cycle of birth and death, for their consciousness has entered into me.*
>
> —BHAGAVAD GITA 12:6-7

Whether it takes ten lives or ten thousand, you cannot fail to achieve your ultimate destiny.

> *No matter where you go, your wandering footsteps will lead you back to God.*
>
> —PARAMAHANSA YOGANANDA

Trust in the Divine wisdom of reincarnation and the fear of death loses its sting. Knowing that we will wake up as if from a dream and reunite with our loved ones adds joy and vibrancy to the rest of our days.

> *Death is not extinguishing the light; it is putting out the lamp because dawn has come.*
>
> —RABINDRANATH TAGORE

EXTERNAL SECURITY IS AN ILLUSION
Living the Lesson

When I was twenty-three, married with an infant daughter, I speculated in the then-volatile gold market and lost $10,000 I didn't have. There was only one thing to do, but the mere thought of it devastated me: I had to sell off my baseball card collection. I realize how trivial this may sound, but I had been collecting cards since I was six years old and they were precious to me.

I remember biking home from the drugstore at seven years old with a box of baseball cards—filled with twenty-four packs at a nickel each—and sitting at our family room table lovingly opening each pack, checking each card against my checklist, and organizing them into appropriate piles. My happiness could not have been more complete. Saying goodbye to my baseball cards felt like I was losing my best friends—and a big piece of my youth as well. I miss them to this day.

In hindsight, however, I am glad I had to let them go. If I hadn't, I would have continued to immerse myself in my hobbies—baseball cards, comic books, coins, and stamps. And chances are I would have continued to be a self-absorbed, unenlightened nerd. Just thinking of the person I used to be makes me cringe. Back then, I didn't have a clue that I didn't have a clue.

Losing my baseball cards was the first time I had to deal with profound loss. I know, that's pretty laughable when compared to people who have lost loved ones, homes, their life savings—and especially their innocence at a young age. But that was my experience, and I didn't have the maturity and wisdom at the time to put it into proper perspective.

But I do now. And I am grateful that life forced me to grow up and get a clue. I see clearly now that every difficult time in my life, whether it was a financial challenge, losing a job, or ending a relationship, carried with it the seeds of opportunity and growth. If life had gone exactly as I planned, I would have had everything I ever wanted, except the one thing I truly needed: myself.

EXTERNAL SECURITY IS AN ILLUSION
Self-Reflection Questions

- In what ways does my focus on obtaining and maintaining a job and financial security prevent me from living life more fully?

- How is my self-esteem tied to my job status, my bank account, and my most valued possessions?

- In what ways do I fear my life changing, and why?

- How can I protect myself from the dangers of complacency?

- How can I remind myself to look beyond the trappings of success and turn my attention to who I am instead of what I have?

- In what ways am I focusing too much on my goals and too little on what I learn along the way?

- How can I find the courage to break through my emotional defenses and confront important personal issues with ruthless self-honesty?

- In what ways have experiences that were painful at the time shaped me into who I needed to be?

- How can I develop the perspective and equanimity to deal with whatever challenges come my way?

- Why do I believe or disbelieve in reincarnation?

- How would I live my life differently if I knew I would reincarnate?

- How would my life change if I could see in advance the consequences of my actions?

EIGHT

LIVE WITH INTEGRITY

The time is always right to do what's right.

—MARTIN LUTHER KING, JR.

LIVE WITH INTEGRITY

Living with integrity means aligning yourself in every moment with all that is good and right.

> *Have you grown to the point where you can unflinchingly stand up for the right, for that which is honorable, honest, truthful, whether it makes you popular or unpopular? Have you grown to the point where absolutely and unreservedly you make truth and honor your standard of thinking and speaking?*
>
> —BOOKER T. WASHINGTON

WITHIN AND WITHOUT

What does living with integrity look like? You speak and act in ways that are wholly consistent with your values, your ideals, and your sense of self.

> *Integrity simply means a willingness not to violate one's identity.*
>
> —ERICH FROMM

You are ferociously honest with yourself. You hold yourself to the highest standard of ethical behavior. You accept full responsibility for your words and actions.

> *Integrity is what we do, what we say, and what we say we do.*
>
> —DON GALER

You live your life from the inside out. You trust your inner wisdom and act upon it with faith and courage.

> *Without courage, wisdom bears no fruit.*
>
> —BALTASAR GRACIAN

You rely on self-reflection to "check in" and stay on track. You live a transparent life with no hidden agendas.

Live so that your friends can defend you but never have to.

—ARNOLD H. GLASOW

You conduct yourself so impeccably that you would not be embarrassed to learn that a hidden television camera was broadcasting your daily life.

Live as if everything you do will eventually be known.

—HUGH PRATHER

Is it realistic to live with that degree of transparency? No, but it is a noble and worthwhile intention nonetheless.

The measure of a man's real character is what he would do if he knew he never would be found out.

—THOMAS BABINGTON MACAULAY

When integrity is integrated into every fiber of your being, you radiate a magnetic presence that attracts and inspires others.

Some people strengthen the society just by being the kind of people they are.

—JOHN W. GARDNER

You become a de facto ambassador of virtuous living who elevates the consciousness of the planet simply by being on it.

Be such a man, and live such a life, that if every man were such as you and every life a life like yours, this earth would be God's Paradise.

—PHILLIPS BROOKS

INTERNAL ETHICS

Your integrity is the revelation of your personal power. Personal power, the polar opposite of power over others, is defined by your capacity to live in harmony with the Divine Mind.

> *He who does not desert his principles when threatened with the*
> *loss of every earthly thing, even to the loss of reputation and life,*
> *is the man of power.*
>
> —JAMES ALLEN

You reach every decision and choose every action as if God's hand were on your shoulder. Day by day, the foundation of your integrity grows ever stronger.

> *Good character is more to be praised than outstanding talent.*
> *Most talents are, to some extent, a gift. Good character, by*
> *contrast, is not given to us. We have to build it piece by piece—*
> *by thought, choice, courage, and determination.*
>
> —JOHN LUTHER

Acting with integrity is the tangible expression of your love for and devotion to God. Integrity is your spiritual practice made visible.

> *The noblest worship is to make yourself as good and as just as*
> *you can.*
>
> —ISOCRATES

Both personally and professionally, you govern yourself internally, relying on the unerring sense of right and wrong that is hardwired into us all.

> *Two things fill the mind with ever new and increasing admiration*
> *and awe, the oftener and the more steadily we reflect on them: the*
> *starry heavens above and the moral law within.*
>
> —IMMANUEL KANT

Trusting Divine guidance, you give precedence to the promptings of your intuition over the protocol of your intellect.

> *It is more important to do the right thing than to do things right.*
>
> —PETER DRUCKER

With your moral compass in working order, external codes of ethical conduct are redundant.

> *Integrity has no need of rules.*
>
> —ALBERT CAMUS

Similarly, the regulations imposed by authorities to ensure proper behavior are superfluous, considering the self-imposed standards you already follow.

> *Laws control the lesser man. Right conduct controls the greater one.*
>
> —CHINESE PROVERB

There is no danger of you violating your personal code of ethics for personal gain even if guidelines, rules, or the letter of the law give you free reign to do so.

> *The right to do something does not mean that doing it is right.*
>
> —WILLIAM SAFIRE

Choices that you once would have perceived as difficult become unmistakably clear. You walk away from a flawed relationship rather than act inauthentically. You pass up a lucrative business deal if a whiff of impropriety hangs in the air.

> *Prefer a loss to a dishonest gain; the one brings pain at the moment, the other for all time.*
>
> —CHILON

VIRTUE AND VICE

Spiritual integrity is a veritable force field that shields you from life's endless parade of enticements.

> *The good man has absolute good, which like fire turns every thing*
> *to its own nature, so that you cannot do him any harm.*
>
> —RALPH WALDO EMERSON

Though no one would be the wiser, you banish self-serving thoughts and impulses the moment you become aware of them.

> *Self-respect is the fruit of discipline, the sense of dignity grows with*
> *the ability to say No to oneself.*
>
> —RABBI ABRAHAM J. HESCHEL

You wisely consider the long-term consequences of short-term temptations and act accordingly.

> *Honor has not to be won; it must only not be lost.*
>
> —ARTHUR SCHOPENHAUER

You honor life when you honor the truth of who you are by living with devotion, discernment, and discipline.

> *Self-reverence, self-knowledge, self-control,*
> *These three alone lead life to sovereign power.*
>
> —ALFRED, LORD TENNYSON

Ultimately, confidence in your rectitude is only wishful thinking until you have forged your character in the furnace of life experiences and fortified it on the anvil of right actions.

> *Life is the only real counsellor . . . wisdom unfiltered through*
> *personal experience does not become a part of the moral tissues.*
>
> —EDITH WHARTON

Indeed, the values and principles you were taught are only words and ideas until you absorb them and become one with them through virtuous living.

> *To be worth any thing, character must be capable of standing firm upon its feet in the world of daily work, temptation, and trial; and able to bear the wear-and-tear of actual life.*
>
> —SAMUEL SMILES

A value is of little value unless you embody it and act in harmony with it reflexively, without the aid of your intellect.

> *Virtues are as dangerous as vices in so far as one lets them rule over one as authorities and laws from without and does not first produce them out of oneself.*
>
> —FRIEDRICH NIETZSCHE

When integrity is woven into your very essence, the ethics of your inner life and the ethics of your public behavior are one and the same.

> *There is no pillow so soft as a clear conscience.*
>
> —FRENCH PROVERB

Choosing virtue over vice is its own reward. The satisfaction of making a principled, disciplined choice is deeper and longer lasting than any fleeting benefit derived from ill-gotten gains.

> *Good feels good.*
>
> —ESTHER HICKS

STRONGER AND DEEPER

Like wisdom, integrity matures as you do. You can possess only as much as the level of your consciousness allows.

In shallow men the fish of little thoughts cause much commotion.
In oceanic minds the whales of inspiration make hardly a ruffle.

—HINDU WISDOM

As your integrity matures and deepens, so too does your longing to express your values through living an active, virtuous life.

Freedom, morality, and the human dignity of the individual
consists precisely in this; that he does good not because he is forced
to do so, but because he freely conceives it, wants it, and loves it.

—MIKHAIL BAKUNIN

Your quest for enlightenment will be stalled until you fiercely commit to a life of truth at all costs.

Honesty is the first chapter in the book of wisdom.

—THOMAS JEFFERSON

Every day brings limitless opportunities to shore up and strengthen your integrity. Every right choice makes you more likely to continue making right choices.

In the mountains of truth you will never climb in vain: either you
will get up higher today or you will exercise your strength so as to
be able to get up higher tomorrow.

—FRIEDRICH NIETZSCHE

As you learn and grow, your capacity to embrace true integrity expands and you become less willing to rationalize away momentary lapses in judgment.

Three things cannot be long hidden: the sun, the moon, and the
truth.

—BUDDHA

Integrity is measured not by your grandest displays of virtue, but in those private moments that no other soul is privy to.

Character may be manifested in the great moments, but it is made in the small ones.

—PHILLIPS BROOKS

The greater your integrity, the more clarity you have about yourself, the world around you, and the role you came to play.

You cannot believe in honor until you have achieved it. Better keep yourself clean and bright: you are the window through which you must see the world.

—GEORGE BERNARD SHAW

You are confident, self-assured, and open to change because you know who you are and you trust God's plan for your life.

Self-knowledge is an anchor that makes unpredictability tolerable.

—DEEPAK CHOPRA

In time, integrity ceases to be a goal and simply becomes who you are. At that point, doing the right thing becomes as natural as breathing.

Integrity is not something that you should have to think about, nor consider doing, but something in the heart that is already done.

—DOUG FIREBAUGH

HONORING OTHERS

Live a life of integrity and you not only conduct yourself with honor, you honor the Divine essence that connects us all by your compassionate, respectful conduct toward others.

You can easily judge the character of a man by how he treats those who can do nothing for him.

—JOHANN WOLFGANG VON GOETHE

Unless they give you a reason not to, you treat every person who crosses your path as if their level of integrity matches your own.

> *Live so that when your children think of fairness and integrity,*
> *they think of you.*
>
> —H. JACKSON BROWN, JR.

Just as every person unconsciously yields to the gravitational pull of Truth, so too do you instinctively recognize those who are worthy of your trust.

> *It is not the oath that makes us believe the man, but the man*
> *the oath.*
>
> —AESCHYLUS

You seek out the good, the beautiful, the virtuous, preferring people and activities that appeal to the better angels of your nature.

> *Finally, brethren, whatever is true, whatever is honorable,*
> *whatever is right, whatever is pure, whatever is lovely, whatever is*
> *of good repute, if there is any excellence and if anything worthy of*
> *praise, dwell on these things.*
>
> —PHILIPPIANS 4:8

The greater your integrity, the greater your capacity to form lasting, meaningful relationships. The bonds of friendship are infinitely more satisfying and rewarding when forged between people of impeccable virtue.

> *There can be no friendship without confidence, and no confidence*
> *without integrity.*
>
> —SAMUEL JOHNSON

The further you move down the path of enlightenment, the more distance you create between your level of awareness and that of others.

There are so many men who can figure costs, and so few who can measure values.

—UNKNOWN

But beware: Greater awareness and deeper understanding do not mean that you are better than, smarter than, or more compassionate than anyone else. You may have an expanded field of vision, but your heart does not leap for joy or weep with sorrow any more intensely than anyone else's.

When the sun rises, it rises for everyone.

—CUBAN PROVERB

CONFLICT AND COMPROMISE

Living with integrity does not mean that every choice you make is nonnegotiable. Most decisions are open to compromise, from where you decide to live to how you spend the holidays.

In matters of style, swim with the current; in matters of principle, stand like a rock.

—THOMAS JEFFERSON

The only issues not open to bargaining are those that would compromise the essence of who you are.

Right is right even if no one is doing it; wrong is wrong even if everyone is doing it.

—SAINT AUGUSTINE

You interact with others confidently, unafraid to tactfully express your true thoughts and feelings.

To know what you prefer, instead of humbly saying Amen to what the world tells you you ought to prefer, is to have kept your soul alive.

—ROBERT LOUIS STEVENSON

Peer pressure does not constrain you. You live your life, as psychologist Abraham Maslow taught, "independent of the good opinion of others."

> *I prefer to be true to myself, even at the hazard of incurring the ridicule of others, rather than to be false, and incur my own abhorrence.*
>
> —FREDERICK DOUGLASS

You recognize that going along to get along will be more stressful in the long run than any momentary discomfort that comes from standing your ground.

> *When I do and say what everyone says and does, then no one calls me irresponsible. But at that time, I am.*
>
> —BARRY STEVENS

Though your decisions may create conflict with those closest to you, you heed the voice of your conscience.

> *With courage you will dare to take risks, have the strength to be compassionate and the wisdom to be humble. Courage is essential for integrity.*
>
> —KESHAVAN NAIR

You trust that a wisdom greater than your own is at work and that the ramifications of your choices and actions will ultimately advance the highest good of everyone involved.

> *How many cares one loses when one decides not to be something but to be someone.*
>
> —GABRIELLE "COCO" CHANEL

You are not deterred from doing what is right even if the outcome may be personally detrimental.

> *It is better to suffer wrong than do it.*
>
> —SOCRATES

Integrity begets valor. When Lewis Morris was warned that the British Army was within cannon shot of his estate and that signing the Declaration of Independence would almost certainly lead to his financial ruin, he shouted, "Damn the consequences, give me the pen."

> *Cowardice asks the question, is it safe? Expediency asks the question, is it politic? Vanity asks the question, is it popular? But conscience asks the question, is it right? And there comes a time when one must take a position that is neither safe, nor politic, nor popular but he must take it because conscience tells him it is right.*
>
> —MARTIN LUTHER KING, JR.

If you inadvertently create conflict or chaos, you immediately accept responsibility and do what you must to set things right.

> *Honor isn't about making the right choices. It's about dealing with the consequences.*
>
> —HIGHLANDER: THE SERIES

You trust that as long as you conduct yourself honorably, the road you find yourself on will always be pointing north.

> *On life's journey faith is nourishment, virtuous deeds are a shelter, wisdom is the light by day and right mindfulness is the protection by night. If a man lives a pure life, nothing can destroy him.*
>
> —BUDDHA

COMPLIMENTS AND CRITICISM

You are concerned with your integrity and yours alone. You are your own harshest critic as well as your most ardent supporter.

> *There is nothing noble in being superior to some other man. The true nobility is in being superior to your previous self.*
>
> —HINDU WISDOM

Your sense of self is not affected one way or the other by what others may think or say about you.

> *Do not let your peace depend on the hearts of men; whatever they*
> *say about you, good or bad, you are not because of it another man,*
> *for as you are, you are.*
>
> —THOMAS À KEMPIS

Should circumstances unjustly besmirch your good name, you repair what damage you can, then walk away in peace, content that your dignity is intact and uncompromised.

> *The world may take your reputation from you, but it cannot take*
> *your character.*
>
> —EMMA DUNHAM KELLEY

You do the right thing not to gain others' approval, but because doing anything other than the right thing never occurs to you.

> *Suppose you scrub your ethical skin until it shines, but inside there*
> *is no music, then what?*
>
> —KABIR

Accepting that the way others view you is out of your control, you challenge yourself to live up to your expectations and yours alone.

> *Reputation is what other people know about you. Honor is what*
> *you know about yourself.*
>
> —LOIS MCMASTER BUJOLD

While seeking the approval of others is not on your radar, you cannot help but receive recognition and accolades.

> *The higher the sun ariseth, the less shadow doth he cast; even so*
> *the greater is the goodness, the less doth it covet praise; yet cannot*
> *avoid its rewards in honours.*
>
> —AKHENATON

You accept compliments gracefully, letting each one serve as a reminder to practice humility. A compliment then becomes useful and serves a greater purpose.

Humility does not mean you think less of yourself. It means you think of yourself less.

—KEN BLANCHARD

You actively solicit constructive criticism in both personal and professional circles, viewing it as valuable feedback that will help you serve the world more effectively.

O would some Power the gift to give us
To see ourselves as others see us!

—ROBERT BURNS

Regardless of the intent of the person providing the feedback, you welcome their comment with gratitude and detachment, either accepting it as true and making changes accordingly or dismissing it as lacking in merit.

Criticism should awaken our attention, not inflame our anger. We should listen to, and not flee from, those who contradict us. Truth should be our cause, no matter in what manner it comes to us.

—MADAME DE SABLÉ

Whether others lavish you with praise or scald you with criticism, you smile politely and keep moving.

The wind cannot shake a mountain. Neither praise nor blame moves the wise man.

—BUDDHA

Your integrity is the guard stationed at the entrance to your mind, keeping it pure and strong and a sanctuary for higher consciousness.

I will not let anyone walk through my mind with their dirty feet.

—MAHATMA GANDHI

You view brickbats and put-downs as evidence that you are actively engaging the world and doing the work you came here to do.

> *To avoid criticism do nothing, say nothing, be nothing.*
>
> —ELBERT HUBBARD

Bow before the altar of integrity and you will remain an island of peace even as storms of public sentiment rage about you.

> *To live in the presence of great truths and eternal laws, to be led by permanent ideals— that is what keeps a man patient when the world ignores him, and calm and unspoiled when the world praises him.*
>
> —HONORÉ DE BALZAC

HONORING THE TRUTH

A truth is relative, dependent on context, and variable as your consciousness evolves. A Truth is absolute, transcendent of context, and innate to consciousness itself.

> *Every issue has its own levels of truth. Levels of truth move in a progression. As one grows and increases in awareness, her or his levels of truth move from the superficial to the more profound.*
>
> —ANNE WILSON SCHAEF

Look through God's eyes and a virtuous circle begins rotating. As you peel away layers of human perceptions, you discern the eternal Truths looming behind the everyday truths that govern your daily life, which yields greater wisdom, which expands your consciousness, which spontaneously leads you to look at the world through God's eyes.

> *There are truths on this side of the Pyrenees which are falsehoods on the other.*
>
> —MICHEL DE MONTAIGNE

You need not travel the world in pursuit of truth. Simply be true to yourself and truth will reveal itself.

> *Truth, like the burgeoning of a bulb under the soil, however deeply sown, will make its way to the light.*
>
> —EDITH PARGETER

How do you know what is true? Divine Intelligence speaks to you through your mind, body, and spirit, and tells you it is so.

> *Truth stands on its own evidences; it does not require any other testimony to attest it; it is self-effulgent. It penetrates into the inmost recesses of our nature, and the whole universe stands up and says, "This is Truth."*
>
> —SWAMI VIVEKANANDA

The truth of a statement or situation resonates within you like a musical note struck in perfect harmony.

> *Truth is not introduced into the individual from without, but was within him all the time.*
>
> —SØREN KIERKEGAARD

Logic can coolly and methodically validate a fact, but it is intuition that validates a truth.

> *We taste and feel and see the truth. We do not reason ourselves into it.*
>
> —WILLIAM BUTLER YEATS

Indeed, logic is not even a pillar of truth, much less its very foundation. In the realm of truth, logic is an afterthought.

> *You can only find truth with logic if you have already found truth without it.*
>
> —G. K. CHESTERTON

As your consciousness expands, you see that truth is a multi-sided gem that reflects the light of perception differently depending on how it is held and turned in your hand.

> *The truth is not simply what you think it is; it is also the circumstances in which it is said, and to whom, why, and how it is said.*
>
> —VACLAV HAVEL

If evidence proves that your confidence in a "truth" was misplaced, you correct your thinking and move on.

> *A very popular error: having the courage of one's convictions; rather it is a matter of having the courage for an* attack *on one's convictions!!!*
>
> —FRIEDRICH NIETZSCHE

Although you consider your truths immutable, you recognize and respect that other people hold other truths that resonate just as deeply with them.

> *Whenever two good people argue over principles, they are both right.*
>
> —MARIE VON EBNER-ESCHENBACH

Trying to corner the market on truth is like trying to wrap your arms around the wind; there will always be more beyond your grasp than within it.

> *Whoever undertakes to set himself up as a judge of Truth and Knowledge is shipwrecked by the laughter of the gods.*
>
> —ALBERT EINSTEIN

Nevertheless, you value your relationship with truth more than any enticements this world has to offer.

> *Rather than love, than money, than fame, give me truth.*
>
> —HENRY DAVID THOREAU

Truth will not demand perfection of you. It asks only for eternal allegiance and purity of intent.

> *There are only two mistakes one can make along the road to truth; not going all the way, and not starting.*
>
> —BUDDHA

Pledge your love to truth, and all that you gaze at reveals an inner beauty visible only to those who see the world through God's eyes.

> *Truth is the vital breath of Beauty; Beauty the outward form of Truth.*
>
> —GRACE AGUILAR

SPEAKING THE TRUTH

Honesty is your best friend. You understand that telling the truth—or what you perceive to be the truth—is a sacred trust.

> *Truth is no theory, no speculative system of philosophy, no intellectual insight. Truth is exact correspondence with reality. For man, truth is unshakable knowledge of his real nature, his Self as soul.*
>
> —PARAMAHANSA YOGANANDA

Truth can never be vanquished. Do what you will: bind it in chains and bury it in the darkest forest. Truth will always rise up and reclaim its throne.

> *The truth comes as conqueror only because we have lost the art of receiving it as guest.*
>
> —RABINDRANATH TAGORE

While you are always prepared to speak the truth, you honor the importance of discretion and timing.

If it is not truthful and not helpful, don't say it.
If it is truthful and not helpful, don't say it.
If it is not truthful and helpful, don't say it.
If it is truthful and helpful, wait for the right time.

—BUDDHA

There will be times when integrity demands that you speak the truth when it is uncomfortable to do so.

Love of the truth puts you on the spot.

—NAROPA INSTITUTE MOTTO

When faced with potentially unpleasant consequences, you humbly trust that the words you feel compelled to speak will play a vital role in the spiritual evolution of those who appear to be adversely affected by your truth-telling.

Make us to choose the harder right instead of the easier wrong,
and never to be content with a half truth when the whole can
be won.

—WEST POINT CADET PRAYER

Not speaking the truth when your conscience requires you to do so is no better than speaking a lie.

Truth can be outraged by silence quite as cruelly as by speech.

—AMELIA BARR

Breathe life into a single lie and your entire sense of self is thrown off kilter. Only the purifying elixir of truth can restore your equanimity.

Remember: one lie does not cost you one truth but the truth.

—FRIEDRICH HEBBEL

Tell the truth and you align yourself with Spirit. Stray from truth and you sacrifice calmness and clarity for chaos and confusion.

If you tell the truth, you have infinite power supporting you; *but, if not, you have infinite power* against you.

—CHARLES GORDON

Are there exceptions to truth-telling? Yes. To use an extreme example, if a Nazi soldier knocked on your door during World War II and asked if you were harboring Jews, you would not be acting with integrity if you answered affirmatively.

Wisdom is knowing what to do next; virtue is doing it.

—DAVID STARR JORDAN

Your integrity is the bridge between truth and justice. Listen to the unerring voice of conscience and you will cross that bridge at the speed of thought.

Justice is conscience, not a personal conscience but the conscience of the whole of humanity. Those who clearly recognize the voice of their own conscience usually recognize also the voice of justice.

—ALEKSANDR SOLZHENITSYN

While you respect society and follow its rules, you recognize Truth as the ultimate authority.

They must find it hard to take truth for authority who have so long mistaken authority for truth.

—GERALD MASSEY

If a choice comes down to following orders or doing what is right, you choose the latter without hesitation.

Never do anything against conscience even if the state demands it.

—ALBERT EINSTEIN

JUDGED AND JUDGING

You honor other people's perspectives and interpretations, never taking an opposing view personally.

> *Let me never fall into the vulgar mistake of dreaming that I am*
> *persecuted whenever I am contradicted.*
>
> —RALPH WALDO EMERSON

When someone challenges your statements or positions, you welcome the opportunity to clarify any misperceptions.

> *Truth is never afraid of questions.*
>
> —PARAMAHANSA YOGANANDA

Even if every choice you make is virtuous, your actions may be misinterpreted by others. That is to be expected—we tend to judge others by their actions and ourselves by our intent.

> *We permit all things to ourselves, and that which we call sin in*
> *others is experiment for us.*
>
> —RALPH WALDO EMERSON

You scrupulously avoid toxic, judgmental thoughts, recognizing that every negative thought about somebody else disturbs your attunement with the Divine current.

> *When you judge another person, you do not define him or her, you*
> *define yourself.*
>
> —WAYNE DYER

Living a life of integrity begins right now. If others continue to define you by your past errors, so be it.

Anyone who proposes to do good must not expect people to roll stones out of his way, but must accept his lot calmly if they even roll a few more upon it.

—ALBERT SCHWEITZER

Do not allow the mistakes of yesterday to sabotage your resolve to do what is right today.

Admitting errors clears the score and proves you wiser than before.

—ARTHUR GUITERMAN

Atone for the errors you can, turn the rest over to God, and serenely surrender to Divine justice.

A man has to live with himself, and he should see to it that he always has good company.

—CHARLES EVANS HUGHES

Embrace absolute integrity and you will find that guilt and regret are inevitably replaced by peace and serenity as naturally as winter gives way to spring.

Just as surely as distress must follow self-deceit, healing must follow self-honesty.

—VERNON HOWARD

On those occasions when you do fall short of your expectations, you view each slip-up as a learning experience that gives you greater insight into your character and values.

All failures are apparent, not real. Every slip, every fall, every return to selfishness is a lesson learned, an experience gained, from which a golden grain of wisdom is extracted.

—JAMES ALLEN

Humbler but wiser, you challenge yourself to minimize, and in due time eliminate, any future backsliding.

The only real mistake is the one from which we learn nothing.

—JOHN POWELL

HOLDING FIRM

You vigorously guard the integrity of your virtue and the virtue of your integrity. Relaxing your ethics, even for trivial matters, is unthinkable.

> *Hold yourself responsible for a higher standard than anybody else*
> *expects of you. . . . Never excuse yourself to yourself. Never pity*
> *yourself. Be a hard master to yourself; be lenient to everybody else.*
>
> —HENRY WARD BEECHER

You do not flaunt your integrity. By definition, integrity is never self-serving or self-aggrandizing.

> *The deepest rivers flow with the least sound.*
>
> —QUINTUS CURTIUS RUFUS

You simply live as you know you should, as you know you must, even if the rest of the world seems to be crumbling around you.

> *Content thyself to be obscurely good. When vice prevails, and*
> *impious men bear sway, the post of honour is a private station.*
>
> —JOSEPH ADDISON

The prevailing winds of public opinion do not even ruffle your hair, much less blow you off course.

> *In matters of conscience the Law of Majority has no place.*
>
> —MAHATMA GANDHI

True integrity does not so much as flinch at attempts to sway it, even if all the riches of the world were to be laid at its feet.

The test of character is the amount of strain it can bear.

—Charles Houston

Hold on to your integrity and you will hold on to your peace of mind, even if all else appears to be lost.

It is possible that the scrupulously honest man may not grow rich so fast as the unscrupulous and dishonest one; but the success will be of a truer kind, earned without fraud or injustice. And even though a man should for a time be unsuccessful, still he must be honest: better lose all and save character. For character is itself a fortune.

—Samuel Smiles

Compromise your ethics, and even a stadium full of people cheering your name cannot begin to restore your sense of self-worth.

Nowhere!
Not in the sky,
Nor in the midst of the sea,
Nor deep in the mountains,
Can you hide from your own mischief.

—Buddha

True integrity is as tough as steel and as fragile as a snowflake. Tough because it is immalleable and unyielding, and fragile because one careless act can melt it away.

The reputation of a thousand years may be determined by the conduct of one hour.

—Japanese proverb

Preserving your integrity may come at a steep cost, but steeper still is the cost of choosing the path of least resistance instead of the road less traveled.

To know what is right and not do it is the worst cowardice.

—Confucius

Inevitably, the easy road is littered with potholes, while the high road offers spectacular views of all you are capable of becoming.

> *No man can purchase his virtue too dear; for it is the only thing whose value must ever increase with the price it has cost us. Our integrity is never worth so much, as when we have parted with our all to keep it.*
>
> —CHARLES CALEB COLTON

NOTHING ELSE MATTERS

You consider yourself successful, regardless of whether you achieve career and financial goals, as long as you stay true to yourself and your ideals.

> *Try to become not a man of success, but try rather to become a man of value.*
>
> —ALBERT EINSTEIN

You recognize that success is determined by the quality of your relationships—with friends and family, with colleagues, with yourself, with God, with the world at large, and, through your words and deeds, even with people you will never personally meet.

> *He has achieved success who has lived well, laughed often, and loved much; who has enjoyed the trust of pure women, the respect of intelligent men, and the love of little children; who has filled his niche and accomplished his task; who has left the world better than he found it, whether by an improved poppy, a perfect poem, or a rescued soul; who has never lacked appreciation of earth's beauty or failed to express it; who has always looked for the best in others and given them the best he had; whose life was inspiration; whose memory a benediction.*
>
> —BESSIE ANDERSON STANLEY

Commit to living a life of complete integrity, and the Universe will test your resolve by presenting you with a series of ethical dilemmas.

*To be yourself in a world that is constantly trying to make you
something else is the greatest accomplishment.*

—Ralph Waldo Emerson

View these challenges as required courses for your Master's degree in integrity from
the College of Divine Knowledge. Dropping out is not an option.

*If you have integrity, nothing else matters. If you don't have
integrity, nothing else matters.*

—Alan Simpson

Staying true to who you are may occasionally weigh heavily upon your shoulders, but
rest assured that your integrity will be a most cherished companion in the winter of
your life.

*If a man can reach the latter days of his life with his soul intact,
he has mastered life.*

—Gordon Parks

LIVE WITH INTEGRITY
Living the Lesson

I loved my job as operations manager for a small investment management firm. Numbers had always been a second language to me, and the work required me to be logical, methodical, and organized—useful traits that continue to serve me well.

However, four years after my high school friend Neil had hired me, my calling came calling. I gradually became consumed with the idea of writing for a living. It wasn't long before the work I was being paid to do no longer held my interest. I didn't have a computer at home so I stayed after work to type my magazine articles and greeting card ideas on my work computer, an arrangement Neil had approved.

Soon, however, my personal use of my work computer began spilling over into my work day. I rationalized that this was okay because it was only for five minutes here and there and I was still getting all of my work done. I was so absorbed in my new passion, however, that my occasional indiscretions began increasing in frequency and length.

One day, as I was typing up a batch of greeting card ideas, Neil opened the closed door to my office, shut it behind him, and gently confronted me. Deeply embarrassed, I apologized; yet I had the temerity to ask if I could finish what I was typing so I could meet a deadline.

I'd like to report that Neil's rebuke slapped some sense into me and prompted me to see the error of my ways, but that would be only partially true. I continued taking occasional liberties whenever my misplaced sense of entitlement deemed it necessary. Yes, I was more careful about stepping over the line but only because I had to be, not because I felt compelled to do what was right.

Some years later, at a small informal gathering of fellow writers, a friend made the statement, "You either have integrity or you don't." It dawned on me that who I thought I was did not sync up with my actual behavior—an unsettling realization, to say the least.

I had always thought of myself as a person of integrity. And it was true, just not completely—I had allowed myself to bend the rules whenever it was convenient to do so. No more. I vowed to never again let myself get away with tiptoeing over the line just because I could. If that meant I had to stop by the library instead of using the copy machine at work, so be it.

Funny how the little things matter so much. Waiting until I left work to do anything of a personal nature made me feel more peaceful, made me feel like I was living a more honorable life. That makes sense. I was.

LIVE WITH INTEGRITY
Self-Reflection Questions

- Under what circumstances are my actions inconsistent with the values of the person I want to be?

- What would I be embarrassed about if I found out my daily life was being broadcast on television?

- How can I stop myself from exploiting and justifying ethical shortcuts?

- What happened the last time I pursued my own selfish interests instead of doing the right thing?

- What is stopping me from committing to a life of truth at all costs?

- Am I better off inherently trusting or distrusting people I meet, and why?

- In what scenarios would I be willing to compromise my principles in order to avoid conflict?

- How can I get better at listening to constructive criticism without getting defensive or angry?

- In what situations would I be tempted to speak untruthfully?

- How can I counteract the negative, judgmental thoughts that pop into my mind?

- How can I guard against making excuses to myself when I take a step backward on the road to integrity?

- How do I define success?

NINE

PURSUE YOUR RIGHT LIVELIHOOD

*There is no scarcity of opportunity to make a living at what you love,
there is only a scarcity of resolve to make it happen.*

—WAYNE DYER

PURSUE YOUR RIGHT LIVELIHOOD

You will find your ideal career when you deepen your self-knowledge, strike the right balance between intuition and intellect, and learn to distinguish the call of your spirit from the fear-based urgings of your ego.

> *When I dare to be powerful, to use my strength in the service*
> *of my vision, then it becomes less and less important whether*
> *I am afraid.*
>
> —AUDRE LORDE

HONORING THE DREAM

The question is not whether you have a talent, but how long it will take you to discover and apply it.

> *The weakest among us has a gift, however seemingly trivial, which*
> *is peculiar to him, and which, worthily used, will be a gift also to*
> *his race for ever.*
>
> —JOHN RUSKIN

Seek your right livelihood by answering these questions: *What kinds of challenges and issues command your attention? What productive activities do you get so immersed in that you lose all sense of time? When do eating and sleeping become nuisances?*

> *If you are doing something you would do for nothing, then you*
> *are on your way to salvation. And if while you are doing it you*
> *are transported into another existence, there is no need for you*
> *to worry about the future.*
>
> —DR. GEORGE SHEEHAN

Do not censor yourself—make the list as long as you would like. List everything that sparks your enthusiasm and adds beauty and joy to your world.

Let yourself be silently drawn
by the stronger pull of what you really love.

—RUMI

Be bold. Close your eyes and watch as your imagination jumps the fence of your comfort zone and gallops toward the vast open fields of your unclaimed potential.

Only as high as I reach can I grow, only as far as I seek can I go,
only as deep as I look can I see, only as much as I dream can I be.

—KAREN RAVN

Next, circle the activities that leap out at you. Know that somewhere, somehow, some people are making a living doing these things.

I learned this, at least, by my experiment; that if one advances
confidently in the direction of his dreams, and endeavors to live
the life which he has imagined, he will meet with a success
unexpected in common hours.

—HENRY DAVID THOREAU

If you were not capable of joining their ranks, you would not have been given the dream to do so.

You are never given a wish without also being given the power to
make it true. You may have to work for it, however.

—RICHARD BACH

When you are aligned with Spirit and long to do meaningful work, the world is in need of whatever it is you need to do.

The place God calls you to is the place where your deep gladness
and the world's deep hunger meet.

—FREDERICK BUECHNER

Until you satisfy your soul's longing to express itself through right livelihood, there will be a giant work-shaped piece missing from the jigsaw puzzle of your life.

> *The pitcher cries for water to carry*
> *and a person for work that is real.*
>
> —MARGE PIERCY

Ultimately, you must follow your heart. Listen closely and you will find that it beats in concert with the heart of all creation.

> *Don't ask yourself what the world needs. Ask yourself what makes*
> *you come alive and then go do that. Because what the world needs*
> *is people who have come alive.*
>
> —HOWARD THURMAN

LEARNING WITHOUT LIMITS

Do not allow yourself to be intimidated and overwhelmed if there is an enormous gap between your current job and the work you aspire to.

> *It is our duty as men and women to proceed as though limits to*
> *our abilities do not exist.*
>
> —PIERRE TEILHARD DE CHARDIN

Keep dreaming big even if you are currently living small. Initiative and ingenuity are infinitely more valuable than any material advantages you could possess.

> *The defining factor is never resources, it's resourcefulness.*
>
> —ANTHONY ROBBINS

You can learn new skills. You can acquire new knowledge. You can meet new people. You can create new experiences.

> *What you can't do you must do; what you must do, you can do.*
>
> —ANTHONY ROBBINS

Jump at opportunities to upgrade your talents. Grab the sledgehammer of self-confidence and smash your self-imposed constraints to smithereens.

As is our confidence, so is our capacity.

—WILLIAM HAZLITT

Demand the best of yourself, but keep working and striving to make your best even better.

> *Plan for more than you can do,*
> *Then do it.*
> *Bite off more than you can chew,*
> *Then chew it.*

—UNKNOWN

When you reach the outskirts of your abilities, press on. Only by testing your limits will you discover that you have no limits.

> *Only those who will risk going too far can possibly find out how*
> *far one can go.*

—T. S. ELIOT

WINNING vs. WISHING

You do not have to be a perfect human being to find or create the job that is perfect for you.

> *Too many people overvalue what they are not and undervalue*
> *what they are.*

—MALCOLM FORBES

Everyone has shortcomings, but no one else has your unique blend of strengths and skills.

> *Instead of looking at life as a narrowing funnel, we can see it*
> *ever-widening to choose the things we want to do, to take the*
> *wisdoms we've learned and create something.*

—LIZ CARPENTER

Do not sell yourself short. Your attitude will spell the difference between a life of winning and a life of wishing.

> *Argue for your limitations, and sure enough, they're yours.*
>
> —RICHARD BACH

Positive thinkers look at a goal and excitedly start mapping out steps they can take to achieve it.

> *The optimist sees the rose and not its thorns; the pessimist stares at the thorns, oblivious of the rose.*
>
> —KAHLIL GIBRAN

They know that no worthy objective can withstand the assault of positive thinking working in tandem with practical action.

> *Thought is fire; use its concentrated power to consume all obstacles to achievement.*
>
> —PARAMAHANSA YOGANANDA

Negative thinkers look at a goal and start rattling off reasons why it is foolish to even attempt it.

> *Self-image sets the boundaries of individual accomplishment.*
>
> —DR. MAXWELL MALTZ

Ignore the naysayers who bray that you will be wading into a cluttered marketplace filled with cutthroat competitors.

> *If you want to stand out, don't be different, be outstanding.*
>
> —MEREDITH WEST

Such skeptics may mean well, but they do not have your passion, your clarity, your vision.

To understand the heart and mind of a person, look not at what
he has already achieved, but at what he aspires to do.

—KAHLIL GIBRAN

Those who caution you not to risk too much or reach too high do not know, as you do, that yours was not meant to be an ordinary life.

Nothing splendid has ever been achieved except by those who
dared believe that something inside themselves was superior to
circumstance.

—BRUCE BARTON

PATIENCE AND PERSEVERANCE

Steadfastly seek the right career, and one day the right career will find you. That *Aha!* moment will part the clouds of doubt and uncertainty and allow the light of clarity and purpose to stream through.

When the deepest part of you becomes engaged in what you are
doing, when your activities and actions become gratifying and
purposeful, when what you do serves both yourself and others,
when you do not tire within but seek the sweet satisfaction of
your life and your work, you are doing what you were meant
to be doing.

—GARY ZUKAV

If there does not seem to be a precedent for your career path, step forward and blaze your own trail. As long as you offer value, people will value what you have to offer.

If you want to put yourself on the map, publish your own map.

—ASHLEIGH BRILLIANT

The instant you take the first step toward a brighter future, the Universe reconfigures itself. The sun comes out. The fog burns off. The next step presents itself.

Whatever you can do, or dream you can, begin it.
Boldness has genius, power, and magic in it.

—JOHANN WOLFGANG VON GOETHE

Even so, do not assume you can skip happily down the yellow brick road of your new career path without encountering any talking trees or wicked witches.

If you can find a path with no obstacles, it probably doesn't lead
anywhere.

—FRANK A. CLARK

The road ahead is paved with both successes and setbacks; do not linger too long on either. With each step, life reveals more of its secrets.

Success is not final; failure is not fatal; it is the courage to continue
that counts.

—WINSTON CHURCHILL

No matter what roadblocks you run up against, you can choose to view hitches, hurdles, and hindrances as occasions for learning and growth.

What we have before us are breathtaking opportunities disguised
as insoluble problems.

—JOHN W. GARDNER

Your right livelihood may feel divinely delivered, but succeeding in it will likely demand significant amounts of study, training, and effort. Beware of any path that does not.

Opportunity is missed by most people because it is dressed in
overalls and looks like work.

—THOMAS EDISON

Mastery cannot be hurried along. Establishing a reputation, building mutually beneficial relationships, and mastering the subtleties of your craft demand time and toil.

*It takes time to succeed because success is merely the natural
reward for taking time to do anything well.*

—JOSEPH ROSS

Success is not achieved overnight, unless by "overnight" you mean a lifetime of learning, experiencing, and becoming.

Success is not a doorway, it's a stairway.

—DOTTIE WALTERS

STEPPING STONES

Your right livelihood calls for you to bring your whole self to the workplace. What does that look like? You speak and act authentically, and value your values more than your paycheck.

*When people go to work, they shouldn't have to leave their hearts
at home.*

—BETTY BENDER

If you are miserable in your current position, recognize that every job you ever had has prepared you for what was to come next.

*The question for each man to settle is not what he would do if he
had means, time, influence and educational advantages; the
question is what he will do with the things he has.*

—HAMILTON WRIGHT MABIE

No matter how much you may dislike it, your current job is also a stepping stone. Do the best you can do and life will give you the opportunity to be the best you can be.

*Making a success of the job at hand is the best step toward the
kind you want.*

—BERNARD BARUCH

Reframe your "negative" job as a training ground for sharpening your skills, and you will discover hidden opportunities for self-improvement.

> *Life is eager to prove your limits false.*
>
> —ALAN COHEN

Choose instead to lose yourself in your misery and you will fail to notice promising circumstances when they present themselves.

> *You can clutch the past so tightly to your chest that it leaves your arms too full to embrace the present.*
>
> —JAN GLIDEWELL

If you despise your job so much that you find yourself wallowing in despair, begin circulating your résumé.

> *Work is love made visible.*
> *And if you cannot work with love but only with distaste, it is better that you should leave your work and sit at the gate of the temple and take alms of those who work with joy.*
>
> —KAHLIL GIBRAN

The vast majority of people who complain about their job are not actively seeking a better one.

> *A rut is a grave with the ends knocked out.*
>
> —LAURENCE J. PETER

They may feel trapped, but the moment they recognize job dissatisfaction as a prison of their own making, thoughts of escape can begin taking shape.

> *There is work that is work, and there is play that is play; there is play that is work, and work that is play. And in only one of these lies happiness.*
>
> —GELETT BURGESS

No workplace rut is so deep that you cannot climb out if it. You *always* have options. A better job is out there, waiting for you to make the effort to find it.

> *Opportunity is as scarce as oxygen; men fairly breathe it and do not know it.*
>
> —UNKNOWN

Your odds of upgrading your work life depend on how you answer two questions: *How bad do you want it?* and *What are you going to do about it?*

> *If you don't like where you are, change it! You're not a tree.*
>
> —JIM ROHN

If you cannot afford to quit your current job, devote every spare moment to creating or landing your dream job.

> *Whatsoever thy hand findeth to do, do it with thy might.*
>
> —ECCLESIASTES 9:10

Odds are that a new job will represent a step up in salary, responsibility, or learning opportunities. But do not rule out taking a pay cut or relocating if your peace of mind is at stake.

> *There is no such thing as can't, only won't. If you're qualified, all it takes is a burning desire to accomplish, to make a change. Go forward, go backward. Whatever it takes! But you can't blame other people or society in general. It all comes from your mind. When we do the impossible we realize we are special people.*
>
> —JAN ASHFORD

When you do land your ideal job, it too may prove to be a stepping stone. As you continue to grow and evolve, so too will the world around you; the work that was once so right for you may give way to an even more satisfying career.

> *Where your talents and the world's needs cross, there lies your vocation.*
>
> —ARISTOTLE

Nothing is certain but this: Each new dream job will leverage the talents and abilities you developed in your previous ideal job.

> *Wherever we are, it is but a stage on the way to somewhere else,*
> *and whatever we do, however well we do it, it is only a preparation*
> *to do something else that shall be different.*
>
> —ROBERT LOUIS STEVENSON

LOVE AND ABUNDANCE

Find work that you love and you will be in harmony with life's soft, sweet melody, adding your instrument to the celestial orchestra that serenades the farthest reaches of the Universe.

> *When you work you are a flute through whose heart the*
> *whispering of the hours turns to music.*
>
> —KAHLIL GIBRAN

If you do not love what you do, you have yet to discover your right livelihood. It is happiness that leads to success, not the other way around.

> *To be successful, the first thing to do is fall in love with your work.*
>
> —SISTER MARY LAURETTA

Love your work and it ceases to be work, becoming instead a vehicle of self-expression and self-actualization.

> *Nothing is really work unless you would rather be doing*
> *something else.*
>
> —J. M. BARRIE

No matter where your right livelihood leads you, doing work that feeds your soul will suffuse your days with joy and soften your nights with the sweet dreams of contentment.

Success based on anything but internal fulfillment is bound to be empty.

—Dr. Martha Friedman

When a hard day's work leaves you exhilarated instead of exhausted, you are on your way to greatness.

Happiness does not come from doing easy work but from the afterglow of satisfaction that comes after the achievement of a difficult task that demanded our best.

—Theodore Isaac Rubin

You know you have found your right livelihood when you enjoy every aspect of your work, even duties you would otherwise dread.

The test of a vocation is the love of the drudgery it involves.

—Logan Pearsall Smith

It is said that if you do what you love, the money will follow. That is true, although the money might not come as fast or be as much as you expected. Proceed cautiously; crawl before you walk, and walk before you run.

The elevator to success is out of order today. You're going to have to take the stairway, one step at a time.

—Wayne Dyer

Rush blindly ahead and you may crash headlong into playwright Dane Stauffer's tongue-in-cheek dictum: "Do what you love, the debt will follow." Then again, you may just hit the jackpot.

You've got to go out on a limb sometimes, because that's where the fruit is.

—Will Rogers

Doing what you love *will* bring abundance, but it may primarily be an abundance of friends, experiences, or opportunities for growth.

*Fill your bowl to the brim and it will spill. Keep sharpening your
knife and it will blunt. Chase after money and security and your
heart will never unclench. Care about people's approval and you
will be their prisoner. Do your work, then step back. The only path
to serenity.*

—LAO TZU

Financial abundance can afford you greater freedom to live as you wish, but wealth is
not the only statistic tallied on the abundance scoreboard. If your sole focus is the
bottom line, you may take life's other gifts for granted.

*No man can tell whether he is rich or poor by turning to his ledger.
It is the heart that makes a man rich. He is rich or poor according
to what he is, not according to what he has.*

—HENRY WARD BEECHER

Even if you never fully succeed at turning your avocation into your vocation, your life
will be more fulfilling and joyous for having made the effort.

*I don't want to get to the end of my life and find that I just lived
the length of it. I want to have lived the width of it as well.*

—DIANE ACKERMAN

Follow your dream, whatever it may be, and you will know a deep satisfaction that
eludes many who have far more "important" careers.

*If it falls your lot to be a street sweeper, go on out and sweep streets
like Michelangelo painted pictures; sweep streets like Handel and
Beethoven composed music; sweep streets like Shakespeare wrote
poetry; sweep streets so well that all the host of heaven and earth
will have to pause and say, "Here lived a great street sweeper who
swept his job well."*

—MARTIN LUTHER KING, JR.

Whatever the size of your paycheck, doing work that you love is one of the greatest gifts
you can give yourself.

Not what we have, but what we enjoy, constitutes our abundance.

—JOHN PETIT-SENN

Success is a state of mind. Listen to your conscience, act with confidence and integrity, and you will know the joy and satisfaction of a life well lived.

Success is simple. Do what's right, the right way, at the right time.

—ARNOLD H. GLASOW

PASSION AND PRODUCTIVITY

Passion is the gateway to success. Every new business originated in the imagination of someone who was passionate enough to bring their vision to fruition.

The greatest achievement was at first and for a time a dream.
The oak sleeps in the acorn; the bird waits in the egg; and in the
highest vision of the soul a waking angel stirs. Dreams are the
seedlings of realities.

—JAMES ALLEN

Creating something out of nothing comes naturally to dreamers who look beyond what is and imagine what could be.

A rock pile ceases to be a rock pile the moment a single man
contemplates it, bearing within him the image of a cathedral.

—ANTOINE DE SAINT-EXUPÉRY

Pour your heart into your work and you serve as a pure channel for the Divine force within you that demands expression.

A man who works with his hands is a laborer; a man who works
with his hands and his brain is a craftsman; but a man who works
with his hands and his brain and his heart is an artist.

—LOUIS NIZER

Celebrate your work as a means of sharing your unique gifts with the world, and your joy and passion will be infused into whatever you produce.

When love and skill work together, expect a masterpiece.

—CHARLES READE

If the quality of your work matches your effort, your services will be in demand. People will always seek out quality and pay generously for it.

If a man can write a better book, preach a better sermon, or make a better mouse-trap than his neighbor, though he builds his house in the woods, the world will make a beaten path to his door.

—RALPH WALDO EMERSON

If you have your own business, satisfied clients will happily recommend you to friends and colleagues.

Ability will never catch up with the demand for it.

—CONFUCIUS

As word of mouth grows, your business will as well, creating an ongoing loop of delighted customers who refer you to soon-to-be-delighted customers.

The reward for work well done is the opportunity to do more.

— DR. JONAS SALK

A word of caution: The siren call of your right livelihood is so alluring that it is tempting to completely give yourself to it. Make a conscious effort to lead a balanced life.

Work, love and play are the great balance wheels of man's being.

—ORISON SWETT MARDEN

Do not let your work consume you so much that you neglect your family, your friends, and the necessities of daily living.

Work is good provided you do not forget to live.

—BANTU PROVERB

The more balanced, centered, and peaceful you become, the more you can offer the world.

Make the most of yourself, for that is all there is of you.

—RALPH WALDO EMERSON

SERVING THE WORLD

Mindfully engaging in your right livelihood with a spirit of humility and service is an integral element of your journey toward enlightenment.

> *True Dharma seekers who live in the world use their daily activity as a polishing tool. Outwardly they may appear to be very busy, like flint striking steel, making sparks everywhere. But inwardly they silently grow, for although they may be working very hard, they are working for the sake of the work and not for the profits it will bring them. Unattached to the results of their labor, they transcend the frenetic to reach the Way's essential tranquility. Doesn't a rough and tumbling stream also sparkle like striking flints—while it polishes into smoothness every stone in its path?*
>
> —HANSHAN DEQING

Unless your work depends on you having some degree of celebrity, consider keeping a low public profile.

> *Obscurity and a competence. That is the life that is best worth living.*
>
> —MARK TWAIN

Seeking fame for the sake of being famous bloats your ego and pulls you off the path of service, devotion, and humility.

I believe the first test of a truly great man is his humility. I do not mean, by humility, doubt of his own power, or hesitation in speaking of his opinions; but a right understanding of the relation between what he can do and say, and the rest of the world's sayings and doings. All great men . . . have a curious undersense of powerlessness, feeling that the greatness is not in them, but through them.

—JOHN RUSKIN

If you must publicize your work to attract new clients, then diligently network and market yourself. Otherwise, let your work speak for itself.

The work praises the man.

—IRISH PROVERB

Even if you are overflowing with optimism, there may be days when you question your sanity for choosing such an arduous path.

Far and away the best prize that life offers is the chance to work hard at work worth doing.

—THEODORE ROOSEVELT

At those times, remind yourself that you did not choose the path so much as the path chose you, and that there is a higher purpose at work.

The highest reward for a man's toil is not what he gets for it, but what he becomes by it.

—JOHN RUSKIN

You are doing the work you were born to do when the work itself is more rewarding than whatever compensation you receive.

See only that thou work, and thou canst not escape the reward:
whether thy work be fine or coarse, planting corn or writing epics,
so only it be honest work, done to thine own approbation, it shall
earn a reward to the senses as well as to the thought: no matter
how often defeated, you are born to victory. The reward of a thing
well done is to have done it.

—RALPH WALDO EMERSON

Your right livelihood, which defines what you do and how you pay the bills, may accelerate the discovery of your life's purpose, which defines who you are and how you serve the world.

We don't know who we are until we see what we can do.

—MARTHA GRIMES

Your work life and your life's work may virtually overlap or they may be mutually exclusive. If your vision is clouded, challenge yourself to view every step on your path through God's eyes. As consciousness grows, so too does clarity.

Not what you do but how you do what you do determines whether
you are fulfilling your destiny. And how you do what you do is
determined by your state of consciousness.

—ECKHART TOLLE

SAFETY vs. SELF-DISCOVERY

Many opt for a "safe" life doing work they do not enjoy, especially when there are children to be raised and a mortgage to be paid.

Chase your passion, not your pension.

—EDWARD JAMES OLMOS

It is easy to make excuses for not developing your talents, for not exploring other opportunities, for not pursuing a more challenging career path.

You can either have your excuses or you can have your dreams.
You can't have both.

—Barbara J. Winter

Yet if you are not actively striving to identify and develop your talents, you are passively engaging in self-sabotage.

The buried talent is the sunken rock on which most lives strike and
founder.

—Frederick William Faber

The time may not be right to act on your dreams, but the time is always right to dream. If hope and resolve are your daily companions, your time will come.

Not only strike while the iron is hot, but make it hot by striking.

—Oliver Cromwell

Pledge your allegiance to the god of practicality and you will one day discover that you have been worshipping a false god.

"Realistic people" who pursue "practical aims" are rarely as
realistic and practical, in the long run of life, as the dreamers
who pursue only their dreams.

—Hans Selye

Yes, leaving your boat chained to the dock appears easier and safer than setting sail in uncharted waters; yet the first choice leads to stagnation while the second leads to salvation.

A ship is safe in harbor, but that is not what a ship is for.

—Thomas Aquinas

Fear not. You are not alone. You are never alone. Pay heed to the angels whispering in your ear, urging you to take that first step in faith.

Leap and the net will appear.

—ZEN PROVERB

Trot contentedly along instead of choosing to gallop, and you will find that a safe life often comes at a steep cost.

The song that I came to sing remains unsung to this day. I have spent my days in stringing and in unstringing my instrument.

—RABINDRANATH TAGORE

You can stick your head in the sand, but know that whether or not you decide to change *your* world, the world around you will continue to advance at breakneck speed.

In a time of drastic change it is the learners who inherit the future. The learned usually find themselves equipped to live in a world that no longer exists.

—ERIC HOFFER

Safety is no friend of growth. If you steadfastly refuse to leave a job that no longer serves you, you may wake up one day to discover that you have become obsolete.

If you don't like change, you're going to like irrelevance even less.

—GENERAL ERIC SHINSEKI

Even worse, you will have denied yourself experiences that would have broadened your horizons and deepened your awareness and self-knowledge.

To dare is to lose one's footing momentarily. To not dare is to lose one's self.

—SØREN KIERKEGAARD

Worse yet, a long history of avoiding challenges prevents you from developing the inner resources needed to deal with the greater challenges that are sure to follow.

We do not fail to dare because [hardships] are difficult, but they are difficult because we do not dare.

—Lucius Annaeus Seneca

True safety lies not in standing still in a futile attempt to protect what cannot be protected, but in bravely pursuing the life you envision when you close your eyes and dare to dream.

Running from safety is the only way to make your last word Yes!

—Richard Bach

It is a virtuous circle. The greater your courage and confidence, the more determined you are to materialize the career that ceaselessly calls your name; the more you apply yourself to learning and mastering new skills, the greater your self-awareness; the farther you travel down the path of self-discovery, the greater your fortitude and self-reliance.

Success is not to be pursued; it is to be attracted by the person you become.

—Jim Rohn

REWARDS AND REGRETS

It becomes especially challenging to follow your heart when you are well established in another career, nestled snugly in your comfort zone, enjoying a comfortable lifestyle.

Or have you only comfort, and the lust for comfort, that stealthy thing that enters the house a guest, and then becomes a host, and then a master?

—Kahlil Gibran

You may tell yourself that you have done everything right, that you have followed all the rules and are entitled to enjoy your hard-earned rewards. All of that may be true. But if your heart still aches for meaning and purpose, the trappings of your success may be equal parts paradise and prison.

*The moment that any life, however good, stifles you, you may be
sure it isn't your real life.*

—ARTHUR CHRISTOPHER BENSON

Ignore the yearning in your soul, and your inner voice grows ever louder and more insistent, echoing that you are marking time, that your talent is being wasted, that you are capable of so much more.

*Vocations which we wanted to pursue, but didn't, bleed, like
colors, on the whole of our existence.*

—HONORÉ DE BALZAC

Every day in which you go through the motions of an unimaginative, uninspired life is another brick to be added to your soul-deadening shrine to mediocrity.

*To try is to risk failure. But risks must be taken, because the
greatest risk in life is to risk nothing. The person who risks
nothing, does nothing, has nothing, is nothing, and becomes
nothing. He may avoid suffering and sorrow, but he simply
cannot learn and feel and change and grow and love and
live.*

—LEO BUSCAGLIA

At the age of forty, to the astonishment of the New York publishing community, Phillip Moffitt honored his intuitive guidance by abandoning his professional identity as CEO and editor-in-chief of *Esquire* magazine to seek greater joy, meaning, and authenticity.

*To the transformed self, as to the artist, success is never a place to
stay, only a momentary reward. Joy is in risking, in making new.*

—MARILYN FERGUSON

After selling *Esquire*, Moffitt had no idea what to do next. All he knew was that a career measured by magazine sales would leave him with more regrets than rewards.

> *I'd rather be a man who has nothing but has it all, than a man*
> *who has it all but has nothing.*
>
> —CICERO LEONARD

As his path unfolded, Moffitt found peace and purpose as a Buddhist meditation teacher and as founder of Life Balance Institute, a nonprofit organization devoted to helping people lead more balanced, meaningful lives.

> *The resistance to change one's life when you're successful is*
> *incredible. It means giving up something known, to take the*
> *chance of achieving something unknown that will provide greater*
> *satisfaction. This resistance is why most people only change their*
> *life as a result of failure. That's really unfortunate. Life is so short*
> *and offers such diversity that repeating anything for a lifetime, no*
> *matter how successful, is ultimately a failure in imagination.*
>
> —PHILLIP MOFFITT

Sacrifice your dreams to the false gods of wealth, fame, and power, and you might as well have auctioned off your soul to the highest bidder.

> *I would be the least among men with dreams and the desire to*
> *fulfill them, rather than the greatest with no dreams and no desires.*
>
> —KAHLIL GIBRAN

Life demands of all of us: *Pay me now or pay me later.* The longer you wait to pursue your passion, the greater the cost.

> *You don't have to fight to live as you wish. Live as you wish and*
> *pay whatever price is required.*
>
> —RICHARD BACH

Train yourself to fear regret more than failure. Fill your dreams with *What is to be*, not *What might have been*.

Don't fear failure so much that you refuse to try new things. The saddest summary of a life contains three descriptions: could have, might have, and should have.

—LOUIS EUGENE BOONE

When the mountain you need to climb seems to grow higher by the day, tell yourself that your anxiety will pale in comparison to the anguish you will surely feel in the years to come—when you face yourself in the mirror and admit that you let your dreams slip away.

Twenty years from now you will be more disappointed by the things you didn't do than by the ones you did do. So throw off the bowlines. Sail away from the safe harbor. Catch the trade winds in your sails. Explore. Dream. Discover.

—UNKNOWN

Begin pursuing your right livelihood today. Before the sun sets, do something, anything, to shrink the distance between you and your dream.

Begin doing what you want to do now. We are not living in eternity. We have only this moment, sparkling like a star in our hand—and melting like a snowflake.

—MARIE BEYNON RAY

Promising yourself, "I'll do it tomorrow," is a promise you never have to fulfill. Why? Because there is always another tomorrow. Until there isn't.

One of these days is none of these days.

—ENGLISH PROVERB

PURSUE YOUR RIGHT LIVELIHOOD
Living the Lesson

My job as operations manager for a small investment management firm provided a steady paycheck in my late twenties when I had a young family and stability was paramount.

In my early thirties, when creative writing started tugging gently and persistently on my sleeve, I threw it a bone now and then by crafting humorous bits for local radio stations and covering the comedy scene for a weekly newspaper. When I started selling ideas to major greeting card companies, the beast became insatiable and demanded daily feedings.

My priorities shifted. The left-brain work that had once satisfied me became a distraction from the right-brain work I was now consumed with. My job performance began to suffer. Soon, my responsibilities were reduced, and eventually I was shown the door. I was equal parts relieved and scared. I knew that the kind of work I needed to do no longer involved balancing bank and brokerage statements.

As I heeded the siren call of my creative muse, my new vocation began taking shape. I began writing feature articles for magazines, advertising copy for catalog companies, and brochures, ads, and other assorted pieces for local businesses.

I accepted every assignment that came my way regardless of subject matter. Delving into so many disparate topics broadened my horizons and helped me form a more cohesive view of how the business world worked.

As the quality of my writing improved, so did my discipline and professionalism. What's more, toggling between creative writing and business writing synthesized my left-brain and right-brain thinking. I felt at home in both worlds.

In time, it dawned on me that earning an income had produced an unanticipated outcome: I now had the tools and maturity I needed to pursue an even greater calling. The irony was poetic; everything I had learned in my work life had prepared me for my life's work.

PURSUE YOUR RIGHT LIVELIHOOD
Self-Reflection Questions

- How can I be confident I'm hearing the voice of Spirit instead of the voice of my own ego?

- What activities engage me so much that I lose track of time while I'm doing them?

- What would my dream job look like?

- What steps can I take now that will help me make my dream job more attainable?

- How can I get better at staying positive and optimistic about my ability to land my dream job?

- How can I train myself to view obstacles as opportunities for learning and growth?

- How can I reframe my current job as a stepping stone to the work I feel called to do?

- How will I know when I have found my right livelihood?

- How can I challenge myself to produce even higher quality work?

- What will I gain and what will I lose if I choose to stay within the safety of my comfort zone instead of advancing in the direction of my dreams?

- What excuses am I making for not pursuing a career I'm passionate about?

- What goals am I capable of achieving that I have been reluctant to pursue?

TEN

FULFILL YOUR DESTINY

Destiny is not a matter of chance, it is a matter of choice;
it is not a thing to be waited for, it is a thing to be achieved.

—WILLIAM JENNINGS BRYAN

FULFILL YOUR DESTINY

Look through God's eyes and you see that destiny has been waiting patiently for you to gain clarity about your place in the world.

> *Everyone has a special purpose, a special talent or gift to give to others, and it is your duty to discover what it is. Your special talent is God's gift to you. What you do with your talent is your gift to God.*
>
> —GAUTAMA CHOPRA

SEEKING CLARITY

You are under contract to contribute to the world in your own unique way. Until you align yourself with this purpose, you are destined to struggle.

> *We can live our lives either acting out of circumstances or acting out of a vision.*
>
> —WERNER ERHARD

According to one African tribe, each soul is born with a song that is uniquely theirs. The tribe sings each person's song to them during important life events to remind them of their identity and purpose.

> *If a man does not keep pace with his companions, perhaps it is because he hears a different drummer. Let him step to the music which he hears, however measured or far away.*
>
> —HENRY DAVID THOREAU

Your destiny may remain elusive until you shift your attention from external gratification to internal exploration.

> *Your vision will become clear only when you can look into your own heart. Who looks outside, dreams; who looks inside, awakens.*
>
> —CARL JUNG

Clues to your destiny are scattered all around you and within you. If you do not see them, you have work yet to do: study, reflect, explore. As awareness grows, the vision of who you were born to be comes into sharper focus.

> *Our destiny exercises its influence over us even when, as yet, we*
> *have not learned its nature: it is our future that lays down the law*
> *to our today.*
>
> —FRIEDRICH NIETZSCHE

Take inventory every so often. Ask yourself, *Am I where I need to be, doing what I need to be doing?*

> *The purpose of life is a life of purpose.*
>
> —ROBERT BYRNE

If your answer is yes, and your calling is clear, you are fortunate indeed. In the midst of your work, you will likely experience transcendent moments when joy spontaneously wells up in your heart from deep within.

> *Authentic empowerment is the knowing that you are on purpose,*
> *doing God's work, peacefully and harmoniously.*
>
> —WAYNE DYER

If your answer is no, whatever is distracting you and commanding your attention may actually be pointing you in the right direction.

> *Whatever keeps you from your work is your work.*
>
> —ALBERT CAMUS

You will find the clarity you seek by heeding the urgings of your heart, not the meanderings of your mind.

> *The most powerful weapon on earth is the human soul on fire.*
>
> —FERDINAND FOCH

When you are in need of guidance and inspiration, listen to your inner wisdom as it urges you to lift your gaze heavenward.

> *Far away there in the sunshine are my highest aspirations. I may not reach them: but I can look up, and see their beauty; believe in them, and try to follow where they lead.*
>
> —LOUISA MAY ALCOTT

AWARENESS DAWNS

Follow your guidance, live with integrity, and your destiny will present itself—not as an option but as a sacred obligation.

> *The mere possession of a vision is not the same as living it, nor can we encourage others with it if we do not, ourselves, understand and follow its truths. The pattern of the Great Spirit is over us all, but if we follow our own spirits from within, our pattern becomes clearer. For centuries, others have sought their visions. They prepare themselves, so that if the Creator desires them to know their life's purpose, then a vision would be revealed. To be blessed with visions is not enough . . . we must live them!*
>
> —HIGH EAGLE

Your destiny does not come *to you* to lift up your own future, it comes *through you* to uplift all of humanity.

> *Blessed is the poem that comes through me but not of me, because the sound of my own music will drown the song of Love.*
>
> —RUMI

When you are ready to know your life's purpose, it will reveal itself by taking up residence in your conscious mind.

[Profound change] may be initiated . . . not through an agonizing decision-making process but by a sudden realization or recognition: This is what I have to do. The decision arrives ready-made, so to speak. It comes through awareness, not through thinking.

—ECKHART TOLLE

Even as your destiny comes into focus, the path to fulfilling it may remain shrouded in mystery.

Sometimes the greatest destiny takes the longest to unfold.

—DANIELLE LEE

In every moment, you are presented with an infinite number of paths. With every step you take, a new set of infinite paths appears. Free will allows you to choose the path of your liking.

We are each given a block of marble when we begin a lifetime, and the tools to shape it into sculpture. . . . We can drag it behind us untouched, we can pound it to gravel, we can shape it into glory.

—RICHARD BACH

If your choice leads you down a dead-end alley, the Universe will create opportunities for you to get back on track. You will also have opportunities to wander further *off* course.

If you do not change direction, you may end up where you are heading.

—LAO TZU

The quality of your choices determines when destiny will tap you on the shoulder, as if to say, *You are ready now, it is time to begin.*

*My will shall shape the future. Whether I fail or succeed shall
be no man's doing but my own. I am the force; I can clear any
obstacle before me or I can be lost in the maze. My choice; my
responsibility; win or lose, only I hold the key to my destiny.*

—ELAINE MAXWELL

Do not protest when that day comes. Though you may not be ready to fulfill your
mission, you will be ready to begin. Otherwise, destiny would not have come calling.

Why always, "not yet"? Do flowers in spring say, "Not yet"?

—NORMAN DOUGLAS

Honoring your sacred contract—the life plan you consented to before incarnating—
may require you to embrace uncertainty and boldness as the dearest of friends.

*It takes courage to push yourself to places that you have never
been before . . . to test your limits . . . to break through barriers.
And the day came when the risk it took to remain tight inside
the bud was more painful than the risk it took to blossom.*

—ANAÏS NIN

To live your grandest destiny, to wear out rather than rust out, you *must* become what
you *can* become.

*The deepest personal defeat suffered by human beings is
constituted by the difference between what one was capable of
becoming and what one has in fact become.*

—ASHLEY MONTAGU

You were blessed with a dream that you might live joyously and purposefully. You were
graced with an indestructible spirit and an indomitable heart that you might pursue
your dream with equal parts reverence and reckless abandon.

*If I could only remember that the days were not bricks to be laid
row on row, to be built into a solid house, where one might dwell
in safety and peace, but only food for the fires of the heart, the fires
which keep the poet alive as the citizen never lives, but which burn
all the roofs of security!*

— EDMUND WILSON

Fearlessly cast aside any self-imposed limitations and preconceived notions and stand ready to answer destiny's call.

*We must be willing to give up the life we've planned, so as to have
the life that is waiting for us.*

—JOSEPH CAMPBELL

ANGELS POINT THE WAY

From the moment it first pierces your awareness, your calling is as much a part of you as your heartbeat.

*From the beginning I had a sense of destiny, as though my life was
assigned to me by fate and had to be fulfilled. This gave me an
inner security, and, though I could never prove it to myself, it
proved itself to me. I did not have this certainty, it had me.*

—CARL JUNG

As you come into alignment with your life's work, you will be given glimpses of what heaven expects from you.

*Ultimately, man should not ask what the meaning of his life is, but
rather he must recognize that it is he who is asked. In a word,
each man is questioned by life; and he can only answer to life by
answering for his own life; to life he can only respond by being
responsible.*

—VIKTOR FRANKL

If your intent is pure and your trust in the Universe complete, you will be intuitively guided to take the steps necessary to bring your vision to fruition.

> *Vision is not enough; it must be combined with venture. It is not enough to stare up the steps; we must step up the stairs.*
>
> —VACLAV HAVEL

The stars align when what you *want* to do is what you *have* to do. Angels point the way and sweep obstacles from your path.

> *Fate itself is like a wonderful wide fabric in which every thread is guided by an infinitely tender hand and laid alongside another thread and is held and supported by a hundred others.*
>
> —RAINER MARIA RILKE

In harmony with Divine Will, your choices become unlimited, your joy becomes uncontainable, and your destiny becomes unstoppable.

> *The possibilities are unlimited as long as you are true to your life's purpose.*
>
> —MARCIA WIEDER

ANSWERING THE CALL

Clarity about your life's work triggers an enduring call to action. You apply a laser-like focus, becoming more productive and proficient.

> *The further we advance, the more difficult and the more important becomes our part in the symphony of life; and the more conscious we are of this responsibility, the more efficient we become in accomplishing our task.*
>
> —HAZRAT INAYAT KHAN

Devotion to your destiny liberates you from the rhythms and routines of an ordinary life.

> *Every sort of mastery is an increase of one's freedom.*
>
> —HENRI FRÉDÉRIC AMIEL

No longer held hostage by the expectations of an unsympathetic world, you answer only to the authority of the voice that speaks to you through your intuitive guidance.

> *Most people see what is, and never see what can be.*
>
> —ALBERT EINSTEIN

The prize is not the culmination of your work, but the work itself. With discipline and devotion, you faithfully answer the call that you alone can hear.

> *You must act as if it is impossible to fail.*
>
> —ASHANTI (WEST AFRICAN) PROVERB

Immersing yourself in your life's work can be exhilarating, but strive to stay grounded. Temper your passion with practicality.

> *It is a mistake to try to look too far ahead. The chain of destiny*
> *can only be grasped one link at a time.*
>
> —WINSTON CHURCHILL

Make plans but stay flexible. Practice stillness, presence, and infinite patience, for the road ahead flows through uncharted territory.

> *Maps are useless where you're going, because the territory ahead is*
> *constantly shifting. You might as well try to map flowing water.*
>
> —DEEPAK CHOPRA

DREAM ON

Nurture your dream. Become one with it. Know that every dream, no matter how insignificant it may sound to others, is a sacred agreement between you and God.

> *Every calling is great when greatly pursued.*
>
> —OLIVER WENDELL HOLMES

Your destiny is nothing more than the organic unfolding of a divine promise. The moment you climb aboard your dream and take aim for the farthest reaches of the sky, you set in motion the effortless manifestation of your grandest vision.

> *Act and God will act!*
>
> —JOAN OF ARC

No matter where your heart leads you, no matter where your imagination takes you, God will be there waiting.

> *You can never outdream God.*
>
> —MELISSA GUYTON

Where there are dreams, there is hope. Where there is hope, there is the recognition that there is something worth hoping for.

> *In the depth of your hopes and desires lies your silent knowledge of the beyond;*
> *And like seeds dreaming beneath the snow your heart dreams of spring.*
>
> —KAHLIL GIBRAN

Whatever is worth dreaming of and hoping for is worth working toward. Destiny demands that the dreamer must do and the doer must dream.

If you have built castles in the air, your work need not be lost; that is where they should be. Now put the foundations under them.

—HENRY DAVID THOREAU

Use the hammer and chisel of persistence to sculpt your dream today and you will find the courage and confidence to apply yourself even more diligently tomorrow.

You must not let your life run in the ordinary way; do something that nobody else has done, something that will dazzle the world.

—PARAMAHANSA YOGANANDA

Your dream was not divinely designed for instant gratification. Your growth while pursuing your dream is every bit as important as its ultimate fulfillment.

Dreams always come one or two sizes too big so you can grow into them.

—DAN CLARK

With gratitude and humility, do what you can with the talent you have, knowing that all destinies are equal in God's eyes.

Use what talents you possess: the woods would be very silent if no birds sang there except those that sang best.

—HENRY VAN DYKE

Your skills were designed to perfectly correspond with your circumstances and yours alone.

In the world to come I shall not be asked, "Why were you not Moses?" I shall be asked, "Why were you not Zusya?"

—RABBI ZUSYA

Surrender joyously to your destiny and give of yourself until you have nothing more to give.

I would like to believe when I die that I have given myself away
like a tree that sows seed every spring and never counts the loss,
because it is not loss, it is adding to future life. It is the tree's way
of being. Strongly rooted perhaps, but spilling out its treasure on
the wind.

—MAY SARTON

Become one with your dream and you will live with peace and purpose all the days of your life.

Hold fast to dreams
For if dreams die
Life is a broken-winged bird
That cannot fly.

—LANGSTON HUGHES

A MIGHTY PURPOSE

The more ardently you throw yourself into your life's work, the more effortless the work becomes.

If a great thing can be done at all, it can be done easily. But it is
in that kind of ease with which a tree blossoms after long years
of gathered strength.

—JOHN RUSKIN

As your mastery deepens, so too does your understanding of the role you came here to play, the work you came here to do, and the urgency of your mission.

Travelers, it is late.
Life's sun is going to set.
During these brief days that you have strength,
be quick and spare no effort of your wings.

—RUMI

Your destiny takes root in your mind, body, and soul, and you methodically reconfigure your life so that your calling becomes priority one.

> What I must do is all that concerns me, not what the people think.
> This rule, equally arduous in actual and in intellectual life, may
> serve for the whole distinction between greatness and meanness.
> It is the harder because you will always find those who think they
> know what is your duty better than you know it. It is easy in the
> world to live after the world's opinion; it is easy in solitude to live
> after our own; but the great man is he who in the midst of the
> crowd keeps with perfect sweetness the independence of solitude.
>
> —Ralph Waldo Emerson

You continue to pursue your career and life goals, but only insofar as they contribute to and are in harmony with your overarching soul goals.

> Be above it! Make the world serve your purpose, but do not
> serve it.
>
> —Johann Wolfgang von Goethe

The days become more precious, and every morning you long to taste the sweet satisfaction of advancing your life's work.

> Your work is to discover your work and then with all your heart to
> give yourself to it.
>
> —Buddha

Heed destiny's soul call and your day's work will conclude with the sweet caress of serenity.

> It is not known how far is the destination, but so much I know:
> That music from afar is coming to my ears.
>
> —Hafiz

As night falls, you peacefully drift off to sleep with a smile upon your lips and the tender kiss of an angel upon your brow.

This is the true joy in life, the being used for a purpose recognized by yourself as a mighty one; the being thoroughly worn out before you are thrown on the scrap heap; the being a force of Nature instead of a feverish selfish little clod of ailments and grievances complaining that the world will not devote itself to making you happy.

—GEORGE BERNARD SHAW

OBJECTIONS AND OBSTACLES

Pursuing your calling is often met with resistance from friends and loved ones who are bewildered by your desire to reinvent yourself.

Those who danced were thought to be quite insane by those who could not hear the music.

—PETER MARTYR

Yes, people closest to you are concerned for your well-being, but also for their own—you stepping out of your comfort zone nudges them out of theirs. Why? On some level, they fear that as you learn and evolve, your relationship with them will change. They are right; it will.

If there's nobody in your way, it's because you're not going anywhere.

—ROBERT F. KENNEDY

The reasons why others say you should *not* do something are often precisely the reasons why you should.

It is not the critic who counts; not the man who points out how the strong man stumbles, or where the doer of deeds could have done them better. The credit belongs to the man who is actually in the arena, whose face is marred by dust and sweat and blood; who strives valiantly; who errs and comes up short again and again, because there is no effort without error or shortcoming; but who does actually strive to do the deeds; who knows the great enthusiasms, the great devotions; who spends himself in a worthy cause; who at the best knows in the end the triumph of high achievement, and who at the worst, if he fails, at least fails while daring greatly, so that his place shall never be with those cold timid souls who know neither victory nor defeat.

—THEODORE ROOSEVELT

Do not allow others to define your capacity for greatness. What they see in you matters not; all that matters is what you see in yourself.

We judge ourselves by what we feel capable of doing, while others judge us by what we have already done.

—HENRY WADSWORTH LONGFELLOW

Only you can detect and decipher the promptings of your soul. While many will raise an eyebrow at your vision, those fortunate few with callings of their own will nod in silent fellowship.

No trumpets sound when the important decisions of our life are made. Destiny is made known silently.

—AGNES DE MILLE

Staying true to your vision in the face of ongoing criticism inevitably produces deeper self-knowledge, positive results, and deep satisfaction.

A successful person is one who can lay a firm foundation with the bricks that others throw at him or her.

—DAVID BRINKLEY

Those you care about may not realize it, but honoring your intuition by humbly and steadfastly pursuing your calling is in their best interests as well.

> *Your greatest contribution to helping other people live their*
> *destiny is for you to live your own.*
>
> —ALAN COHEN

You are modeling a heroic commitment to living harmoniously and congruently, and serving as a shining example of all that is good and right in life.

> *A very great vision is needed and the man who has it must follow*
> *it as the eagle seeks the deepest blue of the sky.*
>
> —CRAZY HORSE

With any luck, your loved ones will come to view your courageous example as a command to rise.

> *Our acts of courage beget courage in others. We never know who's*
> *watching.*
>
> —BARBARA J. WINTER

Ultimately, no matter how much criticism or how many roadblocks you encounter, the only person who can stop you from living your dream is you.

> *Take care to do what you like or you will be forced to like what*
> *you do.*
>
> —GEORGE BERNARD SHAW

Abandoning your calling is unthinkable, no matter what hazards are strewn in your way. Eyes locked on the prize, you press forward, always forward.

> *He turns not back who is bound to a star.*
>
> —LEONARDO DA VINCI

Dangers that once loomed large soften into a shimmering mirage. No matter how harsh your path appears to others, you know that what lies ahead is not danger but destiny.

> *What is necessary is never a risk.*
>
> —CARDINAL DE RETZ

RESISTING THE CALL

There are those who intuitively grasp their life's purpose but turn away from it for any number of reasons—family obligations, low self-esteem, the desire for stability.

> *A smooth life is not a victorious life.*
>
> —PARAMAHANSA YOGANANDA

Yes, there are many sensible, logical, and valid reasons why staying safe at harbor is a good idea. Write them all down. Then tear up the list, burn it, and scatter the ashes.

> *Do not lose hold of your dreams or aspirations. For if you do, you may still exist but you have ceased to live.*
>
> —HENRY DAVID THOREAU

Try as you might, you will never come up with an excuse that is good enough to justify the squandering of your God-given gifts.

> *You were born with wings. Why prefer to crawl through life?*
>
> —RUMI

The only argument that matters is this: If you turn a deaf ear to the whisper of destiny, you will never realize your potential for experiencing fulfilling peace, for you will never experience the peace that comes from fulfilling your potential.

A musician must make music, an artist must paint, a poet must write, if he is to be ultimately happy. What a man can be, he must be.

—ABRAHAM MASLOW

Lasting happiness will stay forever out of reach, waiting patiently for you to commit to a lifetime of service to a wisdom greater than your own.

Many persons have a wrong idea of what constitutes true happiness. It is not attained through self-gratification but through fidelity to a worthy purpose.

—HELEN KELLER

The key word is lifetime. You may retire from your work life but your life's work will gladden your heart until you draw your final breath.

Here is a test to find whether your mission on earth is finished: If you're alive, it isn't.

—RICHARD BACH

When you drift away from your divine purpose, you drift away from your authentic self. Peace and happiness wilt away under the hot sun of inauthenticity.

Too much sanity may be madness. And maddest of all, to see life as it is and not as it should be.

—DALE WASSERMAN

If you feel boxed in by life, know that many have risen up from far more dire conditions to stake their claim to the life they were born to lead.

People are always blaming their circumstances for what they are. I don't believe in circumstances. The people who get on in this world are the people who get up and look for the circumstances they want, and, if they can't find them, make them.

—GEORGE BERNARD SHAW

If anyone was boxed in, it was Tererai Trent. Forbidden to attend school in her rural Zimbabwe village due to her gender, Trent was married off at eleven and bore three children by the age of eighteen to a husband who beat her. She dreamed of going to America and earning a B.S., a Master's, and a Ph.D. She wrote those dreams on a piece of paper, which she placed in a scrap of tin and buried under a rock in a pasture.

> *There is a space between man's imagination and man's attainment that may only be traversed by his longing.*
>
> —KAHLIL GIBRAN

In 1998, seven years after committing her dreams to paper, Trent, her husband (who was later deported for abuse), and their five children moved to Oklahoma. After earning her B.S., Trent returned to Zimbabwe, dug up the tin and checked off that dream. She did the same after attaining her Master's in 2003, and again in 2009 when she was awarded her Ph.D. Happily remarried, she is working as an international consultant specializing in human rights and HIV prevention.

> *If you give more power and attention to your destiny rather than your history, doors will open in amazing ways.*
>
> —ALAN COHEN

Resist your life's purpose and you will never bridge the distance between your own heart and the heart of your very best self who waits patiently in the mists to welcome you home.

> *Change occurs when one becomes what she is, not when she tries to become what she is not.*
>
> —RUTH P. FREEDMAN

Shrink from your calling and you not only deprive yourself, you deprive the world of the contributions you came here to make.

> *Be ashamed to die until you have won some victory for humanity.*
>
> —HORACE MANN

Keep life's call at bay and you will never be able to tap into the full majesty of your true nature.

*What man actually needs is not a tensionless state but rather the
striving and struggling for a worthwhile goal, a freely chosen task.
What he needs is not the discharge of tension at any cost but the
call of a potential meaning waiting to be fulfilled by him.*

—VIKTOR FRANKL

With so much at stake, life will not permit you to give your destiny the cold shoulder indefinitely. Ignore your calling long enough and it will eventually surface as a need.

Aye, the willing soul Fate leads, but the unwilling drags along.

—LUCIUS ANNAEUS SENECA

Resistance is futile. Inevitably, you will find yourself at a crossroads, agonizing over which path to take.

Our destiny is frequently met in the very paths we take to avoid it.

—JEAN DE LA FONTAINE

Reinventing yourself can be intimidating, especially if you believe that destiny has been thrust upon you against your wishes.

*There are two kinds of people: Those who believe their lives are
determined by forces outside themselves, and those who believe
that their lives are determined by a Force inside themselves.*

—ALAN COHEN

Yielding to fate and satisfying your destiny is not a matter of fatalism. But convincing yourself that your destiny does not matter may be fatal to living a satisfying life.

*I do not believe in a fate that falls on men however they act; but
I do believe in a fate that falls on them unless they act.*

—G. K. CHESTERTON

Allow fear to get the best of you and it will sabotage your noblest desires and weigh you down with the awful heaviness of self-loathing and regret.

Fear is the fire that melts Icarian wings.

—FLORENCE EARLE COATES

Even if you manage to chain up the yearning of your soul in the dungeon of your denials, you cannot help but hear, in your quiet moments, the weeping of angels.

Sad will be the day for every man when he becomes absolutely contented with the life that he is living, with the thoughts that he is thinking, with the deeds that he is doing, when there is not forever beating at the doors of his soul some great desire to do something larger; which he knows that he was meant and made to do because he is the child of God.

—PHILLIPS BROOKS

TAKING CARE OF THE NOW

As destiny's call grows more urgent, and the yearning to live your dreams threatens to consume you, once-paralyzing objections and obstacles lose their power over you.

Man is so made that when anything fires his soul, impossibilities vanish.

—JEAN DE LA FONTAINE

Reclaim your spirit and celebrate your liberation from conformity. Cast your fears aside and dance with joyous abandon to the music of your heart.

Life is a great big canvas, and you should throw all the paint on it you can.

—DANNY KAYE

The life you dream of is as real as the life you now lead, provided you have the faith to imagine it and the courage to act.

> *We are very near to greatness: one step and we are safe; can we not take the leap?*
>
> —RALPH WALDO EMERSON

Dreams do not come with how-to instructions. They are, however, laden with the seeds of their own fulfillment.

> *Your job is to say yes, not how. Once you say yes, the Universe takes care of the how.*
>
> —CAROLINE MYSS

Reality is a word embraced by those who have given themselves permission to lose faith in their dreams.

> *If you have within you that faith which is truly divine, and if there is something you desire that is not in the universe, it shall be created for you.*
>
> —SWAMI SRI YUKTESWAR

Embrace your destiny and your every action will be instantly supported by the Divine force that guides and governs all creation.

> *There is one elementary truth, the ignorance of which kills countless ideas and splendid plans: that the moment one definitely commits oneself, then Providence moves too. All sorts of things occur to help one that would never otherwise have occurred. A whole stream of events issues from the decision, raising in one's favour all manner of unforeseen incidents and meetings and material assistance, which no man could have dreamt would have come his way.*
>
> —WILLIAM H. MURRAY

Saying yes to your destiny is akin to standing in front of God and solemnly pledging to do your best to be your best, to squeeze the most out of every day.

*It is easy to say no. To say yes, you have to sweat and roll up your
sleeves and plunge both hands into life up to the elbows. It is easy
to say no, even if saying no means death.*

—JEAN ANOUILH

While the Universe takes care of the *how*, your job is to take care of the *now*. Listen to your inner guidance and follow it faithfully.

*You cannot be too active as regards your own efforts; you cannot
be too dependent as regards Divine grace. Do every thing as if God
did nothing; depend upon God as if He did every thing.*

—JOHN ANGELL JAMES

Focus on the now and you will be led to the wow, for God's plan is bolder and grander than anything your imagination can dream up.

*Destiny grants us our wishes, but in its own way, in order to give
us something beyond our wishes.*

—JOHANN WOLFGANG VON GOETHE

If you have tarried, pull yourself away from your diversions, gather your strength, and step back on your path. Begin today. The world needs you at your best.

*Alas for those that never sing,
But die with all their music in them!*

—OLIVER WENDELL HOLMES

As long as you have breath, you have the power to change, to grow, to serve God—and the duty to share your hard-earned wisdom with others.

*If you genuinely have something to say, there is someone who
genuinely needs to hear it.*

—ARNOLD PATENT

It does not matter how long you have been wandering in the wilderness. Your angels have been waiting patiently to nudge you in the right direction. There is always time to make your way back home.

> *It is never too late to be what you might have been.*
>
> —GEORGE ELIOT

STEPPING FORWARD

Your destiny is rooted in everyday moments. Every thought, every choice, every act influences your life's work and shapes and defines your legacy.

> *We are not permitted to choose the frame of our destiny. But what we put into it is ours.*
>
> —DAG HAMMARSKJÖLD

Your ultimate destiny and your ultimate destination are inseparable. Every time you change your mind, you change your future.

> *The future is not someplace we are going to, but one we are creating. The paths to it are not found but created, and the activity of creating them changes both the maker and the destination.*
>
> —JOHN SCHAAR

As you step forward in faith, know that whatever brings you joy will also bring you peace.

> *I say, follow your bliss and don't be afraid, and doors will open where you didn't know they were going to be.*
>
> —JOSEPH CAMPBELL

As you do what you are called to do, you will feel a deep and abiding sense of gratitude for the opportunity to serve the world as only you can.

To be obsessed with some vision and to have the continuous opportunity of working to realize that vision could be looked upon as God's greatest gift to anyone.

—HENRY MOORE

Much may be asked of you. Do not worry if you do not feel up to the task. All that is expected is the very best you have to offer.

Life only demands from you the strength you possess.

—DAG HAMMARSKJÖLD

Welcome each new challenge that comes your way; it was divinely arranged to teach you, to strengthen you, to draw out the best within you.

I wasn't concerned about the hardships, because I always felt I was doing what I had to do, what I wanted to do and what I was destined to do.

—KATHERINE DUNHAM

Whether you see it or not, there is greatness within you. Trust that you will grow as you go.

I do not pray for a lighter load, but for a stronger back.

—PHILLIPS BROOKS

Give yourself fully to your destiny and you will discover within yourself an inexhaustible reservoir of strength, skills, and wisdom that steadily propels you toward each succeeding summit to be conquered.

It usually happens that the more faithfully a person follows the inspirations he receives, the more does he experience new inspirations which ask increasingly more of him.

—JOSEPH DE GUIBERT

Stride forward in confidence, knowing that success is assured, for you are doing the work that God has assigned to you.

One way to pick a future is to believe it's inevitable.

—RICHARD BACH

Even so, not every quest will culminate in completion and closure. Do not expect destiny to be waiting for you at journey's end in a neatly wrapped package topped with a pretty bow.

A man may fulfill the object of his existence by asking a question
he cannot answer, and attempting a task he cannot achieve.

—OLIVER WENDELL HOLMES

No matter what the result, you will have done your best to do God's work, and peace will be your faithful friend.

Commit yourself to a dream. . . . Nobody who tries to do
something great but fails is a total failure. Why? Because he can
always rest assured that he succeeded in life's most important
battle—he defeated the fear of trying.

—ROBERT H. SCHULLER

On your deathbed, are you going to regret that you led a dull, uneventful, predictable life?

Our repugnance to death increases in proportion to our
consciousness of having lived in vain.

—WILLIAM HAZLITT

Or will you be at peace, grateful that you summoned the courage to follow your heart, chase your dreams, and live a life without limits? Choose meaning. Choose purpose. Choose life.

When you are inspired by some great purpose, some extraordinary
project, all your thoughts break their bonds. Your mind transcends
limitations, your consciousness expands in every direction, and
you find yourself in a new, great, and wonderful world. Dormant
forces, faculties, and talents become alive; and you discover yourself
to be a greater person by far than you ever dreamed yourself to be.

—PATANJALI

FULFILL YOUR DESTINY
Living the Lesson

By my fortieth birthday, I knew what my life's work would be: encouraging and inspiring people to live more positive, loving lives. I began teaching a class on affirmations and spiritual principles at Pathways, a health crisis resource center in Minneapolis. Beyond that my vision was foggy at best.

Slowly, the fog began to lift. First, I realized that I was to write a book on spirituality based on the content of my Pathways class. A few years later, it occurred to me that asking my favorite authors to tell me about a life-changing experience would be a fun project. Shortly after that, Tires Plus founder Tom Gegax asked me to write a business book with him.

Soon after starting work on Tom's book, the sunlight of Divine inspiration burned off the lingering fog and all became clear: I was to write a trilogy of books. First would come *The Big Book of Small Business*. Next would be *Sixty Seconds: One Moment Changes Everything*, a collection of profound, uplifting stories from prominent people. And finally, this book, the most challenging—and most rewarding—of the three.

Ironically, I was to write the books in reverse order of when they entered my consciousness. First would come the business book, which forced me to upgrade my writing skills. Next, the book of life-changing stories expanded my wisdom and deepened my understanding of spiritual principles. Finally, the book you're now holding is the culmination of all that I have learned.

Ten years have passed since I first received my trilogy "assignment," and all has unfolded as I saw it would. I am now gaining clarity about the next phase of my life— getting out in the world and meeting people face to face instead of sitting home alone typing on my laptop.

Fulfilling my destiny is humbling work. Although I am the writer of these three books, I feel as if a power greater than myself has been working through me to bring this wisdom into the world. I was simply chosen to be the instrument, for which I am deeply grateful. Wherever destiny leads me next, I will be honored to go.

FULFILL YOUR DESTINY
Self-Reflection Questions

- How much clarity do I have about my life's purpose?

- How can I do a better job of preparing myself to answer destiny's call?

- How can I work more cooperatively with Divine Intelligence to advance my life's work?

- How can I restructure my life so that pursuing my calling is priority one?

- What are some personal and career goals I had that are no longer as meaningful now that I hear destiny calling my name?

- How can I prepare myself to handle resistance from family and friends who think I should live more conservatively or traditionally?

- In what ways am I allowing others to hinder me from following my dream?

- What rewards will come from staying true to myself in the face of ongoing criticism?

- How is my peace of mind tied to how ardently I follow my destiny?

- If I turn my back on my calling, what will I be risking?

- How are my actions today defining my legacy?

- Why do I feel so exhilarated when I am acting in harmony with my destiny?

ELEVEN

YOUR MIND IS A MAGNET

Have the courage to take your own thoughts seriously,
for they will shape you.

—GERALD HOLTON

YOUR MIND IS A MAGNET

When nurtured with attention and intention, your every thought will find full expression in the physical world.

> *By believing passionately in something which still does not exist, we create it. The nonexistent is whatever we have not sufficiently desired.*
>
> —NIKOS KAZANTZAKIS

LIKE ATTRACTS LIKE

Your thoughts are not just gossamer wisps of nothingness that uneventfully dance and dissolve in the uncharted recesses of your mind.

> *I hold it true that thoughts are things*
> *Endowed with bodies, breath, and wings.*
>
> —ELLA WHEELER WILCOX

Your thoughts (expressions of your individual consciousness) immediately connect you to all of creation through the Unified Field (the omnipresent expression of collective consciousness that includes your "individual" consciousness). This exchange of information mimics the exchange of energy yet operates beyond the boundaries of space and time.

> *Every thought you think reverberates across the universe touching everyone and everything.*
>
> —KATE NOWAK

Ultimately, where your attention goes, "energy" flows. Since every action generates a reaction, every thought produces a response.

> *There are no idle thoughts. All thinking produces form at some level.*
>
> —A COURSE IN MIRACLES

Like energy attracts like energy. Therefore, whatever you think about, you attract into your life.

> *Your thoughts bring your experiences, just like a waiter obediently bringing your order to you. The waiter doesn't argue with you when you order something unhealthy from the menu. He merely nods and brings it to you.*
>
> —DOREEN VIRTUE

The state of your reality, then, is a reflection of your state of mind, which is determined by the quality of your thoughts.

> *The mind fits the world and shapes it as a river fits and shapes its own banks.*
>
> —ANNIE DILLARD

The urgency implicit in this realization cannot be overstated: If you do not control your thoughts, they will control you.

> *Watch your thoughts, for they become words.*
> *Watch your words, for they become actions.*
> *Watch your actions, for they become habits.*
> *Watch your habits, for they become character.*
> *Watch your character, for it becomes your destiny.*
>
> —BUDDHA

CAUSE AND EFFECT

How you see the world determines what you attract. Change the way you look at life and life will change in amazing ways.

> *Our life is shaped by our mind; we become what we think. Suffering follows an evil thought as the wheels of a cart follow the oxen that draw it. Joy follows a pure thought like a shadow that never leaves.*
>
> —BUDDHA

Embody a loving, positive attitude, and you act as a magnet to draw loving, positive people and experiences into your life.

> *Say you are well, or all is well with you,*
> *And God shall hear your words and make them true.*
>
> —ELLA WHEELER WILCOX

Throw mental daggers at your boss and you will continue to be the target of his or her fault-finding missions, never imagining that you are contributing to your own misery.

> *The world thus tends to be your mirror. A peaceful person lives in*
> *a peaceful world. An angry person creates an angry world.*
>
> —KEN KEYES, JR.

This Universal Law is at work in your own life whether or not you are conscious of it. Every thought, every choice, has repercussions.

> *Choice of attention—to pay attention to this and ignore that—is*
> *to the inner life what choice of action is to the outer. In both cases,*
> *a man is responsible for his choice and must accept the*
> *consequences, whatever they may be.*
>
> —W. H. AUDEN

Indeed, your thoughts are like paving stones, shaping a path into a future of your own making.

> *If you want sweet dreams, you've got to live a sweet life.*
>
> —BARBARA KINGSOLVER

Expect nothing but the best to happen, and the Universe interprets your faith and positivity as an invitation to shower you with abundance.

> *Wake up every morning expecting blessings from God and you will*
> *not be able to count them by the end of the day.*
>
> —UNKNOWN

Fear the worst and you might as well send an engraved invitation to the Universe to conjure up the very circumstances that torment your troubled mind.

> *The more wary you are of danger, the more likely you are to meet it.*
>
> —JEAN DE LA FONTAINE

Grow weary of the world and you will experience nothing but the mundane and monotonous. Retain a childlike joy and you will be surrounded at all times by the magical and miraculous.

> *The days . . . come and go like muffled and veiled figures, sent from a distant friendly party; but they say nothing; and if we do not use the gifts they bring, they carry them as silently away.*
>
> —RALPH WALDO EMERSON

SERVICE vs. SELF-GRATIFICATION

Life shifts dramatically when you figure out how to make the law of attraction work *for* you instead of *against* you.

> *The only thing that holds you back from getting what you want is paying attention to what you don't want.*
>
> —ESTHER HICKS

Cultivate a prosperity consciousness by visualizing yourself in the circumstances you desire.

> *Both abundance and scarcity are inner states that manifest as your reality.*
>
> —ECKHART TOLLE

You are reinforcing a scarcity consciousness—and attracting the opposite of what you want—when you picture yourself in situations you are trying to avoid.

You can never get enough of what you don't want.

—WAYNE DYER

A caveat: No matter how skillfully you cultivate the magnet of your mind, you will not be satisfied with what you attract until you align your will with Divine Will, until you are ready to serve the world instead of your own desires.

The turning point of life is when you recognize the relationship between consciousness and results.

—ALAN COHEN

Devote your life to the pursuit of self-gratification, and the compartments of your heart reserved for peace and joy will forever remain arid and hollow.

He who never sacrificed a present to a future good, or a personal to a general one, can speak of happiness only as the blind do of colors.

—HORACE MANN

Place your attention on desires that do not serve your higher purpose, and you wander off your spiritual path into the forests of stagnation.

The quality of one's life depends on the quality of attention. Whatever you pay attention to will grow more important in your life. There is no limit to the kinds of changes that awareness can produce.

—DEEPAK CHOPRA

Your future glows ever more brightly the more pure your desire to be a positive force for good in the world.

Nature magically suits the man to his fortunes, by making these the fruit of his character.

—RALPH WALDO EMERSON

PATTERNS OF PERCEPTION

Since your thoughts define how you show up in the world, the surest way to change who you are is to change the pattern of your thoughts.

> *Nurture your mind with great thoughts. To believe in the heroic makes heroes.*
>
> —BENJAMIN DISRAELI

You may believe that the world is menacing and chaotic, that no one can be trusted, that life is an endless series of bad breaks and hard knocks. After all, rare is the person who has not been bullied at school, fired from a job, or felt rejected and even humiliated in the course of romantic pursuits.

> *People seem not to see that their opinion of the world is also a confession of character.*
>
> —RALPH WALDO EMERSON

Or, you may trust that the Universe is benevolent and orderly, that most people are compassionate and good-hearted, that every day offers countless opportunities to celebrate life and extend kindness to others.

> *The most fundamental question we can ever ask ourselves is whether or not the universe we live in is friendly or hostile.*
>
> —ALBERT EINSTEIN

Each of these outlooks will attract the people, situations, and events that reinforce the worldview of the person doing the attracting.

> *The only reason the same thing keeps happening is that you keep focusing on what happened.*
>
> —ALAN COHEN

What's more, each occurrence will strengthen that person's beliefs, thereby providing even more "proof" that the way they perceive the world is the way the world actually is.

> *Man's mind is a mirror of a universe that mirrors man's mind.*
>
> —JOSEPH CHILTON PEARCE

Their core beliefs will always be perpetuated because people tend to "see" only what they believe and are comfortable with.

> *Everyone hears only what he understands.*
>
> —JOHANN WOLFGANG VON GOETHE

Indeed, when two people with opposing viewpoints witness the same event, they will often interpret it in opposite ways to make it fit their preconceived notions.

> *Life is what we make it, and the world is what we make it. The eyes*
> *of the cheerful and of the melancholy man are fixed upon the same*
> *creation; but very different are the aspects which it bears to them.*
>
> —ALBERT PIKE

Many of us cling ferociously to our worldview because our very identity—how we think, act, and relate to others—is built on the foundation of how we think the world works. Any evidence to the contrary must therefore be sacrificed on the altar of self-preservation.

> *Once someone is sure that the way in which he or she sees the*
> *world is the way things are, then he or she perceives any differences*
> *of opinion as threatening. This results in a closed system and a*
> *rigid approach to life in which all differences must be discounted,*
> *disparaged, or destroyed.*
>
> —ANNE WILSON SCHAEF

When belief hardens into certainty and perception is mistaken for fact, it is only natural to conclude that any reasonable person would agree with our assessment.

What we wish, we readily believe, and what we ourselves think, we imagine others think also.

—JULIUS CAESAR

Those who stridently proclaim that their way is the right and only way are most in need of introspection and least likely to pursue it.

Some not only have closed their minds to new truth, but they sit on the lid.

—DALE TURNER

The gates of wisdom will forever remain locked and bolted to those who brashly assume that only they have been issued the key.

Many men would have attained to wisdom had they not supposed they had already done so.

—LUCIUS ANNAEUS SENECA

You live more consciously as soon as you recognize that your perception of reality is uniquely yours, that the world you live in has a population of one.

Each of us makes his own weather, determines the color of the skies in the emotional universe which he inhabits.

—FULTON J. SHEEN

THE IMPACT OF ATTITUDE

The moment you realize that your outlook on life has shaped every aspect of your existence is the moment you glimpse the incalculable power of your attitude.

Words can never adequately convey the incredible impact of our attitude toward life. The longer I live the more convinced I become that life is 10 percent what happens to us and 90 percent how we respond to it. I believe the single most significant decision I can make on a day-to-day basis is my choice of attitude. It is more important than my past, my education, my bankroll, my successes or failures, fame or pain, what other people think of me or say about me, my circumstances, or my position. Attitude keeps me going or cripples my progress. It alone fuels my fire or assaults my hope. When my attitudes are right, there's no barrier too high, no valley too deep, no dream too extreme, no challenge too great for me.

—CHARLES R. SWINDOLL

Train yourself to monitor your thoughts. When you can observe your thoughts as if they were someone else's, you move from self-absorption to self-awareness.

You are not what you think you are, but what you think, you are.

—NORMAN VINCENT PEALE

Start with your first thought of the day. What runs through your mind upon awakening?

Do not say, "It is morning," and dismiss it with a name of yesterday. See it for the first time as a new-born child that has no name.

—RABINDRANATH TAGORE

As your feet hit the floor, do you dread what lies ahead or are you excited about the brand-new day?

The choice is up to you: It can either be "Good morning, God!" or "Good God, morning."

—WAYNE DYER

Connect the dots between the quality of your daily thoughts and the quality of your daily life, and you will see that moaning about your troubles only makes them more difficult to overcome.

> *If your everyday life seems poor, don't blame it; blame yourself; admit to yourself that you are not enough of a poet to call forth its riches.*
>
> —RAINER MARIA RILKE

A self-defeating attitude becomes a self-fulfilling prophecy. When you do not produce a desired outcome, your self-esteem takes a hit. The lower your self-esteem, the less likely you will produce a desired outcome.

> *Our lack of confidence is not the result of difficulty; the difficulty comes from our lack of confidence.*
>
> —LUCIUS ANNAEUS SENECA

When a negative thought enters your mind, mentally fling it away and replace it with a positive one. With enough practice, thinking more positively becomes second nature.

> *Change your thoughts and you change your world.*
>
> —NORMAN VINCENT PEALE

GIVING EQUALS RECEIVING

Perhaps the best way to get what you want is to give away a portion of what you already have. The message you are sending to the Universe when you give to others is: *I have access to an endless supply of abundance.*

> *To receive everything, one must open one's hands and give.*
>
> —TAISEN DESHIMARU

Since like energy attracts like energy, the Universe responds to your prosperity consciousness by bringing you more of what you have given away.

*If you knew what I know about the power of giving, you would not let
a single meal pass without sharing it in some way.*

—BUDDHA

Keeping the abundance of the Universe circulating is foundational to the practice of tithing. Seen through God's eyes, giving and receiving are one and the same.

*At the deepest level, there is no giver, no gift, and no recipient ... only
the universe rearranging itself.*

—JON KABAT-ZINN

The law of attraction operates in direct proportion to your purity of intent. You will receive more of what you give away only if you offer it with a loving heart and ask nothing in return.

*If you circle your wagons to protect what you have, you can't
venture forward to what you desire.*

—SUZANNE ZOGLIO

Certainly, anyone who is socially adept will at least acknowledge a gift. But when you expect anything more than a grateful nod or a smile, your gift ceases to be a gift and becomes a business transaction.

There is no grace in a benefit that sticks to the fingers.

—LUCIUS ANNAEUS SENECA

When the motive behind your gift is not pure, you disrupt the flow of energy that otherwise would deliver more abundance into your life.

*Whenever I expect something in return, then my inner peace gets
disturbed. And I expect something in return only when I've forgotten
that peace comes from within.*

—DR. DEAN ORNISH

Temper your generosity with common sense. Put yourself in the position of desperately needing what you have just given away and you will continue to desperately need it. Becoming a burden to others defeats the purpose of your gift.

> *Sir, he throws away his money, without thought and without merit.*
> *I do not call a tree generous, that sheds its fruit at every breeze.*
>
> —SAMUEL JOHNSON

You will know what, when, and how much to give by listening to your intuition instead of your ego.

> *It is well to give when asked, but it is better to give unasked,*
> *through understanding.*
>
> —KAHLIL GIBRAN

COMPLETING THE CIRCLE

Generosity is not confined to the sharing of material wealth. A generous spirit finds endless ways to express itself.

> *If you have much, give of your wealth; if you have little, give of your*
> *heart.*
>
> —ARAB PROVERB

Perhaps the most loving and meaningful gift you can give to another is your unhurried time and undivided attention.

> *Rings and other jewels are not gifts, but apologies for gifts. The only*
> *gift is a portion of thyself.*
>
> —RALPH WALDO EMERSON

Follow the wisdom of your heart as it reaches out in joy to share all the beauty and love it possesses with the heart of another.

Give as the rose gives perfume, because it is its own nature, utterly unconscious of giving.

—SWAMI VIVEKANANDA

Give freely of what you have and you will know a joy and satisfaction that transcends any pleasure derived from material possessions.

He is no fool who gives what he cannot keep to gain what he cannot lose.

—JIM ELLIOT

Giving away what you do not need unclutters both your outer and inner environments and creates more space in your life for other blessings to flow through.

People who give are given to.

—MIKE DOOLEY

By definition, what is given must be received. Turn down a well-intentioned gift and you inadvertently break this circle of Divine energy.

To receive a present handsomely and in a right spirit, even when you have none to give in return, is to give one in return.

—LEIGH HUNT

Graciously and gratefully accept every gift and compliment, or you impede the circulation of loving, caring intentions in your life.

The gift is to the giver, and comes back most to him—it cannot fail.

—WALT WHITMAN

This empathy exercise may help: Have you ever been excited about giving someone a gift only to have it refused because the recipient did not feel worthy of receiving it? Remember how disappointed you felt? That is how someone else feels when you yourself protest that a gift is not necessary. Why would you choose to make someone feel that way?

It is not the shilling that I give you that counts, but the warmth that it carries with it from my hand.

—MIGUEL DE UNAMUNO

GIVING IS UNCONDITIONAL

Whatever you own that you cannot bear to part with, owns you. As soon as you vow never to lose it, you have lost yourself in it.

He who obtains has little. He who scatters has much.

—LAO TZU

Eventually, your most prized possessions will fall into the hands of others no matter how tightly you clutch them to your bosom.

What I spent, I had; what I kept, I lost; what I gave, I have still.

—OLD EPITAPH

Every item you own is a hungry beast demanding some portion of your time, attention, and psychic energy.

Have nothing in your houses which you do not know to be useful or believe to be beautiful.

—WILLIAM MORRIS

Giving an object away not only liberates you from the burden of owning it, you simplify your life and receive a more valuable, more permanent gift in return.

While you have a thing it can be taken from you. But when you give it, you have given it. No robber can take it from you. It is yours then for ever when you have given it. It will be yours always. That is to give.

—JAMES JOYCE

In truth, ownership is an illusion; you can no more own a material object than you can own the waves in the ocean or the clouds in the sky.

> Let the stronger man give to the man whose need is greater; let him gaze upon the lengthening path. For riches roll like the wheels of a chariot, turning from one to another.
>
> —RIG VEDA

The instant you give away a possession, your ownership of it ceases as if it had never been.

> How others deal with gifts you've given is not your decision, but theirs.
>
> —RICHARD BACH

True giving is an act of selfless service. The worthiness of the recipient and the consequences of your giving are not your concern.

> You often say, "I would give, but only to the deserving."
> The trees in your orchard say not so, nor the flocks in your pasture.
> They give that they may live, for to withhold is to perish.
> Surely he who is worthy to receive his days and his nights, is worthy of all else from you.
> And he who has deserved to drink from the ocean of life deserves to fill his cup from your little stream. . . .
> For in truth it is life that gives unto life—while you, who deem yourself a giver, are but a witness.
>
> —KAHLIL GIBRAN

True giving has no ulterior motives. You do it because sharing what you have is the right and natural thing to do.

Then there are those who give without any remembrance of what they have done. They are like the vine that has brought forth a cluster of grapes, and having once borne its delicious fruit, seeks nothing more. As the horse that runs its race, the hound that tracks its game, and the bee that hives its honey, so should a man be when he has done an act of kindness—not seeking reward, not proclaiming his virtues, but passing on to the next act, as the vine passes on to bear another cluster of summer grapes.

—MARCUS AURELIUS

Yes, you know that your generosity will be karmically rewarded, but that knowledge in no way influences your actions.

If you help others, you will be helped, perhaps tomorrow, perhaps in one hundred years, but you will be helped. Nature must pay off the debt. . . . It is a mathematical law and all life is mathematics.

—GEORGES IVANOVICH GURDJIEFF

MAKING A DIFFERENCE

The law of attraction also applies to groups. When hundreds, thousands, or even millions of people share a mindset, the combined power of their thoughts can alter their physical environment as well as their collective emotional well-being.

Hope is like a road in the country; there was never a road, but when many people walk on it, the road comes into existence.

—LIN YUTANG

That is why Neale Donald Walsch wrote in *Conversations with God, Book 1* that "fate" can be viewed as an acronym for "From All Thoughts Everywhere."

To say my fate is not tied to your fate is like saying, "Your end of the boat is sinking."

—HUGH DOWNS

This premise has tremendously exciting implications. How many times have you heard or thought that one person cannot make a difference in this world? That global peace is in the hands of politicians, many of whom are corrupt or ineffectual? That the only response to suffering and injustice is righteous anger?

> *Everyone thinks of changing the world, but no one thinks of changing himself.*
>
> —LEO TOLSTOY

Negative energy rabidly feeds on other negative energy, so by railing against a political candidate or engaging in a violent protest, you are unwittingly making the object of your scorn even more imposing and powerful.

> *Fighting any adverse condition only increases its power over us.*
>
> —ERNEST HOLMES

You are also doing no favors for the world at large. Retributive rage generates vast amounts of negative energy, thereby weakening collective consciousness.

> *Returning hate for hate multiplies hate, adding deeper darkness to a night already devoid of stars. Darkness cannot drive out darkness; only light can do that. Hate cannot drive out hate; only love can do that.*
>
> —MARTIN LUTHER KING, JR.

Instead of futilely expending energy and waiting for others to effect change, reclaim your power and be an agent of change, effective immediately.

> *All that you fight weakens you. All that you are for empowers you.*
>
> —WAYNE DYER

Pour your energy into what you support (peace) rather than what you oppose (war), and the world can indeed be transformed.

> *Become peace, for that is the attractor of peace to the world.*
>
> —THE ESSENES

As you raise your own consciousness, you become the Johnny Appleseed of harmonious living, joyously sowing seeds of love and kindness wherever you go.

> When I was a young man, I wanted to change the world. I found it
> was difficult to change the world, so I tried to change my nation.
> When I found I couldn't change the nation, I began to focus on my
> town. I couldn't change the town, and as an older man, I tried to
> change my family. Now, as an old man, I realize the only thing I can
> change is myself, and suddenly I realize that if long ago I had changed
> myself, I could have made an impact on my family. My family and I
> could have made an impact on our town. Their impact could have
> changed the nation and I could indeed have changed the world.
>
> —12TH CENTURY MONK

Every thought you have can make the planet a better place, because every positive, peaceful thought adds that much more loving energy to the Unified Field.

> How wonderful it is that nobody need wait a single moment before
> starting to improve the world.
>
> —ANNE FRANK

This upward tick may barely move the needle of collective consciousness but it keeps the human race moving in the right direction.

> Change yourself and you have done your part in changing the world.
> Every individual must change his own life if he wants to live in a
> peaceful world. The world cannot become peaceful unless and until
> you yourself begin to work toward peace.
>
> —PARAMAHANSA YOGANANDA

Squander your opportunities to add love and light to the world, and all of humankind will be poorer for it.

> We ourselves feel that what we are doing is just a drop in the ocean.
> But the ocean would be less because of that missing drop.
>
> —MOTHER TERESA

As more minds and hearts generate positive thoughts and loving energy, we inch ever closer to critical mass and lasting cultural change.

> *Another world is not only possible, she's on her way. Maybe many of us won't be here to greet her, but on a quiet day, if I listen very carefully, I can hear her breathing.*
>
> —ARUNDHATI ROY

Indeed, the closer you move toward enlightenment, the closer we all move toward an enlightened world.

> *A self-realized being cannot help benefiting the world. His very existence is the highest good.*
>
> —SRI RAMANA MAHARSHI

Your next loving thought may tip the scales. In his groundbreaking book, *Power vs. Force*, Dr. David R. Hawkins scientifically substantiates how the most enlightened 15 percent of the world's population counterbalances the negativity of the remaining 85 percent of the world's people.

> *We change the world not by what we say or do but as a consequence of what we have become. Thus, every spiritual aspirant serves the world.*
>
> —DR. DAVID R. HAWKINS

It is a virtuous circle. Every loving thought you contribute incrementally raises your consciousness; the higher your consciousness, the greater the impact of your contribution and the more likely it becomes that your next thought will also be a positive one.

> *The difference in power between a loving thought and a fearful thought is so enormous as to be beyond the capacity of the human imagination to easily comprehend.*
>
> —DR. DAVID R. HAWKINS

INTERCESSORY PRAYER

Recognize the power of your every thought and you understand why every intercessory prayer you offer delivers love and healing energy to the consciousness of the individual you are praying for.

> *True, whole prayer is nothing but love.*
>
> —Saint Augustine

Granted, mental and spiritual energy operate beyond the scope of what science can measure or language can explain. However, given that we can reach and affect each other through the Unified Field, energy can be considered a metaphor for the instantaneous effect of compassionate human intention.

> *Scores of experiments have verified that our thoughts and prayers do have an impact at a distance, but without the transfer of any known form of physical energy. Because mind and consciousness are nonlocal, which means they're everywhere in space and time, there's no reason for anything to go anywhere or for anything to be "sent" because it's already there.*
>
> —Dr. Larry Dossey

In several of his books, including *Healing Words* and *Reinventing Medicine*, Dr. Larry Dossey, who has spent years researching the relationship between prayer and healing, cites numerous scientific studies that strongly support the power of prayer.

> *Men may spurn our appeals, reject our message, oppose our arguments, despise our persons, but they are helpless against our prayers.*
>
> —J. Sidlow Baxter

An intercessory prayer, when uttered with loving intention and unbroken attention, may potentially be life-saving.

> *More things are wrought by prayer than this world dreams of.*
>
> —Alfred, Lord Tennyson

Yet there are so many factors in play—the recipient's karmic debts, sacred contracts, and will to live, to name a few—that your prayer may not *appear* to affect the ultimate outcome.

> *Praying men must be strong in hope, and faith, and prayer.*
>
> —E. M. BOUNDS

So why bother to pray? Because no matter what the outcome, the loving energy you transmit may ease the recipient's pain, comfort their soul, and bolster their strength and resolve.

> *The time may be delayed, the manner may be unexpected, but sooner or later, in some form or other, the answer is sure to come. Not a tear of sacred sorrow, not a breath of holy desire, poured out in prayer to God, will ever be lost; but, in God's own best time and way, it will be wafted back again in clouds of mercy, and fall in showers of blessings on you and those for whom you pray.*
>
> —WILLIAM SEYMOUR TYLER

Deep healing occurs when you initiate a loving prayer and allow Divine Intelligence to do with it what it will. In the end, every prayer you offer up serves the highest good of the person you are praying for.

> *Our prayers should be for blessings in general, for God knows best what is good for us.*
>
> —SOCRATES

Your intercessory prayer bridges any distance between you and the person you are praying for and strengthens the bond you share.

> *There is nothing that makes us love a man so much, as praying for him.*
>
> —WILLIAM LAW

We are all one spiritual family, so expressing your love for another through intercessory prayer inevitably delivers divine blessings to your own door.

He who prays for his neighbor will be heard for himself.

—THE TALMUD

ACCEPTING RESPONSIBILITY

The law of attraction is absolute. It states that you are absolutely responsible for the circumstances of your life.

> *If you want to meet someone who can fix any situation you don't*
> *like, who can bring you happiness in spite of what other people say*
> *or believe, look in a mirror, then say this magic word: "Hello."*

—RICHARD BACH

Your responsibility begins with the thoughts you think about yourself. As self-employment advocate Barbara J. Winter noted, you cannot outperform your self-image.

> *To be ambitious for wealth and yet always expecting to be poor, to be*
> *always doubting your ability to get what you long for, is like trying to*
> *reach East by traveling West. There is no philosophy which will help*
> *a man to succeed when he is always doubting his ability to do so, and*
> *thus attracting failure. . . . No matter how hard you may work for*
> *success, if your thought is saturated with the fear of failure, it will kill*
> *your efforts, neutralize your endeavors, and make success impossible.*

—ORISON SWETT MARDEN

Until you accept this responsibility, your life will be an endless loop of blaming, shaming, and complaining.

> *Until a person can say deeply and honestly, "I am what I am today*
> *because of the choices I made yesterday," that person cannot say,*
> *"I choose otherwise."*

—STEPHEN R. COVEY

Blame others for your misfortunes and you become your own worst enemy, never realizing that you are subtly engaging in acts of self-sabotage.

> *If it's never your fault, you can't take responsibility for it. If you can't take responsibility for it, you'll always be its victim.*
>
> —RICHARD BACH

Sadly, many turn away from this spiritual truth because it is easier to let things happen and blame others than to make things happen and help others.

> *The fault is in the one who blames.*
> *Spirit sees nothing to criticize.*
>
> —RUMI

This moment, and every moment, is yours to do with as you will. It is the way you spend your moments that has brought you to where you are and that will deliver you to your self-determined destination.

> *Every man is his own ancestor, and every man his own heir. He devises his own future, and he inherits his own past.*
>
> — DR. H. F. HEDGE

What can you do right now, what can you think right now, that will make today and all your tomorrows brighter?

> *I feel it now: there's a power in me to grasp and give shape to my world. I know that nothing has ever been real without my beholding it. All becoming has needed me. My looking ripens things and they come toward me, to meet and be met.*
>
> —RAINER MARIA RILKE

The choice is yours. The only thing standing between you and a brighter future is your very next thought.

> *Everyone is a self-made person, but only the successful admit it.*
>
> —UNKNOWN

YOUR MIND IS A MAGNET
Living the Lesson

I started my adult life in debt and have been scrambling to recover ever since. I don't recall thinking in terms of scarcity or prosperity; money was simply a tool that allowed me to get by for another month.

In my mid-thirties, after reading about the spiritual dynamics of financial abundance, I decided to reprogram the way I looked at money. I'm a big believer in the transformative power of affirmations (see chapter 19) so I regularly affirmed the following:

I am financially independent and free.
I always have much more money coming in than going out.
Thank you, God, for bringing so much money into my life.
I gladly and proudly accept all the abundance the Universe has to offer.
All the money I spend brings me joy.

Did it work? Yes and no. The affirmations significantly reduced my stress level about finances and heightened my appreciation of what did come into my life, but the floodgates of material wealth remained bolted shut. I sensed that I was holding back, but didn't know why.

It took me fifteen years to figure it out. One day I sat down, got quiet, and asked myself why I was resisting wealth and abundance. The answer I got surprised me. Ever since I was little, I had always wanted to be the "good boy" who was liked by everyone (yeah, like that's even possible). Clearly, some part of me presumed that if I were wealthy, there would be those who would resent me for having more money than they did. Thankfully, I had learned to live more authentically and was no longer so concerned about what others may think of me. The moment I shined the light of awareness on this immature, outdated notion, poof!, I let it go.

That flash of insight gave way to another: If I resisted prosperity, I would never be able to move beyond who I once was and walk fully into who I am capable of being. Although I was responsible for the errors that have weighed me down like shackles around my ankles, I must not view those errors with reproach, for they were a necessary part of my maturity process. I cannot allow my psychological, emotional, and spiritual development to be bogged down in the quicksand of insecurity and regret.

I dug deeper and saw that I was also having trouble reconciling the idea of living a spiritual life with the goal of accumulating wealth. Apparently, I believed that I had to choose one over the other. After some reflection, I reached three conclusions.

First, if I continued to struggle financially, I would lack the credibility I needed to inspire others. Why would anyone listen to me about how to create a life of abundance if I hadn't been able to do so myself? It's a question I'm still vulnerable to, although I feel I've been making progress.

Second, by limiting myself financially, I would be limiting the amount of good I could do in the world. Having to continue doing unrelated work just to pay the bills would curtail the time I could devote to my life's work. Not only would my own life be internally and externally impoverished, I would be depriving others of the gifts I was sent here to deliver. What's more, if I were financially comfortable, I could travel more places, meet more people, and offer my books and seminars more inexpensively to those with lower incomes who typically can't afford such luxuries.

Third, blocking myself from tapping into the financial abundance that is available to us all was compromising the quality of every area of my life. After all, living with joy, love, beauty, and abundance is a package deal—if I suppress one I cannot fully embody the others. By definition, a holistic life cannot be compartmentalized.

Once I realized the error of my deep-seated beliefs, I banished them from my consciousness. Instantly, I felt a great joy well up within me and sensed that I was already magnetically attracting the people, events, and experiences that would propel me into a more abundant future.

What does that future look like? It's still too early to tell. But I will welcome it with gratitude, humility, and a deep appreciation for all the abundance the Universe has to offer.

YOUR MIND IS A MAGNET
Self-Reflection Questions

- Why do I believe or disbelieve that my thoughts act as a magnet to attract whatever I think about into my life?

- How do my thoughts influence and control the way I experience reality?

- Given that every thought has repercussions, how can I train myself to think more positively?

- Which came first, my reality or my attitude?

- What is my first thought when I wake up in the morning?

- What are some instances in which my negative thinking led to negative consequences?

- How can I work with the law of attraction to bring good things into my life?

- In what ways have I been limiting my life by assuming that the way I see the world is the only reasonable way to see it?

- Why am I more comfortable giving than receiving, or vice versa?

- What do I need to change about myself to enable me to give to others with no expectation of receiving anything in return?

- How do my positive, loving thoughts help change the world for the better?

- How does praying for others affect my own life?

TWELVE

ASK AND YOU SHALL RECEIVE

*You can have anything you want if you want it
desperately enough. You must want it with an inner
exuberance that erupts through the skin and joins
the energy that created the world.*

—SHEILA GRAHAM

ASK AND YOU SHALL RECEIVE

You set an amazing process in motion by asking the Universe for whatever it is you want. The quality of the outcome hinges on the quality of your efforts to fulfill four conditions.

> *Manifestation is not magic. It is a process of working with natural*
> *principles and laws in order to translate energy from one level of*
> *reality to another.*
>
> —DAVID SPANGLER

FAITH AND OPTIMISM

First, you have unshakable faith that your request will be granted. If you don't believe it, you won't receive it.

> *An active faith can give thanks for a promise even though it be not*
> *yet performed, knowing that God's bonds are as good as ready*
> *money.*
>
> —MATTHEW HENRY

Faith organically produces a bumper crop of optimism, which yields unsinkable expectations, steadfast resolve, and infinite patience.

> *No pessimist ever discovered the secrets of the stars, or sailed to an*
> *uncharted land, or opened a new heaven to the human spirit.*
>
> —HELEN KELLER

It is not your thoughts and words but the conviction behind them that carry the most weight, that ensure that you and your desire become a vibrational match.

I tell you the truth, if anyone says to this mountain, 'Go, throw
yourself into the sea,' and does not doubt in his heart but believes that
what he says will happen, it will be done for him. Therefore I tell you,
whatever you ask for in prayer, believe that you have received it, and
it will be yours.

—JESUS OF NAZARETH
MARK 11:23-24

Such conviction requires that you also have faith in yourself, that you believe in your innate worthiness to receive life's gifts.

Believe in your dreams and they may come true; believe in yourself
and they will come true.

—UNKNOWN

How you feel about yourself determines what shows up in your life. There is always an energetic match between who you are and what you have.

If we go down into ourselves we find that we possess exactly what
we desire.

—SIMONE WEIL

If you sense any resistance on your part, you may be blocking the fulfillment of your desire with a wall built of unwarranted fears and assumptions.

Self-worth comes from one thing—thinking that you are worthy.

—WAYNE DYER

If you do not feel worthy enough to receive what you asked for, or fear that receiving it may alter your life too dramatically, such conflicts can be resolved only by going within and working through your doubts and insecurities.

Accept yourself as you are. Otherwise you will never see opportunity.
You will not feel free to move toward it; you will feel you are not
deserving.

—DR. MAXWELL MALTZ

Self-worth becomes a non-issue when you recognize and accept your Divine nature and inherent virtue.

> *We are Divine enough to ask and we are important enough to*
> *receive.*
>
> —WAYNE DYER

Look through God's eyes and you see that every child of God is deserving of all the riches of the Universe.

> *No matter how qualified or deserving we are, we will never reach*
> *a better life until we can imagine it for ourselves and allow ourselves*
> *to have it.*
>
> —RICHARD BACH

If this were not so, your first instinct would not be lifting your gaze upward and beseeching the heavens when a burning desire stirs your soul.

> *It is the will of our heavenly Father that we should come to Him freely*
> *and confidently and make known our desires to Him, just as we*
> *would have our children come freely and of their own accord and*
> *speak to us about the things they would like to have.*
>
> —OLE HALLESBY

By accepting God's blessings, you honor your Divine heritage and claim what has been promised to you since the dawn of time.

> *Give yourselves permission,*
> *at this very moment,*
> *to touch the world of spirit.*
> *All it takes is your permission. . . .*
> *Your mind does not know the way.*
> *Your heart has already been there.*
> *And your soul has never left it.*
> *Welcome home.*
>
> —PAT RODEGAST (EMMANUEL)

PURITY OF INTENT

Second, you want what you want for the right reasons. Why is intent important? The more genuine your desire to love and serve God, the nearer you approach that sacred space where God's intentions become your intentions.

> *But seek ye first the Kingdom of God and his righteousness, and all these things shall be added unto you.*
>
> —Jesus of Nazareth
> Matthew 6:33

Thus, the closer you move to enlightenment, the greater the positive magnetism of your consciousness and the more likely that your request will be relevant to your life's purpose.

> *The one thing worth living for is to keep one's soul pure.*
>
> —Marcus Aurelius

If your desire is coming from ego instead of spirit, it is likely self-serving and a detriment to your spiritual progress.

> *If your prayer is selfish, the answer will be something that will rebuke your selfishness. You may not recognize it as having come at all, but it is sure to be there.*
>
> —William Temple

Expect the attainment of an ego-driven desire to come with a corrective lesson attached. Is that a price worth paying? Ask King Midas.

> *Take what you want, said God, and pay for it.*
>
> —Spanish proverb

It is tempting to rationalize that satisfying the urges of your ego will not compromise your ability to answer the call of Spirit.

*What we usually pray to God is not that His will be done, but that
He approve ours.*

—HELGA BERGOLD GROSS

Yet peace will remain beyond your reach until you choose to selflessly serve Spirit instead of selfishly serving your ego.

*Just keep asking, "Dear God, if I can't have what I want, then help
me to know what it is you* want *me to have. Help me to receive
whatever it is that You are trying to give me." Know in your heart,
that somewhere inside you there is a treasure much greater than the
one you have been asking for.*

—JOHN E. WELSHONS

Aligning your will with God's will presents an intriguing paradox. On one hand, the more attuned you are to Divine Consciousness, the more accessible are the riches of the Universe.

*Go on a journey from self to Self, my friend . . .
Such a journey transforms the earth into a mine of gold.*

—RUMI

On the other hand, the material items you longed for before you put God first in your life now seem like insignificant trinkets.

*Riches, like glory or health, have no more beauty or pleasure than
their possessor is pleased to lend them.*

—MICHEL DE MONTAIGNE

Your soul yearns not for what is *external* but for what is *eternal*. And it is only God, it is only Love, it is only Joy that is eternal.

*When all your desires are distilled
You will cast just two votes:
To love more, and be happy.*

—HAFIZ

Your desire for earthly possessions diminishes in direct proportion to your yearning for God-intoxication.

> *He who is plenteously provided for from within needs but little*
> *from without.*
>
> —JOHANN WOLFGANG VON GOETHE

You grasp what it means to be in this world but not of it when you find yourself desiring the Giver behind all gifts more than the gifts themselves.

> *The test of whether your life is lived for God alone is that you do*
> *not grieve over any frustrated personal desire, but only when you*
> *have displeased God.*
>
> —PARAMAHANSA YOGANANDA

If seeking God is not your greatest desire, all the treasures of the world will not satisfy the restless aching deep within your soul for meaning, purpose, and Divine communion.

> *Surely there is no greater gift to a man than that which turns all*
> *his aims into parching lips and all life into a fountain.*
> *And in this lies my honour and my reward,—*
> *That whenever I come to the fountain to drink I find the living*
> *water itself thirsty;*
> *And it drinks me while I drink it.*
>
> —KAHLIL GIBRAN

Ultimately, a spiritual seeker's sole desire is to have no desire other than unbroken attunement with the Source of all that is.

> *Have only one desire: to know God. Satisfying the sensory desires*
> *cannot satisfy you, because you are not the senses. They are only*
> *your servants, not your Self.*
>
> —PARAMAHANSA YOGANANDA

Do not be concerned if you feel light years away from the lofty goal of living a God-attuned life. It is called spiritual *practice* for a reason.

Our desire for God is the desire that should guide all other desires. Otherwise our bodies, minds, hearts, and souls become one another's enemies and our inner lives become chaotic, leading us to despair and self-destruction. Spiritual disciplines are not ways to eradicate all our desires but ways to order them so that they can serve one another and together serve God.

—HENRI NOUWEN

Surrender your will to Divine Will and all your desires will be granted in ways that serve your highest good while simultaneously deepening your devotion.

If our petitions are in accordance with His will, and if we seek His glory in the asking, the answers will come in ways that will astonish us and fill our hearts with songs of thanksgiving.

—J. KENNEDY MACLEAN

CLARITY AND VISUALIZATION

Third, you have complete clarity about the desired outcome. Concentrate intensely until you can visualize it in meticulous detail.

Man can only receive what he sees himself receiving.

—FLORENCE SCOVEL SHINN

Keep your desire top of mind by posting visual representations of it where you will see them throughout the day. Clip images from a magazine, locate digital versions, or draw them yourself.

Your thoughts are like the seeds you plant in your garden. Your beliefs are like the soil in which you plant these seeds.

—LOUISE HAY

Why is visualization important? The mind thinks in pictures, which are shaped not by your words, but by the energy—either love or fear—fueling your request.

The soul never thinks without an image.

—ARISTOTLE

If your fears keep you focused on what you do not want—"I am not going to end up broke"—your mind's eye will conjure up that which you are most fearful of.

> *The mental images you form must absolutely support what you want to create and should be visualized with as much detail and clarity as possible. If you give equal time to images contrary to your objective, it would be like trying to dig a hole and fill it at the same time.*
>
> —DR. TAE YUN KIM

Therefore, if the fear of unpaid bills rules your mind, you will be energetically pushing money away instead of attracting it.

> *What you resist sticks to you like glue.*
>
> —JUDITH ORLOFF

A prosperity consciousness is the cause and financial abundance is the effect, not the other way around.

> *The best time to practice being rich is when you're feeling poor.*
>
> —ALAN COHEN

If you feel you need wealth to feel wealthy, you will never feel wealthy no matter how much wealth you acquire.

> *He who doesn't find a little enough, will find nothing enough.*
>
> —EPICURUS

You are more apt to attract wealth when you *already feel wealthy*, when you know that all the wealth you will ever need is even now winging its way toward you.

> *Prosperity in the form of wealth works exactly the same as everything else. You will see it coming into your life when you are unattached to needing it.*
>
> —WAYNE DYER

You will feel wealthy when you are anchored in God and know that you need nothing else to be happy.

> *There's only one reason why you're not experiencing bliss at this present moment, and it's because you're thinking or focusing on what you don't have . . . right now you have everything you need to be in bliss.*
>
> —ANTHONY DE MELLO

Believe that your happiness depends on something other than God, and you will give less attention to God and more attention to what you do not have.

> *He is a wise man who does not grieve for the things he has not, but rejoices for those which he has.*
>
> —EPICTETUS

The law of attraction then delivers a double whammy: You drift further away from God *and* further away from what you desire.

> *If you need it, you can't have it. Claim it, and it's yours.*
>
> —ALAN COHEN

EMBODYING THE ENERGY

Fourth, you *feel* throughout your body—physically and emotionally—every aspect of what you are praying for and visualizing.

> *What we achieve inwardly will change outer reality.*
>
> —OTTO RANK

The Unified Field—that grid of conscious, living intelligence we call creation—responds far more vigorously to your feelings than your thoughts. Speak to it in the language of your heart.

> *Prayers not felt by us, are seldom heard by God.*
>
> —PHILIP HENRY

In humility and gratitude, lose yourself in the energy of your yearning. Feel the feeling of what its attainment feels like with all your senses—see it, touch it, hear it, taste it, smell it.

> *The more willing you are to surrender to the energy within you,*
> *the more power can flow through you.*
>
> —SHAKTI GAWAIN

Your feeling *is* the prayer. You reach the tipping point when your desire *feels* fulfilled in your inner world.

> *A mental picturing of that which we want, with the complete*
> *acceptance and the conviction that it is ours now, will bring it quickly.*
> *See it in its "isness."*
>
> —LESTER LEVENSON

Your calm certainty that fulfillment is imminent signals the Universe to actively manifest your desire in the outer world.

> *Only infinite patience can produce immediate effects.*
>
> —A COURSE IN MIRACLES

Prayer, then, is the gateway to true power. Aligning your will with God's will gives you access to all of creation.

> *Ask, and it shall be given you; seek, and ye shall find; knock, and*
> *it shall be opened unto you.*
>
> —JESUS OF NAZARETH
> MATTHEW 7:7

You are not simply a hapless bystander, buffeted about by the winds of chance. You are a full participant in the creative process.

> *Prayer is not an old woman's idle amusement. Properly understood*
> *and applied, it is the most potent instrument of action.*
>
> —MAHATMA GANDHI

ESSENCE AND EXPECTATIONS

Divine Intelligence is omniscient beyond space and time. Before it even occurred to you to formulate your request, arrangements were in place to fulfill it.

> *Your Father knoweth what things ye have need of, before ye ask him.*
>
> —JESUS OF NAZARETH
> MATTHEW 6:8

Abundance is your divine birthright. All of creation will conspire on your behalf to bring your heart's desire to fruition.

> *Ye have not, because ye ask not.*
>
> —JAMES 4:2

Every prayer is answered. The response, however, is often misinterpreted because the Universe responds to the essence of your request rather than the specifics of it.

> *For my thoughts are not your thoughts, neither are your ways my*
> *ways, saith the Lord. For as the heavens are higher than the earth,*
> *so are my ways higher than your ways, and my thoughts than your*
> *thoughts.*
>
> —ISAIAH 55:8-9

Therefore, what you asked for may be delivered at a time you may not expect and in a package you may not recognize.

Be thankful that God's answers are wiser than your answers.

—WILLIAM CULBERTSON

If you pray for a romantic relationship, for instance, perhaps what you truly desire is to feel loved and cherished. If so, you might not realize that your prayer has been answered when you feel bathed in God's loving presence and when family members and caring friends express how much you mean to them.

She knows Omnipotence hath heard her prayer,
And cries, "It shall be done, sometime, somewhere."

—OPHELIA G. BROWNING

Similarly, an insatiable appetite for riches may stem from a longing for security, freedom, and higher self-esteem: qualities that must be cultivated from within, not without. A series of meditation lessons may take you there faster, and more authentically, than a can't-miss stock tip.

Abundance is not something we acquire. It is something we tune into.

—WAYNE DYER

It sounds contradictory, but a prosperity consciousness and material abundance may be mutually exclusive.

My riches consist not in the extent of my possessions, but in the
fewness of my wants.

—JOSEPH BROTHERTON

True prosperity is recognizing and appreciating that you already have everything you need to fulfill your calling in this life.

We have what we seek. It is there all the time, and if we give it time, it
will make itself known to us.

—THOMAS MERTON

If wealth will help you carry out your life's work, then by all means build your bank account.

See where your own energy wants to go, not where you think it should go. Do something because it feels right, not because it makes sense. Follow the spiritual impulse.

—MARY HAYES GRIECO

If, however, your sacred contract was to serve God and humanity by living and modeling a simple, humble life, then a fat stock portfolio and a stable full of luxury cars may be a hindrance to realizing your spiritual potential.

God give me the strength to withstand the rigors of my answered prayers.

—UNKNOWN

In his speaking engagements, Dr. Bernie Siegel relates how he expresses his sympathy to people who have just been diagnosed with cancer, survived a horrible accident, or won the lottery. He is not kidding about the lottery; too much too soon can send your life spinning out of control.

In this world there are only two tragedies. One is not getting what one wants, and the other is getting it.

—OSCAR WILDE

CLARIFYING THE WHAT

Before formulating a request for what you desire, breathe deeply, quiet your mind, and center yourself.

No prayer is complete without Presence.

—RUMI

Do your best to identify the essence of what you are asking for, then phrase your request accordingly.

I know not by what methods rare,
But this I know: God answers prayer.
I know not if the blessing sought
Will come in just the guise I thought.
I leave my prayer to him alone
Whose will is wiser than my own.

—ELIZA M. HICKOK

God will give you one of three answers: "Yes," "Not yet," or "I have something better in mind."

You say, "But He has not answered." He has, He is so near to you that
His silence is the answer. His silence is big with terrific meaning that
you cannot understand yet, but presently you will.

—OSWALD CHAMBERS

Remember, your job is to clarify the "what" and let God take care of the "how" and the "when."

To bring anything into your life, imagine that it's already there.

—RICHARD BACH

Even so, you must do your share of the heavy lifting by keeping your intention top of mind and by taking whatever steps, if any, you feel guided to take.

God gives every bird his worm, but He does not throw it into
the nest.

—P. D. JAMES

Humbly petitioning God with a pure heart will reshape your internal world as much as, if not more than, your external world.

We impoverish God in our minds when we say there must be
answers to our prayers on the material plane; the biggest answers
to our prayers are in the realm of the unseen.

—OSWALD CHAMBERS

A prayer for a better quality of life, for example, will not only bring you the essence of what you long for, it will inevitably change the essence of who you are.

> It is not so true that "prayer changes things" as that prayer changes me and I change things. God has so constituted things that prayer on the basis of Redemption alters the way in which a man looks at things. Prayer is not a question of altering things externally, but of working wonders in a man's disposition.
>
> —OSWALD CHAMBERS

WANTING vs. HAVING

Fulfilling your desires can produce occasional bursts of happiness, but the pleasures of the material world are both fickle and fleeting.

> We try to cling to pleasure, we try to hug joy, and all we succeed in doing is making ourselves frustrated because, whatever it promises, pleasure simply cannot last. But if I am willing to kiss the joy as it flies, I say, "Yes, this moment is beautiful. I won't grab it. I'll let it go." And I live with a mind at peace and a heart untroubled. Pleasure comes and it goes. When it goes, we don't need to cling to memories of past happiness or dwell on when it may come again.
>
> —EKNATH EASWARAN

Getting exactly what you want may make you happy today, but it may be the opposite of what will make you happy tomorrow.

> More tears are shed over answered prayers than unanswered ones.
>
> —SAINT TERESA OF AVILA

Instead of fretting about *having what you want*, you will be happier and more peaceful if you focus on *wanting what you have*.

> The foolish man seeks happiness in the distance: The wise grows it under his feet.
>
> —JAMES OPPENHEIM

What does that mean? You look for and appreciate the gift in every possession, every encounter, every situation.

> To be upset over what you don't have is to waste what you do
> have.
>
> —KEN KEYES, JR.

You trust that whatever comes into your life has been divinely designed to help you fulfill the promise of all you are capable of becoming.

> "Having" is kindergarten stuff. "Being" is graduate school. "Having"
> is what children want. "Being" is what students of mastery seek.
>
> —NEALE DONALD WALSCH

You humbly acknowledge that you will only be given experiences that are appropriate for your present circumstances, your life's purpose, and the level of your consciousness.

> Seek not that the things which happen should happen as you wish;
> but wish the things which happen to be as they are, and you will
> have a tranquil flow of life.
>
> —EPICTETUS

You recognize that everything that comes your way presents an opportunity to learn and evolve, which further expands your capacity to receive.

> Be content with what you have; rejoice in the way things are. When
> you realize there is nothing lacking, the whole world belongs to you.
>
> —LAO TZU

When a desire surfaces, examine it objectively and learn what you can from it. If a desire leads to a greater appreciation of what you do have or to a deeper understanding of yourself, it will have served its purpose.

> Until you make peace with who you are, you'll never be content with
> what you have.
>
> —DORIS MORTMAN

If you are not satisfied with what you have, attaining all that you want will still leave you unsatisfied.

> *Want is a growing giant whom the coat of Have was never large enough to cover.*
>
> —RALPH WALDO EMERSON

The more unsatisfied you feel, the more you desire. The more you desire, the more you accumulate. The more you accumulate, the more complicated your life. The more complicated your life, the more stress you experience.

> *If your desires be endless, your cares and fears will be so too.*
>
> —THOMAS FULLER

Learning to want what you have requires a major shift in understanding, perception, and attitude.

> *He who knows that enough is enough will always have enough.*
>
> —LAO TZU

A daunting challenge indeed, which makes Roger Delano's triumph over paralysis even more stunning. At fifty-one, Delano contracted a rare condition called transverse myelitis, an incurable inflammation of the spine. A doctor told him he would never walk again, yet nine days later he walked out of the hospital under his own power.

> *Faith isn't faith until it's all you're holding on to.*
>
> —P. B. S. PINCHBACK

In an article for *Self-Realization* magazine, Delano wrote, "I knew that everything that was happening to me was up to God, that He was the only healer. I felt safe, knowing I was surrounded by the overarching mantle of His perfect care. Whatever God brought to me, I wanted. Even if I retained all of the mobility of a flower pot, it didn't matter. 'I' was still the same, the vehicle of expression had changed, that's all. A flower pot can still hold a beautiful flower."

For those who realize that everything is from God, everything is the same.

—RUMI

THE LENS OF GRATITUDE

It is a virtuous circle. The blessing of God's perfect care naturally elicits gratitude; every expression of gratitude heightens your awareness of God's presence; the stronger your attunement with Divine Consciousness, the more you recognize life's blessings.

Gratitude is not only the greatest of virtues, but the parent of all the others.

—CICERO

Nurture your gratitude practice by carrying a gratitude icon—a rock, coin, or other small object—in your pocket. Every time your hand brushes against it, express gratitude for whatever you are experiencing in that moment.

For Zen students a weed is a treasure.

—SHUNRYU SUZUKI

If you are in a grocery store, give silent thanks for the food that sustains you. If you are walking with friends, tell them how much you appreciate their friendship.

God makes three requests of his children: Do the best you can, where you are, with what you have, now.

—AFRICAN-AMERICAN PROVERB

Before long, expressing gratitude becomes a habit. Eventually, it becomes innate and you instinctively view every experience through the lens of gratitude.

If the only prayer you said in your whole life was, "thank you," that would suffice.

—MEISTER ECKHART

A gratitude habit generates countless reminders each and every day that you are amply wealthy in all the ways that matter most.

> *You say grace before meals. All right. But I say grace before the concert and the opera, and grace before the play and pantomime, and grace before I open a book, and grace before sketching, painting, swimming, fencing, boxing, walking, playing, dancing, and grace before I dip the pen in the ink.*
>
> —G. K. CHESTERTON

Inevitably, you find yourself expressing gratitude not only for what is in your life, but what is yet to come.

> *We give thanks for unknown blessings already on their way.*
>
> —SACRED RITUAL CHANT

With increasing frequency, you marvel that every breath you take is a direct gift from God.

> *Gratitude, like faith, is a muscle. The more you use it, the stronger it grows.*
>
> —ALAN COHEN

LIFE BECOMES A CELEBRATION

Opening your mind and your heart to accept life's endless stream of gifts is a priceless gift in itself.

> *Some people are always grumbling that roses have thorns; I am thankful that thorns have roses.*
>
> —ALPHONSE KARR

Never again will you revert to a scarcity consciousness that whispers insidiously that you do not and will not ever have enough.

*Gratefulness is the key to a happy life that we hold in our hands,
because if we are not grateful, then no matter how much we have we
will not be happy—because we will always want to have something
else or something more.*

—BROTHER DAVID STEINDL-RAST

Never again will you suffer the delusion of believing yourself unworthy of receiving all the abundance the Universe has to offer.

*When we stop fighting the inevitable we release energy which enables
us to create a richer life.*

—ELSIE MCCORMICK

Cultivating an attitude of gratitude helps you develop a prosperity consciousness that brings even greater abundance into your life.

*Gratitude unlocks the fullness of life. It turns what we have into
enough, and more. It turns denial into acceptance, chaos to order,
confusion to clarity. It can turn a meal into a feast, a house into
a home, a stranger into a friend. It turns problems into gifts, failures
into successes, the unexpected into perfect timing, and mistakes
into important events. It can turn an existence into a real life,
and disconnected situations into important and beneficial lessons.
Gratitude makes sense of our past, brings peace for today, and
creates a vision for tomorrow.*

—MELODY BEATTIE

The law of attraction dictates that consistently and genuinely expressing thankfulness will magnetically attract even more people, things, and situations to be thankful for.

*Abundance can be had simply by consciously receiving what already
has been given.*

—SUFI WISDOM

Gratitude inevitably produces ever more joy just as constant complaining generates ever more misery.

> *Being ungrateful for what you get never gets you more.*
>
> —ARNOLD H. GLASOW

Life becomes a celebration. You become keenly aware of how each moment presents you with a unique opportunity to express your Divine nature.

> *You've gotta' dance like there's nobody watching,*
> *Love like you'll never be hurt.*
> *Sing like there's nobody listening,*
> *And live like it's heaven on earth.*
>
> —WILLIAM PURKEY

Even when thunderclouds loom, you do not want to waste one minute of life feeling anything other than joy and gratitude.

> *Life isn't about waiting for the storm to pass; it's about learning to*
> *dance in the rain.*
>
> —VIVIAN GREENE

When you are determined to find blessings everywhere, blessings are just as determined to find you.

> *The unthankful heart . . . discovers no mercies; but let the thankful*
> *heart sweep through the day, and as the magnet finds the iron, so it*
> *will find in every hour some heavenly blessings.*
>
> —HENRY WARD BEECHER

While you are grateful no matter what comes to you, you continue to ask for ever more guidance and dream of ever more glorious ways to fulfill your potential.

> *Prayerize, picturize, actualize.*
>
> —NORMAN VINCENT PEALE

In those moments when the magnitude of your gratitude overwhelms you, and you have exhausted your capacity to express it, you realize that your only hope of fully expressing your joy is to live a life of ceaseless gratitude.

The heart that breaks open can contain the whole universe.

—JOANNA MACY

Let every beat of your heart sing out in gratitude, and all of life becomes a heartbreakingly beautiful poem.

To speak gratitude is courteous and pleasant, to enact gratitude is generous and noble, but to live gratitude is to touch Heaven.

—JOHANNES A. GAERTNER

PUTTING IT ALL TOGETHER

The more you believe in, think about, visualize, and feel the manifestation of your desire, the more you subtly reconfigure yourself energetically.

We always attract into our lives whatever we think about most, believe in most strongly, expect on the deepest level, and imagine most vividly!

—SHAKTI GAWAIN

Through your thoughts, words, and actions, you consciously, subconsciously, and unconsciously become a living magnet, growing more powerful by the day.

When the bull's-eye becomes as big in your mind as an elephant, you are sure to hit it.

—ALEJANDRO JODOROWSKY

Inevitably, you reach critical mass, at which point the object of your desire—or opportunities designed to deliver the essence of what you desire—cannot help but show up in your life.

The subjective mind is entirely under the control of the objective mind. With the utmost fidelity it reproduces and works out to its final consequences whatever the objective mind impresses upon it.

—THOMAS TROWARD

No matter what the outcome, every request can bring you that much closer to enlightenment. If the essence of what you desire is granted, that brings you closer to peace, which brings you closer to God.

Joy has nothing to do with material things, or with a man's outward circumstances. It is the simple fact of human experience that a man living in the lap of luxury can be wretched, and a man in the depths of poverty can overflow with joy.

—WILLIAM BARCLAY

If you do manifest a worldly desire, the realization that material pleasures by themselves do not provide complete and lasting happiness may eventually disillusion you, sparking a quest for deeper meaning and purpose.

What you possess in the world will be found at the day of your death to belong to someone else; but what you are will be yours forever.

—HENRY VAN DYKE

If you are dissatisfied with any aspect of your life, look within. Why? Three reasons. First, you are being divinely guided in every moment with infinite wisdom and deep love. Second, you are not separate from God. Third, your thoughts create your reality.

Accept whatever comes to you woven in the pattern of your destiny, for what could more aptly fit your needs?

—MARCUS AURELIUS

Blend those three concepts together, and the inescapable conclusion is that you are a conscious co-creator of every moment in your life and of the world in which you live.

Every person, all the events of your life are there because you have drawn them there. What you choose to do with them is up to you.

—RICHARD BACH

Follow the unerring guidance of your inner wisdom, live to serve God, and all that your soul desires shall be yours.

> *Your willingness to do your part opens the floodgates of God's blessings.*
>
> —Sri Daya Mata

If life appears to unfold otherwise, let your ego scoff if it must. What your ego desires and what your soul desires may be two very different things.

> *I asked God for strength that I might achieve;*
> *I was made weak that I might learn humbly to obey.*
> *I asked for health that I might do greater things;*
> *I was given infirmity that I might do better things.*
> *I asked for riches that I might be happy;*
> *I was given poverty that I might be wise.*
> *I asked for power that I might have the praise of men;*
> *I was given weakness that I might feel the need of God.*
> *I asked for all things that I might enjoy life;*
> *I was given life that I might enjoy all things.*
> *I got nothing that I asked for; but everything I had hoped for.*
> *Almost despite myself, my unspoken prayers were answered;*
> *I am, among all men, most richly blessed.*
>
> —The Prayer of an
> Unknown Confederate Soldier

Do not look exclusively to the material plane for answers to your prayers. There is a greater wisdom at work. In time, all will become clear.

> *As white snow flakes fall quietly and thickly on a winter day, answers to prayer will settle down upon you at every step you take, even to your dying day. The story of your life will be the story of prayer and answers to prayer.*
>
> —Ole Hallesby

ASK AND YOU SHALL RECEIVE
Living the Lesson

Driving home to Minneapolis from Chicago in early December, I was forced to stay overnight at a Wisconsin motel when a snowstorm made the highway too treacherous. The next morning, soon after I hit the road, I started to pull off the highway to get to a gas station; but my car skidded and I plowed right into a snowbank separating the highway and the exit lane.

Relieved that nothing dangerous had been lurking under the snowbank, I dropped my cell phone in my jacket pocket, got out of the car, and thumbed a ride up to the top of the exit and over to the gas station. Nobody at the station was helpful, but I did manage to procure a list of towing companies from the phone book.

Glancing at the first number on my list, I reached into my jacket pocket for my phone. The pocket was empty. Puzzled, I checked every pocket I had, twice. I was already feeling a bit dazed and out of my element, and the mystery of the vanishing cell phone only added to the surrealism of the moment.

I felt compelled to return to my car before deciding what I should do next. As I started walking, I thought of Roger Delano's story from this chapter, which helped put my predicament in perspective. Over and over, I said out loud, "Whatever God brings to me, I want." After all, there was some reason why all this was happening and I was intent on keeping my awareness high so as not to miss any clues.

As I turned the corner to walk down the steep exit ramp, I was startled to see a police car and a tow truck already on the scene. I waved to them, and when I got down to my car, I explained what had occurred. Before hooking his chain up to my car, the tow truck driver asked me if I had lost a phone. He had found it in the snow right outside the front passenger door.

It's a good thing I dropped it. Otherwise, I would have been up at the gas station calling towing companies, oblivious to the fact that my car was being towed away. I'm sure I would have panicked a bit had I walked back and found an empty snowbank.

After towing my car up to the gas station parking lot, the driver filled out his paperwork, had me sign it, and I was on my way as if nothing had happened. After arriving home, I was pleased to discover that the towing rider I had added to my auto insurance policy just weeks before at the suggestion of a friend would fully reimburse me for the towing costs.

By staying calm and positive, surrendering to the moment, and letting the Universe take care of the "how," I ended up with a nice little story to tell instead of a miserable experience that would have ruined my day. To this day, my snowy adventure serves as a cheerful reminder to welcome everything that comes into my life with open arms, a trusting heart . . . and a zippered jacket pocket.

ASK AND YOU SHALL RECEIVE
Self-Reflection Questions

- If I doubt that I will receive what I ask for, what is likely to happen and why?

- What issues are preventing me from feeling worthy of receiving all the abundance the Universe has to offer?

- How can I wean myself from focusing so much of my time and energy on self-indulgent desires?

- What do I need to learn in order to value treasures of the spirit more than pleasures of the ego?

- How can I develop a prosperity consciousness regardless of how much money I have?

- How can I make time in my day to lose myself in the imagery and energy of my desires?

- Given that I am a participant in the creative process, what does what I now have in my life tell me about myself?

- How can I learn to identify the essence of what I desire so I can phrase my request for it more relevantly?

- How was one of my prayers answered in an unexpected way?

- How can I train myself to value what I already have more than what I don't yet have.

- How can I challenge myself to look for the subtle lessons behind my desires?

- How can I develop the habit of expressing gratitude for all the many blessings in my life?

THIRTEEN

SEE EVERY MOMENT AS A GIFT

*The greatest discovery of my generation is that
a human being can alter his life by altering his attitude.*

—Unknown

SEE EVERY MOMENT AS A GIFT

When you surrender to Divine Will with unwavering faith and trust, every moment becomes a gift.

> *The Master gives himself up to whatever the moment brings.*
>
> —LAO TZU

MAKING THE SHIFT

All it takes is a shift of perspective to recognize and appreciate life's gifts, even when—especially when—what you are experiencing seems like anything but a gift.

> *Though outwardly a gloomy shroud,*
> *The inner half of every cloud*
> *Is bright and shining:*
> *I therefore turn my clouds about*
> *And always wear them inside out*
> *To show the lining.*
>
> —ELLEN THORNEYCROFT FOWLER

Caroline Myss urges her readers to develop "symbolic sight," to probe beneath the surface of experiences so they can better understand how life events are woven into the tapestry of Divine design.

> *Discovery consists of seeing what everybody has seen and thinking*
> *what nobody has thought.*
>
> —ALBERT SZENT-GYÖRGYI

Interpreting events, relationships, and challenges symbolically, rather than literally, helps you perceive the deeper meaning of life experiences.

*Every now and then a man's mind is stretched by a new idea or
sensation, and never shrinks back to its former dimensions.*

—OLIVER WENDELL HOLMES

Every event has a purpose; sometimes you get to see the reason, sometimes you don't.
The scope of your symbolic sight is relative to your level of consciousness.

*Experience is the toughest teacher because she gives the test first, and
then the lesson.*

—UNKNOWN

Unplug from the need to know why something happened and trust that behind the
event is a message of Divine empowerment. As soon as you make that shift, the message
can be delivered.

*The universe is like a safe to which there is a combination. But the
combination is locked up in the safe.*

—PETER DEVRIES

Developing your symbolic sight opens wide the gates of wisdom. But beware: Approach
these gates with humility and reverence or they will slam shut as quickly as they
opened.

*If you forget your feelings about things of the world, they become
enlightening teachings. If you get emotional about enlightening
teaching, it becomes a worldly thing.*

—MUSO KOKUSHI

ACCENTUATE THE POSITIVE

Look beyond the illusory "negative" aspects of an event and you may discover the
golden nugget of Divine Wisdom lying just beneath the details.

Everything has beauty, but not everyone sees it.

—CONFUCIUS

Seek to find beauty in everything you look at and you will find it. Invite beauty into your life and your life becomes more beautiful.

Why do some people always see beautiful skies and grass and lovely flowers and incredible human beings while others are hard-pressed to find anything or any place that is beautiful?

—LEO BUSCAGLIA

Accepting whatever life delivers to you with humility and gratitude naturally leads you to act more positively in every situation, which in turn produces more favorable outcomes.

Things turn out best for the people who make the best out of the way things turn out.

—ART LINKLETTER

Every ordinary moment is bursting with extraordinary opportunities to reinvent yourself. The only thing stopping you, the only thing that *can* stop you, is the self-imposed limit of your imagination.

A day dawns, quite like other days; in it a single hour comes, quite like other hours; but in that day and in that hour the chance of a lifetime faces us.

—MALTBIE D. BABCOCK

The beauty of reframing even the most challenging of moments as a gift is that doing so is a gift in itself. Even if the "divine purpose" you identify is wildly off the mark, the act of searching for meaning and purpose raises your consciousness, which ultimately leads you to live your life with more meaning and purpose.

It's not what you look at that matters, it's what you see.

—HENRY DAVID THOREAU

Granted, such an exercise is unthinkable in the wake of tragic events. At such times, we must go deeper into our faith and turn to our loved ones in the hope of finding some measure of comfort and healing.

> *Don't think that the person who is trying to comfort you now lives*
> *untroubled among the simple and quiet words that sometimes give*
> *you pleasure. His life has much trouble and sadness, and remains*
> *far behind yours. If it were otherwise, he would never have been*
> *able to find those words.*
>
> —RAINER MARIA RILKE

In this way, even if only a sliver of light penetrates our darkest moments, there is light nonetheless; and where there is light, there is the gift of hope.

> *Two men look out through the same bars:*
> *One sees the mud, and one the stars.*
>
> —FREDERICK LANGBRIDGE

FRESH APPRECIATION

In time, viewing every moment as a gift orchestrated by Divine Intelligence becomes ingrained in your consciousness.

> *The happiest man is he who learns from nature the lesson of*
> *worship.*
>
> —RALPH WALDO EMERSON

No matter where you are, no matter what the circumstances, you see the hand of God at work.

> *Whoever does not see God in every place does not see God in any*
> *place.*
>
> —RABBI ELIMELECH

Look at the world through God's eyes and the beauty and majesty of a falling leaf will leave you breathless.

> *We look too much to museums. The sun coming up in the morning is*
> *enough.*
>
> —ROMARE BEARDEN

The sun has risen every morning since the world began; yet if we were fully present and our vision were pure, we would greet each sunrise with rejoicing.

> *Where others see but the dawn coming over the hill, I see the sons of*
> *God shouting for joy.*
>
> —WILLIAM BLAKE

Walk through nature and listen as the meadows, trees, and birds serenade you with the celebratory song that echoes joyously throughout all creation.

> *Where is the fountain that throws up these flowers in a ceaseless*
> *outbreak of ecstasy?*
>
> —RABINDRANATH TAGORE

Some of life's greatest gifts lie hidden in unpleasant obligations, waiting for you to activate your symbolic sight and greet them with reverence rather than reluctance.

> *If you begin to live life looking for the God that is all around you,*
> *every moment becomes a prayer.*
>
> —FRANK BIANCO

You need not look far for examples. Washing a sink full of dirty dishes may mean you have enjoyed a night surrounded by loved ones. Paying the bills could mean you have been blessed with a source of income to provide for your family.

> *Most human beings have an almost infinite capacity for taking things*
> *for granted.*
>
> —ALDOUS HUXLEY

Expressing gratitude for such opportunities as they occur adds depth and meaning to even the most mundane tasks.

> *This is the day which the Lord hath made; we will rejoice and be glad in it.*
>
> —PSALMS 118:24

Similarly, frustrations and disappointments with loved ones can be reframed as opportunities to foster empathy and intimacy.

> *Change the way you look at things, and the things you look at change.*
>
> —WAYNE DYER

Instead of allowing your buttons to get pushed, set aside your fears and respond with love. A less-than-stellar report card is an invitation to deepen your bond with your child through extended study sessions. A maxed-out credit card sets the stage for a breakthrough discussion with your spouse about values and unfulfilled emotional needs.

> *The more sand has escaped from the hourglass of our life, the clearer we should see through it.*
>
> —JOHANN RICHTER

A TIMELESS, ETERNAL REALM

Savoring little moments throughout the day does not slow down time; it just feels like it does.

> *We do not remember days, we remember moments.*
>
> —CESARE PAVESE

Slipping a loving note in your child's lunchbox or squeezing your spouse's hand during a movie makes your heart sing and also brings you closer to God. Why? Consciously adding love to the world puts you squarely in the present moment; and that is where God lives.

> *Love is the ultimate force at the heart of the universe.*
>
> —DEEPAK CHOPRA

The present moment has no duration; in a flash, it is gone, and yet all of life is contained within the borders of the ever-changing now.

> *The passage of time, though absolute and inescapable, is more*
> *a function of psychology and perspective than a physical reality.*
>
> —TOBY JOHNSON

The present moment is the only moment you have ever had, and the only moment you will ever have.

> *My friend, the sufi is the son of the present moment:*
> *to say tomorrow is not our way.*
>
> —RUMI

The present moment is both ephemeral and infinite; it exists outside of time, which means presence is a timeless state of being.

> *If past to future is on a horizontal line, then the present moment*
> *is not in time, but a vertical movement transcending time.*
>
> —OSHO

Timelessness is your natural state, and the present moment patiently waits to welcome you home.

You would measure time the measureless and the immeasurable.
You would adjust your conduct and even direct the course of your
spirit according to hours and seasons.
Of time you would make a stream upon whose bank you would sit
and watch its flowing.
Yet the timeless in you is aware of life's timelessness,
And knows that yesterday is but today's memory and tomorrow is
today's dream.
And that that which sings and contemplates in you is still dwelling
within the bounds of that first moment which scattered the stars
into space.

—KAHLIL GIBRAN

Through its link to the Divine Mind, the present moment is a portal to infinity and life everlasting.

If we take eternity to mean not infinite temporal duration but
timelessness, then eternal life belongs to those who live in the present.

—LUDWIG WITTGENSTEIN

Step into the stillness, the timelessness, of the present moment and you will be perfectly positioned to view the world through God's eyes.

One instant is eternity; eternity is in the now. When you see through
this one instant, you see through the one who sees.

—WU MEN HUI-K'AI

Your capacity to be fully present expands dramatically when you stop identifying yourself as a time-bound human being separate from others, and start experiencing life as a timeless spiritual being at one with all creation.

There are three words that convey the secret of the art of living, the
secret of all success and happiness: One With Life. Being one with life
is being one with Now. You then realize that you don't live your life,
but life lives you. Life is the dancer, and you are the dance.

—ECKHART TOLLE

It is your intuition that is your lifeline to Spirit, to the ever-alert, ever-present observer within you. Deepak Chopra describes this "observer in the midst of observation" as "the timeless factor in every time-bound experience."

> Just as a person can watch through a screen a crowd of people in front of him, without himself being seen by them, so the soul through the screen of intuition watches all its thoughts.
>
> —PARAMAHANSA YOGANANDA

The timeless, eternal realm of the present moment is so saturated with Spirit that the ego, forever bound to the material world of space and time, is, by definition, barred from entering.

> God himself culminates in the present moment, and will never be more divine in the lapse of all the ages.
>
> —HENRY DAVID THOREAU

The ego looks only to the past or the future. Your past perceptions, memories, and experiences, after all, are the source of the ego's body-bound identity.

> Yesterday and tomorrow are humanity's downfall. Today you may be aroused toward God. But yesterday and tomorrow pull you back.
>
> —REBBE NACHMAN OF BRESLOV

It is your future that is the ego's favorite destination, because if *you* have a future, *its* survival is assured.

> To be identified with your mind is to be trapped in time: the compulsion to live almost exclusively through memory and anticipation. This creates an endless preoccupation with past and future and an unwillingness to honor and acknowledge the present moment and allow it to be. The compulsion arises because the past gives you an identity and the future holds the promise of salvation, of fulfillment in whatever form. Both are illusions.
>
> —ECKHART TOLLE

ANCHORED IN THE PRESENT

While being fully present is a goal worth striving for, it is *how* you live in the moment that matters most.

> *Let your life lightly dance on the edges of Time like dew on the tip of a leaf.*
>
> —RABINDRANATH TAGORE

Abide in the *now*, surrender to Divine Will, and your thoughts, words, and actions will naturally align with that which is right.

> *Things which matter most must never be at the mercy of things which matter least.*
>
> —JOHANN WOLFGANG VON GOETHE

Melt into oneness with the Divine Mind and you gather the entirety of the Universe in your loving embrace. Distinctions of self and Self drop away as if they had never been.

> *All that is, is holy.*
>
> —ANCIENT WISDOM

You are serenely centered yet intensely aware that every moment is imbued with infinite depth and power.

> *Look at everything as though you are seeing it for the first or last time. Then your time on earth will be filled with glory.*
>
> —BETTY SMITH

Stay anchored in the present moment and you will know the joy of living a life without limits.

> *Everything you wish to eventually achieve, you can have right now, if you don't refuse it to yourself. And this means taking no notice of the past, trusting the future to providence, and living now in union with faith and justice.*
>
> —MARCUS AURELIUS

You are fully present in those moments when love and joy consume you and bliss is your only option.

> *Time is a factory where everyone slaves away*
> *Earning enough love to break their own chains.*
>
> —HAFIZ

In those transcendent moments, there is no past, there is no future, there is only the welcoming embrace of eternity.

> *"Why aren't you dancing with joy at this very moment?" is the only*
> *relevant spiritual question.*
>
> —VILAYAT INAYAT KHAN

How do you practice being present and mindful, especially when juggling your daily obligations demands all your mental energy? *Pay attention to what you are paying attention to.*

> *The moment one gives close attention to anything, even a blade*
> *of grass, it becomes a mysterious, awesome, indescribably*
> *magnified world in itself.*
>
> —HENRY MILLER

When your attention wanders and you feel pulled in multiple directions, your awareness is fragmented and your happiness is compromised by the stresses of past events and the weight of future expectations.

> *We do not rest satisfied with the present. We anticipate the future*
> *as too slow in coming, as if in order to hasten its course; or we*
> *recall the past, to stop its too rapid flight. So imprudent are we*
> *that we wander in the times which are not ours, and do not think*
> *of the only one which belongs to us; and so idle are we that we*
> *dream of those times which are no more, and thoughtlessly*
> *overlook that which alone exists.... The present is never our end.*
> *The past and the present are our means; the future alone is our*
> *end. So we never live, but we hope to live; and, as we are always*
> *preparing to be happy, it is inevitable we should never be so.*
>
> —BLAISE PASCAL

Certainly, it is useful and often necessary to look at the past (for analyzing) or the future (for planning). As long as you maintain acute awareness, your mind and spirit remain fully engaged in the *now*.

> *It's okay to glance backward, just don't stare.*
>
> —STEPHEN M. POLLAN AND MARK LEVINE

Dive joyously into the boundless depths of the present moment, and the past and the future will serenely bow before you.

> *Yesterday is but a dream, tomorrow is only a vision. But today, well lived, makes every yesterday a dream of happiness, and every tomorrow a vision of hope. Look well, therefore, to this day, for it is life, the very life of life.*
>
> —SANSKRIT PROVERB

A RUSHING RIVER

When you walk into the present moment, the scattered imaginings of your anxious mind fall away and life unfolds effortlessly and harmoniously.

> *When you live fully focused in the present, instead of always in plans and efforts for the future, things begin to flow to you from that very future, it seems. Full awareness from moment to moment seems to put you in the cosmic flow where things happen without pushing.*
>
> —ELISABET SAHTOURIS

The less you resist what life has given you, the greater your presence. That does not mean that you stop trying to change things for the better; it means accepting that you cannot change what has already happened.

> *Now is a rushing river. There are those who would hug the shore, but there is no shore. Push off into the stream. Hold your head above the fray. See who else is in the midst of things, and celebrate.*
>
> —NATIVE AMERICAN WISDOM

Living in the rushing river of the present moment requires diligence and will power; it is all too easy to get swept away by the crosscurrents of daily living.

> *The golden moments in the stream of life rush past us, and we see nothing but sand; the angels come to visit us, and we only know them when they are gone.*
>
> —GEORGE ELIOT

Let regular occurrences and daily rituals—a ringing phone, brushing your teeth, starting your car—serve as reminders to return to the *now*.

> *This moment deserves your full attention, for it will not pass your way again.*
>
> —DAN MILLMAN

When you are fully present, fears and worries evaporate and you are "in the zone," operating at peak capacity.

> *Present-moment living, getting in touch with your "now," is at the heart of effective living. When you think about it, there really is no other moment you can ever live. Now is all there is, and the future is just another present moment to live when it arrives.*
>
> —WAYNE DYER

You are authentically being who you are, and on the fast track to becoming all that you are meant to be.

> *All that you are, you are right now. All that you can be, begins in this moment. Now is a great place to be. For when you live it fully, with love, with gratitude, with purpose, anything is possible.*
>
> —RALPH MARSTON

With the clarity of higher consciousness, you honor every moment as sacred, and recognize every act of concentration as an act of consecration.

The art of life is to live in the present moment, and to make that moment as perfect as we can by the realization that we are the instruments and expression of God Himself.

—EMMET FOX

When you inhabit the present moment, life is always fresh and new and brimming over with opportunities for adventure.

The passing moment is all we can be sure of; it is only common sense to extract its utmost value from it.

—W. SOMERSET MAUGHAM

Indeed, the present moment is laden with gifts. Resolve to unwrap each one with anticipation and gratitude.

Whatever the present moment contains, accept it as if you had chosen it. Always work with it, not against it. Make it your friend and ally, not your enemy. This will miraculously transform your whole life.

—ECKHART TOLLE

Look beyond the present moment for life's treasures and you will find only pale imitations.

The value of moments, when cast up, is immense, if well employed; if thrown away, their loss is irrevocable.

— PHILIP LORD CHESTERFIELD

Defer the peace, joy, and contentment available to you *right now* and you defer life itself.

A life uncommanded now is uncommanded; a life unenjoyed now is unenjoyed; a life not lived wisely now is not lived wisely.

—DAVID GRAYSON

A GIVING HEART

Appreciation of the moment naturally expresses itself through appreciation of others. You recognize the fragility of life on this earth and vow that you will not leave any words unspoken with those you love.

> *If you had an hour to live and could make just one phone call, who would it be to, what would you say . . . and why are you waiting?*
>
> —STEPHEN LEVINE

A grateful heart is a giving heart. As awareness of God's presence grows, so too does generosity of spirit.

> *Do things for people not because of who they are or what they do in return, but because of who you are.*
>
> —RABBI HAROLD S. KUSHNER

As your heart expands, so does your capacity for joy, empathy, patience, and respect for others.

> *We can only be said to be alive in those moments when our hearts are conscious of our treasure.*
>
> —THORNTON WILDER

Every step toward enlightenment deepens your appreciation for the unique gifts, hopes, and dreams that every individual brings to the world.

> *Your neighbor's vision is as true for him as your own vision is true for you.*
>
> —MIGUEL DE UNAMUNO

Look at every person you meet through God's eyes, and you will view every encounter as a reminder to be kinder.

Wherever there is a human being, there exists the opportunity for an act of kindness.

—Lucius Annaeus Seneca

Touching another's heart through kindness is one of the most precious and wonderful gifts you can offer.

To touch the soul of another human being is to walk on holy ground.

—Stephen R. Covey

Knowing that God is working through you to let others know that they are loved and cherished changes you, makes you better, and brings you to your knees in humility and gratitude.

Kindness can become its own motive. We are made kind by being kind.

—Eric Hoffer

WHOM SHALL YOU BLESS?

Sharing the joy in your heart through kindness to others is the equivalent of sending a thank you card to God.

When a person does a good deed when he doesn't have to, God looks down and says, "For this moment alone, it was worth creating the world."

—The Talmud

The more you consciously practice kindness, the more you unconsciously become kinder.

Perfect kindness acts without thinking of kindness.

—Lao Tzu

Each act of kindness naturally leads to another. There is nothing so satisfying as making someone's day.

> *You cannot live a perfect day without doing something for someone*
> *who will never be able to repay you.*
>
> —JOHN WOODEN

When you feel guided to perform a kindness, act on it at once. Wait too long and circumstances may fan the flames of remorse.

> *You cannot do a kindness too soon because you never know how soon*
> *it will be too late.*
>
> —RALPH WALDO EMERSON

Whom shall you bless with your kindness? Whoever is in front of you and in need of your compassion. They have crossed your path for a reason.

> *Since you cannot do good to all, you are to pay special regard to those*
> *who, by the accidents of time, or place, or circumstance, are brought*
> *into closer connection with you.*
>
> —SAINT AUGUSTINE

You may never know how your simple acts of kindness—a friendly smile and greeting, carrying someone's groceries, offering a few quarters to an exasperated driver at a parking meter—touches others' hearts or restores their faith in humanity.

> *The world needs all of our power and love and energy, and each of us*
> *has something to give. The trick is to find it and use it, to find it and*
> *give it away, so there will always be more. We can be lights for each*
> *other, and through each other's illumination we will see the way.*
> *Each of us is a seed, a silent promise, and it is always spring.*
>
> —MERLE SHAIN

Your kind words and actions may prove to be life-changing—and perhaps even life-saving—to those whom society considers invisible or irrelevant.

Seek to do brave and lovely things which are left undone by the majority of people. Give gifts of love and peace to those whom others pass by.

—Paramahansa Yogananda

When you are kind to another, the message you deliver is: *You are worthy of receiving special attention.*

Everyone has an invisible sign hanging from his or her neck saying, "Make me feel important!" Never forget this message when working with people.

—Mary Kay Ash

It is not the act of kindness itself that touches people, it is the caring, the love, the compassion that accompanies it.

They may forget what you said, but they will never forget how you made them feel.

—Frederick Buechner

THE KARMA OF KINDNESS

Your kind gestures may inspire others to act in kind, and perhaps set off chain reactions of good will that karmically circle back to you.

One of the most difficult things to give away is kindness—it is usually returned.

—Cort R. Flint

Before your kindness returns to you, it will gladden hearts, uplift spirits, and energetically connect you to countless others who would have otherwise remained strangers.

> *Start some kind word on its travels. There is no telling where the good*
> *it may do will stop.*
>
> —WILFRED GRENFELL

Though your kindnesses may fade into the mists of time, they will live on in the hearts and souls of those who were fortunate enough to be graced by your generous spirit.

> *On that best portion of a good man's life,*
> *His little nameless unremembered acts*
> *Of kindness and of love.*
>
> —WILLIAM WORDSWORTH

Kindness is the greatest legacy that you can bequeath to the countless generations yet to come.

> *A single act of kindness throws out roots in all directions, and the*
> *roots spring up and make new trees. The greatest work that kindness*
> *does to others is that it makes them kind themselves.*
>
> —AMELIA EARHART

Kindness, by definition, requires humility, purity of intent, and a willingness to put another person's needs before your own.

> *Humility must accompany all our actions, must be with us*
> *everywhere; for as soon as we glory in our good works they are of*
> *no further value to our advancement in virtue.*
>
> —SAINT AUGUSTINE

An act of kindness tainted by your ego's desire for recognition or reward will karmically backfire faster than you can say, "Look how thoughtful I am."

> *Verily the kindness that gazes upon itself in a mirror turns to stone,*
> *And a good deed that calls itself by tender names becomes the parent*
> *to a curse.*
>
> —KAHLIL GIBRAN

When your intent is pure, you become a channel of Divine love, and your every act of kindness is imbued with God's grace.

> *Be kind, for everyone you meet is fighting a hard battle.*
>
> —Rev. John Watson

Ultimately, we are all messengers. Let kindness be the message you deliver to the world. From this moment forward, consider yourself an emissary of the angels.

> *You may be the only Bible somebody else reads.*
>
> —Mark Twain

THE KINDNESS CHALLENGE

Your life as an earth angel will begin when you learn how to think with your heart as well as your mind.

> *The prudence of the best heads is often defeated by the tenderness of the best hearts.*
>
> —Henry Fielding

Of course, no matter how kind you are, others may be having a bad day. Or a bad life. Let their rudeness serve as a good reminder to never treat others that way yourself.

> *Be kind whenever possible. It is always possible.*
>
> —His Holiness the 14th Dalai Lama

Indeed, this is why many people enter your life, to challenge you to look through God's eyes, transcend human pettiness, and serve as a channel of Divine loving energy.

Let no one ever come to you without leaving better and happier.
Be the living expression of God's kindness; kindness in your face,
kindness in your eyes, kindness in your smile, kindness in your
warm greeting.

—MOTHER TERESA

Even if those people walk away scowling, the love and light you sent them is helping them in some small way to heal.

Treat people as if they were what they ought to be and you help them
to become what they are capable of being.

—JOHANN WOLFGANG VON GOETHE

Choose kindness, and you are acting selflessly in ways that serve God and all the world.

What sunshine is to flowers, smiles are to humanity. They are but
trifles, to be sure; but scattered along life's pathway, the good they
do is inconceivable.

—JOSEPH ADDISON

Choose to be anything but kind, and you are acting selfishly in ways that serve only your own ego.

In a controversy the instant we feel anger we have already ceased
striving for the truth, and have begun striving for ourselves.

—BUDDHA

Think, speak, or act in a mean-spirited way and you harm yourself as well as others. When meanness takes up residence in your heart, peace and kindness are evicted and God is barred from entering.

Nobody appears inferior to us when our heart is kindled with
kindness.

—HAZRAT INAYAT KHAN

You cannot begin to grasp the meaning and purpose of life until kindness has touched your soul and softened your heart.

> *Kindness is more important than wisdom, and the recognition of this is the beginning of wisdom.*
>
> —THEODORE ISAAC RUBIN

MYSTERIES AND MIRACLES

Welcoming every moment as a gift provides revealing glimpses into the mysteries of the Universe.

> *A mature sense of wonder does not need the constant titillation of the sensational to keep it alive. It is most often called forth by a confrontation with the mysterious depth of meaning at the heart of the familiar and quotidian.*
>
> —SAM KEEN

Slip any random moment under a metaphysical microscope and you will find that it contains the DNA of God's master plan.

> *Life will give you whatever experience is most helpful for the evolution of your consciousness. How do you know this is the experience you need? Because this is the experience you are having at this moment.*
>
> —ECKHART TOLLE

You would then understand why every thought you think, every word you speak, every step you take is an outright miracle cloaked in the guise of an ordinary moment.

> *Our true home is in the present moment. To live in the present moment is a miracle. The miracle is not to walk on water. The miracle is to walk on the green Earth in the present moment, to appreciate the peace and beauty that are available now.*
>
> —THICH NHAT HANH

This awareness presents a thought-provoking choice. You can view ordinary moments as miracles or miracles as ordinary moments.

> *The invariable mark of wisdom is to see the miraculous in the common.*
>
> —RALPH WALDO EMERSON

Your perspective depends on how you define "ordinary." The higher you elevate your consciousness, the more naturally you behold the ordinary as extraordinary.

> *Miracles . . . rest not so much upon faces or voices or healing power coming suddenly near to us from afar off, but upon our perceptions being made finer, so that for a moment our eyes can see and our ears can hear what is there about us always.*
>
> —WILLA CATHER

Of course, you also view the extraordinary as ordinary. No matter how complex a situation may appear to our human eyes, the manifestation of Divine Will is effortless and instantaneous.

> *There is no order of difficulty in miracles.*
>
> —A COURSE IN MIRACLES

Look through God's eyes with purity of mind and spirit and a deeply rooted sense of unity with all creation, and all becomes clear.

The deep thinkers of all ages have therefore held one principle of awakening to life, and that principle is: emptying the self. In other words, making oneself a clearer and fuller accommodation in order to accommodate all experiences more clearly and more fully. All the tragedy of life, all its sorrows and pains belong mostly to the surface of the life in the world. If one were fully awake to life, if one could respond to life, if one could perceive life, one would not need to look for wonders, one would not need to communicate with spirits; for every atom in this world is a wonder for the one who sees with open eyes.

—HAZRAT INAYAT KHAN

What once would have wowed you as metaphysical magic now simply elicits a smile of reverence and gratitude.

If you learn what this world is, how it works, you automatically start getting miracles, what will be called miracles. But of course nothing is miraculous. Learn what the magician knows and it's not magic anymore.

—RICHARD BACH

The word "miracle" defines an event that transcends the natural operation of the Universe, which implies that we have an exhaustive understanding of Universal Law.

Miracles are not contrary to nature, but only contrary to what we know about nature.

—SAINT AUGUSTINE

Yet each new generation of scientists continues to unearth startling new discoveries—not only about the world around us but also about the world within us.

As Western science would put it, coherent human emotion, which occurs when what we are thinking, feeling, and expressing are all in alignment, produces a chemical change in our bodies, and that chemical change has quantum effects that extend beyond our bodies and bring about changes in our physical world—and now it's no longer a "miracle."

—GREGG BRADEN

Ultimately, a miracle is nothing more than a shift in perception. It is simply God manifesting another aspect of God. God can do anything because God is everything.

> *Miracles in fact are a retelling in small letters of the very same*
> *story which is written across the whole world in letters too large*
> *for some of us to see.*
>
> —C. S. Lewis

Viewing every decision, every conversation, every incident as an occasion for insight and growth deepens your wisdom, expands your capacity to enjoy life, and inspires you to seize every opportunity to create, achieve, and become.

> *To me every hour of the light and dark is a miracle,*
> *Every cubic inch of space is a miracle.*
>
> —Walt Whitman

When you live every day of your life viewing every moment as a gift, you become a gift to the world.

> *If perchance you see no reason for giving thanks, rest assured the fault*
> *is in yourself.*
>
> —Wabasha

SEE EVERY MOMENT AS A GIFT
Living the Lesson

At thirty-four, I was unemployed with a wife and twelve-year-old daughter to support. I didn't have highly marketable skills and was feeling more desperate by the day. Two months after I lost my job, my tax guy told me I needed to make a $2,500 payment to the IRS in thirty days. I was already heavily in debt and had no idea how I was going to pay that month's rent, much less the looming IRS bill. I had to repeatedly remind myself to keep breathing.

A few weeks later, my dad asked me to meet him for lunch. We lived seventy miles apart so we met at a Wendy's in Monticello, a town halfway in between. We sat down and, without question, without judgment, he handed me a check for $2,500. I was stunned. I knew he couldn't afford to give me so much. As I sat there, blinking back tears, he told me he believed in me and that he loved me. It was the most unexpected, generous, and loving gift I had ever received, and it deepened the already strong bond between us.

Fast-forward nearly six years. I asked my dad to meet me at the Wendy's in Monticello at three o'clock. He hadn't a clue why. We sat down, and I thanked him again for that day and told him how much his loving gesture had meant to me. Then I handed him a check for $2,500. It was his turn to be stunned. He tried to thank me but was too overcome with emotion, so much so that he lowered his head to the table and began sobbing. Tenderly, I leaned over and kissed the top of his head. The gift of that moment remains one of the highlights of my life.

I am now grateful for those dark days of no job and no money. Enduring such a stressful period, with fear gnawing at the pit of my stomach for days on end, was a small price to pay for such beautiful moments of love, grace, and redemption. My dad is gone now, but the memories of those lunches at Wendy's continue to nourish me and feed my soul. Even if I were in debt the rest of my life, I'd still feel like the richest man on earth.

SEE EVERY MOMENT AS A GIFT
Self-Reflection Questions

- How can I shift my perspective so I can notice the gifts embedded in every life experience?

- How would my life change if I interpreted situations symbolically rather than literally?

- How has the correlation between positive thinking and positive outcomes affected my life?

- How can I become better at discerning evidence of God's handiwork in everything I observe?

- What would happen if I reframed ordinary moments and disputes with loved ones as opportunities to celebrate my life and relationships?

- How can I learn to be more mindful of the present moment?

- Which of my everyday rituals can serve as triggers to remind me to live more consciously?

- How does being fully present help me live more authentically?

- If I only had an hour to live, what would I say to each of my family members and friends?

- What is one thing I can do in the next hour to make someone's day?

- When I am kind and generous to others, how am I also being kind and generous to myself?

- What is the message I am delivering to others by the way I live my life?

FOURTEEN

DETACH FROM OUTCOMES

Faith is letting down our nets into the transparent
deeps at the Divine command, not knowing what
we shall draw.

—François Fénelon

DETACH FROM OUTCOMES

If your happiness depends on achieving your goals precisely as you have envisioned, on events playing out according to your wishes, or on other people doing exactly what you want them to do, you are condemning yourself to a lifetime of misery.

> *When everything has to be right, something isn't.*
>
> —STANISLAW JERZY LEC

BOWING TO WISDOM

Try to control circumstances that are beyond your control, and you are proclaiming to the Universe that you know better than God what is best for you.

> *If you want to make God laugh, tell Him your plans.*
>
> —YIDDISH PROVERB

Detaching from outcomes does not mean that you are apathetic and unmotivated. Quite the contrary. Detachment means that you care deeply, but from an objective, enlightened perspective.

> *By detachment I mean that you must not worry whether the desired result follows from your action or not, so long as your motive is pure, your means correct.*
>
> —MAHATMA GANDHI

Enlightened detachment flows out of heightened awareness and the conviction that life is unfolding as it should.

> *When you realize how perfect everything is you will tilt your head back and laugh at the sky.*
>
> —BUDDHA

You are fully engaged in life while humbly acknowledging that a greater wisdom than your own is at work.

> *All journeys have secret destinations of which the traveller is unaware.*
>
> —MARTIN BUBER

Let go of the need to control outcomes, and fear and insecurity naturally give way to faith, trust, and hope.

> *Hope is definitely not the same thing as optimism. It is not the conviction that something will turn out well, but the certainty that something makes sense, regardless of how it turns out.*
>
> —VACLAV HAVEL

ATTACHMENT AND ATTUNEMENT

Looking through God's eyes, you recognize that everything in the material world is ultimately impermanent.

> *To renounce things is not to give them up. It is to acknowledge that all things go away.*
>
> —SHUNRYU SUZUKI

Therefore, your emotional attachment to whatever you desire must also be impermanent.

> *One who has finally learned that it is in the nature of objects to come and go without ceasing, rests in detachment and is no longer subject to suffering.*
>
> —ASHTAVAKRA GITA

Attachment to desires typically produces anxiety and anguish along the way, no matter how things work out.

> *Life is not suffering; it's just that you will suffer it, rather than enjoy it, until you let go of your mind's attachments and just go for the ride freely, no matter what happens.*
>
> —Dan Millman

Attachment and desire feed on each other. The more attached you become to a desire, the more attractive the object of your desire becomes, which intensifies your attachment to it.

> *Attachment is blinding; it lends an imaginary halo of attractiveness to the object of desire.*
>
> —Swami Sri Yukteswar

Obsessing about specific outcomes blocks you from aligning your will with Divine Will. Attachment and attunement cannot coexist.

> *The soul that is attached to anything, however much good there may be in it, will not arrive at the liberty of divine union. For whether it be a strong wire rope or a slender and delicate thread that holds the bird, it matters not, if it really holds it fast; for, until the cord be broken, the bird cannot fly.*
>
> —Saint John of the Cross

The moment you realize that worldly attachment is an obstacle to Self-realization is the moment you make a quantum leap in your ability to see life through God's eyes.

> *When we come to that non-attachment, then we can understand the marvelous mystery of the universe; how it is intense activity and vibration, and at the same time intensest peace and calm; how it is work every moment and rest every moment. That is the mystery of the universe—the impersonal and personal in one, the infinite and finite in one. Then we shall find the secret.*
>
> —Swami Vivekananda

STAYING ACTIVE, STAYING OPEN

When a certain outcome is desired, some people choose to "let go and let God" while others adopt an aggressive "do it yourself" mindset.

> *Pray as though everything depended on God. Work as though everything depended on you.*
>
> —SAINT AUGUSTINE

Although these perspectives seem to be perched on opposite ends of the goal-getting spectrum, they actually dovetail perfectly.

> *Prayer is not a substitute for action. Action is not a substitute for prayer.*
>
> —ALAN COHEN

Reconcile this "free will vs. Divine Will" conundrum by doing what you feel guided to do while staying open to unanticipated outcomes.

> *You have to take it as it happens, but you should try to make it happen the way you want to take it.*
>
> —GERMAN PROVERB

Think and act with a pure heart, noble intentions, and unwavering faith in Divine Wisdom, and you will be at peace with whatever life brings you.

> *When you live by the highest you know, the outcome of the game doesn't matter. However it comes out, it came out right.*
>
> —RICHARD BACH

If your sights are set on the prize behind door number one, your job is to work your way up to the door, not to kick it in. Why? Two reasons. First, by the time you reach the door, it may be locked and bolted.

> *Don't spend time beating on a wall, hoping to transform it into a door.*
>
> —GABRIELLE "COCO" CHANEL

Second, once you are at the threshold of what you wanted so badly, you may see three other doors you had not realized were there, and behind each of those doors are three more doors, and so on.

> *Just because you can't see what you're looking for doesn't mean what you're looking at isn't what you should see.*
>
> —CAROLINE MYSS

Refusing to avert your gaze from your original goal clouds your judgment, causing you to ignore or overlook encounters, experiences, and situations that might have led to more favorable outcomes.

> *Too many people miss the silver lining because they're expecting gold.*
>
> —MAURICE SETTER

Let go of the belief that success is measured by specific results and you awaken to a wondrous new world bursting with adventure and opportunity.

> *When the outcome drives the process, we will only ever go to where we've already been.*
>
> —BRUCE MAU

Fixate on outcomes and you risk stagnation. Dedicate yourself to continual self-improvement and the outcomes will exceed your initial expectations.

> *If you focus on results, you will never change. If you focus on change, you will get results.*
>
> —JACK DIXON

The path of self-discovery is by definition a quest for the undiscovered; and what is undiscovered cannot be neatly labeled and categorized on a "To Do" list.

I am willing to put myself through anything; temporary pain or discomfort means nothing to me as long as I can see that the experience will take me to a new level. I am interested in the unknown, and the only path to the unknown is through breaking barriers, an often-painful process.

—Diana Nyad

RIPPLES AND REPERCUSSIONS

In the chess game of life, you are faced with a particular universe of choices at any given moment.

Life is like a game of cards. The hand that is dealt you represents determinism; the way you play it is free will.

—Jawaharlal Nehru

With every move, that universe is reconfigured, creating new possibilities and eliminating old ones.

Every turn in your life, every time you decide, you become parent to all your alternate selves who follow.

—Richard Bach

The grand masters, having learned to see the world through God's eyes, welcome each moment with acceptance and gratitude.

The less you know about the game, and the less you remember you're a player, the more senseless living becomes.

—Richard Bach

Accepting and appreciating every outcome often leads to greater emotional and material rewards than a mindset intent on specific results.

> *To offer no resistance to life is to be in a state of grace, ease, and lightness. This state is then no longer dependent upon things being in a certain way, good or bad. It seems almost paradoxical, yet when your inner dependency on form is gone, the general conditions of your life, the outer forms, tend to improve greatly.*
>
> —ECKHART TOLLE

Your thoughts, words, and actions are pebbles tossed into the lake of your daily life, creating ripples that extend far beyond your immediate vision.

> *Nothing is ever lost. Not time; for what seems to have passed, lives on in the wisdom of future decisions. Not money; for what seems to have been spent, was only invested. And not love; for what seems to have vanished, has only moved so close you must look within your heart to see it.*
>
> —MIKE DOOLEY

Each of these pebbles subtly alters the Unified Field, presenting you with fresh new opportunities and experiences that can heighten your awareness, expand your perspective, deepen your wisdom, and rearrange your priorities.

> *Goals are a means to an end, not the ultimate purpose of our lives. They are simply a tool to concentrate our focus and move us in a direction. The only reason we really pursue goals is to cause ourselves to expand and grow. Achieving goals by themselves will never make us happy in the long term; it's who you become, as you overcome the obstacles necessary to achieve your goals, that can give you the deepest and most long-lasting sense of fulfillment.*
>
> —ANTHONY ROBBINS

Hence, by the time a long-sought-after goal is within reach, you may find its attainment not as meaningful as you expected it to be.

> *To live only for some future goal is shallow. It's the sides of the mountain which sustain life, not the top.*
>
> —ROBERT M. PIRSIG

Perhaps your original goal is ill-suited for your current level of consciousness. Or perhaps there is a more desirable and appropriate result waiting behind a door that has yet to reveal itself.

> *It is good to have an end to journey towards; but it is the journey that matters, in the end.*
>
> —URSULA K. LE GUIN

Do what you feel compelled to do, and trust that whatever awaits you at journey's end is in your best interests.

> *We must walk consciously only part way toward our goal, and then leap in the dark to our success.*
>
> —HENRY DAVID THOREAU

FAITH AND SURRENDER

Some goals may stay beyond your reach because achieving them would delay your awakening to the wonders that lie beyond material existence.

> *Prosperity knits a man to the world.*
>
> —C. S. LEWIS

In the ensuing darkness of disappointment and regret, the beckoning light of detachment glows ever more brightly.

> *In detachment lies the wisdom of uncertainty . . . in the wisdom of uncertainty lies the freedom from our past, from the known, which is the prison of past conditioning. And in our willingness to step into the unknown, the field of all possibilities, we surrender ourselves to the creative mind that orchestrates the dance of the universe.*
>
> —DEEPAK CHOPRA

If life continues to play out against your wishes, you have a choice: You can either surrender to despair or surrender to Divine Will.

> *Aim at Heaven and you will get earth "thrown in": aim at earth and you will get neither.*
>
> —C. S. LEWIS

Surrendering to God floods your heart with peace and invigorates your weary spirit. With humility and gratitude, you place your goals in God's hands.

> *It constantly happens that the Lord permits a soul to fall so that it may grow humbler.*
>
> —SAINT TERESA OF AVILA

You boldly and confidently move forward, trusting that Divine Intelligence is directing you to the people, situations, and events that will serve your highest good.

> *I seldom end up where I wanted to go, but almost always end up where I need to be.*
>
> —DOUGLAS ADAMS

Attuned to the Divine current, you are so focused on doing work that matters that the actual results of that work may feel anticlimactic.

> *To live my life for the outcome is to sentence myself to continuous frustration. . . . My only sure reward is in my actions, not from them.*
>
> —HUGH PRATHER

While you are proud of the work you do, you take no more ownership of the outcome than cows take of milk or bees take of honey.

> *The roots below the earth claim no rewards for making the branches fruitful.*
>
> —RABINDRANATH TAGORE

The more deeply you surrender to Divine Will, the stronger your conviction that all that truly matters is adding love to the world and serving God and humankind through your life's work.

> *Happy people plan actions, they don't plan results.*
>
> —DENNIS WHOLEY

Any attachments that distract you from lovingly serving the world spontaneously release their hold on you.

> *Better indeed is knowledge than mechanical practice. Better than knowledge is meditation. But better still is surrender of attachment to results, because there follows immediate peace.*
>
> —BHAGAVAD GITA 12:12

You find yourself loving God for the sheer joy of loving God, with no expectation of rewards.

> *There is not in the world a kind of life more sweet and delightful than that of a continual conversation with God.*
>
> —BROTHER LAWRENCE

Detaching from results in no way hinders your enjoyment of the process that leads to those results.

> *The really happy man is one who can enjoy the scenery on a detour.*
>
> —UNKNOWN

Just the opposite is true: Detachment liberates you from worrying about the outcome, which frees you up to savor the present moment instead of looking past it.

*When we turn to the past in yearning, we are running away
from the present. When we propel ourselves into the future in
anticipation, we are running away from the present. This is the
secret of what the world's spiritual traditions call detachment:
if we don't cling to past or future, we live entirely here and now,
in "Eternity's sunrise."*

—EKNATH EASWARAN

Giving your best and learning along the way are more important than the ultimate outcome of your efforts.

*And what if I did run my ship aground; oh, still it was splendid to
sail it!*

—HENRIK IBSEN

Inner peace is a greater prize than outer results; and it is the process, not the result, that brings peace and fulfillment.

*Need and struggle are what excite and inspire us; our hour of
triumph is what brings the void.*

—WILLIAM JAMES

Live serenely in the present moment and let your expectations take flight, trusting that you are karmically contributing to a happy, healthy, and harmonious future.

If we take care of the moments, the years will take care of themselves.

—MARIA EDGEWORTH

DETACHING FROM DRAMA

The more you can step back and view whatever happens as an impartial observer, rather than as a victim, the more peaceful your life will be.

Much of our inner turbulence reflects the fear of loss: our dependence on people, circumstances, and things not really under our control. On some level we know that death, indifference, rejection, repossession, or high tide may leave us bereft in the morning. Still, we clutch desperately at things we cannot finally hold. Nonattachment is the most realistic of attitudes. It is freedom from wishful thinking, from always wanting things to be otherwise.

—MARILYN FERGUSON

Paramahansa Yogananda urged his devotees to look dispassionately at the drama of their lives "from the balcony of introspection."

To become a spectator of one's own life is to escape the suffering of life.

—OSCAR WILDE

Embracing this wisdom is the gateway to a greater understanding of God's plan and how to play your role in it.

Let's not look back in anger, or forward in fear, but around in awareness.

—JAMES THURBER

Impartially observing the circumstances of a loved one's life may be more difficult; after all, you may care about their well-being more than your own. Peace comes when you understand that you can be caring and supportive while respecting that your loved ones have their own path to walk, their own lessons to learn, and agendas, values, and priorities that may diverge widely from your own.

Detachment is not apathy or indifference. It is the prerequisite for effective involvement. Often what we think is best for others is distorted by our attachment to our opinions; we want others to be happy in the way we think they should be happy. It is only when we want nothing for ourselves that we are able to see clearly into others' needs and understand how to serve them.

—EKNATH EASWARAN

Detaching from the drama generated by a loved one can mean the difference between living a peaceful, happy life and making yourself sick from worry, stress, and grief.

> *You can't get sick enough to make another person healthy. You can't get sad enough to make another person happy. You can't get poor enough to help one person on the planet get rich. You can't get hungry enough to feed one starving child.*
>
> —WAYNE DYER

You may tell yourself that you are being compassionate by caring so much it hurts; but in truth, your excessive empathy deprives your loved one of the strong, emotionally healthy support they need.

> *Just think of the trees: they let the birds perch and fly, with no intention to call them when they come and no longing for their return when they fly away. If people's hearts can be like the trees, they will not be off the Way.*
>
> —LANGYA

Of course, if your loved one's life is in danger, your emotions will take center stage, and rightly so. When the focus shifts from learning a lesson to losing a life, detachment is devalued.

> *There is no instinct like that of the heart.*
>
> —LORD BYRON

Learn to view life's dramas through God's eyes and your enlightened detachment may be misconstrued by those who allow themselves to be swallowed whole by one crisis after another.

The thinking mind cannot understand Presence and so will often misinterpret it. It will say that you are uncaring, distant, have no compassion, are not relating. The truth is, you are relating but at a level deeper than thought and emotion. In fact, at that level there is a true coming together, a true joining that goes far beyond relating. In the stillness of Presence, you can sense the formless essence in yourself and in the other as one. Knowing the oneness of yourself and the other is true love, true care, true compassion.

—ECKHART TOLLE

CONTROLLING CRAVINGS

Pursuing desires is an integral part of the dance of life. There is no need to live monastically.

Desire is what leads you through life until the time comes when you desire a higher life. So do not be ashamed that you want so much, but do not fool yourself into thinking that what you want today will be enough tomorrow.

—DEEPAK CHOPRA

Sense pleasures are to be enjoyed, unless and until you are dependent on them for your sense of identity or your desire for them threatens to consume you.

Desires are insatiable. They keep growing as we try to satisfy them just as the fire becomes more inflamed when oil is poured into it.

—MANU SMRITI

It is not the pleasures of material existence that must be renounced, but the idea that those pleasures are the source of lasting happiness and fulfillment.

A life directed chiefly toward the fulfillment of personal desires will sooner or later always lead to bitter disappointment.

—ALBERT EINSTEIN

Detachment reorders your priorities so that even as you delight in worldly pleasures, you are keenly aware that they pale in comparison to the ever-new joy of Divine communion.

> *The process of practice is to see through, not to eliminate, anything to which we are attached. We could have great financial wealth and be unattached to it, or we might have nothing and be very attached to having nothing. Usually, if we have seen through the nature of attachment, we will tend to have fewer possessions, but not necessarily.*
>
> —CHARLOTTE JOKO BECK

Our baser human cravings lead us away from God; our desire for what truly has value asserts its dominance only when we mature.

> *Paradise is surrounded by what we dislike;*
> *the fires of hell are surrounded by what we desire.*
>
> —RUMI

When you tune in to your cravings, you break off attunement with the Divine current. You are no longer serving God, you are serving only your own desires.

> *I found God more tempting than temptation.*
>
> —PARAMAHANSA YOGANANDA

In this state of mind, the karmic consequences generated by your actions inevitably lead to regret and remorse.

> *Self-denial is a kind of holy association with God; and by making him your partner interests him in all your happiness.*
>
> —ROBERT BOYLE

Your strongest cravings—typically those that have a consciousness-lowering effect— will boldly resist your efforts to overcome them.

Involuntary thought is an affection of the mind, and curbing of thought, therefore, means curbing of the mind which is even more difficult to curb than the wind.

—MAHATMA GANDHI

Strive to rise above your craving, and it will ceaselessly whisper, "Just once more, and I will release you."

Grant me chastity and continence, but not yet.

—SAINT AUGUSTINE

Two things are certain: One, when tomorrow comes, the urge will return full force. Two, tomorrow always comes.

Just as a tree, though cut down, can grow again and again if its roots are undamaged and strong, in the same way if the roots of craving are not wholly uprooted sorrows will come again and again.

—BUDDHA

Your cravings are like tentacles that wrap themselves around you and drag you backward as you struggle to reach the doorway to your very best self.

If you do not conquer self, you will be conquered by self.

—NAPOLEON HILL

Ironically, to liberate yourself from such seductively urgent desires, you may first have to yield to them.

Plunge into the world, and then, after a time, when you have suffered and enjoyed all that is in it, will renunciation come; then will calmness come. So fulfill your desire for power and everything else, and after you have fulfilled the desire, will come the time when you will know that they are all very little things; but until you have fulfilled this desire, until you have passed through that activity, it is impossible for you to come to the state of calmness, serenity and self-surrender.

—SWAMI VIVEKANANDA

By giving in to temptation, you may discover that the combined pleasure of the expectation and the act itself is trumped by the pain of the consequence—whether that manifests as an upset stomach, an awkward social encounter, a guilty conscience, or the disappointment of not living up to your ever-evolving standards.

> *How like herrings and onions our vices are in the morning after we have committed them.*
>
> —SAMUEL TAYLOR COLERIDGE

Recalling that pain, you will be less likely to allow this desire to consume you when next it rears up and demands fulfillment.

> *The followers of the Way are like dry straw, and must be protected against the fires of desire. One must put distance between oneself and the object of his desire.*
>
> —BUDDHA

Fending off your cravings through sheer force of will may grant you a temporary reprieve, but truly transcending such desires requires conscious fidelity to a higher purpose.

> *Opportunity may knock only once, but temptation leans on the doorbell.*
>
> —UNKNOWN

The best way to add distance between you and the object of your desire is to view your options and their likely consequences through God's eyes.

> *A man is a slave to anything he cannot part with that is less than himself.*
>
> —GEORGE MACDONALD

No matter how intoxicating your desire, thinking through the chain reaction of emotions and experiences your actions would set in motion often has a sobering effect.

Do not bite at the bait of pleasure till you know there is no hook beneath it.

—THOMAS JEFFERSON

When your intuition tells you that what you crave is not in harmony with Divine Will, your desire may relax its grip just enough to tilt the balance of power back in your favor.

If you can't pray a door open, don't pry it open.

—LYELL RADER

The deeper your devotion and the stronger your yearning for oneness with the Divine, the better your chances of transcending your craving.

Strength does not come from physical capacity. It comes from an indomitable will.

—MAHATMA GANDHI

The further you travel on your spiritual path, the closer looms your day of reckoning. No matter how many textbooks on swimming technique you have studied, you cannot claim to know how to swim until you find yourself in deep water. Similarly, you cannot claim to be spiritually advanced until you can stand toe to toe with your cravings without blinking.

A man who knows all goods and all truths, as many as can be known, but does not shun evils, knows nothing.

—EMANUEL SWEDENBORG

Listen intently after slaying the dragon of your craving with the righteous sword of higher consciousness and you will hear a chorus of angels rejoicing.

He who conquers others is strong. He who conquers himself is mighty.

—LAO TZU

Identify with ego and denial of sense pleasures is excruciating. Surrender to Spirit and the same denial can become exhilarating, steeped in meaning and purpose.

> *To become free of attachment means to break the link identifying you*
> *with your desires. The desires continue; they are part of the dance of*
> *nature. But a renunciate no longer thinks that he is his desires.*
>
> —RAM DASS

You are on the road to peace when you learn to control your cravings instead of allowing your cravings to control you.

> *Conscience is the voice of the soul, the passions are the voice of*
> *the body. Is it surprising that these two voices should sometimes*
> *contradict each other, or can it be doubted, when they do, which*
> *ought to be obeyed?*
>
> —JEAN-JACQUES ROUSSEAU

In time, it occurs to you that what you once ached for has as much power over you as the whistling of the wind.

> *We never lose an attachment by saying it has to go. Only as we gain*
> *awareness of its true nature does it quietly and imperceptibly wither*
> *away; like a sandcastle with waves rolling over, it just smooths out*
> *and finally—where is it? What was it?*
>
> —CHARLOTTE JOKO BECK

THE MYTH OF MISTAKES

Letting go of the need to produce specific outcomes erases any trepidation or guilt about making mistakes.

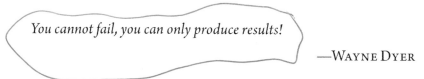

> *You cannot fail, you can only produce results!*
>
> —WAYNE DYER

Every action simply recalibrates the Unified Field, redirecting you to other possible outcomes. Trust this process; it is the road to wisdom.

> *Good judgment comes from experience. And where does experience come from? Experience comes from bad judgment.*

—MARK TWAIN

Missteps, misfires, and mishaps are invaluable teachers. Learn what you can from each one so you do not make the same mistake twice.

> *Mistakes are natural. Mistakes are how we learn. When we stop making mistakes, we stop learning and growing. But repeating the same mistake over and over is not continuous learning—it's not paying attention.*

—WALLY "FAMOUS" AMOS

Architect and visionary Buckminster Fuller explained the value of mistakes through the analogy of a ship's rudder. A ship tends to continue moving in the direction it is angled. The helmsman has to steer the ship back toward the intended destination, acting and reacting, adjusting and reorienting, in a never-ending process of course correction.

> *If error is corrected whenever it is recognized as such, the path of error is the path of truth.*

—HANS REICHENBACH

By doing something the wrong way, you learn how to do it the right way. Not learning is not possible.

> *I have not failed 10,000 times. I have successfully found 10,000 ways that will not work.*

—THOMAS EDISON

More important than a mistake itself is your reaction to having made it. Objectively analyzing what happened while keeping your emotions in check allows the calm, clear voice of your intuitive guidance to reveal the next best step.

> *Mishaps are like knives, that either serve us or cut us, as we grasp them by the blade or the handle.*

—JAMES RUSSELL LOWELL

If you choose instead to wallow in self-pity and evade responsibility for your error, you are signaling to the Universe that failing is your natural state.

> A man can fail many times, but he isn't a failure until he begins to blame somebody else.
>
> —JOHN BURROUGHS

Beat yourself up for mistakes, and the Universe will impartially see to it that you continue to experience "negative" results that make you miserable.

> If you have made mistakes, even serious mistakes, there is always another chance for you. And supposing you have tried and failed again and again, you may have a fresh start any moment you choose, for this thing we call "failure" is not the falling down, but the staying down.
>
> —MARY PICKFORD

Welcome your mistakes. They remind you that perfection is an unreasonable goal and that humility is a necessary portal to enlightenment.

> Once we realize that imperfect understanding is the human condition, there is no shame in being wrong, only in failing to correct our mistakes.
>
> —GEORGE SOROS

With humility comes maturity. With maturity comes wisdom. With wisdom comes the awareness to learn not just from your own mistakes but from the mistakes of others.

> Is there anyone so wise as to learn by the experience of others?
>
> —VOLTAIRE

Even the gravest of mistakes can be a blessing if you use it as a key to unlock inner storehouses of fortitude and resolve.

> Failure is God's own tool for carving some of the finest outlines in the character of his children.
>
> —THOMAS HODGKIN

Behind every successful person is a trail of spectacular blunders that would have laid low less adventurous souls.

> *We are all failures—at least, all the best of us are.*
>
> —J. M. Barrie

Avoid taking risks to avoid making mistakes, and you will never achieve the greatness that beckons to you from the other side of failure.

> *But as in most things, it may take a bundle of mistakes to arrive at something sublime, just as it takes thousands of flowers to produce a few drops of perfume.*
>
> —Thomas Moore

You live risk-free when you follow your guidance, reframe your errors as lessons, and have faith that Divine Wisdom will deliver the right results.

> *And the trouble is, if you don't risk anything, you risk even more.*
>
> —Erica Jong

THE DESIRE FOR DETACHMENT

Buddha stated that the core message of his teaching was, "Nothing should be clung to as me or mine." Indian guru Nisargadatta Maharaj sagely added that enlightenment was also reachable through the mindset of "*Everything* should be clung to as me or mine."

> *Contradiction is not a sign of falsity, nor the want of contradiction a sign of truth.*
>
> —Blaise Pascal

These seemingly competing statements present a compelling paradox of perspectives; yet, upon closer examination, they coexist in perfect harmony.

*Spiritual maturity lies in the readiness to let go of everything. The
giving up is the first step. But the real giving up is in realizing that
there is nothing to give up, for nothing is your own.*

—NISARGADATTA MAHARAJ

Buddha's dictum implies the complete vanquishing of the ego; Nisargadatta's maxim
assumes total identification with Spirit. The only difference between the two asser-
tions is a matter of emphasis.

*To my extreme happiness,
My Lord has come to tell me
That from now on
 I must stand apart from my actions,
Divine and undivine.
He alone is the Doer;
I am a mere observer.*

—SRI CHINMOY

Paradox is nothing more than the same truth viewed from different angles. It is an invitation to expand your perspective, to recast seemingly contradictory statements like
"Everything matters" and "Nothing matters" as complementary. "Everything matters"
because your every action generates karmic repercussions. "Nothing matters" because
no matter what you do or do not do, you will ultimately melt into Divine union.

*Every experience is a paradox in that it means to be absolute, and
yet is relative; in that it somehow always goes beyond itself and yet
never escapes itself.*

—T. S. ELIOT

Detachment is a natural consequence of spiritual advancement; it cannot be hurried
along or forced.

*The sages call that man wise whose pursuits are all without selfish
plan or longings for results, and whose activities are purified by the
fire of wisdom.*

—BHAGAVAD GITA 4:19

Allow your ego to rule your mind, and detachment will remain a mystery. Allow your spirit to reign in your heart, and detachment will flow from mastery.

> *Like two golden birds perched on the selfsame tree,*
> *Intimate friends, the ego and the Self*
> *Dwell in the same body. The former eats*
> *The sweet and sour fruits of the tree of life*
> *While the latter looks on in detachment.*
>
> —THE MUNDAKA UPANISHAD

Consciously working to develop detachment is more of an exercise in self-discipline than a means of hastening enlightenment.

> *Detachment is a plant of slow growth; if you pluck the tender*
> *plant to look for the pods, you will be disappointed.*
>
> —SRI SATHYA SAI BABA

Detachment is the transcendence of desire, but a desire to achieve detachment is itself a desire, and may circle back as frustration and guilt.

> *Getting rid of things and clinging to emptiness*
> *Is an illness of the same kind;*
> *It is just like throwing oneself into a fire*
> *To avoid being drowned.*
>
> —YUNG-CHIA TA-SHIH

Whatever you do, do it for God, do it to serve the world, and trust that a wisdom greater than your own will govern the outcome.

> *On earth we have nothing to do with success or with results, but only*
> *with being true to God, and for God. . . . Defeat in doing right is*
> *nevertheless victory.*
>
> —FREDERICK WILLIAM ROBERTSON

Judge yourself not on material wealth or public approval, but on the purity of your intent.

'Tis the motive exalts the action.
'Tis the doing, not the deed.

—MARGARET JUNKIN PRESTON

Until you escape from Planet Me, you will not achieve the higher consciousness necessary to understand and appreciate the meaning and purpose of detachment.

People are often unreasonable, illogical, and self-centered;
. . . Forgive them anyway.
If you are kind, people may accuse you of selfish, ulterior motives;
. . . Be kind anyway.
If you are successful, you will win some false friends and some true
enemies;
. . . Succeed anyway.
If you are honest and frank, people may cheat you;
. . . Be honest and frank anyway.
What you spend years building, someone could destroy overnight;
. . . Build anyway.
If you find serenity and happiness, they may be jealous;
. . . Be happy anyway.
The good you do today, people will often forget tomorrow;
. . . Do good anyway.
Give the world the best you have, and it may never be enough;
. . . Give the world the best you've got anyway.
You see, in the final analysis, it is between you and God;
It was never between you and them anyway.

—KENT M. KEITH

DETACH FROM OUTCOMES
Living the Lesson

On an otherwise ordinary Thursday night, my dad slept in his own bed in his own home for the last time. He didn't realize it, and never would. He was to spend Friday night—and all the rest of his nights—in a nearby nursing home.

His memory had been failing for at least a decade but it wasn't until a warm September evening six years before that I truly became alarmed. In my mind, it was the night he veered off the main highway of life and began weaving erratically down Alzheimer's Avenue.

He had headed the stats crew for University of Minnesota Gopher football games for forty years, and, as was his custom, he was going to drive the twenty minutes to my townhouse after the game and sleep over rather than drive an additional seventy miles to his home in St. Cloud.

I didn't expect him until after midnight; at a quarter to one, the phone rang. He was lost. He was calling from the Hopkins House Hotel a couple of miles away. I cheerfully told him that all he had to do was head east on Highway 7. He said he didn't know which way east was, which startled me. I then heard five words that sent a chill up my spine. In a soft, sweet voice, he said, "I'll never make it, hon." I paused for a second, then said, "I'll be right there." I drove over and he followed me home.

It was another couple of years before he stopped driving altogether. A year after that, my mom began bringing him to the St. Cloud Veterans Administration Medical Center for adult day care. It was a godsend for both of them. He loved the staff, loved to swim and exercise, and best of all, loved to while away the time working on arts and crafts projects. My parents' house is filled with these little treasures. I too shared in the bounty; a pink ceramic piggy bank he painted stares happily down at me from a shelf as I write this.

My dad was very happy at the V.A. for a few years. But when he no longer could follow simple instructions and began needing one-on-one attention just to color a picture, the staff gently told my mom that other arrangements needed to be made. My mom hoped to keep my dad at home as long as she could but when he was unable to shower in the morning without help, she knew she had run out of options. With a heavy heart, she drove him to a nursing home that Friday morning.

Some would say that my dad's slow descent into oblivion was a tragedy. I prefer to view it as the natural unfolding of a Divine plan, the details of which I am not privy to. From the very start, as his mental capacities diminished, my mother, sister, and I surrendered to the process. Clinging to any expectations would have been counterproductive. Instead, we focused our attention simply on loving him in the moments we had together.

Inevitably, the glimmer of recognition in my dad's eyes began to flicker and fade. But that was okay. With a hug, a kiss on the cheek, and a shoulder rub, I could still communicate with him through the language of the heart. Besides, I knew who he was—and that he would forever be who he always was.

We got the call from the nursing home eight weeks before his seventy-ninth birthday. His eyes were glazing over and he was having difficulty breathing. It was his time to go.

I was fortunate to have a few minutes alone with him as he lay on the bed in his room for the last time. I snuggled up beside him, rested my head on his chest, told him how much I cherished him, and shared some of my favorite memories of our life together. I like to think that, on some level, he was able to hear and understand me.

At one point he jerked up his head, and for a moment, his panicked eyes were filled with terror. In a soothing voice, I told him that it was okay, that I was here, and that everything would be all right. The fear passed from his eyes and he lowered his head to the pillow. I remember feeling honored that I could comfort him in his hour of need.

Soon, the family gathered around his bed and the vigil began. One minute before midnight, the changeless, eternal essence of who he was burst forth, free to soar once again. Hours later, alone and in silent gratitude, I hit my knees and thanked God for giving me the gift of being my father's son.

DETACH FROM OUTCOMES
Self-Reflection Questions

- Why do I resist the idea of detaching from results?

- In what ways do I try to control my interactions with others, and why?

- If I open myself to the possibility that there may be better outcomes than the one I have in mind, how would that change my life?

- How would partnering with Divine Intelligence—doing what I feel guided to do and turning over responsibility for the outcome—change the way I interpret the consequences of my actions?

- How can I get in the habit of gratefully and graciously accepting whatever comes into my life?

- How can I shift my focus so that I extract more value from the process of pursuing my goals?

- How can I get better at stepping back and allowing my loved ones to learn the lessons they need to learn?

- What is an example of a situation in which too much empathy would be unhealthy?

- What do I value about worldly pleasures that I cannot get from spiritual pleasures, and vice versa?

- How can I remind myself to reframe my mistakes as learning opportunities?

- Why is humility a pivotal element in how I deal with mistakes?

- How can I expand my vision so that my goals serve the world instead of just serving myself?

FIFTEEN

WELCOME ADVERSITY

Adversity causes some men to break;
others to break records.

—William Arthur Ward

WELCOME ADVERSITY

Though adversity may scramble the puzzle pieces of your life, it arrives bearing a gift: a shift in consciousness that deepens your understanding and appreciation of Universal forces.

> *In every crisis there is a message. Crises are nature's way of forcing change—breaking down old structures, shaking loose negative habits so that something new and better can take their place.*
>
> —SUSAN L. TAYLOR

PROBLEMS HAVE PURPOSE

The value of adversity has long been the stuff of legend. In the Bhagavad Gita, Kunti, mother of heroic Arjuna, prays to Lord Krishna to bless her with a never-ending series of sorrows, reasoning that her thoughts will then always be turned to Him.

> *What is required of us is that we love the difficult and learn to deal with it. In the difficult are the friendly forces, the hands that work on us.*
>
> —RAINER MARIA RILKE

Yes, battling through adversity can bring you closer to God. But while Kunti's devotion is admirable, her wish is impractical and misguided.

> *Experience may be hard but we claim its gifts because they are real, even though our feet bleed on its stones.*
>
> —MARY PARKER FOLLETT

Ideally, unlike Kunti, you will transition from being reactive and learning through pain to being proactive and learning through joy.

Sooner or later, a time arises in every person's life when a connection with that Higher Power suddenly becomes of utmost urgency, bringing him to his knees through painful desperation or worshipful devotion—the choice is his.

—Paramahansa Yogananda

Until you make that transition, a calamity may be the only way for the Universe to get your attention.

A good scare is worth more to a man than good advice.

—Edgar Watson Howe

Odds are that your search for deeper meaning and purpose did not kick into overdrive until a crisis turned your world inside out and upside down.

God whispers to us in our pleasures, speaks in our conscience, but shouts in our pains: it is His megaphone to rouse a deaf world.

—C. S. Lewis

As awareness grows, you realize that adversity may be a signal that your current path leads someplace other than your highest good.

It is often better to have a great deal of harm happen to one than a little; a great deal may rouse you to remove what a little will only accustom you to endure.

—Grenville Kleiser

You begin viewing frustrations, difficulties, and impediments as clues that the Universe is nudging you to make better choices.

One of the secrets of life is to make stepping stones out of stumbling blocks.

—Jack Penn

You tackle each obstacle with equal parts detachment, discernment, and determination, recognizing that it contains divinely encoded instructions designed to further your growth.

> *The problem is not that there are problems. The problem is expecting otherwise and thinking that having problems is a problem.*
>
> —THEODORE ISAAC RUBIN

The higher your consciousness, the greater the chance you will recognize the Divine reason behind your misfortune, thus learning the intended lesson.

> *Your pain is the breaking of the shell that encloses your understanding. Even as the stone of the fruit must break, that its heart may stand in the sun, so must you know pain.*
>
> —KAHLIL GIBRAN

Learning a lesson and taking it to heart eliminates the need for you to endure future situations designed to deliver the same message—unless you drift back into old, familiar patterns and need another wake-up call.

> *Aversion, also, is a form of bondage. We are tied to what we hate or fear. That is why, in our lives, the same problem, the same danger or difficulty, will present itself over and over again in various aspects, as long as we continue to resist or run away from it instead of examining and solving it.*
>
> —PATANJALI

The moment you understand why you repeatedly find yourself in the same types of dysfunctional relationships, unfulfilling jobs, or needless conflicts, you can choose to break the pattern, start living more consciously, and free yourself up for healthier experiences.

> *Blame yourself if you have no branches or leaves; don't accuse the sun of partiality.*
>
> —CHINESE PROVERB

THE BIG PICTURE

By definition, the circle of life demands that we experience the full range of what this life has to offer.

> *To round itself out, life calls not for perfection but for*
> *completeness; and for this the "thorn in the flesh" is needed,*
> *the suffering of defects without which there is no progress*
> *and no ascent.*
>
> —CARL JUNG

Adversity is an integral part of the natural order of things. No one escapes its bittersweet embrace.

> *There is a time for expanding and a time for contraction; one*
> *provokes the other and the other calls for the return of the*
> *first. . . . Never are we nearer the Light than when the darkness*
> *is deepest.*
>
> —SWAMI VIVEKANANDA

While you cannot prevent adversity from knocking on your door, you can prepare for its arrival by living your life as an unceasing prayer of gratitude.

> *Be grateful even for hardship, setbacks, and bad people. Dealing with*
> *such obstacles is an essential part of training in the art of Peace.*
>
> —MORIHEI UESHIBA

The greater your alignment with the Divine Mind, the greater your ability to serenely accept, work through, and transcend whatever challenges come your way.

> *Misfortune is never mournful to the soul that accepts it; for such do*
> *always see that every cloud is an angel's face.*
>
> —LYDIA M. CHILD

As you become more attuned to Divine Consciousness, you become better equipped to counsel and support others who are struggling.

> *Each difficult moment has the potential to open my eyes and open my heart.*
>
> —MYLA KABAT-ZINN

The road to enlightenment is by no means a linear path; adversity and triumph melt into one another until they are all but indistinguishable.

> *Some of you say, "Joy is greater than sorrow," and others say, "Nay, sorrow is the greater."*
> *But I say unto you, they are inseparable.*
> *Together they come, and when one sits alone with you at your board, remember that the other is asleep upon your bed.*
>
> —KAHLIL GIBRAN

Thus, while you do not necessarily rejoice whenever life steers you into a ditch, you at least challenge yourself to view each plight with symbolic sight.

> *Suffering is but another name for the teaching of experience, which is the parent of instruction and the schoolmaster of life.*
>
> —HORACE

Granted, activating your symbolic sight may be difficult to do in the midst of an emotional maelstrom.

> *Even loss and betrayal can bring us awakening.*
>
> —BUDDHA

Still, the instant you unplug from reacting out of pure emotion and begin objectively observing a situation, your fears and anxieties loosen their steely grip and you start to regain your mental clarity.

> *To see your drama clearly is to be liberated from it.*
>
> —KEN KEYES, JR.

COURAGE AND CHARACTER

How you feel about a challenge depends on how you choose to deal with it. You can call upon the best in you, or let it get the best of you.

> *Providence has hidden a charm in difficult undertakings, which is appreciated only by those who dare to grapple with them.*
>
> —MADAME SWETCHINE

It matters not whether you are caught in a spring shower or a raging thunderstorm. What matters is whether you seize the opportunity to better yourself.

> *The things that happen to us do not matter; what we become through them does.*
>
> —SRI GYANAMATA

Viewed through God's eyes, every challenge becomes a vehicle for self-expression, a chance to react to the circumstances at hand with love, courage, and integrity.

> *It is almost more important how a person takes his fate than what it is.*
>
> —WILHELM VON HUMBOLDT

No matter how much discomfort it brings, every difficulty calls forth the heroic, noble qualities of your soul.

> *Ultimately, there is no way to avoid the hero's quest. It comes and finds us if we do not move out bravely to meet it.*
>
> —CAROL PEARSON

How heroically you answer that call determines how fully you realize your divine potential.

> *Difficulty, my brethren, is the nurse of greatness; a harsh nurse, who roughly rocks her foster-children into strength and athletic proportion.*
>
> —WILLIAM CULLEN BRYANT

Celebrate the difficult moments, for they are where the missing pieces of your greatness can be found.

> *Things don't go wrong and break your heart so you can become bitter and give up. They happen to break you down and build you up so you can be all that you were intended to be.*
>
> —CHARLIE "TREMENDOUS" JONES

Greeting every challenge as a character-building exercise deepens your wisdom, sets the stage for inner victories, and summons the hero that lies within.

> *If God asks that you bend, bend and do not complain. He is making you more flexible, and for this be thankful.*
>
> —MERIEL STELLIGER

Adversity does not strengthen character so much as reveal it. As storm clouds gather, the radiant light of integrity shines ever more brightly.

> *People are like stained-glass windows. They sparkle and shine when the sun is out, but when the darkness sets in, their true beauty is revealed only if there is a light from within.*
>
> —ELISABETH KÜBLER-ROSS

In contrast, many who think themselves honest and law-abiding will happily slip through an ethical loophole if given the chance, rationalizing that nobody's perfect, anyone else would do the same, and besides, life isn't fair.

> *Adversity is the trial of principle. Without it a man hardly knows whether he is honest or not.*
>
> —HENRY FIELDING

It is true that life is not fair. It is also true that it is. It all depends on whether you are looking through God's eyes or your own. Human justice can look very different than Divine justice.

> *Life is not fair, but life is not fair for everyone. That makes life fair.*
>
> —UNKNOWN

ELEVATING YOUR GAME

Every tussle with adversity is designed to further buff the perfectly formed diamond of your soul.

> *If you are irritated by every rub, how will you be polished?*
>
> —RUMI

Athletes elevate their game not by practice alone, but by competing against stronger opponents.

> *He that wrestles with us strengthens our nerves, and sharpens our skill. Our antagonist is our helper.*
>
> —EDMUND BURKE

Embrace your inner David and rise up to meet Goliath. The satisfaction of triumphing over so great an adversary will taste that much sweeter.

> *The harder the conflict, the more glorious the triumph.*
>
> —THOMAS PAINE

You may even look forward to finding yourself knee-deep in misfortune just so you can know the joy of overcoming it.

> *God turns you from one feeling to another and teaches by means of opposites, so that you will have two wings to fly, not one.*
>
> —RUMI

Every squall you are forced to navigate better prepares you for the next storm brewing just over the horizon.

> *Smooth seas do not make skillful sailors.*
>
> —AFRICAN PROVERB

Indeed, it may be advantageous to find yourself adrift in troubled waters rather than relaxing contentedly on shore.

> *Adversity has the effect of eliciting talents which in prosperous circumstances would have lain dormant.*
>
> —HORACE

When you manage to crawl out of the surf, take whatever time you need to catch your breath and regain your equilibrium. Then build a better ship, and set sail again.

> *The purpose of life is to be defeated by greater and greater things.*
>
> —RAINER MARIA RILKE

EMERGING STRONGER

Our greatest lessons are often embedded in our greatest pain. We cry to the heavens, unaware that we are growing stronger and wiser even as we plead for mercy.

> *We rarely gain a higher or larger view except as it is forced upon us through struggles which we would have avoided if we could.*
>
> —CHARLES HORTON COOLEY

You would not be the person you are today if you had never been brought to your knees by the vicissitudes of life.

> *If life teaches us anything, it may be that it's necessary to suffer some defeats. Look at a diamond: It is the result of extreme pressure. Less pressure, it is crystal; less than that, it's coal; and less than that, it is fossilized leaves or just plain dirt.*
>
> —MAYA ANGELOU

Even the most dedicated and disciplined spiritual aspirants must do battle with adversity to touch the upper limits of their strength and wisdom.

> *Character cannot be developed in ease and quiet. Only through experience of trial and suffering can the soul be strengthened, vision cleared, ambition inspired, and success achieved.*
>
> —HELEN KELLER

The most capable and courageous among us have likely lived through punishing experiences, the simple telling of which would make the rest of us faint dead away.

> *That which does not kill me, makes me stronger.*
>
> —FRIEDRICH NIETZSCHE

If you cannot change what you are faced with, then you must face that you are meant not to change it, but to experience it.

> *For after all, the best thing one can do when it's raining is to let it rain.*
>
> —HENRY WADSWORTH LONGFELLOW

You cannot choose when adversity will pay you a visit. Your only choice is how to deal with it when it arrives.

> *We say that we cannot bear our troubles but when we get to them we bear them.*
>
> —NING LAO T'AI-T' AI

Just as Atlas was able to bear the weight of the entire world, trust that you too can shoulder whatever comes your way.

> *God gave burdens, also shoulders.*
>
> —YIDDISH PROVERB

Adversity compels you to dig deep within until you tap into the bottomless well of tenacity and fortitude that is a hallmark of the human spirit.

> *Pain nourishes courage. You can't be brave if you've only had wonderful things happen to you.*
>
> —MARY TYLER MOORE

In the worst of times, you may surprise yourself by your boundless capacity for strength and endurance.

> *Our strength often increases in proportion to the obstacles imposed upon it.*
>
> —PAUL DE RAPIN

Meet hardship with dignity and grace, and you will emerge from your trials with greater reverence, humility, and clarity of purpose.

> *Life is a grindstone, and whether it grinds a man down or polishes him up, depends on what he is made of.*
>
> —JOSH BILLINGS

Misfortune also brings the gift of clarity to your relationships. Your bonds of love and friendship are forever deepened and strengthened with those who rally to your side.

> *Adversity draws men together and produces beauty and harmony in life's relationships, just as the cold of winter produces ice-flowers on the window-panes, which vanish with the warmth.*
>
> —SØREN KIERKEGAARD

FIGHTING THE FEAR

Fear is the moat full of alligators between you and the castle where your greatest self resides.

> *You gain strength, courage, and confidence by every experience in which you really stop to look fear in the face. You are able to say to yourself, "I lived through this horror. I can take the next thing that comes along." . . . You must do the thing you think you cannot do.*
>
> —ELEANOR ROOSEVELT

There may be many who fear less than you, but no human being has ever been truly fearless.

> *Courage is resistance to fear, mastery of fear—not absence of fear.*
>
> —MARK TWAIN

Summon the courage to look squarely at the challenge in front of you, lest you slip into avoidance, escapism, and, inevitably, denial.

> *Be willing to have it so. Acceptance of what has happened is the first step to overcoming the consequences of any misfortune.*
>
> —WILLIAM JAMES

Face adversity with fear instead of fortitude and you obscure the accompanying lessons, depriving yourself of valuable learning experiences.

> *Troubles are often the tools by which God fashions us for better things.*
>
> —HENRY WARD BEECHER

It is always in your power to reframe a hardship so that you instantly transition from fearing the worst to expecting the best.

> *Sometimes when the world is dark it is for a purpose. Otherwise you would not see the light of the tunnel you're supposed to choose.*
>
> —KRISTA BELLES

Fear relaxes its hold on you when, in the midst of crisis, you can look beyond the pain of the moment and think, *There is value in this.*

> *Bad times have a scientific value. These are occasions a good learner would not miss.*
>
> —RALPH WALDO EMERSON

Fear is nothing more than a bully spewing empty threats. Take even one step toward it and fear begins slinking away like the coward that it is.

> *Do the thing you fear, and the death of fear is certain.*
>
> —RALPH WALDO EMERSON

Turn away in fear from a challenge that must be faced and it only grows more formidable, swallowing up more of your emotional energy with each passing day.

Courage is being scared to death . . . and saddling up anyway.

—JOHN WAYNE

As the circumstances of your evasion sink to the bottom of your memory, your fear gradually softens into vague feelings of uneasiness and regret that block you from bringing more peace into your life.

Every difficulty slurred over will be a ghost to disturb your repose later on.

—FRÉDÉRIC CHOPIN

Fear can only be conquered if it is seized and wrestled to the ground. Shrink away from it and fear becomes your master.

Look into your fears, dare them to do their worst and cut them down when they try. If you don't, they'll clone themselves, mushroom till they surround you, choke the road to the life you want. Every turn you fear is empty air, dressed to look like jagged hell.

—RICHARD BACH

Beating your chest, gnashing your teeth, and howling at the injustice of it all only exacerbates your plight.

Wisdom never kicks at the iron walls it can't bring down.

—OLIVE SCHREINER

Even worse, your resistance sweeps your mind out to sea, short-circuiting your intuitive guidance and rendering you incapable of rational response.

Facing it—always facing it—that's the way to get through. Face it!

—JOSEPH CONRAD

Continue to say yes to life no matter what it delivers to your door, and fear remains locked in the cellar, its muffled threats only dimly piercing your consciousness.

Courage, in its final analysis, is nothing but an affirmative answer to the shocks of existence.

—Dr. Kurt Goldstein

WORRY IS SELF-PERPETUATING

Fretting about what could go wrong is a self-fulfilling prophecy that needlessly produces suffering.

He who foresees calamities suffers them twice over.

—Beilby Porteus

The more you worry about bad things happening, the more likely that bad things will happen.

We act in such a way that people finally comply and act in the way we feared they would act. You fear a person will leave you, and because of that fear, you act in such a way that finally causes the person to actually leave.

—Bill Harris

The law of attraction will ensure that your fears energetically draw hardship and suffering into your life.

This I have seen in life—he who is overcautious about himself falls into dangers at every step; he who is afraid of losing honour and respect, gets only disgrace; he who is always afraid of loss always loses.

—Swami Vivekananda

Yet your greatest fears, the monsters that plague your days and wreck your nights, rarely, if ever, materialize.

We poison our lives with fear of burglary and shipwreck . . . and the house is never burgled, and the ship never goes down.

—JEAN ANOUILH

Even if the cataclysms that haunt your mind never comes to pass, the damage has been done.

Who feareth to suffer, suffereth already, because he feareth.

—MICHEL DE MONTAIGNE

Worry bumps you out of the present moment, stripping you of your capacity to feel peaceful and loving.

Worry does not empty tomorrow of its sorrow. It empties today of its strength.

—CORRIE TEN BOOM

Worrying is an insurance policy against happiness. Even when tomorrow brings nothing but bluebirds and rainbows, the back of your mind remains fixated on the storm clouds that are surely gathering somewhere within striking distance.

Real difficulties can be overcome; it is only the imaginary ones that are unconquerable.

—THEODORE NEWTON VAIL

Whatever you worry about grows larger every time you worry about it. Worrying can quickly inflate a relatively insignificant issue into an ulcer-inducing ordeal.

Worry gives small things a big shadow.

—SWEDISH PROVERB

Worry often enough for long enough and you program your subconscious to accept worrying as the natural and proper response to life.

Worry is a thin stream of fear trickling through the mind. If encouraged, it cuts a channel into which all other thoughts are drained.

—ARTHUR SOMERS ROCHE

Worrying never helps and always hurts. It ruins good times, intensifies bad times, and recasts life's challenges as waking nightmares.

If you can solve your problem, then what is the need of worrying?
If you cannot solve it, then what is the use of worrying?

—SHANTIDEVA

When worries beset you, be still and go within. Invite your fears in one by one and watch them dissolve in the rarefied air of higher consciousness.

Any negative state, like worry, is like your shadow. If you run away, it pursues, but by standing still you see that it has no movement except that which you give it by running away.

—VERNON HOWARD

Motivational pioneer Dale Carnegie observed that when you have identified and accepted the worst that can happen in a given situation, you have nothing more to lose, which automatically means that you have everything to gain.

You'll break the worry habit the day you decide you can meet and master the worst that can happen to you.

—ARNOLD H. GLASOW

God is always willing to make a trade. Give God your worries; in exchange, you will receive a heart filled with peace.

When trust removes fear, faith flows in.

—ANN-MARGRET

LESSONS OF LOSS

Every one of us has suffered losses—a job, a romance, a friendship, cherished posses-sions, money, health, or all of the above—and desperately prayed for what we lost to be returned to us.

> *This being human is a guest house.*
> *Every morning a new arrival.*
>
> *A joy, a depression, a meanness,*
> *some momentary awareness comes*
> *as an unexpected visitor.*
>
> *Welcome and entertain them all!*
> *Even if they're a crowd of sorrows,*
> *who violently sweep your house*
> *empty of its furniture,*
> *still, treat each guest honorably.*
> *He may be clearing you out*
> *for some new delight.*

—Rumi

Yet every one of us can look back at a particularly painful loss and see that it was a blessing in disguise.

> *If you want the rainbow, you gotta put up with the rain.*

—Dolly Parton

In time, you found a new job, a new relationship, a new outlook on life that served you better. Your consciousness was expanded, your awareness was heightened, and you learned how to make healthier choices.

> *He who suffers much will know much.*

—Greek proverb

Every staggering loss you have endured has played a major role in shaping who you are. Pain and purpose walk hand in hand.

> *Perhaps all the dragons in our lives are princesses who are only*
> *waiting to see us act, just once, with beauty and courage.*
>
> —RAINER MARIA RILKE

By simple virtue of enduring what must be endured, you activate your powers of self-discovery and mastery.

> *When you pull a propeller through compression, don't be surprised*
> *when the engine starts.*
>
> —RICHARD BACH

You come to see and appreciate the value of loss, and honor it as a necessary and important element in your journey toward wholeness.

> *One may not reach the dawn save by the path of the night.*
>
> —KAHLIL GIBRAN

RESCUING LOVED ONES

We pray for our children to live easy, uncomplicated lives. We may be doing them a disservice.

> *At every step, the child should be allowed to meet the real experience*
> *of life; the thorns should never be plucked from his roses.*
>
> —ELLEN KEY

We serve our children better by praying that the hardships they *do* endure make them stronger, wiser, and better equipped to fulfill their sacred contracts and share their unique gifts with the world.

Prosperity is a great teacher; adversity is a greater. Possession pampers the mind; privation trains and strengthens it.

—WILLIAM HAZLITT

Be an endless source of love and compassion, but think twice before donning a super-hero costume and saving the day.

The truest help we can render an afflicted man is not to take his burden from him, but to call out his best energy, that he may be able to bear the burden.

—PHILLIPS BROOKS

If someone had swooped in and saved you from experiencing every hardship, would you be as strong and as wise as you are today?

God doesn't want us merely to "get" through our problems. He wants us to "grow" through them.

—GARY OLIVER

Just as the Universe treats all of God's children with loving detachment, so must we guide and support our children while recognizing that "rescuing" them from difficulties can thwart the maturation process and prevent them from learning vital life lessons.

Then that which caused us trial shall yield us triumph; and that which made our heart ache shall fill us with gladness; and we shall then feel that there, as here, the only true happiness is to learn, to advance, and to improve; which could not happen unless we had commenced with error, ignorance, and imperfection. We must pass through the darkness, to reach the light.

—ALBERT PIKE

Indeed, we may inadvertently be creating an endless loop of dependence and entitlement that retards their psychological and spiritual growth.

Too many parents make life hard for their children by trying, too zealously, to make it easy for them.

—JOHANN WOLFGANG VON GOETHE

Ultimately, fighting the battles that were theirs to fight may prevent our children from becoming all that they were born to be.

Do not free a camel of the burden of his hump; you may be freeing him from being a camel.

—G. K. CHESTERTON

Instead, let us encourage our children to venture outside their comfort zone and experience all the richness and complexities that life has to offer.

"Come to the edge."
"We can't. We are afraid."
"Come to the edge."
"We can't. We will fall."
"Come to the edge."
And they came.
And he pushed them.
And they flew.

—CHRISTOPHER LOGUE

GOD IS THERE

Medieval Roman philosopher Boethius wrote in *Consolation of Philosophy* that the wheel of life, which represents the mercurial nature of fortune, is always in motion. The only changeless portion is the wheel's center where God presides, offering you protection from the vagaries of life on earth.

The Master sees things as they are, without trying to control them.
She lets them go their own way, and resides in the center of the circle.

—LAO TZU

In your darkest hour, you may feel desolate and abandoned, but isolation is an illusion. God is as near to you as the air you breathe.

> God's promises are like the stars; the darker the night, the brighter
> they shine.

—DAVID NICHOLAS

The very thought of God can lead you back to the peace and comfort in your own soul, that individualized spark of the Divine within you.

> I wish I could show you,
> When you are lonely or in darkness,
> The Astonishing Light of your own Being.

—HAFIZ

The moment you reach for God's hand, you gain clarity and perspective. You begin to feel stronger, wiser, and less fearful.

> If you knew Who walks beside you on this way, which you have
> chosen, fear would be impossible.

—A COURSE IN MIRACLES

Bathed in the healing, protective glow of God's love, you recognize fear for the illusion that it is.

> Clouds don't worry about falling into the sea because they can't
> (a) fall or (b) drown. But they are free to believe they can, and they
> may fear if they wish.

—RICHARD BACH

You realize it is not the adversity that needs to be changed, it is you that needs to be changed in order to face the adversity with greater courage and faith.

> It is quite useless knocking at the door of Heaven for earthly
> comfort: it's not the sort of comfort they supply there.

—C. S. LEWIS

Not asking for God's help and guidance is like choosing to sail across the ocean on a rickety raft instead of a luxury yacht.

> *If God brings you to it, He will bring you through it.*
>
> —UNKNOWN

If you do not feel God's hand in yours, stay strong. God is there, guiding you and loving you with infinite tenderness.

> *Faith is the bird that feels the light*
> *and sings when the dawn is still dark.*
>
> —RABINDRANATH TAGORE

You may remain unaware of God's presence until the precise moment it will benefit you most.

> *When you walk to the edge of all the light you have*
> *and take that first step into the darkness of the unknown,*
> *you must believe that one of two things will happen:*
> *There will be something solid for you to stand upon,*
> *or, you will be taught how to fly.*
>
> —PATRICK OVERTON

Coming to God only when life forces you to lift your gaze heavenward is like starving yourself for days only to be dragged kicking and screaming to the most delicious meal you could ever imagine.

> *The creature finally turns to his Creator, if for no other reason than to*
> *ask in anguish: "Why, Lord, why?" By ignoble whips of pain, man is*
> *driven at last into the Infinite Presence, whose beauty alone should*
> *lure him.*
>
> —THE PERFUME SAINT

If you stopped trusting God when life punched you in the gut, you never truly trusted God to begin with.

> *The will of God will not take you where the grace of God cannot keep you.*
>
> —UNKNOWN

Unconditional, spiritually mature faith is rooted in love. Conditional, fair-weather faith is rooted in fear.

> *Fear knocked at the door. Faith answered. And lo, no one was there.*
>
> —UNKNOWN

Your faith, both in God and in yourself, will lead you from fear and self-doubt to courage and self-confidence.

> *To be thrown upon one's own resources is to be cast into the very lap of fortune, for our faculties then undergo a development and display an energy of which they were previously unsusceptible.*
>
> —BENJAMIN FRANKLIN

Faith alone is not enough, of course. To the extent that you can, you must take appropriate action.

> *Call on God, but row away from the rocks.*
>
> —INDIAN PROVERB

Do whatever you feel will move you in the right direction, no matter how insignificant it may seem.

> *It is better to light a single candle than to curse the darkness.*
>
> —MOTTO OF THE CHRISTOPHERS

Stronger still is faith bolstered not only by action but by purpose as well. In *Man's Search for Meaning*, psychiatrist and concentration camp survivor Viktor Frankl explained that prisoners whose minds were fixated on an all-consuming reason to live—reuniting with loved ones, completing unfinished work, alerting the world to atrocities—were most apt to survive.

If we possess our why of life we can put up with almost any how.

—FRIEDRICH NIETZSCHE

COURSE CORRECTIONS

If you believe that you are one with God, that you co-create whatever comes into your life, and that everything happens for a reason, then it follows that hardships are nothing more than course corrections on your spiritual path.

There is no such thing as a problem without a gift for you in its hands. You seek problems because you need their gifts.

—RICHARD BACH

If you could but look through God's eyes, you would see God's fingerprints everywhere and glimpse the beauty and perfection inherent in every trial and tribulation.

We turn to God for help when our foundations are shaking, only to learn that it is God who is shaking them.

—CHARLES C. WEST

Knowing you will be presented only with obstacles you are capable of overcoming is immeasurably comforting.

I know God will not give me anything I can't handle. I just wish that He didn't trust me so much.

—MOTHER TERESA

You may feel overwhelmed at the time, but everything in your life has led you to that moment, has prepared you for the challenge at hand.

Love the moment. Flowers grow out of dark moments. Therefore, each moment is vital. It affects the whole. Life is a succession of such moments and to live each, is to succeed.

—CORITA KENT

Hold on to even a fragment of faith and a sliver of hope, and despair can only nip at your heels.

> There is not enough darkness in all the world to put out the light of even one small candle.
>
> —ROBERT ALDEN

Hope and faith will always triumph over adversity just as good will always triumph over evil, for implicit in the duality of material existence is the promise that this, too, shall pass.

> Good and evil must ever be complements on this earth. Everything created must bear some guise of imperfection. How else could God, the Sole Perfection, fragment His one consciousness into forms of creation distinguishable from Himself? There can be no images of light without contrasting shadows. Unless evil had been created, man would not know the opposite, good. Night brings out the bright contrast of day; sorrow teaches us the desirability of joy.
>
> —PARAMAHANSA YOGANANDA

Rise to the occasion and you will emerge victorious, no matter what the results look like and no matter how others perceive the outcome.

> Man is not fully conditioned and determined but rather determines himself whether he gives in to conditions or stands up to them. In other words, man is ultimately self-determining. Man does not simply exist but always decides what his existence will be, what he will become in the next moment.
>
> —VIKTOR FRANKL

When that day dawns, you will see the perfection in your path and raise your arms to the heavens in gratitude.

> Never to suffer would never to have been blessed.
>
> —EDGAR ALLAN POE

WELCOME ADVERSITY
Living the Lesson

Not long after starting my freelance writing career, I was asked to write a script for a non-linear, interactive video presentation in which the viewer would be able to jump seamlessly from segment to segment—sort of like clicking on website links today. It was a rush job; I had two days to complete a draft.

I listened carefully to the instructions but this was brand-new territory for me and I was a bit confused. When I got home, I stared at the computer screen, not knowing how or where to begin. Fighting off a wave of panic, I dove in, not sure that what I was doing was what needed to be done. I called my client for clarification but hung up the phone even more confused. Still, I managed to put together some semblance of a script and showed up at the appointed time, draft in hand.

To my horror, my client's face began souring as he read what I had written. Finally, he looked up with an expression that I interpreted as, *I can't believe I trusted this project to such a bozo.* Heart pounding and palms sweating, I tried to remain calm as he patiently explained that what I had given him was off target. Somehow, I managed to restrain myself from bolting out the front door.

Fortunately, my client remained calm. We moved to the conference room and began working together to revise the script. As I listened to his input, I started gaining clarity about the format and approach he was looking for. Slowly, the script began taking shape; we were in sync and the work flowed smoothly. By the end of the day, the project was completed and my client was happy. Best of all, I had increased my skills and gained confidence in a new market segment.

I felt great leaving that office. From that day on, I actively sought out opportunities to knock down the walls of my comfort zone. I was excited about expanding my horizons, and that meant tackling work I had never done before.

My enthusiasm for professional growth spilled over into my personal life. I began reframing every relationship glitch, every financial blunder, every health setback as a chance to get smarter and wiser. Was it easy? Certainly not. In times of adversity, I still have to remind myself to breathe slowly and view the situation with symbolic sight. Ah, but when I manage to do that, awareness diminishes fear, peace displaces frustration, and stress gives way to resolve. And all is right with the world.

WELCOME ADVERSITY
Self-Reflection Questions

- What role did adversity play in awakening my interest in spirituality?

- How can I begin learning and growing on my own initiative instead of waiting for adversity to give me a wake-up call?

- Why do I believe or disbelieve that walking a spiritual path will protect me from adversity?

- What do I need to change about myself so that I am better able to deal with adversity?

- What was a challenge that got the best of me, and how could I have handled it better?

- How can I rise to the challenge of meeting adversity with love, courage, and integrity?

- How can I remind myself to reframe challenging situations so that I expect the best instead of fearing the worst?

- What challenges in my life am I doing my best to avoid?

- How can I train myself to worry less about what could go wrong?

- What difficult losses have I suffered only to realize later that they were blessings in disguise?

- What is an example of how I rescued a friend or family member only to realize later that my help prevented them from discovering and expressing their own resourcefulness and strength of character?

- How has facing adversity helped me grow as a person?

SIXTEEN

TRANSCEND YOUR SUFFERING

*May every wound bring wisdom
and may every trial bring triumph.*

—KATE NOWAK

TRANSCEND YOUR SUFFERING

The moment you recognize the blessings inherent in your suffering, the greater your capacity to transcend your anguish, even as grief and pain threaten to consume you.

> *Whenever evil befalls us, we ought to ask ourselves, after the first*
> *suffering, how we can turn it into good. So shall we take occasion,*
> *from one bitter root, to raise perhaps many flowers.*
>
> —LEIGH HUNT

THE FOUR NOBLE TRUTHS

The core of the Buddha's teachings are known as the Four Noble Truths. The first is that life means suffering. It is true indeed. No one escapes this life without experiencing anguish and sorrow.

> *There is no tree that the wind has not shaken.*
>
> —HINDU PROVERB

The second of the Buddha's Four Noble Truths is that attachment to desire is the origin of suffering.

> *The moment you place your happiness in the fulfillment of any want*
> *or wish, that is, outside yourself, outside the Way, in anything but the*
> *thing as it is, as it is becoming, at that moment your balance is lost*
> *and you fall straight from Heaven to Hell.*
>
> —REGINALD HORACE BLYTH

The Buddha's third Noble Truth is that suffering can be overcome, a promise that offers hope and comfort to troubled souls everywhere.

> *Although the world is full of suffering, it is full also of the overcoming*
> *of it.*
>
> —HELEN KELLER

The last of the Buddha's Four Noble Truths is that there is a path of practice that leads to enlightenment and an end to suffering.

> *There are two kinds of suffering: the suffering that leads to more suffering and the suffering that leads to the end of suffering. If you are not willing to face the second kind of suffering, you will surely continue to experience the first.*
>
> —AJAHN CHAH

Implicit in the Buddha's teachings is the distinction between pain and suffering. Pain is physical and cannot be avoided; suffering is emotional and can be transcended.

> *You do not suffer, only the person you imagine yourself to be suffers. You cannot suffer.*
>
> —NISARGADATTA MAHARAJ

You begin transcending your suffering when, as author and meditation teacher Phillip Moffitt explains, you condition yourself to mindfully *respond* to suffering rather than emotionally *react* to it.

> *Pain makes man think. Thought makes man wise. Wisdom makes life endurable.*
>
> —JOHN PATRICK

Yet even with the unshakable faith that you are being guided with infinite wisdom and deep love, your grief may be every bit as intense when faced with a great loss.

> *We are not necessarily doubting that God will do the best for us; we are wondering how painful the best will turn out to be.*
>
> —C. S. LEWIS

The difference is, if you are supported by a solid spiritual foundation as you sink to your knees, you will likely heal and recover more rapidly.

> *You cannot prevent the birds of sadness from passing over your head, but you can prevent them from nesting in your hair.*
>
> —SWEDISH PROVERB

THE OTHER SIDE OF PAIN

Suffering can be a springboard for growth and self-discovery that ultimately enriches your life.

> *The burden of suffering seems a tombstone hung about our necks,*
> *while in reality it is only the weight which is necessary to keep down*
> *the diver while he is hunting for pearls.*
>
> —JOHANN RICHTER

A physical or emotional crisis can jolt you out of your comfort zone and, whether you like it or not, compel you to explore an inner world that initially seems like foreign territory.

> *A man may perform astonishing feats and comprehend a vast*
> *amount of knowledge, and yet have no understanding of himself.*
> *But suffering directs a man to look within. If it succeeds . . . then*
> *there, within him, is the beginning of his learning.*
>
> —SØREN KIERKEGAARD

Suffering can reorder your priorities, spur you to make sweeping life changes, and deepen your trust in God's plan for your life.

> *Just as the plough furrows the earth deeply, purifying it of weeds and*
> *thistles, so suffering and tribulation free man from the petty affairs of*
> *this worldly life until he arrives at a state of complete detachment.*
>
> —ABDU'L-BAHÁ

Walking a spiritual path does not grant you immunity from suffering. The nature of your sufferings may shift, but you will suffer nonetheless.

> *Let me not pray to be sheltered from dangers but to be fearless in*
> *facing them.*
> *Let me not beg for the stilling of my pain but for the heart to*
> *conquer it.*
>
> —RABINDRANATH TAGORE

As inspirational author and speaker Andy Andrews playfully reminds us, we are either in a crisis, coming out of a crisis, or heading for a crisis.

> *No Winter lasts forever, no Spring skips its turn.*
>
> —HAL BORLAND

While actively seeking wisdom may help you avoid certain crises, you cannot know the karmic debts you have accrued in life's ledger.

> *Suffering becomes beautiful when anyone bears great calamities with cheerfulness, not through insensibility but through greatness of mind.*
>
> —ARISTOTLE

No two people suffer alike or for the same reasons. What causes heartbreak in one person may elicit nothing but wistfulness and gratitude in another.

> *Fiery trials burn off the dross of our lives so that we can look at the gold more purely.*
>
> —UNKNOWN

One person's suffering cannot be compared to another's. As Viktor Frankl wrote in *Man's Search for Meaning*, an individual's suffering is similar to the behavior of gas. If gas is pumped into an empty chamber, it will fill the chamber completely and evenly, no matter how big the chamber. Likewise, suffering completely fills the human soul and conscious mind, no matter the size of the suffering.

> *Nothing that grieves us can be called little: by the eternal laws of proportion a child's loss of a doll and a king's loss of a crown are events of the same size.*
>
> —MARK TWAIN

Do not fear suffering. The more you try to shield yourself from it, the smaller your world becomes.

> *The truth that many people never understand, until it is too late, is that the more you try to avoid suffering, the more you suffer, because smaller and more insignificant things begin to torture you, in proportion to your fear of being hurt.*
>
> —THOMAS MERTON

View suffering as an enemy and you distance yourself from the richer, more fulfilling life that waits patiently on the other side of pain.

> *The deeper that sorrow carves into your being, the more joy you can contain.*
>
> —KAHLIL GIBRAN

Refuse to acknowledge your suffering and you learn nothing—except that struggling against suffering only creates more suffering.

> *I do not believe that sheer suffering teaches. If suffering alone taught, all the world would be wise, since everyone suffers. To suffering must be added mourning, understanding, patience, love, openness, and the willingness to remain vulnerable. All these and other factors combined, if the circumstances are right, can teach and can lead to rebirth.*
>
> —ANNE MORROW LINDBERGH

The moment you embrace your vulnerability, you widen your vision and expand your awareness of the entire spectrum of human experience.

> *If you had not suffered as you have, there would be no depth to you as a human being, no humility, no compassion.*
>
> —ECKHART TOLLE

In this way, suffering forces you to humbly acknowledge that you are not exempt from the human condition. Hence, through your own suffering, you gain insight into the suffering of others.

Suffering and joy teach us, if we allow them, how to make the leap
of empathy, which transports us into the soul and heart of another
person. In those transparent moments we know other people's joys
and sorrows and we care about their concerns as if they were our own.

—Fritz Williams

Suffering then becomes a potent reminder to step outside yourself and treat others with love and compassion.

Those who have suffered
understand suffering
and thereby extend their hand.

—Patti Smith

GRIEF AND GROWTH

Grief, whether for the loss of a relationship, a loved one, or your health, is a necessary bridge between the life you once enjoyed and the life that even now extends a welcoming embrace.

The world breaks everyone and afterward many are strong at the
broken places.

—Ernest Hemingway

Yet, immersed in sorrow, you fear that you may never again drink deeply of the cup of life.

There is no pain so great as the memory of joy in present grief.

—Aeschylus

Those who have lost a loved one may tenderly wrap their arms around their grief and resist all efforts to pry them loose, believing on some level that by holding on to their grief they are holding on to their beloved.

Grieving is not about forgetting. Grieving allows us to heal, to remember with love rather than pain.

—DR. RACHEL NAOMI REMEN

Grief is often tinged with regret. We dream of traveling back to happier times and making the most of second chances. Spare yourself such anguish by making the most of first chances.

When we lose one we love, our bitterest tears are called forth by the memory of hours when we loved not enough.

—MAURICE MAETERLINCK

Grief will not be ignored. Turn in any direction and grief is there, fencing you in. Only when you give grief your full attention will it give up its gifts.

Mourning is not forgetting. . . . It is an undoing. Every minute tie has to be untied and something permanent and valuable recovered and assimilated from the knot.

—MARGERY ALLINGHAM

While you did not consciously choose to suffer, you have no other choice but to follow the lead of your suffering once it has you in its grip.

Life dances and you must dance with it.

—PHILLIP MOFFITT

Pretend that grief is not pounding on the door to your heart and you jeopardize your physical health as well as your emotional well-being.

The sorrow which has no vent in tears may make other organs weep.

—HENRY MAUDSLEY

Look through God's eyes and you realize that had you never been blessed with what you have lost, your life would have been much poorer. Grief and celebration are two sides of the same coin.

When you are joyous, look deep into your heart and you shall find
it is only that which has given you sorrow that is giving you joy.
When you are sorrowful look again in your heart, and you shall see
that in truth you are weeping for that which has been your delight.

—KAHLIL GIBRAN

Indeed, every blossoming circumstance in the garden of life is implanted with both seeds of joy and seeds of sorrow.

Where there is sunshine, there is also shade.

—KASHMIRI PROVERB

AN INVINCIBLE SUMMER

Fighting your suffering disrupts the flow of life. Surrender to your suffering and the gates of understanding swing open.

Suffering is magnificent music—the moment you give ear to it. But
you never listen to it: you always have a different, private, stubborn
music and melody in your ear which you will not relinquish and with
which the music of suffering will not harmonize.

—HERMANN HESSE

Accepting that what is, *is*, leads to greater presence, a deeper peace, and the end of suffering.

He knew that insofar as one denies what is, one is possessed by what
is not, the compulsions, the fantasies, the terrors that flock to fill the
void.

—URSULA K. LE GUIN

Heidi von Beltz, a former championship skier and aspiring actor, was paralyzed from her earlobes down in a two-vehicle head-on collision while working as a stunt double in *The Cannonball Run* in 1980. Unbowed by her doctors' prognosis that she had perhaps five years to live, von Beltz routinely endured a grueling regimen of physical therapy and muscle stimulation for up to ten hours a day. Nine years later, she was able to sit up on her own. Six years after that, outfitted with lightweight aluminum leg braces, she taught herself to stand.

> *In the depths of winter, I finally learned that within me there lay an invincible summer.*
>
> —ALBERT CAMUS

Sixteen years after the crash, while promoting her memoir, *My Soul Purpose*, von Beltz, who had devoured countless books on philosophy and spirituality, said she considered herself lucky and wouldn't have wanted to miss the experience of her paralysis for anything. "I'm the happiest I've ever been," she said. "I was always so active that I would never have sat down long enough to learn what I've learned. I can't imagine going through this life and not knowing what I know now. I just had to break my neck to do it."

> *Suffering is not good for the soul, unless it teaches you how to stop suffering.*
>
> —JANE ROBERTS (SETH)

Former triathlon champion Jim MacLaren was also grateful for the two vehicular accidents that rendered him a quadriplegic. "Even though both accidents were devastating at the time, I now view them as gifts and not tragedies," he said in an interview.

> *Pure Divine Love is no meek priest*
> *Or tight banker.*
> *It will smash all your windows*
> *And only then throw in the holy gifts.*
>
> —HAFIZ

MacLaren insisted he would not trade his years of paralysis for a restored, healthy body. "Having to admit to my own dependency and vulnerability actually made me more powerful," he said. "For me, the journey has always been about going deeper and becoming more of a human being."

People with diseases like AIDS and cancer feel an urgency in straightening out their lives, examining their purpose, and confronting the reality of death. Ironically, in spite of the physical and emotional pain they experience, many of these patients express gratitude for this opportunity. The encounter with their own mortality changes their priorities in life, their values and aspirations. For many, it makes them truly cherish life and the ability to give and receive love.

—JEFF SEIBERT

Expressing gratitude for such horrific experiences is incomprehensible to most of us. Yet it is undeniable that when we look for beauty, even in the most challenging of times, it is there to be found.

Barn's burnt down—now I can see the moon.

—MIZUTA MASAHIDE

Recognizing, much less appreciating, the upside of suffering requires great maturity and wisdom.

I saw grief drinking a cup of sorrow,
and I called out,
It tastes sweet, does it not?
You have caught me, grief answered,
and you have ruined my business.
How can I sell sorrow
when you know it is a blessing?

—RUMI

It may take years to realize that what was calamitous at the time was instrumental in your spiritual growth.

Sorrow is a fruit. God does not allow it to grow on a branch that is too weak to bear it.

—VICTOR HUGO

Rare is the soul who serenely reframes burdens as blessings even as they unfold. As Dr. Bernie Siegel points out, "It's not like you get hit by a truck, wake up in the hospital in a body cast, and shout, 'Thank you, God!'"

> *If God said,*
> *"Rumi, pay homage to everything that has helped you enter my arms,"*
> *there would not be one experience of my life,*
> *not one thought,*
> *not one feeling,*
> *not any act,*
> *I would not bow to.*
>
> —RUMI

Hold fast to your reverence for life, even as darkness descends, and suffering will take its place at your table and sit quietly with folded hands.

> *And could you keep your heart in wonder at the daily miracles of*
> *your life, your pain would not seem less wondrous than your joy.*
>
> —KAHLIL GIBRAN

THE DAWN WILL BREAK

While a damaged body or a broken heart may signal that the life you once knew is over, it does not mean that life itself is over.

> *Every exit is an entrance somewhere else.*
>
> —TOM STOPPARD

Once you have regained your equilibrium and have adjusted to the "new normal," alternative paths reveal themselves.

Turn your losses into opportunities. If you can't run, then swim.
Don't be one of those people who curse and say, "I can't do that
anymore." Be like a river. When a tree falls down in front of you, find
another avenue to continue. Even if the new activity isn't as fulfilling
as the old one, you're still engaging the world.

—FATHER PAUL MORRISSEY

While the courage and grace embodied by Heidi von Beltz and Jim MacLaren are remarkable, countless others have also found reason to be thankful for hardships that initially seemed insurmountable.

Nothing happens to any man which he is not formed by nature to bear.

—MARCUS AURELIUS

No matter how deeply you are wounded, there are great forces at work that you can tap into for comfort and support.

Healing . . . is not a science, but the intuitive art of wooing Nature.

—W. H. AUDEN

Granted, an abiding faith in the perfection of God's plan may be of little comfort when your body is wracked with unbearable pain or when the world is not large enough to contain your grief.

When we lose God, it is not God who is lost.

—UNKNOWN

But it is the light of that faith, no matter how dimly it flickers in the darkness of your despair, that carries with it the promise of a better day.

However long the night, the dawn will break.

—AFRICAN PROVERB

In the throes of despair, the idea that time will heal your pain may be inconceivable. And yet, the voice of Spirit calls to you, tells you it is so.

> *Even the cry from the depths is an affirmation: Why cry if there is no hint or hope of hearing?*
>
> —MARTIN MARTY

No matter how intolerable your suffering, do not lose heart. The human spirit is imbued with more power to overcome than you have troubles to overcome.

> *The spirit of man is an inward flame; a lamp the world blows upon, but never puts out.*
>
> —MARGOT ASQUITH

Strive to free yourself from the quicksand of your sorrow, for hope waits patiently, lovingly at the edge, reaching for your hand.

> *When you get into a tight place, and everything goes against you till it seems as if you couldn't hold on a minute longer,* never give up then, *for that's just the place and time that the tide'll turn.*
>
> —HARRIET BEECHER STOWE

Summoning the strength to make it through just one more day brings you that much closer to finding some measure of peace and acceptance.

> *If you're going through hell, keep going.*
>
> —WINSTON CHURCHILL

BEWARE WOUNDOLOGY

Regrettably, there are those who use the authenticity of their suffering as an excuse for not healing. Caroline Myss coined the term "woundology" to describe how some people define themselves by their physical, emotional, or social wounds.

> *No one can solve problems for someone whose problem is that they don't want their problems solved.*
>
> —RICHARD BACH

In *Why People Don't Heal and How They Can*, Myss wrote that many people hoping to heal "are striving to confront their wounds, valiantly working to bring meaning to terrible past experiences and traumas, and exercising compassionate understanding of others who share their wounds. But they are not healing. They have redefined their lives around their wounds and the process of accepting them. They are not working to get beyond their wounds. In fact, they are stuck in their wounds."

> *The healthy life consists of meeting and resolving crises as early as possible so that we can get on to the next one.*
>
> —M. Scott Peck

As shocking as it sounds, the last thing that many who are wounded, grieving, or ill are seeking is the full recovery of their health.

> *It is part of the cure to wish to be cured.*
>
> —Lucius Annaeus Seneca

Pain is their primary "relationship currency" and, consciously or not, they fear making their way in the world without it.

> *Men make use of their illnesses at least as much as they are made use of by them.*
>
> —Aldous Huxley

Pain has its privileges. Those who adopt a victim mentality may use their wounds to manipulate and control people and situations. Suffering can be a convenient excuse for dodging unwanted responsibilities.

> *Most of the shadows of this life are caused by our standing in our own sunshine.*
>
> —Ralph Waldo Emerson

Others embrace pain because, after a lifetime of attending to others, they relish being attended to.

Many ordinary illnesses are nothing but the expression of a serious dissatisfaction with life.

—PAUL TOURNIER

Pain is the ticket that gains the wounded entrance into well-meaning support groups where members receive, perhaps for the first time, validation, understanding, and acceptance.

People have a hard time letting go of their suffering. Out of a fear of the unknown, they prefer suffering that is familiar.

—THICH NHAT HANH

A support group's purpose is to help members heal so they can move freely on in life, and many participants do just that, often serving as positive role models and providers of hope for those who continue to struggle.

Hope is the feeling you have that the feeling you have isn't permanent.

—MIGNON MCLAUGHLIN

But other support group members choose not to heal because that would mean leaving the only community that has ever offered them love and support.

Use pain as a stepping stone, not a campground.

—ALAN COHEN

There is a huge difference between glorifying your pain and honoring what you feel; the former is driven by ego, the latter by spirit.

A warrior acknowledges his pain but he doesn't indulge in it.

—CARLOS CASTANEDA

THE FIRE BECKONS

It takes courage to explore your suffering, to peel away layer after layer of beliefs, behaviors, and assumptions and rigorously hold yourself accountable to life.

> *Deep, unspeakable suffering may well be called a baptism, a regeneration, the initiation into a new state.*
>
> —GEORGE ELIOT

Suffering cannot be compartmentalized. Refuse to deal with your pain and you poison every aspect of your life.

> *When you deny emotional pain, everything you do or think as well as your relationships become contaminated with it. You broadcast it, so to speak, as the energy you emanate, and others will pick it up subliminally.*
>
> —ECKHART TOLLE

Ignore your suffering, numb it with distractions and addictions, and the sentry who guards your heart will not yield his post even when joy comes calling.

> *Those who don't know how to weep with their whole heart don't know how to laugh either.*
>
> —GOLDA MEIR

Suffering always has meaning and always has your best interests in mind. You would not be experiencing it otherwise.

> *God brings men into deep waters, not to drown them, but to cleanse them.*
>
> —REV. JOHN HILL AUGHEY

Allow the energy of your suffering to descend upon you, to seep into your emotional pores as surely as water overtakes a sponge, for suffering is as purposeful as it is unstoppable.

That is why the sadness passes: the new presence inside us, the
presence that has been added, has entered our heart, has gone into
its innermost chamber and is no longer even there, is already in our
bloodstream. And we don't know what it was. We could easily be
made to believe that nothing happened, and yet we have changed, as
a house that a guest has entered changes. We can't say who has come,
perhaps we will never know, but many signs indicate that the future
enters us in this way in order to be transformed in us, long before it
happens.

—RAINER MARIA RILKE

When your suffering has washed over you, has moved through you, let the worst of it
have its way with you.

Don't surrender your loneliness so quickly.
Let it cut more deep.
Let it ferment and season you
As few human or even divine ingredients can.

—HAFIZ

When you have experienced your grief as intensely as you can, brace yourself, and walk
into it.

We are healed of a suffering only by experiencing it to the full.

—MARCEL PROUST

Take heart; the further you travel into your suffering, the closer you are to overcoming it.

You can only go halfway into the darkest forest; then you are coming
out the other side.

—CHINESE PROVERB

Just as a silversmith holds a piece of silver in the middle of a fire to burn away its impuri-
ties, so must you lean into the fire of your pain . . . and burn.

But gentle flames are not enough for iron;
it eagerly draws to itself the fiery dragon's breath.
That iron is the dervish who bears hardship:
under the hammer and fire, he happily glows red.

—RUMI

Only the searing flames of relentless self-honesty can cauterize your wounds, blunt the jagged edges of your agony, and prepare you for the journey back to wholeness.

Truth, that fair goddess who comes always with healing in her wings.

—ANNE SHANNON MONROE

The higher the flames, the deeper your healing. If you do not advance beyond your perceived capacity to tolerate pain, you will not be purified.

The purest ore is produced from the hottest furnace, and the brightest thunderbolt is elicited from the darkest storm.

—CHARLES CALEB COLTON

Nobly enduring suffering bestows wisdom; and wisdom provides insight into the value and the necessity of suffering.

God, whose law it is that he who learns must suffer. And even in our sleep, pain that cannot forget falls drop by drop upon the heart, and in our own despite, against our will, comes wisdom to us by the awful grace of God.

—AESCHYLUS

Conversely, drowning in self-pity defeats the purpose of your suffering and brings your spiritual development to a screeching halt.

To suffer, is a necessity entailed upon thy nature, wouldst thou that miracles should protect thee from its lessons? or shalt thou repine, because it happeneth unto thee, when lo! it happeneth unto all? Suffering is the golden cross upon which the rose of the Soul unfoldeth.

—AKHENATON

Feeling sorry for yourself instead of working though your suffering delivers a sledge-hammer blow to the bridge leading from where you are now to your whole, healed self.

> *The longer we dwell on our misfortunes, the greater is their power to harm us.*
>
> —VOLTAIRE

ILLNESS IS INFORMATION

As Louise Hay explained in *You Can Heal Your Life*, your beliefs and ideas about yourself are often the cause of your emotional problems and physical maladies.

> *I see rejection in my skin, worry in my cancers, bitterness and hate in my aching joints. I failed to take care of my mind, and so my body now goes to hospital.*
>
> —TERRI GUILLEMETS

Illness often—*but not always*—serves as a red flag, a metaphysical memo that some part of your life is out of sync with your higher purpose.

> *Diseases can be our spiritual flat tires—disruptions in our lives that seem to be disasters at the time but end by redirecting our lives in a meaningful way.*
>
> —DR. BERNIE SIEGEL

In this context, illness is information. Perhaps your emotional needs are not being met, or you need a crash course in empathy, or your eyes are on the wrong prize.

> *A bodily disease, which we look upon as whole and entire within itself, may, after all, be but a symptom of some ailment in the spiritual part.*
>
> —NATHANIEL HAWTHORNE

If you have fended off destiny's call, the Universe may choose to galvanize your spirit into action by invoking a health-crisis clause in your sacred contract.

So it is that an illness can come into our lives not because of negativity but because Heaven is demanding more of us.

—CAROLINE MYSS

Indeed, when you live inauthentically, when you do not heed the urgings of your heart, when you live somebody else's idea of what your life should be, the unavoidable clash between your true self and the life that you lead cannot help but wreak havoc on your physical health.

When one is pretending the entire body revolts.

—ANAÏS NIN

Gaining clarity about the emotional root of an illness, and tending to it as well as to your physical symptoms, often accelerates healing.

You can't recover from what you do not understand.

—LILLIAN HELLMAN

The notion that every moment is a gift may ring hollow when that "gift" brings with it a serious illness.

You will not grow if you sit in a beautiful flower garden and somebody brings you gorgeous food on a silver platter. But you will grow if you are sick, if you are in pain, if you experience losses and still don't put your head in the sand, but take the pain and learn to accept it, not as a curse or a punishment, but as a gift to you with a very, very specific purpose.

—ELISABETH KÜBLER-ROSS

Challenge yourself to remain open and inquisitive, for suffering is a great teacher and learning melts pain.

Do not weep; do not wax indignant. Understand.

—BARUCH SPINOZA

Some people reject this cause-and-effect notion, complaining that they should not have to feel guilty for becoming ill. True enough; guilt is irrelevant because they did not intentionally, consciously get sick.

> *If you want to see what your body will look like tomorrow, look at your thoughts today.*
>
> —NAVAJO PROVERB

Yet, while their rational mind disputes the theory that they have co-created their own illness, the ever-present observer within them merely nods in silent understanding.

> *Every human being is the author of his own health or disease.*
>
> —BUDDHA

It is inescapable that your life history—the cumulative and synergistic blending of your feelings, experiences, and perceptions—has culminated in the body you are walking around in today.

> *Your biography becomes your biology.*
>
> —CAROLINE MYSS

Elevate your consciousness and you will understand that while you are not responsible *for* your illness, you are responsible *to* it. Your soul may be calling your attention to a lesson in need of learning.

> *From the perspective of a healer, illness is the result of imbalance. Imbalance is a result of forgetting who you are. Forgetting who you are creates thoughts and actions that lead to an unhealthy lifestyle and eventually to illness. . . . Illness can thus be understood as a lesson you have given yourself to help you remember who you are.*
>
> —BARBARA ANN BRENNAN

CURING vs. HEALING

You may argue that there is little point in learning a lesson if your body cannot be cured and you are teetering on the threshold of death's door.

> *There is nothing the body suffers that the soul may not profit by.*
>
> —GEORGE MEREDITH

Here is where the distinction between curing and healing comes into play. Curing relates to the repair of your physical body; healing relates to the care of your soul.

> *Medicine is dealing with what's wrong with you. Healing is dealing with what's right with you.*
>
> —INGRID DILLEY

The healing of your spirit may or may not be accompanied by the curing of your physical malady.

> *Healing is far more than a return to a former condition. True healing means drawing the circle of our being larger and becoming more inclusive, more capable of loving. In this sense, healing is not for the sick alone, but for all humankind. . . . In the end, healing must be a ceaseless process of relationship and rediscovery, moment by moment. The more we "know" about healing, the more we are simultaneously carried toward something unknowable. For this reason all healing is in essence spiritual.*
>
> —RICHARD MOSS

Look through God's eyes and you comprehend that the deterioration of your body may be a necessary catalyst in the awakening of your spirit.

> *Sickness may be the solemn occasion of God's intervention in a person's life.*
>
> —PAUL TOURNIER

Accepting the possibility that you have co-created your disease may be a life-saving realization. After all, if your beliefs can make you ill, it stands to reason that they can also make you well.

> *Belief kills and belief cures.*
>
> —JAMAICAN PROVERB

Countless research studies have demonstrated that your will to live is often a determining factor in how quickly and how well you recover.

> *Our bodies are our gardens, to which our wills are gardeners.*
>
> —WILLIAM SHAKESPEARE

Modern science is only now confirming what has been recognized for millennia: The mind plays a major role in the curing of the body.

> *He who can believe himself well, will be well.*
>
> —OVID

Nothing demonstrates this mind-body connection more effectively than the placebo effect. When patients are told that a sugar pill or bogus medical procedure will promote healing or reduce pain, it very often does. It is undeniably the expectation associated with the pill or procedure that produces the positive result.

> *Belief becomes biology.*
>
> —NORMAN COUSINS

The human body is an amazing work of art. It has an intelligence all its own and continually strives to achieve optimal health. A positive attitude boosts your immune system and might just tip the scales in your favor.

> *The greatest force in the human body is the natural drive of the body
> to heal itself—but that force is not independent of the belief system,
> which can translate expectations into physiological change.*
>
> —NORMAN COUSINS

Your likelihood of recovery dramatically improves when, through alignment of mind, body, and spirit, you become a proactive partner in the healing process.

> *Almost every type and condition of illness has been in some way or other related to our pattern of thinking, a pattern of thinking that apparently is contradictory to the spiritual pattern of a perfect and healthy body. . . . We must get ourselves and our limited human thinking out of the way so that the Divine pattern of perfection can fully express itself in us. . . . The doctor can assist the body mechanically through surgery and medication; we can assist through how we think and act.*
>
> —ERNEST HOLMES

Traditional medicine certainly plays a crucial role in curing the body. Yet for all the remarkable advances in medical science, love remains the best medicine.

> *I am convinced that unconditional love is the most powerful known stimulant of the immune system. If I told patients to raise their blood levels of immune globulins or killer T cells, no one would know how. But if I can teach them to love themselves and others fully, the same changes happen automatically. The truth is: love heals.*
>
> —DR. BERNIE SIEGEL

A PORTAL TO PEACE

No matter how lost, scared, vulnerable, or powerless you feel, you can treat this very moment as a portal to peace, wisdom, and healing.

> *This place where you are right now, God circled on a map for you.*
>
> —HAFIZ

The opportunity to choose healing is always in front of you. It is never too late to learn and apply life lessons.

It is God's kindness to terrify you in order to lead you to safety.

—RUMI

Your body may be broken, but if your spirit is healed and whole, you are serving God by radiating love and hope, and demonstrating that suffering can be transcended.

To be able to stand in the midst of darkness and live as though all about you was light is the final test of the human spirit.

—EDWARD H. GRIGGS

Your very existence will inspire others to find the strength they need to overcome their own challenges and live their best lives.

In some way, suffering ceases to be suffering at the moment it finds a meaning, such as the meaning of a sacrifice.

—VIKTOR FRANKL

Begin today to live the life you were born to live. There is no need to wait for suffering to gather you in its arms.

If you're going to do something different with your life because you've found out you've got a disease, then you're not living as you should be.

—ARLO GUTHRIE

Your journey may be arduous, but be a friend to suffering and, when you least expect it, suffering may be a friend to you.

Our way is not soft grass, it's a mountain path with lots of rocks. But it goes upwards, forward, toward the sun.

—DR. RUTH WESTHEIMER

TRANSCEND YOUR SUFFERING
Living the Lesson

At a 1998 weekend workshop conducted by spiritual healer Dr. Ibrahim Jaffe, I learned about energy healing, the practice of balancing the energy field that surrounds the human body. On the final day, Ibrahim demonstrated his healing method on a few of the participants. One woman he brought up to the front of the class had sustained injuries in a car accident that restricted the use of various parts of her body, including her hands.

After only a minute or so of working with her energy, Ibrahim, who is clairvoyant, stopped and gently said, "You could be healed right now, but you're not ready for that, are you?" To my astonishment, she agreed. She explained that she had obsessive-compulsive disorder and was actually thrilled when she could no longer use her hands because that meant she didn't have to touch doorknobs. She added that the thought of being healthy was such a foreign concept to her that she was afraid of it, that she wouldn't know how to think or act in the absence of her maladies.

I was dumbfounded. For the first time, I realized that some people would prefer *not* to be healthy. Her confession affirmed that the best outcomes occur when healing the mind and spirit precedes the curing of the body, and that if the underlying reasons for the body's ills are not addressed, the same problems may resurface after the body is repaired. That day, I understood that healing is a choice, and the more consciously we make that choice, the healthier we will be.

TRANSCEND YOUR SUFFERING
Self-Reflection Questions

- What is the relationship between my desires and my sufferings?

- How have my sufferings rearranged my priorities?

- How can I challenge myself to hold on to my faith in God's plan for my life even in the worst of times?

- How has suffering affected my level of empathy?

- What are some ways in which suffering has accelerated my spiritual growth?

- In what ways have I resisted healing my life because of the benefits I derived from remaining unhealed?

- How can I get better at facing my suffering and moving through it?

- How can I train myself to view illness as information instead of a heartless enemy?

- What is the difference between being responsible *for* an illness and *to* an illness?

- How is curing different from healing?

- How does my attitude affect my immune system and my overall health?

- How can I take an active role in healing my life?

SEVENTEEN

FIND FREEDOM THROUGH FORGIVENESS

He that cannot forgive others breaks the bridge over which
he himself must pass if he would ever reach heaven;
for everyone has need to be forgiven.

—GEORGE HERBERT

FIND FREEDOM THROUGH FORGIVENESS

Forgiveness is a great purifier. It matters not how long you have hated or how deep the hurt runs. A room can be dark for ten seconds or ten years; the moment that light floods the room, the darkness disappears as though it had never been.

One moment of true forgiveness can erase years of guilt, pain, or fear.

—ALAN COHEN

REFRAME, RELEASE, REWRITE

"Forgiveness" is a loaded word that may anger those who have endured great wrongs. Anyone with a trace of empathy can appreciate how difficult it must be to forgive the unforgivable.

When a deep injury is done us, we never recover until we forgive.

—ALAN PATON

Substituting the word "release" for "forgiveness" short-circuits the emotional charge and reframes the act as a blessing that you bestow on yourself rather than one bestowed on your antagonist.

Forgiveness is an act of self-love.

—WAYNE DYER

Many balk at forgiveness, associating it with weakness, with losing, with giving in and giving up.

The weak can never forgive. Forgiveness is the attribute of the strong.

—MAHATMA GANDHI

True forgiveness is the noblest of acts, requiring great wisdom, spiritual strength, and an intuitive understanding of the human condition.

To heal the wounded memory is as natural to the human spirit as it is for the cells of the human body to heal themselves.

—LEWIS B. SMEDES

Forgiveness is not an intellectual decision. It is an act of the heart, reflecting the infinite love and compassion of your spirit.

Forgiveness defies your mind. You have to break through your mind to forgive. Without forgiveness, a genuine healing cannot happen.

—CAROLINE MYSS

The moment you forgive, you reinvent yourself. Your psyche is flooded with light, forever dispelling the darkness that had emotionally crippled you.

Someone may have stolen your dream when it was young and fresh and you were innocent. If someone has damaged the innocence of your dreams,
Anger is natural.
Grief is appropriate.
Healing is mandatory.
Restoration is possible.

—JANE RUBIETTA

Instead of identifying yourself by past injuries and injustices, you are free to rewrite the story of who you are and who you wish to be.

Forgiveness is a rebirth of hope, a reorganization of thought, and a reconstruction of dreams. Once forgiving begins, dreams can be rebuilt. When forgiving is complete, meaning has been extracted from the worst of experiences and used to create a new set of moral rules and a new interpretation of life's events.

—BEVERLY FLANIGAN

Writing a new story is more difficult if the person you are forgiving remains in your life and continues to act in ways that require forgiveness. A thoughtless relative is one thing, an abusive spouse is quite another. Forgiveness does not equal tolerance. If your antagonist treats your forgiveness as a welcome mat for further abuse, your new story must be written from a safe distance.

You must not lose faith in humanity. Humanity is an ocean. If a few drops are dirty, the ocean does not become dirty.

—MAHATMA GANDHI

SELFISH AND SELFLESS

Forgiveness is ultimately a selfish act, requiring you to free your imprisoned spirit and reclaim your dignity, power, and sense of self-worth.

When we forgive, we set a prisoner free and discover that the prisoner we set free is us.

—LEWIS B. SMEDES

If you do not forgive, you are bound to the person who injured you as surely as if you were handcuffed together.

As long as you don't forgive, who and whatever it is will occupy rent-free space in your mind.

—ISABELLE HOLLAND

Forgiveness is ultimately a selfless act, requiring you to look through God's eyes and not your own.

I pardon him, as God shall pardon me.

—WILLIAM SHAKESPEARE

Then, instead of judging others, you will be adding much-needed loving energy to collective consciousness.

Forgiveness is holiness; by forgiveness the universe is held together.

—PARAMAHANSA YOGANANDA

In this light, forgiving the imperfections of others contributes to the perfection of your own path as well as to God's ultimate plan for the world.

When we forgive we ride the crest of love's cosmic wave; we walk in stride with God.

—LEWIS B. SMEDES

THE PRICE OF RESENTMENT

There is no middle ground for forgiveness. Resentment and forgiveness cannot coexist. You must choose one or the other.

"I can forgive, but I cannot forget," is only another way of saying, "I will not forgive." A forgiveness ought to be like a cancelled note, torn in two and burned up, so that it never can be shown against the man.

—HENRY WARD BEECHER

Grudgingly attempting forgiveness while refusing to relinquish your resentment fools no one. Your insincerity will carry more weight than your words or actions.

You cannot shake hands with a clenched fist.

—INDIRA GANDHI

Resentment exacts a steep cost. Investing your emotional energy in angrily clinging to past events saps your life force, ages you, and weakens your immune system.

Resentment is like taking poison and waiting for the other person to die.

—MALACHY McCOURT

Unresolved anger has a corrosive effect on your body. It elevates your blood pressure and increases the likelihood of heart attacks and strokes.

You will not be punished for your anger, you will be punished by your anger.

—BUDDHA

You cannot know real peace without forgiveness. Until you release your resentments, the external world will always remain a threat.

> *When you make peace with yourself, you make peace with the world.*
>
> —MAHA GHOSANANDA

The price of resentment is unending suffering. The priceless gift of forgiveness is lasting peace.

> *Forgiveness is the economy of the heart. . . . Forgiveness saves the expense of anger, the cost of hatred, the waste of spirits.*
>
> —HANNAH MOORE

Hold on to grudges and grievances and you restrict your life. You will never know the joy and freedom of a soul unburdened by pain.

> *When you harbor bitterness, happiness will dock elsewhere.*
>
> —UNKNOWN

Refusing to forgive your antagonist compromises all your other relationships. Some part of you will always hold back, limiting your capacity to be emotionally available.

> *When we judge, we are pushing people away; we are creating a wall, a barrier. When we forgive we are destroying barriers; we come closer to others.*
>
> —JEAN VANIER

You may argue that your resentment is justified—indeed, that you are *entitled* to it. Defiantly, you wrap your anger around your heart, unwittingly blocking out the sunlight of Divine love and mercy.

*We attach our feelings to the moment when we were hurt, endowing
it with immortality. And we let it assault us every time it comes to
mind. It travels with us, sleeps with us, hovers over us while we make
love, and broods over us while we die. Our hate does not even have
the decency to die when those we hate die—for it is a parasite sucking
our blood, not theirs. There is only one remedy for it.*

—LEWIS B. SMEDES

You may think that you are protecting yourself by refusing to forgive. The opposite is true: Your every hostile thought boomerangs back, causing incalculable damage to mind, body, and spirit.

To carry a grudge is like being stung to death by one bee.

—WILLIAM H. WALTON

Then again, refusing to release your resentment *is* a form of protection. Choosing resentment over recovery protects you from the discomfort of facing and working through your emotional trauma.

*I imagine that one of the reasons people cling to their hates so
stubbornly is because they sense, once hate is gone, that they will
be forced to deal with pain.*

—JAMES BALDWIN

Unchecked, your righteous anger takes root and stealthily expands, blotting out all the beauty and wonder of life, and insidiously choking off avenues of peace and love like a cancerous tumor.

The man who opts for revenge should dig two graves.

—CHINESE PROVERB

You cannot carry resentment without it permeating your consciousness and influencing the way you think, speak, and act. You become contaminated with rage. You wonder why your life seems stuck, why you cannot attune yourself to the Divine current, why you focus so much of your attention on those you scorn rather than on those you love.

Don't ruin the present with the ruined past.

—ELLEN GILCHRIST

By living like this, by mentally returning to the scene of the crime over and over again, you enable your antagonist to wreak ever more havoc with your life and psyche. Like a marionette, you allow someone else to pull your strings, even from the grave.

When we hate our enemies, we are giving them power over us: power over our sleep, our appetites, our blood pressure, our health, and our happiness. Our enemies would dance with joy if only they knew how they were worrying us, lacerating us, and getting even with us! Our hate is not hurting them at all, but our hate is turning our own days and nights into a hellish turmoil.

—DALE CARNEGIE

Brand your attacker as unforgivable and you become an accomplice to the crime. By passionately defending your hatred and anger, you are snatching the knife from your attacker's hand and plunging it deeper into your own heart.

It's not only injustice that causes problems; often our vengeful response to injustice creates even greater and more enduring problems.

—ROBERT ENRIGHT

Yet you continue to cling desperately to your antagonist, fearful that if he breaks free of your grasp he will go unpunished, and *that* you cannot permit.

Anger is always fear, and fear is always fear of loss.

—RICHARD BACH

Ah, but here is the ironic twist. While you are maintaining a death grip on your resentment, thereby inflicting untold damage on your physical and emotional well-being, your adversary is oblivious to your wrath.

The one who throws the stone forgets; the one who is hit remembers forever.

—ANGOLAN PROVERB

REVENGE AND REMORSE

Acting on resentment by pursuing revenge is akin to dropping a huge boulder in the middle of your spiritual path. It blocks out the sun and halts all progress.

> *People who fight fire with fire usually end up with ashes.*
>
> —ABIGAIL VAN BUREN

By striking back at those who have harmed you, you harm yourself. Your obsession with getting even rips open your original wounds and inflames them further with the venom of vengeance.

> *Revenge . . . is like a rolling stone, which, when a man hath forced up a hill, will return upon him with a greater violence, and break those bones whose sinews gave it motion.*
>
> —REV. JEREMY TAYLOR

No matter how justified you feel your actions are, meting out your own brand of vigilante justice lowers your consciousness, attracts toxic consequences, and paves the way for future regrets.

> *How much more grievous are the consequences of anger than the causes of it.*
>
> —MARCUS AURELIUS

Worst of all, there will be a stain in your memory that will not wash out no matter how desperately you scour it with remorse.

> *If the other person injures you, you may forget the injury; but if you injure him you will always remember.*
>
> —KAHLIL GIBRAN

Look through God's eyes and you understand that Divine justice may not require your assistance. Ultimately, the perpetrator will be held karmically responsible for his or her actions. Of course, if the action was criminal or if you are in a position to prevent others from being victimized, follow your guidance accordingly.

If a man sin against thee, speak peaceably to him, and in thy soul hold not guile; and if he repent and confess, forgive him. . . . But if he be shameless and persisteth in his wrong-doing, even so forgive him from the heart, and leave to God the avenging.

—GAD, THE NINTH SON OF JACOB

Refuse to forgive someone who has wronged you, and you cannot expect to be forgiven by someone whom you have wronged. We all must learn to forgive, just as we all must need to be forgiven.

The gift of being forgiven and love's power to forgive are like yin and yang. Each needs the other to exist. To receive the gift without using the power is absurd; it is like exhaling without inhaling or like walking without moving your legs.

—LEWIS B. SMEDES

ADVERSARIES OR ALLIES

How do you begin the process of forgiveness, of release? It may help to view your adversary in a new light: not as a powerful monster, but as a flawed, insecure human being in need of love and compassion. In other words, much like yourself.

If only there were evil people somewhere insidiously committing evil deeds, and it were necessary only to separate them from the rest of us and destroy them. But the line dividing good and evil cuts through the heart of every human being. And who is willing to destroy a piece of his own heart?

—ALEKSANDR SOLZHENITSYN

In fact, you may be your own antagonist. Resentment is the inability to forgive others; guilt is the inability to forgive yourself.

Every guilty person is his own hangman.

—LUCIUS ANNAEUS SENECA

If you are wracked with guilt and remorse, it may help to view your former self as a separate person, as someone who no longer resembles you, a person whose sense of integrity had not yet fully formed and who did not have the knowledge and wisdom you now possess.

> *The day the child realizes that all adults are imperfect, he becomes an adolescent; the day he forgives them, he becomes an adult; the day he forgives himself, he becomes wise.*
>
> —ALDEN NOWLAN

Reframing your transgression by recognizing the limitations of the person you used to be may give you the distance you need to apply these principles, heal your emotional scars, and find some measure of peace.

> *I do not want the peace which passeth understanding. I want the understanding which bringeth peace.*
>
> —HELEN KELLER

Looking through God's eyes, you realize that adversarial relationships are an illusion, and that every difficult encounter has been divinely orchestrated.

> *No one at one with himself can even conceive of conflict.*
>
> —A COURSE IN MIRACLES

Before incarnating, you agreed to participate in situations on earth that would help you learn pivotal lessons, achieve your life's purpose, and advance your spiritual growth.

> *We choose our joys and our sorrows long before we experience them.*
>
> —KAHLIL GIBRAN

In light of these sacred contracts, every quarrel, every betrayal, every hostility becomes a gift, an occasion to grow and evolve.

> *Forgiveness is born of increased awareness. The more you can see, the easier it is to forgive.*
>
> —DEEPAK CHOPRA

Remember too, that virtually everyone, no matter how horribly misguided they may be, believes that the way they conduct their life is the right way, the best way, and wholly consistent with the way the world works.

> *Pardon him . . . he is a barbarian, and thinks that the customs of his tribe and island are the laws of nature.*
>
> —GEORGE BERNARD SHAW

Therefore, do not take every transgression so personally; the way someone treats you says far less about you than it does about them.

> *If we could read the secret history of our enemies, we should find in each man's life sorrow and suffering enough to disarm all hostility.*
>
> —HENRY WADSWORTH LONGFELLOW

Even though the act that needs forgiving *involved* you, it often is not *about* you. You were simply an obstacle in the way or a convenient vehicle used in the self-absorbed pursuit of a self-centered desire.

> *How people treat you is their karma; how you react is yours.*
>
> —WAYNE DYER

NOTHING TO FORGIVE

Your sacred contracts offer a wealth of opportunities to transcend your human nature by expressing your Divine nature.

> *You know quite well, deep within you, that there is only a single magic, a single power, a single salvation, and a single happiness, and that is called loving. Well, then, love your suffering. Do not resist it, do not flee from it. Taste how sweet it is in its essence, give yourself to it, do not meet it with aversion. It is only your aversion that hurts, nothing else.*
>
> —HERMANN HESSE

If you accept that these pre-incarnation agreements exist and that we cross paths with those whom we are to learn from, then there is nothing to forgive.

> *Remember you come here having already understood the necessity*
> *of struggling with yourself—only with yourself. Therefore thank*
> *everyone who gives you the opportunity.*
>
> —GEORGES IVANOVICH GURDJIEFF

You stop seeing yourself as a victim, and view every person in conflict with you as an instrument of God.

> *We do not and cannot know the agenda of each individual soul—*
> *but we can know that the agenda of each individual soul serves the*
> *agenda of every other soul.*
>
> —NEALE DONALD WALSCH

With this understanding, you learn to welcome conflict as an opportunity for self-reflection and honor it as a reminder of the Universal Intelligence that guides your way.

> *Another illusion is that external events have the power to hurt you,*
> *that other people have the power to hurt you. They don't. It's you who*
> *give this power to them.*
>
> —ANTHONY DE MELLO

You realize that everyone you encounter, no matter how unlikely it seems to your earthbound sensibilities, is your teacher, your collaborator, your ally.

> *You know you have forgiven someone when he or she has harmless*
> *passage through your mind.*
>
> —REV. KARYL HUNTLEY

On a soul level, you and your adversary have agreed to challenge and confront each other in ways that benefit you both.

What is a good man but a bad man's teacher?
What is a bad man but a good man's job?
If you don't understand this, you will get lost,
however intelligent you are.

—LAO TZU

Years from now when you have left this world, you shall meet again; only this time you will bow in gratitude for serving each other in that way.

Out beyond ideas of wrongdoing and rightdoing,
there is a field. I'll meet you there.

—RUMI

Our challenge in the present moment is to resist responding with rage, resentment, and retaliation, and instead view conflict through God's eyes, with loving detachment.

Never does the human soul appear so strong and noble as when it
forgoes revenge and dares to forgive an injury.

—EDWIN HUBBELL CHAPIN

THE ASHES OF ATROCITY

It takes courage to forgive, to cast aside the insistent judgments of ego in favor of the infinite wisdom of Spirit.

If you want to see the brave, look at those who can forgive.

—BHAGAVAD GITA

Granted, that is all well and good for garden-variety dustups, but the concept is harder to swallow when applied to shockingly brutal individual acts and crimes against humanity.

I believe in the sun—even when it does not shine;
I believe in love—even when it is not shown;
I believe in God—even when he does not speak.

—SCRATCHED INTO A BASEMENT WALL
BY A HOLOCAUST VICTIM

Throughout history, people with malicious intent have exercised their free will to hurt others. God does not directly interfere because, by definition, free will would be rendered meaningless if it were interfered with.

God created the law of free will, and God created the law of cause and effect. And he himself will not violate the law. We need to be thinking less in terms of what God did and more in terms of whether or not we are following those laws.

—MARIANNE WILLIAMSON

Consequently, God's plan for each of us may weather continual course corrections, just as each move on a chess board reconfigures our universe of choices going forward. In extreme cases, our life's plan may be adapted, rewritten, or postponed. Even then, however, karmic forces are at work and angels hover near.

It can even come about that a created will cancels out, not perhaps the exertion, but the result of divine action; for in this sense, God himself has told us that God wishes things which do not happen because man does not wish them!

—JOSEPH DE MAISTRE

One way or another, in this life or another, our soul lessons will play out as planned. Fulfillment is certain; circumstances and timing are not.

When you mix free will you get certain deviants. . . . You may believe that just because there is an absence of good, for example, that evil exists. This is not so. In fact, things are far more intricate.

—LENA LEES

It is insensitive at best and cruel at worst to suggest to those who have suffered horrifically that there may be even a modicum of meaning behind unspeakable crimes. And yet, even as we honor another's grief, it is an argument that must be considered, even if it remains unspoken.

> *The mark of your ignorance is the depth of your belief in injustice and tragedy. What the caterpillar calls the end of the world, the master calls a butterfly.*
>
> —RICHARD BACH

We cannot profess that we are co-creators of everything that comes into our lives . . . except this. Or that everything happens for a reason . . . except that. Or that we are being divinely guided in every moment . . . except then.

> *Within each of us lives a skeptic inclined toward reason—and a believer drawn to faith.*
>
> —DAN MILLMAN

Clearly, any attempt to look through God's eyes has its limits; and any purpose behind incomprehensible suffering may remain beyond the capacity of human beings to grasp. But a purpose we cannot wrap our minds around is a purpose nonetheless.

> *You've got to look hard for the sparks of divinity in the ashes of atrocity.*
>
> —RABBI HAROLD M. SCHULWEIS

FINALLY FREE

Paradoxically, to attain the enlightened perspective that forgiveness is unnecessary, it is necessary to practice forgiveness.

> *Forgiveness is humanity's highest achievement because it shows true enlightenment in action.*
>
> —WAYNE DYER

Every act of forgiveness expands your awareness, understanding, and appreciation of Divine Wisdom.

> *Be assured that if you knew all, you would pardon all.*
>
> —THOMAS À KEMPIS

You come to see that, while forgiveness cannot alter past events, it can alter your interpretation of them.

> *You change the past when you change the way you see it.*
>
> —ALAN COHEN

You become more willing to forgive until, finally, you will yourself to a place beyond suffering, beyond forgiveness.

> *Forgiveness does not change the past, but it does enlarge the future.*
>
> —PAUL BOESE

In any context, Eva Kor's act of forgiveness is stunning. On January 27, 1995, in a public ceremony marking the fiftieth anniversary of the liberation of Auschwitz by Soviet troops, Kor declared her forgiveness toward the Nazis who murdered her parents and two older sisters.

> *Genuine forgiveness does not deny anger but faces it head-on.*
>
> —ALICE MILLER

Standing by the ruins of a gas chamber at the infamous death camp, Kor also forgave Josef Mengele, the Nazi doctor who used her and her twin sister Miriam as guinea pigs for genetic experiments.

> *When we forgive evil we do not excuse it, we do not tolerate it, we do not smother it. We look the evil full in the face, call it what it is, let its horror shock and stun and enrage us, and only then do we forgive it.*
>
> —LEWIS B. SMEDES

Kor's forgiveness allowed her to release the heartache and hatred she had carried for five decades. She said, "I read my document of forgiveness and signed it. I immediately felt the pain lift from my shoulders. Finally, I was no longer a prisoner of Auschwitz. I was finally free. So I say to everybody, 'Forgive your worst enemy. It will heal your soul and set you free.'"

> *Holding on to anger is like grasping a hot coal with the intent of throwing it at someone else; you are the one who gets burned.*
>
> —BUDDHA

Later that year, Kor opened the CANDLES Holocaust Museum in Terre Haute, Indiana. (*CANDLES is an acronym for Children of Auschwitz Nazi Deadly Lab Experiments Survivors.*) In 2003, the museum was burned to the ground by a fire that was deliberately set. Kor forgave the arsonist and rebuilt the museum. She said, "For most people there is a big obstacle to forgiveness because society expects revenge. Forgiveness is nothing more and nothing less than an act of self-healing, an act of self-empowerment. I call it a miracle medicine. It's free, it works, and it has no side effects."

> *Resentment, whether cold fury or smoldering rage, hardens your emotions. . . . Tragically, you become one with anger; you are now its servant.*
>
> —PHILLIP MOFFITT

As Eva Kor learned, forgiveness does not mean that you condone what was done to you or that you absolve the perpetrator of responsibility for his or her actions.

> *Forgiveness does not equal forgetting. It is about healing the memory of the harm, not erasing it.*
>
> —KEN HART

How deserving your assailant is of your forgiveness is irrelevant. Forgiveness is a gift to yourself. It is an indispensable element in your enlightened self-care toolkit.

*We must forgive those we feel have wronged us, not because they
deserve to be forgiven, but because we love ourselves so much we don't
want to keep paying for the injustice. Forgiveness is the only way to
heal.*

—Don Miguel Ruiz

It is always within your power to forgive someone, even for things that one human being should never do to another.

*There is nothing that in the end, cannot be forgiven, but there remains
much that is inexcusable.*

—Vladimir Jankélévitch

Forgiveness allows you to recall your spirit back to present time, which energizes and heals you in profound ways, both physically and emotionally.

I have always found that mercy bears richer fruits than strict justice.

—Abraham Lincoln

Eva Kor captured the true meaning of forgiveness when she said, "Forgiveness means to me that whatever was done to me is no longer causing me such pain that I cannot be the person I want to be."

*A wise man will make haste to forgive, because he knows the true
value of time, and will not suffer it to pass away in unnecessary pain.*

—Samuel Johnson

It took Eva Kor fifty years to forgive her tormentors. Grief and rage demand their due. Be patient; forgiveness cannot be forced. Listen to your heart and you will know when it is time to forgive.

I worry about fast forgivers. They tend to forgive quickly in order to avoid their pain.... And their instant forgiving only makes things worse.... People who have been wronged badly and wounded deeply should give themselves time and space before they forgive.... There is a right moment to forgive. We cannot predict it in advance; we can only get ourselves ready for it when it arrives.

—LEWIS B. SMEDES

CHOOSING LOVE

Forgiveness is another word for love. It is about choosing to love when love seems like an impossible choice to make.

We cannot love unless we have accepted forgiveness, and the deeper our experience of forgiveness is, the greater is our love.

—PAUL TILLICH

It is easy to love someone who is lovable, but you can never fully embody love and forgiveness until you learn to love the unlovable.

People need loving the most when they deserve it the least.

—MARY C. CROWLEY

When you are treated poorly, when you are not respected, when you are ignored or mocked or scorned, recognize that such behavior speaks to the other person's character, not your own.

To be wronged or robbed is nothing unless you continue to remember it.

—CONFUCIUS

Do not take such boorish behavior personally. As an ambassador of God's love, it is your great privilege to respond to insensitivity and mean-spiritedness with kindness.

Start learning to love God by loving those whom you cannot love.

—MEHER BABA

Your antagonist is playing the role that must be played if you both are to grow and evolve as planned.

> *I have learned silence from the talkative, toleration from the intolerant, and kindness from the unkind; yet strange, I am ungrateful to these teachers.*

—KAHLIL GIBRAN

As you model graciousness and generosity of spirit, you inspire and change others who are fortunate enough to find themselves in your presence.

> *Forgiveness is the fragrance that the violet sheds on the heel that has crushed it.*

—MARK TWAIN

You cannot release a hurt until you send love to the source of that hurt, as if you were a parent sending unconditional love to your child. How do you do that? Like this: "I send you love and light, from my heart to yours—to love you, to protect you, to guide you, to heal you, to cherish you, to comfort you. God bless you. You are beautiful and you are loved."

> *And I saw the river over which every soul must pass to reach the kingdom of heaven and the name of that river was suffering; and I saw a boat which carries souls across the river and the name of that boat was love.*

—SAINT JOHN OF THE CROSS

If you are more visually oriented, ask God to guide your soul to meet the other person's soul on a bridge of light between your hearts. Visualize the two of you meeting halfway on that bridge and embracing in divine friendship.

> *If we really want to love, we must learn how to forgive.*

—MOTHER TERESA

You break the hold that people have over you by bathing them in love and asking that these conflicts be resolved for the highest good of everyone involved.

> *Forgiveness finishes unfinished business.*
>
> —STEPHEN LEVINE

Whether or not you witness any changes in these relationships, they have been forever altered.

> *When we are firmly established in nonviolence, all beings around us cease to feel hostility.*
>
> —PATANJALI

Forgiveness unsupported by love is only a word. If your love is not genuine, your forgiveness will be shallow and transient.

> *We pardon to the extent that we love.*
>
> —FRANÇOIS DE LA ROCHEFOUCAULD

It is not necessary to tell the people whom you are forgiving that you are forgiving them. The loving energy you broadcast through the Unified Field reaches people, changes them, makes them better.

> *Sincere forgiveness isn't colored with expectations that the other person apologize or change. Don't worry whether or not they finally understand you. Love them and release them. Life feeds back truth to people in its own way and time.*
>
> —SARA PADDISON

If sending love to someone who betrayed you or harmed you seems inconceivable, step aside and ask God to use you as a conduit.

> *Forgiveness is not always easy. At times, it feels more painful than the wound we suffered, to forgive the one who inflicted it. And yet, there is no peace without forgiveness.*
>
> —MARIANNE WILLIAMSON

By allowing the pure love of God to flow through you and into that person's heart, you are surrendering to a higher form of justice.

> *There is no love without forgiveness, and there is no forgiveness without love.*
>
> —BRYANT H. MCGILL

You do not have to like the other person, you simply have to acknowledge that God loves him or her the way all of God's children are loved.

> *An overflowing love which seeks nothing in return,* agape *is the love of God operating in the human heart. At this level, we love men not because we like them, nor because their ways appeal to us, nor even because they possess some type of divine spark; we love every man because God loves him. At this level, we love the person who does an evil deed, although we hate the deed that he does.*
>
> —MARTIN LUTHER KING, JR.

Resolve to be an instrument of Divine love and mercy regardless of your personal feelings for those who have harmed you.

> *You will know that forgiveness has begun when you recall those who hurt you and feel the power to wish them well.*
>
> —LEWIS B. SMEDES

Granted, no matter how much you long for the peace and release that forgiveness brings, the words "I forgive you" can stick in your throat, even if you intend to only say them silently.

> *Wisdom is harder to do than it is to know.*
>
> —YULA MOSES

Think of God as the supreme love of your life, and your love and compassion for others will flow more naturally and effortlessly.

> *Love is an act of endless forgiveness, a tender look which becomes a habit.*
>
> —PETER USTINOV

In time, this intention of love and forgiveness will take up lasting residence in your mind and heart.

> *Forgiveness is not an occasional act; it is a permanent attitude.*
>
> —MARTIN LUTHER KING, JR.

In this state of awareness, resentment against your adversaries drops off your radar. Indeed, you no longer *have* adversaries. You see that everyone who crosses your path does so to deliver a message divinely crafted just for you.

> *Whoever approaches Me walking, I will come to him running;*
> *and he who meets Me with sins equivalent to the whole world,*
> *I will greet him with forgiveness equal to it.*
>
> —MISHKAT AL-MASABIH

FIND FREEDOM THROUGH FORGIVENESS
Living the Lesson

From the beginning, my mom and my wife were at odds with each other, and neither had any qualms about offering her opinion. I often felt caught in the middle. The conflict finally reached critical mass after I had a particularly bitter argument with my mom. I smugly wrote her a letter telling her she would no longer be in my life, and felt completely justified in sending it. What a clueless, self-righteous dolt I was! My dad told me later that my mom cried when she read the letter and had trouble sleeping for days afterward.

It didn't take long for my mom and me to start talking again, but something important was missing. She had doted on me from the day I was born and we had always had a wonderful, loving relationship. But there was now a distance between us. I even stopped telling her I loved her because I couldn't pretend that the purity of our relationship had been restored.

I don't remember how long the rift between us lasted. It may have been months, but it seemed like years. Over time, it gradually dissipated until one day there was no longer any resentment or bruised feelings. We both had awakened to the understanding that love is what matters most. We also understood that we both had acted very foolishly.

My mom traces her wake-up call to the day a friend of hers explained the tradition of Yom Kippur, a day of atonement in Judaism that follows a ten-day period of reflection, repentance, and reconciliation. Realizing that her constant criticism was poisoning our relationship, my mom decided she would stop judging us and allow us to live our lives as we saw fit. The moment she committed to that decision, she felt an enormous burden lift. More importantly, her heart was at peace.

Writing that letter to my mom is perhaps the greatest regret of my life. Now that my daughter is grown, I can't begin to imagine the excruciating heartache I would feel if I received such a letter from her. If anything could destroy me, that would be it. I recently told my mom that I still felt anguish about putting her through such torment. She waved off my concern with a loving smile. We were both wrong, she said, but none of that mattered anymore.

I can no longer remember what feeling angry at my mom felt like. The power of unconditional love vaporizes any and all non-loving feelings as if they had never existed. I can attest that pure, loving forgiveness washes away every last trace of hurt.

My mom and I aren't the only ones who experienced the healing balm of forgiveness. My now ex-wife feels nothing but love and affection for my mom. We've been divorced for more than sixteen years but we all still get together for the holidays when we can and consider ourselves one big happy family. Indeed, that is exactly what we are.

FIND FREEDOM THROUGH FORGIVENESS
Self-Reflection Questions

- Who have I not forgiven and cannot imagine ever forgiving?

- How is forgiving both selfish and selfless?

- How does holding on to past hurts and resentments affect my mental, emotional, and physical well-being?

- How does refusing to forgive prevent me from fully living in the present moment?

- How do my anger and resentment allow the person who harmed me to continue to exercise power over my life?

- Why are acts or even thoughts of revenge harmful to me?

- How can learning to forgive myself affect how I show up in the world?

- How is my antagonist a collaborator in my spiritual development?

- How would viewing a conflict through God's eyes instead of my own affect the way I react to it?

- If I believe that everything happens for a reason, why do I believe or not believe there are exceptions to that rule?

- Why does forgiveness have far more to do with me than the person I am forgiving?

- How does love release the hold my antagonist has on me?

EIGHTEEN

BEHOLD YOUR BELOVED

To cheat oneself out of love is the most terrible deception;
it is an eternal loss for which there is no reparation,
either in time or in eternity.

—Søren Kierkegaard

BEHOLD YOUR BELOVED

Take a leap of faith and dive headlong into the ocean of romantic love. The waters may be choppy from time to time, but an exhilarating world of unimaginable beauty awaits.

> *A life without love, without the presence of the beloved, is nothing but a mere magic-lantern show. We draw out slide after slide, swiftly tiring of each, and pushing it back to make haste for the next.*
>
> —JOHANN WOLFGANG VON GOETHE

LOVE ATTRACTS LOVE

Like most of the human race, you likely have yearned for a soulmate: someone to love, to be intimate with, to share your life with.

> *Love is an irresistible desire to be irresistibly desired.*
>
> —ROBERT FROST

The urge to find your beloved is not merely a human instinct, it is a Universal force that connects you to the deep love of God through the gateway of your heart.

> *Loving another person is not separate from loving God. One is a single wave, the other is the ocean.*
>
> —DEEPAK CHOPRA

If your longing for a worthy spiritual partner is to find expression, you must first believe that you yourself are worthy of being loved.

> *The most enlightened prayer isn't "Dear God, send me someone wonderful," but, "Dear God, help me realize that I am someone wonderful."*
>
> —MARIANNE WILLIAMSON

Your ideal partner is patiently waiting for you to see and appreciate the beauty and perfection of your own soul.

We must be our own before we can be another's.

—RALPH WALDO EMERSON

Loving your own life naturally leads to loving all that life has to offer, a signal to the Universe that you are ready for a loving relationship.

Love attracts love, and when you cultivate love from the inside out, the universe will deliver it from the outside in.

—ALAN COHEN

When you are one with love, you will find the one you love. Until then, trust that the person you yearn to be with yearns to be with you.

You will be in love when you know that you are love.

—DEEPAK CHOPRA

SEEKING A SOULMATE

Your search for a romantic partner will move closer to fruition once you direct your attention within.

Those who go searching for love only find their own lovelessness. But the loveless never find love; only the loving find love, and they never have to search for it.

—D. H. LAWRENCE

You dramatically improve the odds of meeting your soulmate when you stop trying to *find* the right person and start trying to *be* the right person.

To be loved, be worthy to be loved.

—OVID

Prepare yourself in body, mind, and spirit to welcome your beloved. Commit to a life of absolute integrity, vigilant self-awareness, and continual self-improvement.

> *When you realize you want to spend the rest of your life with*
> *somebody, you want the rest of your life to start as soon as possible.*
>
> —NORA EPHRON

You cannot fully and confidently give your heart to another until you assume total responsibility for your own happiness and well-being.

> *You can love only in proportion to your capacity for independence.*
>
> —ROLLO MAY

Your maturity reaches the tipping point when you recognize the difference between being self-centered and being centered in your self.

> *The purpose of relationship is not to have another who might*
> *complete you; but to have another with whom you might share*
> *your completeness.*
>
> —NEALE DONALD WALSCH

As awareness grows, you naturally develop greater empathy, compassion, and generosity of spirit. Ultimately, any tendency to be controlling, demanding, or self-serving vanishes in a puff of higher consciousness.

> *The most important ingredient we put into any relationship is not*
> *what we say or what we do, but what we are.*
>
> —STEPHEN R. COVEY

The greater your autonomy, self-knowledge, and self-confidence, the greater the likelihood you will attract a compatible, emotionally healthy partner.

> *Love is for people who know who they are.*
>
> —NATHANIEL BRANDEN

Too many lonely, frustrated souls are unwilling to do the self-work that spiritual partnership demands. Instead, they chase a fairy-tale fantasy and wonder why it continues to elude them.

> *True love is like ghosts, which everyone talks about but few have seen.*
> —FRANÇOIS DE LA ROCHEFOUCAULD

Every day that you follow your guidance and do the hard work of self-development brings you one day closer to encountering your beloved.

> *Don't rush into any kind of relationship. Work on yourself. Feel*
> *yourself, experience yourself and love yourself. Do this first and*
> *you will soon attract that special loving other.*
> —RUSS VON HOELSCHER

The more effort you put into making yourself lovable, the more effortlessly love will show up in your life.

> *When love comes it comes without effort, like perfect weather.*
> —HELEN YGLESIAS

DRAWN TOGETHER

At the right time, the right partner will come into your life. You will be drawn to each other, spirit to spirit, heart to heart.

> *Lovers don't finally meet somewhere.*
> *They're in each other all along.*
> —RUMI

You may have potentially found your beloved when an unanticipated, unexplainable shock of recognition roots you to the ground.

> *I seem to have loved you in numberless forms, numberless times, in life after life, in age after age forever.*
>
> —RABINDRANATH TAGORE

On some level, you will sense an instantaneous connection, as if the final two pieces of a puzzle had just clicked into place.

> *Intellect, in its effort to explain Love, got stuck in the mud like an ass. Love alone could explain love and loving.*
>
> —RUMI

Though your initial attraction may be driven by passion, you will have come together for a greater purpose.

> *It is wrong to think that love comes from long companionship and persevering courtship. Love is the offspring of spiritual affinity and unless that affinity is created in a moment, it will not be created in years or even generations.*
>
> —KAHLIL GIBRAN

Romantic love has its own agenda and an exquisite sense of timing. Sacred contracts will be played out; karmic scales will be balanced.

> *If it is your time, love will track you down like a cruise missile.*
>
> —LYNDA BARRY

Your soulmate is a means to your destiny, the only person who can reveal and draw out parts of you that you have yet to explore.

> *Our partner is essential to the discovery of our own calling, and in a curious way shows us what we want, or more exactly, shows us what is wanted of us from within ourselves and our world.*
>
> —THOMAS MOORE

Love may come naturally, but sustaining and deepening a loving relationship requires concentrated effort—and the maturity and wisdom that only experience can bestow.

*For one human being to love another human being: that is perhaps
the most difficult task that has been entrusted to us, the ultimate task,
the final test and proof, the work for which all other work is merely
preparation. That is why young people, who are beginners in
everything, are not yet capable of love: it is something they must
learn.*

—RAINER MARIA RILKE

The younger the lovers, the greater the struggle to reach the summit of true love. Your
first love is typically but a glimpse, a promise, of the riches that await.

*Loving does not at first mean merging, surrendering, and uniting
with another person (for what would a union be of two people who
are unclarified, unfinished, and still incoherent—?), it is a high
inducement for the individual to ripen, to become something in
himself, to become world, to become world in himself for the sake of
another person; it is a great, demanding claim on him, something
that chooses him and calls him to vast distances.*

—RAINER MARIA RILKE

Over the years, the adoration and affection that flow and grow between soulmates
will outswell the initial waves of passion that so urgently and desperately crashed
upon their shores.

*Let your love be like the misty rains, coming softly, but flooding the
river.*

—MALAGASY PROVERB

COMMITTING TO LOVE

Committing to a romantic relationship expands your capacity to love—not only your
beloved, but eventually all of humanity, and ultimately and most importantly, the
Divine Beloved.

> *If we love one another, God dwelleth in us, and his love is perfected in us.*
>
> —1 JOHN 4:12

When two people give themselves fully to each other, they offer not only their minds, hearts, and bodies, but also the safekeeping of their souls.

> *He felt now that he was not simply close to her, but that he did not know where he ended and she began.*
>
> —LEO TOLSTOY

Spiritual partners gaze into each other's eyes and behold the majesty of God's presence.

> *To love another person is to see the face of God.*
>
> —VICTOR HUGO

Spiritual unions are timeless. When two people are connected through divine romance, the past and future drop away and they touch eternity through the portal of the present moment.

> *Love vanquishes time. To lovers, a moment can be eternity, eternity can be the tick of a clock.*
>
> —MARY PARRISH

Soulmates are certain that no one else in the history of the world has ever loved more truly, more madly, more deeply.

> *The lover is a monotheist who knows that other people worship different gods but cannot himself imagine that there could be other gods.*
>
> —THEODOR REIK

Romantic partners view each other like Jim Carrey's character in *Bruce Almighty* learned to do. He had taken his girlfriend for granted but when God asks him if he wants her back, he selflessly replies, "I want her to meet someone who will see her always as I do now, through your eyes."

> *You come to love not by finding the perfect person, but by seeing an imperfect person perfectly.*
>
> —SAM KEEN

Wise words, for when we view our partner through God's eyes, we see infinite, breath-taking beauty.

> *Oh! Death will find me, long before I tire*
> *Of watching you.*
>
> —RUPERT BROOKE

A romantic relationship is not only a vehicle for deeper, richer expressions and explorations of self, it is an opportunity for life itself to manifest more profoundly.

> *The point of relationship is the added power that life gets in working with it as a channel. A good relationship gives life more power. If two people are strong together, then life has a more powerful channel than it has with two single people. It's almost as though a third and larger channel has been formed.*
>
> —CHARLOTTE JOKO BECK

DOING THE WORK

Spiritual partners make nourishing their relationship a priority and revel in dreaming up new ways to express their love for each other.

> *Knowing how to keep our excitement for another person alive is not different from knowing how to keep alive our excitement for life.*
>
> —NATHANIEL BRANDEN

They know that the full potential of their life together will be achieved only through consistent attention, intention, and effort.

> *We need more than love to make love last.*
>
> —NATHANIEL BRANDEN

They appreciate that the two elements required for maintaining and building intimacy are time and proximity.

> *Love is like a campfire: It may be sparked quickly, and at first the kindling throws out a lot of heat, but it burns out quickly. For long lasting, steady warmth (with delightful bursts of intense heat from time to time), you must carefully tend the fire.*
>
> —MOLLEEN MATSUMURA

They view their relationship as a blossoming plant that requires daily watering, not as a cactus that they can splash a few drops of water on every few weeks.

> *Love doesn't just sit there, like a stone, it has to be made, like bread; remade all the time, made new.*
>
> —URSULA K. LE GUIN

They know that the right time to express affection is right now, that romance lives in ordinary moments, waiting for a stolen kiss, a loving touch, a knowing glance.

> *Love is for those who understand that it is now or never.*
>
> —NATHANIEL BRANDEN

Intimacy deepens with effort, but love itself grows effortlessly when the very thought of your beloved can make your heart sing with joy.

> *Joy is a nutrient of love: it makes love grow.*
>
> —NATHANIEL BRANDEN

Communication is the linchpin of spiritual unions. No subject is off limits. Soulmates do not argue, they discuss.

The first duty of love is to listen.

—PAUL TILLICH

Spiritual partners encourage their beloved to share their innermost thoughts and feelings, knowing that transparently revealing the essence of who they are is the bedrock of emotional intimacy.

Four of the most loving words in the world are: "Tell me about it."

—NATHANIEL BRANDEN

By definition, transparency requires absolute honesty. Both partners understand that any short-term pain produced by speaking truthfully pales in comparison to the long-term damage that would certainly be wrought by the slightest hint of dishonesty.

Where there is love, there is pain.

—SPANISH PROVERB

They know that sharing what they are thinking is important, but not as important as sharing what they are feeling.

Only from the heart can you touch the sky.

—RUMI

Each partner feels free to express their fears, frustrations, and longings, knowing that the other will listen carefully and respond thoughtfully.

The ultimate test of a relationship is to disagree but hold hands.

—ALEXANDRIA PENNEY

Recognizing that wants can be sacrificed but needs cannot, they give special attention to exploring how each other's needs can be fulfilled.

Relationships are a day-to-day work of art.

—WILLIAM SHOCKLEY

Each partner acts to clear the air at the slightest indication of tension, welcoming the opportunity to address and resolve any issue, no matter how small, that threatens the purity of their interactions.

> *Love is more than just a feeling: it's a process requiring continual attention. Loving well takes laughter, loyalty, and wanting more to be able to say, "I understand" than to hear, "You're right."*
>
> —MOLLEEN MATSUMURA

Each challenges the other to grow intellectually, emotionally, and spiritually. They cannot wait to share with each other new insights, new discoveries, new passions.

> *To be enjoyable, a relationship must become more complex. To become more complex, the partners must discover new potentialities in themselves and in each other. To discover these, they must invest attention in each other—so that they can learn what thoughts and feelings, what dreams reside in their partner's mind. This in itself is a never-ending process, a lifetime's task. After one begins to really know another person, then many joint adventures become possible: traveling together, reading the same books, raising children, making and realizing plans all become more enjoyable and more meaningful.*
>
> —MIHALY CSIKSZENTMIHALYI

REACHING A CROSSROADS

Only when you are comfortable with who you are can you truly be comfortable with who your beloved is.

> *The beginning of love is to let those we love be perfectly themselves, and not to twist them to fit our own image. Otherwise we love only the reflection of ourselves we find in them.*
>
> —THOMAS MERTON

The more authentic you both are, the safer you both will feel and the stronger your relationship will be.

A soulmate is someone who has locks that fit our keys, and keys to fit our locks. When we feel safe enough to open the locks, our truest selves step out and we can be completely and honestly who we are; we can be loved for who we are and not for who we're pretending to be. Each unveils the best part of the other. No matter what else goes wrong around us, with that one person we're safe in our own paradise. Our soulmate is someone who shares our deepest longings, our sense of direction. When we're two balloons, and together our direction is up, chances are we've found the right person. Our soulmate is the one who makes life come to life.

—LESLIE PARRISH

Therein lies the paradox. You will not attain your ideal relationship until you learn and evolve. But the best way to learn and evolve is by being in a relationship.

However good or bad you feel about your relationship, the person you are with at this moment is the "right" person, because he or she is a mirror of who you are inside.

—DEEPAK CHOPRA

The simultaneous demand for learning and loving is why "opposites" attract, although the contrasts in question are actually complementary differences. If, for example, one partner is gregarious and the other is shy, they can learn together that there is a healthy middle ground.

What counts in making a happy marriage is not so much how compatible you are, but how you deal with incompatibility.

—GEORGE LEVINGER

We are drawn to those who possess qualities we admire and wish to possess for ourselves. Such a person may have a different temperament, sensibility, or lifestyle, or simply offer contrasting life experiences.

But, once the realization is accepted that even between the closest
human beings infinite distances continue to exist, a wonderful living
side by side can grow up, if they succeed in loving the distance
between them which makes it possible for each to see the other whole
and against a wide sky!

—RAINER MARIA RILKE

As both partners learn what they can from each other, the union reaches critical mass; either the relationship has run its course and the participants agree to go their separate ways, or they begin a more fulfilling life together strengthened and enriched by their newfound similarities and synergies.

The best relationship is one in which your love for each other exceeds
your need for each other.

—H. JACKSON BROWN, JR.

LOVED AND CHERISHED

A spiritual union is a divine friendship between two people who are equally devoted to each other's well-being and best interests.

All love that has not friendship for its base,
Is like a mansion built upon the sand.

—ELLA WHEELER WILCOX

Hand in hand, they step down from pedestals of preconceived notions and delight in continually rediscovering each other.

A successful marriage requires falling in love many times, always with
the same person.

—MIGNON MCLAUGHLIN

Both partners accept each other's flaws and idiosyncrasies, and acknowledge that while neither of them is perfect, they are perfect for each other.

I love you not only for who you are,
but for what you are when I am with you.
I love you not only for what you have made of yourself,
but what you are making of me.

—ERICH FRIED

The only expectations they have for each other are that they will at all times authentically be themselves and act with complete integrity.

When a match has equal partners then I fear not.

—AESCHYLUS

Even when their love, loyalty, and support for each other are unconditional, the relationship will inevitably deteriorate unless each truly admires the other.

To love is to admire with the heart; to admire is to love with the
mind.

—THÉOPHILE GAUTIER

Admiration is the cornerstone of a lifelong love affair. In the absence of admiration, desire and passion grow ever more hollow.

Tell me who admires you and loves you, and I will tell you who you
are.

—CHARLES AUGUSTIN SAINTE-BEUVE

The relationship will continue to flourish as long as both participants feel loved and cherished.

To love and be loved is to feel the sun from both sides.

—DAVID VISCOTT

While both partners cherish their time together, they respect each other as individuals who need time alone to reflect, recharge, and relate to the world on their own terms in their own way.

> *Give your hearts, but not into each other's keeping.*
> *For only the hand of Life can contain your hearts.*
> *And stand together yet not too near together:*
> *For the pillars of the temple stand apart,*
> *And the oak tree and the cypress grow not in each other's shadow.*
>
> —KAHLIL GIBRAN

They give each other plenty of space, both literally and figuratively, for uninterrupted time to think, to dream, to simply be.

> *I hold this to be the highest task of a bond between two people:*
> *that each should stand guard over the solitude of the other.*
>
> —RAINER MARIA RILKE

Striking the right balance between independence and interdependence is an ongoing dance featuring constantly changing choreography.

> *A long marriage is two people trying to dance a duet and two solos at*
> *the same time.*
>
> —ANNE TAYLOR FLEMING

The dance must flow organically, with each partner following the other's lead while simultaneously honoring their own rhythms and the rhythms of life itself.

> *A good relationship has a pattern like a dance and is built on some of*
> *the same rules. The partners do not need to hold on tightly, because*
> *they move confidently in the same pattern . . . To touch heavily would*
> *be to arrest the pattern and freeze the movement, to check the*
> *endlessly changing beauty of its unfolding. There is no place here for*
> *the possessive clutch, the clinging arm, the heavy hand; only the*
> *barest touch in passing.*
>
> —ANNE MORROW LINDBERGH

While each longs for the other during long stretches apart, they know they are separated by distance only, that such breaks can enrich their relationship.

Absence is to love what wind is to fire; it extinguishes the small, it
kindles the great.

—ROGER DE BUSSY-RABUTIN

Whether they are miles apart or in each other's arms, they inwardly bow to the other, honoring one another's spirit.

But let there be spaces in your togetherness,
And let the winds of the heavens dance between you.
Love one another, but make not a bond of love:
Let it rather be a moving sea between the shores of your souls.
Fill each other's cup but drink not from one cup.
Give one another of your bread but eat not from the same loaf.
Sing and dance together and be joyous, but let each one of you be alone,
Even as the strings of a lute are alone though they quiver with the
same music.

—KAHLIL GIBRAN

They trust each other with their lives and view their relationship as an opportunity to serve one another.

In reality, the only way a relationship will last is if you see your
relationship as a place that you go to give, and not a place that
you go to take.

—ANTHONY ROBBINS

LOVE AND SUPPORT

Joining hands, spiritual partners step into the world together, certain only that no matter what comes their way, they will not be alone in facing it.

Love does not consist in gazing at each other but in looking
outward together in the same direction.

—ANTOINE DE SAINT-EXUPÉRY

When life serves up a crisis, love finds a way through it. In times of struggle, soulmates draw closer together and feel even more at home in each other's arms.

> *Love, like a river, will cut a new path whenever it meets an obstacle.*
>
> —CRYSTAL MIDDLEMAS

If one partner is in need of comfort or support, their beloved is at their side in a heartbeat.

> *Trouble is part of your life, and if you don't share it, you don't give the person who loves you enough chance to love you enough.*
>
> —DINAH SHORE

If one is grieving the loss of something held dear, the other does not offer solutions, but simply listens.

> *Let us love and be loved: benefiting ourselves by loving, and others by being loved. We find rest in those we love, and we provide a resting place in ourselves for those who love us.*
>
> —SAINT BERNARD OF CLAIRVAUX

If the world deems one partner a failure, the other takes their hand, looks them in the eye, and says, "I believe in you."

> *To love a person is to learn the song that is in their heart and to sing it to them when they have forgotten.*
>
> —UNKNOWN

As their knowledge of each other grows, so too does their love. Each becomes more beautiful in the other's eyes; each becomes more cherished in the other's heart.

> *Love must be as much a light as a flame.*
>
> —HENRY DAVID THOREAU

As selfishness gives way to selflessness, love grows and deepens in ways that ego would have you believe are not possible.

Our wedding was many years ago. The celebration continues to this day.

— GENE PERRET

No matter how many years they have been together, their hearts occasionally still skip a beat when they catch a glimpse of their beloved's face.

Nobody has ever measured, even the poets, how much a heart can hold.

— ZELDA FITZGERALD

NO RULES

Spiritual partners place no restrictions upon each other. They grant each other complete freedom to do whatever they like with whomever they choose.

Him that I love, I wish to be
Free—
Even from me.

— ANNE MORROW LINDBERGH

First, however, they thoroughly discuss the compatibility of their values and desires and clearly specify the boundaries of what they cannot live with.

Love is always open arms. With arms open you allow love to come and go as it wills, freely, for it'll do so anyway. If you close your arms about love you'll find you are left only holding yourself.

— LEO BUSCAGLIA

By agreeing to these terms, they are telling each other that they never wish to impose their will upon the other.

Where love rules, there is no will to power; and where power predominates, there love is lacking. The one is the shadow of the other.

— CARL JUNG

They trust that each of them values the relationship enough to forgo acting on any desire that would jeopardize it.

> *The best proof of love is trust.*
>
> —Dr. Joyce Brothers

Thus, they vow to never do or say anything that they would not do or say in front of the other.

> *Love at first sight is easy to understand; it's when two people have been looking at each other for a lifetime that it becomes a miracle.*
>
> —Amy Bloom

Recognizing that change and growth are as enriching as they are inevitable, they neither resist nor resent each other's budding new interests and aspirations.

> *If we have the self-confidence and the wisdom to be the friend of our partner's growth, then growth is no threat. If we set ourselves against it, we invite tragedy.*
>
> —Nathaniel Branden

Viewing their life together as an ever-evolving adventure, they encourage each other to follow their bliss wherever it might lead.

> *Relationships, of all kinds, are like sand held in your hand. Held loosely, with an open hand, the sand remains where it is. The minute you close your hand and squeeze tightly to hold on, the sand trickles through your fingers. You may hold on to some of it, but most will be spilled. A relationship is like that. Held loosely, with respect and freedom for the other person, it is likely to remain intact. But hold too tightly, too possessively, and the relationship slips away and is lost.*
>
> —Kaleel Jamison

Knowing that the only shared interests that truly matter are their fundamental values and loving devotion to each other, they explore options and discover ways to integrate any new avocation or activity into their lives.

*If one does not wish bonds broken, he should make them elastic
and thereby strengthen them.*

—CHARLES JEAN JACQUES JOSEPH ARDANT DU PICQ

They realize that freedom in a mature, loving relationship is less about allowing each other to *do* what they want to do, and more about allowing each other to *be* who they really are.

Love rules without rules.

—ITALIAN PROVERB

HEALING A BROKEN HEART

The love and mutual respect between spiritual partners may not always bridge the chasm of their differences. People change; desires change. Paths cross and paths diverge.

*The value of a relationship lies in the joy it affords, not in its
longevity.... The ending of a relationship does not mean that
someone has failed. It means only that someone has changed,
perhaps for the better.*

—NATHANIEL BRANDEN

Just because a relationship ends does not mean that beginning it was a mistake. Each relationship expands your self-awareness and clarifies what you do and do not desire in a partner.

*Each relationship you have with another person reflects the
relationship you have with yourself.*

—ALICE DEVILLE

Life may present you with a series of romantic partners, each of them a soulmate, each of them coming into your life at precisely the right time to take you deeper into the mysteries of your own heart.

> *When something is missing in your life, it usually turns out to be someone.*
>
> —ROBERT BRAULT

Every romantic relationship, no matter how long it lasts, showers you with untold blessings.

> *There are no failed relationships. Every person who enters and exits your life does so in a mutual sharing of life's divine lessons.*
>
> —WAYNE DYER

Even if you later part ways, joining your heart with another's allows you to express and experience your deepest desires for emotional and physical intimacy.

> *When love beckons to you, follow him,*
> *Though his ways are hard and steep.*
> *And when his wings enfold you yield to him,*
> *Though the sword hidden among his pinions may wound you.*
> *And when he speaks to you believe in him,*
> *Though his voice may shatter your dreams as the north wind lays*
> *waste the garden.*
>
> —KAHLIL GIBRAN

Sometimes hearts are broken and there is nothing to be done except express gratitude for the gift you were given and move on.

> *I hold it true, whate'er befall;*
> *I feel it, when I sorrow most;*
> *'Tis better to have loved and lost*
> *Than never to have loved at all.*
>
> —ALFRED, LORD TENNYSON

A spiritual person is generous of spirit with a former partner, wishing that the rest of their days be filled with peace and purpose and that their life be graced with ever greater and deeper love.

There is no remedy for love but to love more.

—HENRY DAVID THOREAU

Pledging your love to another in a healthy way always leads to positive repercussions, even when circumstances may suggest otherwise.

Sometimes with one I love, I fill myself with rage, for fear I effuse unreturned love;
But now I think there is no unreturned love—the pay is certain, one way or another;
(I loved a certain person ardently, and my love was not returned;
Yet out of that, I have written these songs.)

—WALT WHITMAN

Whether you leave a relationship feeling relief or heartache, you are presented with a tremendous opportunity for growth and renewal.

To love and win is the best thing, to love and lose is the next best.

—WILLIAM MAKEPEACE THACKERAY

Step out of your emotions as best you can and challenge yourself to interpret the relationship with symbolic sight.

Spiritual partners bond with an understanding that they are together because it is appropriate for their souls to grow together. They recognize that their growth may take them to the end of their days in this incarnation and beyond, or it may take them to six months. They cannot say that they will be together forever. The duration of their partnership is determined by how long it is appropriate for their evolution to be together. All of the vows that a human being can take cannot prevent the spiritual path from exploding through and breaking those vows if the spirit must move on.

—GARY ZUKAV

Not only will you gain clarity about why things unfolded as they did, but also about what you want the rest of your life to look like.

> *If you cry because the sun has gone out of your life, your tears will prevent you from seeing the stars.*
>
> —RABINDRANATH TAGORE

With fresh insight and clarity of purpose, you can take yourself apart, then put yourself together in a new and better way.

> *When a marriage comes to an end, we're free to call it a failure. We're also free to call it a graduation.*
>
> —RICHARD BACH

In time, your grief gives way to understanding and acceptance. Your broken heart heals and becomes stronger and more resilient.

> *Relationships are like Rome—difficult to start out, incredible during the prosperity of the "golden age," and unbearable during the fall. Then, a new kingdom will come along and the whole process will repeat itself until you come across a kingdom like Egypt . . . that thrives, and continues to flourish. This kingdom will become your best friend, your soulmate, and your love.*
>
> —HELEN KELLER

Do not allow the fear of heartbreak to stop you from promising your love to another. By protecting your heart, you may end up losing it.

> *To love at all is to be vulnerable. Love anything, and your heart will certainly be wrung and possibly be broken. If you want to make sure of keeping it intact, you must give your heart to no one, not even to an animal. Wrap it carefully round with hobbies and little luxuries, avoid all entanglements, lock it up safe in the casket or coffin of your selfishness. But in that casket—safe, dark, motionless, airless— it will change. It will not be broken; it will become unbreakable, impenetrable, irredeemable. The alternative to tragedy, or at least to the risk of tragedy, is damnation.*
>
> —C. S. LEWIS

BEHOLD YOUR BELOVED
Living the Lesson

My second marriage ended months after it began. I didn't want it to, but the gap between our lifestyles kept widening, and splitting up soon became inevitable. I was heartbroken, but even as sadness seeped through me, I saw value in my grief.

By facing my grief head on, I healed myself in four months, which is better than suffering for four years . . . or forever. I hope my story of recovery offers comfort to others who are hurting. You *can* recover from a broken heart. You *can* heal. You *can* be whole again.

Every day for four months I drilled deeply into my grief. I challenged myself to discover how much of my grief was genuine and how much of it was just me feeling sorry for myself. I knew that wallowing in my emotional pain, even just a bit, was a huge barrier to healing. I asked myself questions like:

- What is the source of my grief and why am I so invested in whatever that is?

- What is the essence of what I lost and how much do I need whatever that is in my life?

- What am I missing more—her presence or what she or the marriage represented?

- What exactly am I afraid of? Being alone? People's reactions? Not being able to find another soulmate?

- What are the expectations I had going into the marriage that turned out to be wishful thinking?

- Were my expectations of her realistic?

- Where did those expectations come from?

- How and why did my expectations differ from hers?

- How did I fail to meet her expectations?

- In what ways did I impact the relationship by being selfish or self-absorbed?

- What did she need from me that I was unable or unwilling to give her, and vice versa?

- What did she need in her life that was unacceptable to me, and vice versa?

It helped tremendously that we both had been completely upfront and honest with each other from day one of our relationship. There were no untruths spoken, no betrayal of trust. We were just two people who crossed paths at precisely the moment when our needs and desires perfectly overlapped. For fifteen months, we were in perfect sync.

Yet all along, we both had been subtly moving, in opposite directions, toward the life we each desired to lead. It was only a matter of time before we stepped beyond the boundaries of the common ground we shared.

You may be wondering how I could marry someone and not know how vastly different our lifestyle preferences were. The truth is, I did. But because we were clicking on all levels, I naively assumed that we would do so indefinitely and that I could handle any challenges that did come along. So that's on me.

After the relationship ended, I saw clearly that I had seen only what I wanted to see, and that I had ignored red flags that, in hindsight, were painfully obvious. We simply had different ways of looking at relationships and at life in general. It was unavoidable that we'd begin authentically expressing ourselves in ways that added distance between us.

To her credit, she was always willing to answer all of my questions even as the relationship deteriorated and my grief deepened. I will always be grateful to her for that. Those discussions provided much-needed insight and clarity that accelerated my healing. Most people trying to recover from a broken heart do not have the luxury of open, honest communication with their former partner. I fully realize how fortunate I was.

Toward the end, when we knew we would be parting ways, I told her that if I had known from the start that it would end like this, I still would have signed up for it in a heartbeat. "So would I," she said. I cherish that moment.

The lessons I learned in my four months of grief were invaluable. Before the marriage unraveled, I thought I was living a spiritually mature life and authentically embodying the principles I planned to write and speak about. I was fooling myself. I discovered I had a lot more work to do if I wanted to get to where I thought I already was. If I had not endured the breakup of my marriage, I would not have become the person I needed to be in order to do the work I feel called to do; I would have lacked the credibility to legitimately speak to others about spiritual and personal growth.

I also realized that experiencing the fulfillment, however briefly, of what I had wished for in a relationship liberated me from wanting it so badly ever again. That doesn't mean that I don't want to be in another relationship; it means that I am now in control of that desire rather than having the desire control me. If I ever do enter into another relationship, it will be because I want to, not because I need to.

Some other life-transforming lessons I needed to learn were:

- See every moment as a gift. If I believe that everything happens for a reason, which I do, then I must learn to look for the blessings in every situation.

- Be unconditionally accepting and loving, even when another person's words or actions are deeply hurtful.

- Remain peaceful and joyful in even the most challenging and stressful of times.

- Be ruthlessly honest about my flaws and work hard to correct them.

- Be more concerned with wanting what I have than with having what I want.

- Expect nothing from people other than to authentically be who they are.

- I cannot have my heart set on having my time with someone turn out a certain way. Trying to control what I cannot control will always end badly.

Looking back, it's obvious to me that everything unfolded exactly as it should have. I see the perfection in why we came together . . . and why we came apart. To this day, I feel blessed that, through the alchemy of symbolic sight, my leaden grief was transmuted into the gold of inner peace.

BEHOLD YOUR BELOVED
Self-Reflection Questions

- What value do I get out of sharing my life with a soulmate?

- How does learning to love myself affect my relationship with my beloved?

- How does a romantic relationship expand my capacity to love?

- How can I do a better job of viewing my beloved through God's eyes instead of my own?

- What are three things I could do to deepen intimacy with my beloved?

- What is the correlation between authenticity and a healthy relationship?

- What do I have yet to learn from my beloved, and vice versa?

- How can I get better at demonstrating my love and admiration for my romantic partner?

- How can my beloved and I improve the balance between our independence and interdependence?

- What restrictions do my partner and I place on each other, and how do these rules hurt or help our relationship?

- In what ways did a failed romance help me to learn, grow, and become better equipped to be in a healthy relationship?

- How can I challenge myself to learn even more from my romantic relationships?

NINETEEN

PRACTICE AFFIRMATIONS

*I have always found that an affirmation
is much more effective than a mere petition
in drawing inspiration while composing.*

—JOHANNES BRAHMS

PRACTICE AFFIRMATIONS

Your thoughts are a powerful, creative force that set the course and tone of your life. We all think thousands of thoughts per day, the vast majority of which are repetitive. Over time, this relentless self-chatter—too often negative and self-limiting—forms the patterns of our thinking.

My thoughts are loving and positive.
I believe in myself and I am unstoppable.
I grow wiser, stronger, and more loving every day.

Affirmations help you tame the chaotic rumblings on the edge of your consciousness and replace your negative thought patterns with positive ones. What is an affirmation? It is a positive statement that a specific intention is already true.

I see beauty and perfection wherever I look.
The love I radiate to others heals them and brings them peace.
I am blessed with gifts and abilities that enable me to
serve the world as only I can.

Affirmations are an easy and effective way to reshape the way you look at the world. Train yourself to think more positive, loving thoughts and you will live a more positive, loving life.

I choose love in every moment.
I always choose the path of most love.
Everything I do adds love to the world.

Affirmations were popularized by Émile Coué, a French pharmacist and self-trained psychologist whose book, *Self-Mastery Through Conscious Autosuggestion*, was published in 1920. Known as the "Father of Autosuggestion," Coué instructed his patients to repeat the following affirmation twenty times, three times a day: "Every day, in every way, I am getting better and better." Coué observed that "whatever we think becomes true for us."

The work I do helps heal the world.
I am an instrument of God, humble and steadfast.
I am a source of love, hope, and healing energy to
every soul I encounter today.

The operative word in describing affirmations is "positive"; you must affirm what you do want, not what you do not. For instance, "I no longer spend my money foolishly," is a constant, negative reminder that you used to waste your money. A better choice is, "I spend my money wisely." A successful affirmation does not recall past troubles; it is a positive statement phrased in the present tense that states that from this moment forward you are choosing a better way.

Everything I do leads to success and happiness.
As I do my life's work, great abundance flows freely to me.
I gladly and proudly accept all the abundance
the Universe has to offer.

Notice that the above affirmation was not phrased, "I *will* spend my money wisely." If an affirmation becomes a promise to change at some undetermined point in the future rather than a statement that the change has already been made, the affirmation is rendered powerless. Why? Affirming "I will spend my money wisely" implies that, starting that afternoon, or next week, or the month after that, you will finally begin to spend your money wisely. The affirmation becomes a promise you never have to fulfill, a giant loophole that gives you free reign to continue spending your money foolishly until you finally decide that you are ready to act responsibly. If a change is envisioned in the future, that is where it will remain.

I am a beloved child of God.
God's inexhaustible love flows through me and into the hearts of others.
I am lovingly guided to be a force for all that is good and right in the world.

Similarly, beginning an affirmation with "I want" announces to the Universe that you are coming from a position of lacking whatever it is you want. Remember, the law of attraction states that the Universe is a giant copy machine; it does not judge your desires, it simply responds to your thoughts by giving you more of the same. Therefore, if you affirm, "I want lots of money," you will continue to have the experience of wanting lots of money. You will always be "wanting" and never "having" because you are affirming that you "want" the money, not that you "have" it already.

I trust and follow my intuitive guidance.
I put forth my best effort no matter the circumstances.
Every setback is an opportunity to gain greater clarity
about my life's work.

A powerful way to begin an affirmation is with the words, "I am." As Joel Osteen, pastor of Lakewood Church in Houston, Texas, put it, "What follows the 'I am' will always come looking for you. . . . When you say, 'I am healthy,' health starts heading your way. When you say, 'I am strong,' strength starts tracking you down." Indeed, the Universe does not judge, it simply responds. "Okay," says the Universe, "if that is what you are, I will give you experiences that support that statement." Hence, the affirmation, "I am thoughtful and considerate," is more potent than "I will be thoughtful and considerate" or "I want to be thoughtful and considerate."

I am a shining example of spiritual and physical well-being.
I am boundless love. I am infinite joy. I am unlimited wisdom.
I am radiant health. I am eternal youth. I am inexhaustible energy.

But, you might protest, such statements are not true; you do not spend your money wisely and you are not thoughtful and considerate. So isn't it dishonest to phrase such affirmations as if you have already made the changes? Not in the least. You are not lying to yourself, you are reprogramming your subconscious; each time you repeat an affirmation, you are positively reinforcing that programming.

I am beautiful and I am loved.
I am Spirit. I am a drop of God in a sea of God.
I naturally attract loving relationships into my life.

More importantly, remember that your soul, your essence, that spark of the Infinite within you, is perfect and magnificent, with capacities beyond your comprehension. Therefore, whatever you affirm will indeed be true on the deepest, most meaningful level imaginable. Looking through God's eyes, you realize that affirmations are simply reminders of your true nature. Even so, if an affirmation feels too grandiose, scale it down to whatever you are comfortable with. For instance, affirm that your loving energy is healing your family instead of the world.

I take great joy in hearing about the good fortune of others.
I see the beauty and presence of God in every soul
who crosses my path.
I see everyone experiencing the happiness with which
I have been blessed.

An affirmation is a self-fulfilling prophecy. Gradually, through the consistent use of affirmations, your conscious intent is absorbed by your unconscious mind. Over time, you grow into and finally become the person you wish to be. Indeed, affirmations are more about internal transformation than external outcomes. Telling yourself, "I spend my money wisely" or "I am thoughtful and considerate" day in and day out cannot help but change your self-image. As you authentically become what you affirm, the affirmation evolves from a desire for change to an expression of gratitude.

Everything God sends to me is a treasure.
All the riches of the Universe are as close to me as my next thought.
My success inspires and empowers others to
achieve their highest potential.

Some people prefer calling an affirmation a prayer. Both are ways of asking for Divine guidance. Whichever term you choose, you will get better results if you phrase your request as if it has already been fulfilled. For instance, instead of pleading, "God, please show me how to control my weight," affirm, "God, thank you for showing me how to control my weight." The distinction is a powerful one. It is a question of positioning the carrot stick just beyond your reach versus taking firm control of your life right here, right now.

Everything I do, I do for God.
I serve God through service to others.
The instant I set a goal, my angels spring into action.

How many affirmations should you use? Whatever number works for you. Whether you start with one or six or twenty, keep experimenting until you arrive at just the right comfort level. How often should you practice affirmations? Twice a day is a good start. If you still feel scattered or anxious, run through them as often as you need to until you feel grounded. For amazing results, use an activity you engage in multiple times a day, such as walking through your bedroom door, as a trigger to repeat your favorite affirmations. As you consciously devote more of your attention to attaining and maintaining attunement with Divine Will, your need for affirmations will diminish.

I am immersed in the deep love of God.
The deep love of God is alive and vibrant deep within my heart.
Thank you, God, for bathing me in the healing, protective glow
of your deep love.

Affirmations can be repeated silently, spoken out loud, or even sung. Some swear that writing down an affirmation significantly increases its power. Be creative and go with whatever works for you. Cover your bathroom mirror and bedroom wall with them. Record them on a CD with a musical background and listen to them in your car or while you do house chores.

The wisdom of the world lies within me.
I was born to serve humanity in my own unique way.
I have access to all the creativity and beauty of the Universe.

Paramahansa Yogananda recommended that an affirmation be said repeatedly, first in a loud voice, then gradually softer and slower until your voice becomes a whisper. Then keep affirming it mentally only without moving the tongue or lips until you have attained deep, unbroken concentration.

God, I welcome your loving spiritual guidance.
Thank you, God, for loving me so very, very deeply.
God, I trust completely in your infinite wisdom and your deep love.

Yogananda's method is powerful because the potency of an affirmation lies not in the words themselves but in your relationship to them. Invest your emotional energy in each word. Inhabit each affirmation and let it inhabit you. Feel it resonate within you until it takes root, repeating it until, as Yogananda wrote, "you finally realize the meaning of your utterance in every fiber of your being."

Not my will, God, but yours.
I surrender my will to Divine Will, unconditionally and with great joy.
Thank you, God, for guiding me to be a messenger of your deep love.

Granted, there will be times when circumstances do not allow you to concentrate fully on your affirmations—driving across town, taking a break at work, waiting in line at a grocery store. Even so, practicing affirmations for even a few minutes in less-than-ideal surroundings is still an effective way to center yourself and get back on track.

Whatever God brings to me, I want.
I do God's work effortlessly, with great joy, love, skill,
enthusiasm, and humility.
I think and live in ways that guide me to love and serve God
in the highest way possible.

Creating an accompanying visualization can make an affirmation even more effective. For instance, if you affirm, "Thank you, angels, for laying your hands of light on me and sending me your love and healing energies," closing your eyes and imagining angels coming to you and comforting you can produce a deep sense of inner peace and well-being.

I am deeply attuned to Spirit in each and every moment.
I am safe and protected, for I have great work to do in this life.
I honor my skills by consistently improving them and
using them to serve the world.

Do not let your affirmations get stale. If you repeat the same ones over and over, you may get into a rut, gradually lose interest, and abandon the practice altogether. Create a list of affirmations that resonate with you, then keep it fresh and meaningful by revising it often. If an affirmation loses its power, replace it with a new one relevant to your current circumstances. Keep your antennae up while reading personal-growth books; when an idea for an affirmation jumps out at you, add it to your collection.

Whatever I need to know is revealed to me.
Whatever I need comes to me in divine right order.
Thank you, God, for blessing me with every moment of this sweet life.

Affirmations are a wonderful way to neutralize years of bad mental habits and the negative internal chatter that plagues us all. Besides, you're going to talk to yourself one way or another, so you might as well have something positive to say!

I honor God in every moment of my life.
I honor God with every thought, every word, every deed.
I am so honored, I am so blessed, I am so grateful to be loved so much.

CLOSING THOUGHTS

I love those moments when everything changes. While reading Gerald Jampolsky's book, *Teach Only Love*, a particularly compelling passage jumped off the page and into my heart. The gist of it was this: *In every encounter we have with another human being, that person is either offering love to us or is in need of love from us.* In that instant, I became a better person.

I imagine you can recall moments of your own when you read or heard a phrase, a quote, or a concept that immediately reframed the way you looked at the world. With any luck, you found a few of those life-altering insights in these pages. Individually and collectively, these ideas certainly changed my life for the better. I hope they do the same for you.

But don't stop there. Each concept we touched on can be explored further. Indeed, countless books have been written about each chapter topic. To further deepen your understanding of these timeless spiritual principles, I recommend the books listed below.

- *A Return To Love: Reflections on the Principles of "A Course in Miracles"* by Marianne Williamson

- *Anatomy of the Spirit: The Seven Stages of Power and Healing* by Caroline Myss, Ph.D.

- *Autobiography of a Yogi* by Paramahansa Yogananda

- *The Bridge Across Forever: A True Love Story* by Richard Bach

- *Conversations with God: An Uncommon Dialogue (Book 1)* by Neale Donald Walsch

- *Creating Money: Attracting Abundance* by Sanaya Roman and Duane Packer

- *Creative Visualization: Use the Power of Your Imagination to Create What You Want in Your Life* by Shakti Gawain

- *Dancing with Life: Buddhist Insights for Finding Meaning and Joy in the Face of Suffering* by Phillip Moffitt

- *Healing Words: The Power of Prayer and the Practice of Medicine* by Larry Dossey, M.D.

- *Jesus, Buddha, Krishna, Lao Tzu: The Parallel Sayings* by Richard Hooper

- *Kitchen Table Wisdom: Stories That Heal* by Rachel Naomi Remen, M.D.

- *Man's Search for Meaning* by Viktor Frankl

- *The Power of Now: A Guide to Spiritual Enlightenment* by Eckhart Tolle

- *Power vs. Force: The Hidden Determinants of Human Behavior* by David R. Hawkins, M.D., Ph.D.

- *The Prophet* by Kahlil Gibran

- *The Spontaneous Fulfillment of Desire: Harnessing the Infinite Power of Coincidence* by Deepak Chopra, M.D.

- *Teach Only Love: The Twelve Principles of Attitudinal Healing* by Gerald G. Jampolsky, M.D.

- *There's a Spiritual Solution to Every Problem* by Wayne W. Dyer

I hope you enjoy these authors as much as I do. Over the years, as your journey progresses, I hope you also return to these pages whenever you are in need of comfort, clarity, and inspiration.

I imagine that some of you may be leaning toward embracing this ancient wisdom but just cannot make that leap of faith. After all, this spiritual stuff sounds good, but what if it isn't true? What if we are *not* being divinely guided in every moment and there are no soul lessons to be learned from adversity? I would still contend that applying these spiritual laws and trusting that a greater purpose is at work makes suffering more bearable.

Then, of course, there is the big question: What if the only thing waiting for you at the end of your life is, well, the end of your life? Even in the absence of definitive proof, wouldn't you prefer to live in a benevolent and orderly Universe rather than suffer through a random, pinball-like existence in a world devoid of ultimate purpose and meaning?

There are those who think that they do not deserve God's grace, that these principles apply to everyone but them. This may be the most common hurdle preventing people from living life to the fullest. Hopefully, through study, introspection, meditation, affirmations, and other spiritual practices, those who feel unworthy will begin to heal and come to the inescapable conclusion that God's love is their birthright. As Paramahansa Yogananda noted, "You have a claim on God as valid as that of the greatest saint."

No matter how determined you are to embody these teachings, it is unlikely you will achieve complete mastery in this lifetime. I do my best to live up to the standards spelled out in these pages, but I still find myself leading with my ego and judging others far too often. My meditation practice is uneven at best, and Paramahansa Yogananda's counsel to remain "calmly active and actively calm" is more difficult to put into practice than I expected.

The point is, no matter how far you progress in your quest for enlightenment, you will have made a quantum leap in the quality of your daily life by consciously choosing to live with kindness, compassion, and a positive, loving attitude. When you choose to fill your days with love, there is no downside, and the upside is experiencing heaven on earth.

> *While there is a chance of the world getting through its troubles*
> *I hold that a reasonable man has to behave as though he was sure*
> *of it. If at the end your cheerfulness is not justified, at any rate you*
> *will have been cheerful.*
>
> —H. G. WELLS

SOURCES OF QUOTES FROM SELF-REALIZATION FELLOWSHIP PUBLICATIONS

Page 10

The vast ocean of truth can be measured only according to the capacity of one's own cup of intelligence and perception.
Paramahansa Yogananda

Whispers from Eternity—First Version, 1929; hardcover edition 2005, page 5

Page 15

If you doubt, you won't see; and if you see, you won't doubt.
Paramahansa Yogananda

Sayings of Paramahansa Yogananda, 1980; hardcover edition 1994, page 64

Page 17

If I were to display the powers God has given me, I could draw thousands. But the path to God is not a circus. I gave the powers back to God, and I never use them unless He tells me to. My mission is to awaken love for God in the soul of man. I prefer a soul to a crowd, and I love crowds of souls.
Paramahansa Yogananda

Finding the Joy Within You by Sri Daya Mata, 1990; hardcover edition 2008, "Paramahansa Yogananda—As I Knew Him," page 259

Page 21

We have no sense that can reveal knowledge of Him; the senses give knowledge only of His manifestations. No thought or inference can enable us to know Him as He truly is, for thought cannot go beyond the data of the senses; it can only arrange and interpret the impressions of the senses.
Paramahansa Yogananda

Self-Realization magazine, Fall 2011, "Beyond Thought and Intellect: The Unlimited Insight of Soul Intuition," page 17

Page 22

If you don't invite God to be your summer Guest, He won't come in the winter of your life.
Lahiri Mahasaya

Autobiography of a Yogi by Paramahansa Yogananda, 1946; hardcover edition 2008, "I Become a Monk of the Swami Order," page 194

Page 28

The wave cannot say, "I am the ocean," because the ocean can exist without the wave. But the ocean can say, "I am the wave," because the wave cannot exist without the ocean.
Paramahansa Yogananda

The Divine Romance, 1986; hardcover edition 2002, "How You Can Approach God," page 367

Page 31

All that separates us from others, as Indian yogi Paramahansa Yogananda noted, are "partitions of ego consciousness."

Self-Realization magazine, Winter 2010, quoted by Sri Daya Mata in back-page letter as follows:

Friendship is God's trumpet call, bidding the soul destroy the partitions of ego consciousness that separate it from all other souls and from Him.

Page 35

As moving pictures are sustained by a beam of light coming from the projection booth of a movie house, so are all of us sustained by the Cosmic Beam, the Divine Light pouring from the projection booth of Eternity.
Paramahansa Yogananda

Man's Eternal Quest, 1975; hardcover edition 2001, "Healing by God's Unlimited Power," page 90

Page 44

The very foundation of the spiritual life is humility. Without humility the cup of one's consciousness is so filled with "I, I, I" that there is no room for "Thou, Thou, Thou."
Sri Daya Mata

Finding the Joy Within You, 1990; hardcover edition 2008, "Death: Mystery Portal to a Better Land," page 143

Page 46

It is on the anvil of this gross earth that struggling man must hammer out the imperishable gold of spiritual identity.
Paramahansa Yogananda

Autobiography of a Yogi, 1946; hardcover edition 2008, "The Years 1940-51," page 417

Page 56

You are a wildflower, a beauty unsurpassed. In each soul is the unique imprint of the grace of God.
Paramahansa Yogananda

A Thursday evening talk at Self-Realization Fellowship Temple, Encinitas, California

Self-Realization magazine, Summer 2007, "Divine Devotion: The Love for God That Sets You Free," page 9

Page 60

Human friendship is the echo of God's friendship.
Paramahansa Yogananda

Metaphysical Meditations, 1964; hardcover edition 1998, "Friendship and Service," page 97

Page 67

No matter which way you turn a compass, its needle points to the north. So it is with the true yogi. Immersed he may be in many outer activities, but his mind is always on the Lord.
Paramahansa Yogananda

Sayings of Paramahansa Yogananda, 1980; hardcover edition 1994, page 87

Page 68

In your silence God's silence ceases.
Paramahansa Yogananda

In the Sanctuary of the Soul, 1998; hardcover edition 2010, page 45

Page 69

If you pray to God as though your heart and mind will burst with longing, He will respond.
Paramahansa Yogananda

Self-Realization magazine, Winter 2002, quoted by Sri Daya Mata in "Mastering the Life-changing Power of Prayer," page 31

Page 70

O Father, when I was blind I found not a door that led to Thee. Thou hast healed my eyes; now I discover doors everywhere; the hearts of flowers, the voices of friendship, memories of lovely experiences.

Each gust of my prayer opens a new entrance to the vast temple of Thy presence.
Paramahansa Yogananda

Whispers from Eternity, 1986; hardcover edition 2011, "Doors Everywhere," page 219

Page 72

It is only when you go deep within, in meditation, that you suddenly realize how completely you had forgotten what you really are. You will be astonished to find what a tremendous gap there is beyond ordinary consciousness, which is of the world, and that consciousness in which you feel that just behind the restless mind, just behind the limited physical awareness, is a vast realm of divine awareness, of divine bliss.

Sri Daya Mata

Self-Realization magazine, Spring 2009, "Pranayama: Bridge to Divine Consciousness," page 20

Page 73

The sun shines, but if I close my eyes I see only darkness. When I open my eyes, the sunlight is there. It was always there; the darkness existed merely because I had my eyes closed. That is the way it is with the light of God's presence. Your eyes are closed; but if you open your spiritual eye by meditation, you will behold Him shining within you and everywhere.

Paramahansa Yogananda

Self-Realization magazine, Fall 2005, "Living the Divine Existence God Planned for You," pages 17-18

Page 74

Striving, striving, one day behold! the Divine Goal.

Lahiri Mahasaya

Autobiography of a Yogi by Paramahansa Yogananda, 1946; hardcover edition 2008, "Founding a Yoga School in Ranchi," page 221

Page 74

If you follow the way of meditation that we teach, you shall find that one day, when you are least expecting it, God will drop both His hands to lift you up. It is not only that you are seeking God, but that God is seeking you—more than you are seeking Him.

Paramahansa Yogananda

Convocation banquet speech, January 3, 1937

The Divine Romance, 1986; hardcover edition 2002, "I Am Blessed to Behold Him," page 408

Page 75

By meditation we connect the little joy of the soul with the vast joy of the Spirit.

Paramahansa Yogananda

Spiritual Diary, 1982; softcover edition 2007, August 20 entry

Pages 76 and 515

Meditation teaches you how to be, in Yogananda's words, "calmly active and actively calm."

God Talks With Arjuna: The Bhagavad Gita, 1995; hardcover edition 2005, Chapter 3, Verse 5, page 341, as follows:

The calm yogi can whirl his body and mind into intense action without being identified with them, and can then instantly return to his inner action-free state of meditative communion with Spirit. He is ever calmly active and actively calm.

Page 91

Let my soul smile through my heart and let my heart smile through my eyes, that I may scatter Thy rich smiles in sad hearts.

Paramahansa Yogananda

Metaphysical Meditations, 1964; hardcover edition 1998, "Spreading Divine Joy," pages 88-89

Page 92

The essence of spirituality is to love God supremely and to love all souls as a part of Him.

Sri Daya Mata

Christmas 2006 letter to devotees

Page 92

Only spiritual consciousness—realization of God's presence in oneself and in every other living being—can save the world. I see no chance for peace without it. Begin with yourself. There is no time to waste. It is your duty to do your part to bring God's kingdom on earth.

Paramahansa Yogananda

Man's Eternal Quest, 1975; hardcover edition 2001, "Self-realization: Criterion of Religion," page 110

Page 97

Be so drunk with the love of God that you will know nothing but God; and give that love to all.

Paramahansa Yogananda

Finding the Joy Within You by Sri Daya Mata, 1990; hardcover edition 2008, "Paramahansa Yogananda—As I Knew Him," page 262

Page 100

Cultivate the desire to do for others as you would do for your own loved ones. Expand the little cup of your love into an ocean of love divine for all beings.

Sri Daya Mata

Self-Realization magazine, Winter 2006, "Christmas in the Spirit of Yoga," page 25

Page 102

The faraway sun, seemingly small in the sky, radiates beyond its sphere to give us light and warmth. The stars share with us the joy of their jewel-like luster. All of God's expressions in nature send out a vibration that in some way serves the world. You are His highest creation; what are you doing to reach out beyond yourself?

Paramahansa Yogananda

To Be Victorious in Life, 2002; softcover edition 2010, "Expanding Your Consciousness for All-Round Success," pages 7-8

Page 136

Lord, I will reason, I will will, I will act; but guide Thou my reason, will, and activity to the right thing I should do.

Paramahansa Yogananda

God Talks With Arjuna: The Bhagavad Gita, 1995; hardcover edition 2005, Chapter 6, Verse 1, page 588

Page 147

Stillness is the altar of Spirit.

Paramahansa Yogananda

Rajarsi Janakananda: A Great Western Yogi, 1996; softcover edition 2009, page 96

Page 160

A child of God "bears witness" *by his life*. He embodies truth; if he expound it also, that is generous redundancy.

Paramahansa Yogananda

Autobiography of a Yogi, 1946; hardcover edition 2008, "The Years 1940-51," page 419

Page 168

Possession of material riches without inner peace is like dying of thirst while bathing in a lake.

Paramahansa Yogananda

Journey to Self-Realization, 1997; hardcover edition 2000, "Business, Balance, and Inner Peace: Restoring Equilibrium to the Work Week," pages 75-76

Page 178

If you don't discover the pearl by one or two divings, don't blame the ocean; find fault with your diving. You haven't yet plunged deep enough.

Paramahansa Yogananda

Sayings of Paramahansa Yogananda, 1980; hardcover edition 1994, page 89

Page 183

So love God inwardly that nothing will ever be able to touch you outwardly.

Paramahansa Yogananda

Finding the Joy Within You by Sri Daya Mata, 1990; hardcover edition 2008, "The Guru: Guide to Spiritual Freedom," page 254

Page 184

As Paramahansa Yogananda wrote, when you can "stand unshaken midst the crash of breaking worlds," then nothing can touch you where you live, and nothing of value can be taken from you.

The Divine Romance, 1986; hardcover edition 2002, "The Yoga Ideal of Renunciation Is for All," page 239, as follows:

The successful yogi can stand unshaken midst the crash of breaking worlds.

Page 190

Though God is the Creator and Sustainer of man, He has ordained the law of cause and effect, or karma, to govern life so that man himself is the judge of his own actions.
Paramahansa Yogananda

The Second Coming of Christ, 2004; hardcover edition 2007, Discourse 35, page 646

Page 191

In the course of natural righteousness, each man, by his thoughts and actions, becomes the molder of his destiny. Whatever universal energies he himself, wisely or unwisely, has set in motion must return to him as their starting point, like a circle inexorably completing itself.
Paramahansa Yogananda

Autobiography of a Yogi, 1946; hardcover edition 2008, "Kashi, Reborn and Discovered," page 227

Page 191

Seeds of past karma cannot germinate if they are roasted in the fires of divine wisdom.
Paramahansa Yogananda

Autobiography of a Yogi, 1946; hardcover edition 2008, "Outwitting the Stars," page 146

Page 192

No matter where you go, your wandering footsteps will lead you back to God.
Paramahansa Yogananda

Songs of the Soul, 1983; hardcover edition 2006, "My Soul Is Marching On," page 5

Page 201

In shallow men the fish of little thoughts cause much commotion. In oceanic minds the whales of inspiration make hardly a ruffle.
Hindu wisdom

Autobiography of a Yogi by Paramahansa Yogananda, 1946; hardcover edition 2008, "Years in My Master's Hermitage," page 102

Page 213

Truth is no theory, no speculative system of philosophy, no intellectual insight. Truth is exact correspondence with reality. For man, truth is unshakable knowledge of his real nature, his Self as soul.
Paramahansa Yogananda

Autobiography of a Yogi, 1946; hardcover edition 2008, "The Years 1940-51," page 419

Page 216

Truth is never afraid of questions.
Paramahansa Yogananda

Sayings of Paramahansa Yogananda, 1980; hardcover edition 1994, page 5

Page 230

Thought is fire; use its concentrated power to consume all obstacles to achievement.
Paramahansa Yogananda

A Thursday evening inspirational service at Self-Realization Fellowship headquarters in Los Angeles, California

Self-Realization magazine, Spring 2008, "How to Succeed in Finding God," page 9.

Page 263

You must not let your life run in the ordinary way; do something that nobody else has done, something that will dazzle the world.
Paramahansa Yogananda

Man's Eternal Quest, 1975; hardcover edition 2001, "Increasing the Power of Initiative," page 357

Page 269

A smooth life is not a victorious life.
Paramahansa Yogananda

Self-Realization magazine, Spring 2002, "The Help and Blessings of an Ever-Living Guru," Letter to Ananda Mata, page 8

Page 274

If you have within you that faith which is truly divine, and if there is something you desire that is not in the universe, it shall be created for you.
Swami Sri Yukteswar

Man's Eternal Quest by Paramahansa Yogananda, 1975; hardcover edition 2001, "Increasing the Power of Initiative," page 355

Page 299

Change yourself and you have done your part in changing the world. Every individual must change his own life if he wants to live in a peaceful world. The world cannot become peaceful unless and until you yourself begin to work toward peace.
Paramahansa Yogananda

Para-Grams

Page 315

The test of whether your life is lived for God alone is that you do not grieve over any frustrated personal desire, but only when you have displeased God.
Paramahansa Yogananda

The Divine Romance, 1986; hardcover edition 2002, "The Yoga Ideal of Renunciation Is for All," page 238

Page 315

Have only one desire: to know God. Satisfying the sensory desires cannot satisfy you, because you are not the senses. They are only your servants, not your Self.
Paramahansa Yogananda

Sayings of Paramahansa Yogananda, 1980; hardcover edition 1994, page 61

Page 326

I knew that everything that was happening to me was up to God, that He was the only healer. I felt safe, knowing I was surrounded by the overarching mantle of His perfect care. Whatever God brought to me, I wanted. Even if I retained all of the mobility of a flower pot, it didn't matter. "I" was still the same, the vehicle of expression had changed, that's all. A flower pot can still hold a beautiful flower.
Roger Delano

Self-Realization magazine, Fall 1999, "A Healing Gift," pages 70-71

Page 333

Your willingness to do your part opens the floodgates of God's blessings.
Sri Daya Mata

Self-Realization magazine, Winter 2002, back-page letter

Page 346

Just as a person can watch through a screen a crowd of people in front of him, without himself being seen by them, so the soul through the screen of intuition watches all its thoughts.
Paramahansa Yogananda

God Talks With Arjuna: The Bhagavad Gita, 1995; hardcover edition 2005, Chapter 2, Verse 25, page 225

Page 355

Seek to do brave and lovely things which are left undone by the majority of people. Give gifts of love and peace to those whom others pass by.
Paramahansa Yogananda

Spiritual Diary, 1982; softcover edition 2007, April 8 entry

Page 368

Attachment is blinding; it lends an imaginary halo of attractiveness to the object of desire.
Swami Sri Yukteswar

Autobiography of a Yogi by Paramahansa Yogananda, 1946; hardcover edition 2008, "Years in My Master's Hermitage," page 93

Page 377

Paramahansa Yogananda urged his devotees to look dispassionately at the drama of their lives "from the balcony of introspection."

In Sri Daya Mata's back-page letter in the Summer 2001issue of *Self-Realization* magazine, she wrote: "Gurudeva Paramahansa Yogananda taught that if we would control our destiny, we must take time to look dispassionately at this drama from the balcony of introspection. Then we discover, hidden in even difficult or enigmatic scenes, the guidance of our loving Father-Mother-God that can lift us to new levels of understanding."

Yogananda's use of the phrase "balcony of introspection" also appears in:

• *Journey to Self-Realization*, 1997; hardcover edition 2000, "Why God Created the World," page 48; and

• *Whispers from Eternity*, 1986; hardcover edition 2011, "We Are Actors in Thy Cosmic Pictures," page 119

Page 380

I found God more tempting than temptation.
Paramahansa Yogananda

Convocation banquet speech, January 3, 1937

The Divine Romance, 1986; hardcover edition 2002, "I Am Blessed to Behold Him," page 407

Page 388

The sages call that man wise whose pursuits are all without selfish plan or longings for results, and whose activities are purified by the fire of wisdom.
Bhagavad Gita 4:19

God Talks With Arjuna: The Bhagavad Gita by Paramahansa Yogananda, 1995; hardcover edition 2005, page 471

Page 397

Sooner or later, a time arises in every person's life when a connection with that Higher Power suddenly becomes of utmost urgency, bringing him to his knees through painful desperation or worshipful devotion—the choice is his.
Paramahansa Yogananda

The Second Coming of Christ, 2004; hardcover edition 2007, Discourse 34, page 621

Page 401

The things that happen to us do not matter; what we become through them does.
Sri Gyanamata

Only Love by Sri Daya Mata, 1976; hardcover edition 2006, page 74

Page 417

The creature finally turns to his Creator, if for no other reason than to ask in anguish: 'Why, Lord, why?' By ignoble whips of pain, man is driven at last into the Infinite Presence, whose beauty alone should lure him.
The Perfume Saint

Autobiography of a Yogi by Paramahansa Yogananda, 1946; hardcover edition 2008, "A 'Perfume Saint' Displays His Wonders," page 39

Page 420

Good and evil must ever be complements on this earth. Everything created must bear some guise of imperfection. How else could God, the Sole Perfection, fragment His one consciousness into forms of creation distinguishable from Himself? There can be no images of light without contrasting shadows. Unless evil had been created, man would not know the opposite, good. Night brings out the bright contrast of day; sorrow teaches us the desirability of joy.
Paramahansa Yogananda

God Talks With Arjuna: The Bhagavad Gita, 1995; hardcover edition 2005, Chapter 5, Verse 15, pages 552-553

Page 454

Forgiveness is holiness; by forgiveness the universe is held together.
Paramahansa Yogananda

God Talks With Arjuna: The Bhagavad Gita, 1995; hardcover edition 2005, Chapter 16, Verses 1-3, page 967

Page 510

Feel it resonate within you until it takes root, repeating it until, as Yogananda wrote, "you finally realize the meaning of your utterance in every fiber of your being."

Cosmic Chants, 1974; softcover edition 2011, Introduction, page xviii

Page 514

You have a claim on God as valid as that of the greatest saint.
Paramahansa Yogananda

A talk at Self-Realization Fellowship Temple, Encinitas, California

Self-Realization magazine, Spring 2006, "Destroying the Consciousness of Fear," page 15

The above quotes are used with permission from Self-Realization Fellowship, Los Angeles, California (yogananda-srf.org).

Sources of all other quotes in this book can be found at GodsEyesQuotes.com.

INDEX

NOTES

NOTES

NOTES

NOTES